TIGERS IN RED
WEATHER

TIGERS IN RED WEATHER

A Quest for the Last Wild Tigers

Ruth Padel

Walker & Company
New York

For my mother, who taught us to look
at animals and plants

'Tiger Drinking at Forest Pool'

Water, moonlight, danger, dream.
Bronze urn, angled on a tree-root: one
Slash of light, then gone. A red moon
Seen through clouds, or almost seen.
Treasure found but lost, flirting between
The worlds of lost and found. An unjust law
Repealed, a wish come true, a lifelong
Sadness healed. Haven, in the mind,
To anyone hurt by littleness. A prayer,
For the moment, saved; treachery forgiven.
Flame of the crackle-glaze tangle, amber
Reflected in grey milk-jade. An old song
Remembered, long debt paid.
A painting on silk, which may fade.

CONTENTS

PART III   SOUTH
South-East Asia, Indonesia – Indo-Chinese, Malayan, Sumatran; and the
Extinct Tigers: Javan, Balinese and (out of place) the Caspian

PART IV   RETURN TO SOUTH INDIA
Tigers Today and Tomorrow

ACKNOWLEDGEMENTS

For reading, listening and commenting, whether on paragraphs, chapters or whole drafts, many thanks to Volta Bone, Amanda Bright, Gwen Burnyeat, Mrinal Chatterjee, Sarah Christie, Elaine Feinstein, John Goodrich, Lavinia Greenlaw, Kerin Hope, Peter Jackson, Ullas Karanth, Tom Maddox, Debbie Martyr, Dale Miquelle, Miranda Seymour, Jo Shapcott, Valmik Thapar; to everyone at Kindlings; and, over and over again, Patrick Walsh.

For help in the field, everyone in the book; and many more. I had to keep some people out of the pages for the sake of brevity, but I am very grateful to them all, which means:

In Bangladesh: Rubaiyat Mansur of the Guide Tours, Dhaka.

In Bhutan: the Kingdom of Bhutan for its kind invitation to visit; Hishey Tshering of Bhutan Heritage Travels, Thimphu; Karma Tshering, Head of Park Management Planning and Integrated Conservation and Development Programme; Sharap Wangchuk, Tiger Programme (Nature Conservation Division); Sangay Wangchuk, Joint Director Nature Conservation Division; Tshewang Norbu, Deputy Park Ranger in Jigme Singye Wangchuck National Park; Sangai, ranger in Thrumshingla National Park; Chadho Tensin of WWF Bhutan; Karma Phuntso and his parents; Princess Kunzang Choden.

In China: Endi Zhang, Aili Kang, Bing Li and staff of the WCS, Shanghai; in Hunchun, students Liu Yu (also for magnificent interpreting) and Yue, studying ungulates (just as important as tigers themselves); the Director and staff of Hunchun Tiger Reserve, Jilin province, especially Li Zhi Xing, Director of Policy and Education; in

Yihuang, the Director and staff of Yihuang Reserve, Jiangxi province; and Wang and Cao, translators from Nanchang.

In India: Amanda Bright and Carole Elliott of GTP; Anil, resident naturalist of Tuli Tiger Resort, Kanha; Mrinal Chatterjee and the crew of his boat; Raghu Chundawat, Vinnie and Anil of the Ken River Lodge, Panna; Vipul Jain, guide to Ranthambhore National Park; Lee and Stephen Emery; Ullas Karanth of WCS; all members and Trustees of Wildlife First; and the Wildcats, especially Shreedev Hulikere; Ayappa Paniker, D. V. Girish, P. K. Sen, Fateh Singh Rathore, Jaisal Singh and the staff at Sher Bagh, Ranthambhore; Valmik Thapar.

In Laos: Changsavi Vongkhamheng of WCS; Boatang in Phou Loei Biodiversity Reserve; Arlyne and Mike Johnson of WCS; and Toh, who saw me safe through the Nam Ha Bio-diversity Reserve.

In Nepal: Charles 'Chuck' McDougal; John Roberts, Field/Guest Relations Officer at Tiger Tops; all the staff, especially trackers, naturalists and mahouts, at Tiger Tops Jungle Lodge, Royal Chitwan National Park.

In Russia: Olga Bekhtereva of Dalintourist Travel, Vladivostock; Sergei Bereznuk of the Phoenix Fund; Dale Miquelle; John Goodrich and the staff of WCS Vladivostock and Terney; Michiel Hötte of the Tigris Foundation; Yevgeny and Tamara of Terney; Dr Yudin of the Russian Academy of Biological Sciences, Gaivoron village, near Khanka Nature Reserve, Primorye; Sergei Zubtsov, Head of Inspection Tiger.

In Sumatra: Tom Maddox, and everyone working for ZSL; Sean Marron and Ian Rowland of PT Asiatic Persada; Elva Gemita, Volta Bone; Debbie Martyr of FFI and all the Tiger Team members; Ibu Lystia Kusumardhani of the Indonesian Forest Service; Ramla of J. L. Sumur, Aceh Village no. 34, Lahat; Vera of PT Trijaya Travel Medan, and Lilik for interpreting and guidance under difficult circumstances; and, backstage and *in absentia*, Jeremy Holden.

In Thailand: Tim Redford of Wildaid; Tony Lynam of WCS.

For advice, help, and answering ignorant emails or phone calls out of the blue, Anthony Aris, Debbie Banks of EIA, Alan Blanchard of Tiger Trails, Amanda Bright of GTP, Judy Mills, Tessa McGregor, Dan Cao of the WWF Traditional Chinese Medicine Programme, Andy Fisher, Head of the Metropolitan Police Wildlife Unit at New Scotland

Yard, the Harrison Institute; Peter Jackson, Chairman Emeritus, Cat Specialist Group, World Conservation Union (IUCN); Monirul Khan; John Lewis of the International Veterinary Group; John Keeble; Karma Phuntso; Li Quan of Save China's Tigers; Alan Rabinowitz and Linde Ostro of WCS; Frances Wood of the British Library. And two people who put me in touch with other tiger people all over the world, and were unfailingly generous with their time, advice, knowledge and judgement: Sarah Christie of ZSL and Valmik Thapar.

Thanks also to the Calouste Gulbenkian Foundation for a grant from their 'Arts and Science' programme, shared with Dr Ullas Karanth. And to those who extended invitations to give poetry readings, through which I learned about countries and people in a different way: the British Council in Mandalay, Yangon and Shanghai; Elena Vasil'eva and the Grey Horse Poetry Circle, Vladivostock; Ayappa Paniker and the Poetry Chain, Trivandrum; Dr Yusrita Yanti of Bung Hatta University, Padang; and to the Environmental Investigation Agency for permission to reproduce arrows from their map in *The Tigerskin Trail*.

Thanks also for information, and permission to visit the Jambi plantation, to Sean Marron, President Director of PT Asiatic Persada, and Ian Rowland, Environment Manager, PT Asiatic Persada. A few paragraphs in three chapters derive from short stories I published in *Dublin Review*, *Prospect Magazine* and *Hyphen: Short Stories by Poets*, edited by Ra Page (Comma and Carcanet Press, 2003). Many thanks to three editors it was a pleasure to work with. Finally, to my agent and friend Patrick Walsh, creative, merciless and patient critic; my beloved editor Antonia Hodgson, intuitive, generous, always supportive however far away; to Stephen Guise, for work on an intricately messy manuscript; Vanessa Neuling of Time Warner; to Myles Burnyeat for help, translation and support in Russia; and to Gwen, as always, for comments, criticism, excellent judgement and constant support.

ABBREVIATIONS AND NOTE
ON PLACE NAMES

BKSDA	Department for Conservation of Natural Resources, Indonesia
CEC	Central Empowered Committee (set up by Supreme Court of India in 2002 to investigate abuse of India's forest land)
CITES	Convention of International Trade in Endangered Species
DFO	deputy forest officer, India
EIA	Environment Investigation Agency
FFI	Flora and Fauna International
GTP	Global Tiger Patrol (a UK charity)
MoEF	Ministry of Environment and Forests, India
NGO	non-governmental organization
TCM	traditional Chinese medicine
TWP	temporary working permit (for mines in India)
UXO	unexploded ordnance (dropped in Cambodia and Laos during the Vietnam War)
WCS	Wildlife Conservation Society, USA
WWF	World Wildlife Fund
ZSL	Zoological Society of London

Among so many unfamiliar names, I have used the old Anglicized forms for place names which Western audiences in the past have generally recognized, such as Calcutta, Bombay, Rangoon, or the Irrawaddy River.

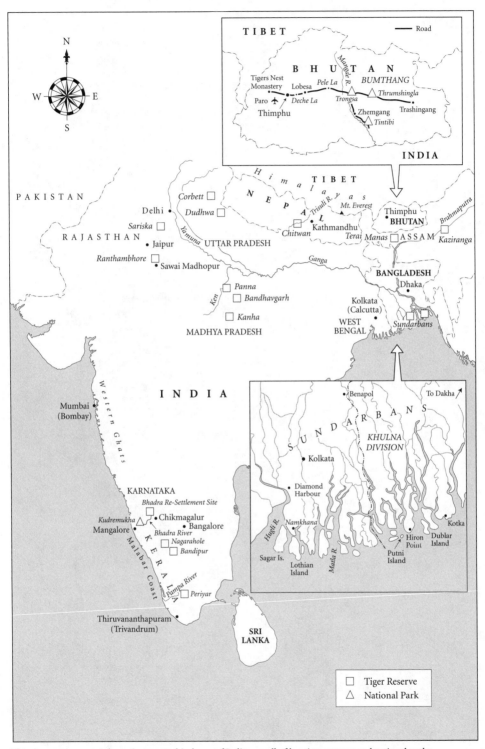

This does not represent the entire geographical area of India, nor all of her tiger reserves and national parks

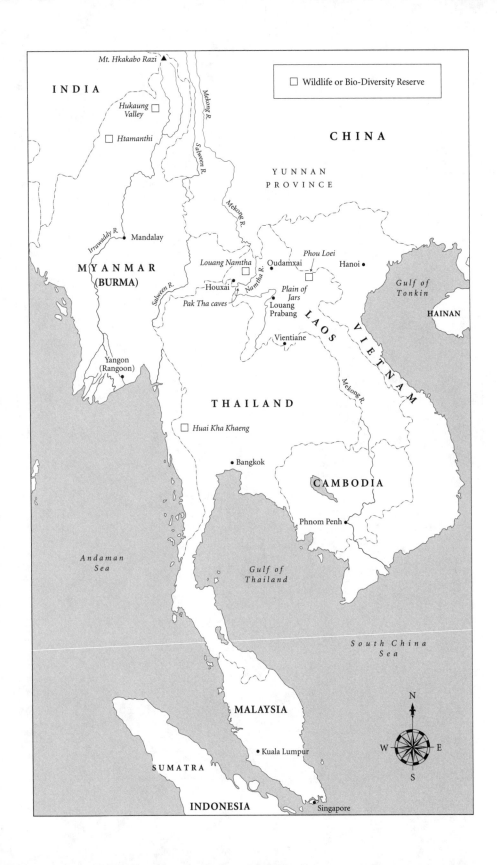

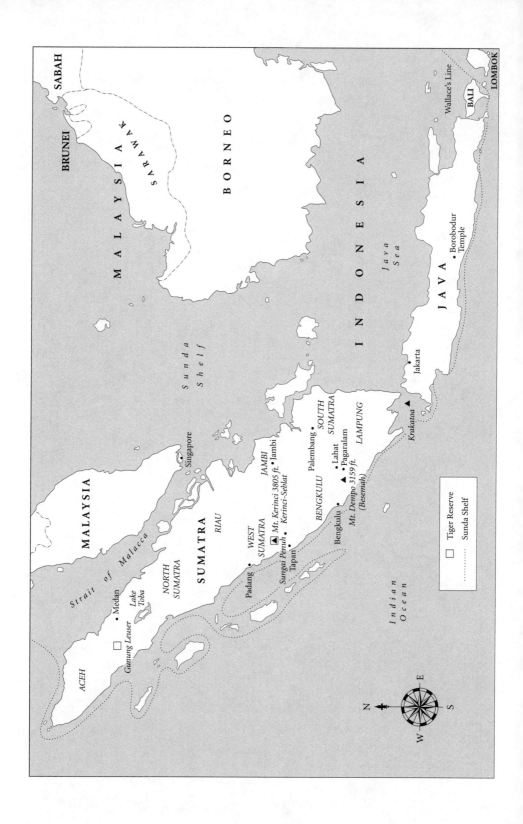

PROLOGUE
TEENAGER

St Lucy's Day, the winter solstice. How did Lucy get the day of least light? But this is India, a forest in Madhya Pradesh highlands. If you pressed your face against a map of the country it would meet your nose. At three thirty in the afternoon even St Lucy is full of light here. It falls on red-gold and snowy fur: one of the two or three thousand wild Indian tigers alive at the beginning of the new millennium. He lies on his back by a stream, his massed paws floppy, innocent as leaves.

Daylight usually means sleep for tigers but this is a young male, sixteen months, restless and curious like young males everywhere. He rolls over. Amber-tipped grasses rustle above. His mother is asleep nearby, his sister's cheek on her hock. Sun slips through leaves making a familiar jigsaw of light and dark. Cats' eyes are differently made from ours but do have colour rods. He is looking at a comforting muddle of gently breathing gold – as we would see it – and burnished green.

Whatever artist dreamed up the tiger face exaggerated the eyes. White butterfly patches wing up like higher, bigger eyes above surprisingly small real ones of ochre. Black hieroglyphs in these patches vary from tiger to tiger. Over his right eye is a blurry black triangle with three crescent moons above. Over the left a worm of black flame.

Biologists classify him as *Panthera tigris*. They once classed tigers with cats in genus *Felis*. But after studying the cat larynx they put tigers in another genus, *Panthera*, with lions, leopards, jaguars. In most cats the hyoid bone, which supports the back of the tongue, is held close to the skull by a series of short, joined bones. In *Panthera*, these are imperfectly ossified; an elastic ligament of gristle fixes jaw to larynx, letting the larynx pulse like a rattly exhaust: *Panthera* cats roar. But tigers do not do it often. The molecular and gene structures of pantherine cats suggest that lion, leopard and jaguar have more in common with each other. The tiger's main call audible to us is a low *aoom*, which vibrates through forest like a foghorn.

This one rears on hind legs, unsheathes claws from cream-coloured fur of huge front feet, and stretches, six foot of him, scoring cuts in the fissured *sal* tree. When he is in his prime, five years (if he gets there), he may reach nine foot or ten. Belly and back dip like a swag of washing. He is making his mark. He drops down and sniffs a bush his mother sprayed a few hours ago. The muscles of his upper lip draw back in the spasm called *flehmen* by the tiger-observation trade. He stays in this grimace a moment, upper lip wrinkled above his teeth, deep furrows up his nose. With nerve-cells in his nose called his Jacobson's organ, he is savouring fragrance from which, older and alone, he will get his crucial social news: age, sex, size and physical condition – maybe emotional condition, how do we know? – of another tiger.

Tigers are too heavily armed to meet often. Like nuclear powers, they depend on peaceful co-existence with their only peers, each other, avoiding conflict by a silent gossip of scent marks ruled by conventions as byzantine as NATO protocol. Their currency is a mix of urine and anal-gland secretion. Females squirt a pyramid of fine drizzle, a male reverses his penis to shoot a more focused jet. These tangy hieroglyphs are the basis of tiger social code, augmented by scratches on trees and scrapes along a path: graffiti blazonings of territory. His mother makes them constantly, updating her boundaries. They are tiger ABC. He is learning to read and to write.

His mother holds ideal territory, thirty-five square kilometres with water, full of deer. She maintains it vigilantly. But she is lucky. If this were Russia, she would be hunting sparse deer in two hundred square kilometres instead. Where prey is scarce, tigers live further apart. They evolved as forest animals and need forested real estate where they can sleep, drink, hunt and shelter cubs. Territory means cover, food, water, sex. Females want one large enough to feed cubs. Males want a super-territory, with several breeding females and cubs they know are theirs, and can protect. If a new male usurps an old one's territory he kills its cubs and mates with their mothers to spread his genes. Females defend their cubs bitterly, sometimes to the death, but cannot help coming into heat for him if the cubs die.

This tigress opens her eyes, raises her head. The neural flows and synapses that take care of long-term planning in her brain say this is the moment for a swim. Her face, framed by a wide white ruff, has perfectly symmetrical markings: yellow eyes, kohl outline round a rose-brown nose, black hammer-and-sickle curls in white wings above her eyes. She yawns. The outer skin of her lips is gleaming black. Below yellow-fissured bottom canines the gum is pink.

Tigers would be no good at Whiskas. Their teeth evolved for tearing and scraping. They have the largest canines of all big cats, two and a half to three inches long, threaded with pressure-sensitive nerves to find the precise place between vertebrae to sever a spinal cord. Leaving two pink dips under the canines, the black skin of her lower gum swoops up to the centre, to four small whiter teeth between the canines: the incisors, which pluck feathers and scrape flesh off bone. If you looked from behind, the white target spots on the backs of her ears would match white blobby seed-heads scattered through grasses rippling in this breeze like keys on a pianola. Two paces back, and you'd miss her entirely. On her, and her sisters throughout Asia, the future of wild tigers depends.

She is the ideal teacher. He learns how to be a tiger from her. How his ears are the best information-gatherers, picking up high-frequency rustles in undergrowth, low-frequency calls from other tigers; he can judge sound geometry by rotating his pinnae, the external ear flaps. He learns, too, from playing with his sister: all those forehand swipes, leaps, rolls, play-snarls. Tigers are solitary but have strong relationships, likes and dislikes. A tiger meeting a friend waves its tail slowly. Personalities vary. Some tigers bond with adult siblings, even share food. Wild tigers are hard to see, and even harder to watch systematically over a long period. There is much scientists do *not* know about how tigers communicate, how flexible they are in their social being. Learning, without disturbing them, is tricky.

This one is not ready to leave his mother. He is all potential. He looks like a tiger but he has no ruff, his paws are too big for his legs, his bones and brain are still growing. He is a possible tiger. He could not kill deer by himself. He will probably strike off on his own before his second birthday, in 'dispersal': the beginning of his adult life. Young females stay closer to mother, may share her territory, move next door. But for him, the time is coming when father, and mother too, will want him out. He will become a transient. Of all tigers a dispersing transient male is most at risk. He and his sister have learned this territory together, stone by stone. She may stay here all her life. He will go to unknown zones. The journey he was born for: to find and hold new territory, spread *his* genes. But the best territory will be occupied and defended by heavier experienced males. He will have to travel far, and find food in places where other males, for good reason, do not go. He will be vulnerable to them, but also to the other creatures pressing constantly at the forest edge. He may have to enter their territory to eat. Like the robin in your garden, he has to kill to live. If he cannot get wild prey he will approach cows, dogs, goats. He will have no idea how dangerous this is.

His mother has been lying against a rock. Now she gets to her feet. She walks slowly, and her teenagers follow, suede shoulder to suede shoulder, towards a rubbery brown pool. Tigers love water. They are brilliant swimmers and never lie far from water if they can help it. She stares at the far bank to check for danger, turns round like a combine harvester parking, slips in backwards. It looks clumsy, but this is tiger practice. Tigers like their whiskers dry. The cubs follow, they copy everything, they learn by mimesis. She is exacting: she teaches every needed tiger thing. They slip into bloodwarm water and swim side by side, three heads calm as paint. The lapping light picks up their wake as long wrinkles, liquid rubber bands skimmering the surface.

Tiger life is alternation, long quiet followed by furious action. Fast, then feast. She is preparing herself, and them, for an evening hunt. She has problems with them now, especially the male. She cannot leave them in bushes, they have to come with her and learn, but he ruins things at the last minute, bursting out of hiding. His sister is more cautious. She crouches, learning self-restraint till the last second: a hard lesson for young males of any species.

She comes to rest against the bank. The cubs lie against her, half in

half out of bright weed. Tiger families are very physical, very affec-
tionate. Their paws rest on hers, heads against her chest and shoulder.
Her body is their touchstone. Branches over the pool rustle, dropping
sun-spokes over mud and floating weed.

The young male moves first, rubs his cheek against his mother's
and climbs out, staggering and ungainly a moment on the bank till he
gets his balance. Brown water drops fall like cappuccino from his
belly on split-end grass. A racket-tailed drongo calls, the mimic of
the Indian jungle, a black glossy bird with tail-feathers like two black
lollipops. A sentinel langur monkey barks from a *sal* tree over the
pool. Both have seen the movement: a tiger, a predator, jumping. The
tigress's whiskers twitch in irritation. Alarm calls cross the species
barrier: they are the jungle's lingua franca. Everyone wants to know
when a predator is near. Grey langurs, the silky, silvery monkeys of
Indian forests, large as Labradors, are the eyes of the jungle, packing
the trees with black judgemental faces. They have their own territories
and social worries but are always watching for predators. They bark
to say where predators are. Deer listen. What this tigress would like is
no langurs, and deer shapes at the water's edge. She gets out, followed by her daughter. They shake themselves, lie down. It is not
time yet.

Most tigers hunt in early morning or late evening. They are cre-
puscular: active in half-light. They can be nocturnal too: tigers often
walk and hunt at night. There is no fast rule: some move in daylight.
It depends on the forest, prey, temperature, the tiger's personality,
and human activity. Any disturbance, and tigers fall back on the
night.

Light rain begins to fall on the pool surface. Small animals, voles,
frogs, slender secret snakes, breathe differently now the gods have
left. Humbler, shyer life comes back to normal in the grass.

But the male stands, restless. You could say, I could say, he is waiting for me. He does not know that. He is a gold vase filling with
knowledge. Every breath he takes he is learning, from the forest, the
langurs, the grasses, prey killed by his mother. But he has not much
sense of a future; and tigers, though many are very curious, did not
evolve to be that interested in human beings.

*

I do not know it either. England is five and a half hours behind India. I am filling an electric kettle in London with no thought of tigers. I know little about them except Jim Corbett's *Man-Eaters of Kumaon,* which I read as a child. I am not thinking about tigers. There are other things on my mind.

PART I

OUT OF THE WEST

India, Bangladesh, Nepal, Bhutan

Bengal Tigers

1

SUNDOWN

Only the tiger in the jungle is lonely as the samurai.

Alain Delon, *The Samurai*

In London, St Lucy's was the darkest, coldest day as well as the shortest, and the last working day before Christmas. While that teenage tiger was waking, a carpenter was painting my cupboards. After months of kitchenless chaos we had a floor and worktop, but at the end of a very dark year. My father had died of a rare leukaemia. My friend Kay, a Greek writer I had travelled and laughed with for twenty years, was on a round-the-clock line of oxygen in an Athens flat with emphysema. I'd sat by her bed, stopping her throwing herself off it. Another old friend who lived far away died of a tumour in the foot. And my dog Jenny, bought from a pet shop at six weeks old, terrified all her sixteen years of losing me, found that her back legs and bowels no longer worked. She was deaf, confused, embarrassed. 'You can do this for her,' said the vet, tilting the needle.

Other things might have been just black vaudeville, any other time. A roofer took the top off the house then disappeared, leaving plastic over it. My daughter's bedroom flooded. I cut the heart out of her carpet before it brought down the ceiling below, and got another roofer to finish. The first refused to remove his scaffolding unless I paid for work he had not done. The new one found beer cans all over the gutters. *And* we had rats. We could hear them but couldn't use poison because of my daughter's spaniel, who had cheered Jenny's last years. She tracked rat babies at play in the walls, cocking her ears as if this entertainment was laid on specially. I caught the mother in a trap and drowned her in a dustbin of water. She died standing up, trying to get out. I was also very short of money. I had done some work, but would not get the money till after Christmas. Still, we had a kitchen. Joe, the carpenter, diabetic, bald and kind, was on his tummy with a spirit level. My teenage daughter was out. And at noon I would see the person who for five years had been the other centre of my life. We did not live together but we travelled together, and in London saw each other twice a week, in six-hour slices of time. Our Christmases were a rushed lunch fitted round our different families.

His parents came from the West Peloponnese. His mother from a mountain village, his father from Pylos, overlooked by the Palace of King Nestor. (I had been there once with my own father.) But he had never seen Pylos. His parents emigrated young; their kids became more English than the English, relishing establishment and inner circles. 'In the loop,' he'd say. 'That's where I want to be.' He did not learn his parents' language or go back to Greece. He worked in the City, a director of various businesses and charities I knew little about. His outside was all suits and Oxford accent; I loved the inside, quick, inquisitive, ebullient. *Pylos!* I thought he was so lucky.

Just now, though, not so lucky. Two weeks ago we had been in New Orleans, magically happy. When we got back the rest of his life blew up around him because, he said, of me. Other people were involved. He told me on the phone. We were each other's inner life; I never wanted to disturb his outer one, and now walked to the wine bar petrified for him, for us.

He was under a ceiling painted with Toulouse-Lautrec dancers kicking legs over champagne glasses and leopards. Fifty, in a dark suit. Crisp close curls – they, at least, were Greek – grizzled at the temples. Black shaggy eyebrows, wire Armani glasses we'd chosen together. A swirly tie I'd given him. He loved surface, sparkle, clothes, swagger; he brought intensity to the slightest thing. He was biting his nails. He asked the waiter to do lunch in thirty minutes.

Red wine came. Ancient Greeks foretold the future from reflections in basins of water. I saw only my own eye in the red-black surface. He finished his drink in one gulp as if his throat had no flap, ordered another, heaped butter on walnut bread. I held my hands round my glass. Puddled olive and gold sparkled from the green amber ring he had given me. It came with a leaflet saying amber was the tears of gods. A heap of ivory linguini sat in front of me.

'You're going to eat all that up. You're too thin, young lady. You never eat all I give you.'

He often said this. We looked into each other over glass rims as we had looked all over the world. Whenever our eyes met, we were in a good place. Now was different.

'Why do my wine-glasses never shine like this?' When we had people to dinner he rewashed my glasses. If we changed wines he rewashed again, drying them with clean cloths. Women, he said, never take seriously enough the wine men bring.

'Let's have another glass.'

'But the time . . .' Christmas shopping, for both our houses: turkeys, wrapping paper.

'Indulge me.'

'I got you all this in twenty minutes,' said the waiter. 'Now you've stayed an hour.'

'Glass of house red and a spritzer,' he said coldly.

I pushed linguini round my plate.

He started shaking. 'What's happening to me?'

'Maybe, just for a moment, you're letting go.'

If it makes sense to talk of hearts breaking, mine was for him. For myself, but most for him. He lived for getting away with things. Now there was no way out. A thought-bubble, CRISIS, hung over our heads. There was only one gift to give. I had not realized; now I did. For his sake, I had to break these bars – like Bagheera in the maharajah's cage at Udaipur.

The Jungle Book was my favourite childhood reading. My hero, Bagheera the black leopard, had a bare patch under his chin from past captivity. A collar rubbed. Until, he says, 'I broke the silly lock with one blow of my paw.' Yes. If I let this moment go it would not come again.

I said, 'You've got to stop seeing me.'

Walls had not fallen. This would solve things for him. I had no idea what it would do to me. The bar went on with its wine-bar life. The ceiling billowed with leopards. He held the idea to the light, a wine-taster swirling a glass. He spotted a flaw.

'But we'd be very unhappy.'

'It's the only way.'

He looked at my mouth as if treasure were buried there. I looked at folds of cheek familiar as my own hands; lips that free-associated fragments from dreams into my ear, when we slept like double almonds in one shell.

'I must go.' He drained his glass, called for the bill, got up. His coat swung over the table. He made eight times what I did in a year; paying made him feel in charge. I felt like my own ghost. From one sip of house red to the next I had rushed into an ending. His Christmas present: life without me for ever. I looked over my shoulder at pushed-back chairs, my unfinished wine. We walked down the hill to his car.

'Look,' I said. 'I'm holding your heart.'

'Have I still got one?'

'I'm holding it in.'

One minute more, the last of five years. A barn owl's lifespan, Darwin's *Beagle* voyage.

'We're so happy together,' he said, as he drove. 'Even in a crisis.'

'Dancing on the precipice,' I said, backing out, car door against my hip, mouth on his ear. This was where it stopped, life with love at its centre that made the world dazzle.

'We're so fab,' he said. 'We said all the right things.'

His car joined the rosary of tail-lights. Two geese overhead honked to each other. Wind whistled in their wings. *Are you there?* What is reassurance, for a goose? I eased his ring off my finger, dropped it into my pocket and walked through darkening streets towards lunch-for-twenty-five and getting down decorations from a now-dry attic. That was my St Lucy's Day.

St Lucy was Sicilian, martyred in the persecutions of Diocletian. Her rejected pagan lover betrayed her as a Christian. Dangerous thing to do, reject a man. I did not know this: my eyes were going to be opened for St Lucy is the divine eye-specialist. She holds a plate with eyes on it. Her name comes from *lux*, light. But like the winter solstice she stands for the darkness before new light. In a poem about losing his beloved, John Donne calls her day the year's midnight. 'The world's whole sap is sunk.' He is 'every dead thing, in whom love wrought new alchemy'. Donne says everything best about love, including losing it.

For us, the alchemy seemed endless. Now I felt amputated, but also desperately anxious for my lost limb. There had been medical tests. I worried about the results as I followed his Christmas in my mind. On Boxing Day, *I* fell ill. The day I got up, a letter lay on the mat by the front door he had entered night after night for five years, rushing arms round me as if he panning for gold beneath my spine.

Winter sunlight fell on ten accusing, self-pitying pages. Writing I had only ever seen saying loving things was blaming me: not for break-ing it off (he seemed not to have noticed that), but for having a relationship with him. 'We're so close,' he used to say, 'it's like having a second skin.' His voice was still on my mobile saying, 'You're every-thing I've ever loved.' Generous and tender had been everything. Now he too saw we had to be apart; he was making this decision his own. He had to. But no word of care, here, for anyone but him. 'I've lost all my mirth and you helped. You can phone me at work, if you like. Not any other way.'

What *was* this? I imagined him writing at night in the garden shed. Saw the colour-trailed glass I'd given him empty on the desk as he licked the envelope, feeling sorry for himself but proud he'd done it: given up the love of his life. This sign-off to his longest ever faithful relationship, the one by which he'd tried to redefine himself, was eye-opening. 'You've made me good,' he would say. 'You don't know how you've changed me.' I had not asked him to change. He'd wanted that.

Like most British poets I live freelance. Teaching, talks, radio, poetry readings, schools, art shows, all sorts of things, wherever poetry is useful. Work that had been commissioned by a charity weeks ago was suddenly jettisoned. I would not get the fee – money that would have been all I earned in December. Our worlds hardly overlapped, but he happened to direct that charity. 'You were spectacularly wrong-headed', he wrote now, 'for doing that work.'

When I broke it off, I imagined, dimly, what it would feel like; the way (I imagine) you know it will hurt before you jump under a train.

I thought we parted with care for each other. Suttee. A lovers' leap. Like the end of another Donne poem:

> But think that we
> Are but turned aside to sleep;
> They who one another keep
> Alive, ne'er parted be.

We looked after each other. I assumed we would go on caring.

'In Buddhism,' said a friend, 'you are your actions. His show what he's really like.' I was ashamed for him. Showing his true colours was his last gift. But not one he meant to give.

The world looks dead when you've walked around it for years with love. Every road reminded me of him. I needed a clean-sheet world. A newspaper ad offered a fortnight's bed and breakfast on the Malabar coast for four hundred pounds, flights included. I borrowed the cash; the office was above a second-hand car firm in a back street. Its name was Go A Way. It had one ticket left. The visa section of the Indian consulate had a tiger on the wall: amber, charcoal, big gold stare. The *Rough Guide* said a tiger reserve lay eight hours' bus ride from where I would stay.

I was a Fellow of the Zoological Society but had used this only to entertain children. Now I was a different person, things I had not had time to investigate could show themselves. I consulted the Sumatran tigers in London Zoo. There were repairs to the gibbon cage nearby; the tigers sat under bushes fuming. Over the road was the Fellows' library, where I had never been. I showed my Fellow's card, found the mammal bay, borrowed four tiger books to go with Go A Way. What did it matter *what* I did now, except adore my daughter and support her, best I could, through being a teenager? This was the dark. 'Nor will my Sun renew,' says Donne's St Lucy poem. Everything, except my daughter, was midnight now.

Only it wasn't. I finished my tiger books, borrowed four more, mostly by someone called Valmik Thapar. I was being pulled towards the great animal solitary. Tigers were about surviving, alone.

*

'There is another Loneliness', says Emily Dickinson, 'that many die without.' Her poems are about surviving pain. Would she have written them without solitude?

> Water, is taught by Thirst –
> Land – by the Oceans passed –
> Transport – by Throe –
> Peace – by its Battles told –
> Love, by Memorial Mold –
> Birds, by the Snow.

Maybe the important things come at the bottom of the pit, when you discover what's in the sump. What I saw was the tiger's glow.

Borges's poem 'The Other Tiger' is set in a library. The poet longs to touch a real tiger walking in river-mud in Bengal, but can't bridge the gap between imagined and real. His poem is about that gap. I can only dream you, he tells the tiger:

> and yet,
> I keep hunting
> the other tiger, the one not in my poem.

He is writing about writing a poem about a tiger:

> The tiger I summon in my poem
> is a tiger of symbols and shadows,
> a series of literary metaphors,
> memories of encyclopedias.

I wanted to cross that divide. Poems help you re-see things but the world has its own reality too. Trying to forget the presence in my city of someone around whom I had drawn my own symbols and shadows, I suddenly wanted real forests, real tigers.

The night before I left I had a drink with someone who led Buddhist retreats in Bhutan. He sketched a map on a beer-mat.

'You'd love Bhutan. There are tigers on the wall of every house. In their Buddhism, tiger is the ground you start from, where there's nothing to lose. That's where the curiosity, the sniffing-things-out a tiger does, can begin. The tiger is the broken heart.'

'You're kidding.'

Was he telepathic? Telling me what I wanted to hear? All I said was I wanted to see tigers. I forgot they lived outside India too.

'Not at all. The tiger's the beginning of change, and you can't change without suffering. The tiger is the beginning of the journey; tiger is where you start.'

St Lucy was sundown, the light that failed. But sundown is when the jungle comes alive, the tiger begins to roam.

You bring to India what is in you. The people, animals, gods and bacteria you meet there decide what you do with it. I came feeling lost. What should I do in Kerala? The person I loved was in the underworld, or in Elysium, as lost as I was, and irrecoverable.

I got off the plane in light brighter than I'd ever seen. Kerala was created when a god flung an axe at the sea. The sea drew back leaving land that had never seen sky before. I felt like that too. Uncovered land, the person I would be without him. A taxi with tweed seats drove me along causeways dotted with cows and wasp-yellow autorickshaws. Painted temples, palms, a sand dune dead-end where I and the driver carried my bags into a cupped-hand bay of steep sand and boisterous foam: the Arabian Sea. Then mud alleys, tiny canals, people selling mineral water and Ayurvedic massage, to a courtyard in a marsh of twilit palms, a bare small room with cement floor, Formica table and ragged yellow curtain, satisfyingly unlike anywhere I had been with him.

He travelled for work; I went with him. He adored glamour and luxury, felt he had a right to them. His work could afford it, so we did that and loved it. He would *hate* this. We had once met in an Irish pub I suggested. 'What are we doing in this scabby boozer?' he asked. That was how he would see this. To me it was a refuge. There was a wall-safe I could lock the laptop in, wild tigers down the road, and I could not pick up a phone. Here I could begin to let myself feel at last the moral shock.

As Malabar night fell, I balanced the laptop lead on the table and a suitcase so it reached the high electric plug. Outside seemed extreme, unknown; I could not look for dinner in the dark.

In fact, of course, it was fine. The place was run by kind, careful people, who knew exactly what they were doing. But I turned inwards, to books. When in India, find out about tigers.

Tigers live wild only in Asia. There are none in Africa, never have been. Their fourteen countries today are India, Bangladesh, Nepal, Bhutan; Russia, Korea, China, including Tibet; South-East Asia (Burma, Thailand, Vietnam, Laos, Cambodia); Malaysia; Indonesia as far as Sumatra. They once lived also in Mongolia, Afghanistan, Pakistan, Persia, around the Caspian Sea. They stretched from east Turkey to east Russia; they flourished on Java and Bali.

By the mid-twentieth century tigers were classified into eight sub-species according to apparent physical differences in size, skull-shape, colour, stripe-patterns. The northernmost tigers, Siberians, were considered to be the largest and palest, with widest-apart stripes; the southerners, Sumatrans, were smaller and darker, with closer stripes. But individual tigers vary, and what distinguishes the subspecies now is genetic and molecular sequence. Recent DNA tests reveal there are nine sub-species. Javanese, Balinese and Caspian tigers are extinct. But six others are still around: Bengal (India, Himalayas), Siberian or Amur (Russian far east, north-east China), South China, Indo-Chinese (northern South-East Asia), Malayan (the newest, recently distin-guished from Indo-Chinese), and Sumatran. None are white. White tigers are not a sub-species but a mutation – and, in some countries, a significant myth. Zoos have bred them artificially, for cuteness. White tigers in circuses today are a human artefact.

Tigers evolved in the Pleistocene era when the climate varied dram-atically. Ice came and went, sea levels went down and up, and cut-off animal families developed differently. This was speciation. Deer and cattle families expanded, exploring different kinds of tropical forest, creating a niche for a large forest predator who could handle them all. Enter the tiger. In different climates and forests – deserts, wet saline forest, snow, dense rainforest – and isolated from the populations they left behind as they spread south into India and South-East Asia, tigers in different places came to vary genetically. The names we give them mainly reflect human geography. This is the tiger's problem: that where it lives, people live too.

I slept, but went on seeing tigers. Only gold ones: I am glad to say I never dreamed white. First I was in a ship. Tigers swam below among peacock sparkles. I had to jump down to them. I was afraid. Then I was in a train; tigers looked at me from fields outside. Then one took refuge in my bedroom. I had to protect him, help him escape to a forest.

I woke to Hindi pop music outside. Protect and set free? I had been there, done that. Finally I dreamed I had treasure hidden in an Arabian Nights cave. (The Arabian Ocean was getting to me.) I did not know what the treasure was, but did have a key – no, a magic word, to open the cave. Then I forgot the word. As I woke I remembered but it was too late, the treasure was lost; my eyelashes were wet with tears. The only thing left of my treasure was a fading word. Then not even a word: a number. Four digits, like the safe-lock. I lay listening to crashing waves, repeating the number as the sun came through holes in the curtains.

Then I realized what number it was. For years, I'd rung it every day. Ringing it was like breathing. Of course my eyes were wet. Even on a Kerala morning St Lucy, patron of opened eyes and men who thought they were rejected, was at work.

The wall-safe was damp as a Turkish bath. I wrapped the laptop in a plastic bag and followed a canal past cows, jungle crows, a small grey snake. I left my sandals outside the phone shack, booked nights at Periyar Tiger Reserve, and rang a poet whose number I had been given.

'Come,' he said.

First day in India, first auto-rickshaw, a causeway full of lorries. We broke down and stood in blazing sun with two humped cows. The driver flagged another, who took me to Ayappa Paniker, Kerala's Seamus Heaney.

Ayappa is a Keralan name and Keralan deity, Shiva's son by an enchantress who abandoned him by the Pampa river. A childless king found him and reared him as his, then had a son of his own. To get rid of the foundling, the queen pretended she was ill. Hoping tigers would eat Ayappa, she sent him to the forest to find the only cure: tiger's milk. But Hindu gods were created to destroy particular demons and Ayappa was born to conquer one called Mahishi. In the forest he killed Mahishi, then returned with tiger's milk. The royal couple realized he was divine, begged forgiveness, pressed him to stay. But, mission accomplished, he departed, promising to protect the kingdom. What I liked was that he carried back tiger's milk riding the tigress.

Ayappa Paniker was small with a cloudy grey beard, sitting on a porch beside a wall-tile of Ganesh, elephant-headed god of propitious beginnings. A Ganesh swinging his trunk, dancing and merry.

We talked poetry, swapped books. A small saucer between us held mixed granules of salt and sugar.

'The Sanskrit for feeling is *bhava*, related to imagination, *bhavana*. In English, "imagination" is related to *imago*, "the visual".'

We talked of how different cultures mingle imagination and feeling, word and thought, sweet and sour. India was suddenly less strange. On his mobile, Ayappa arranged a reading for me at the local poetry society. 'Would you like to meet Rama Iyer?' he asked. 'Director of Margi?'

An Indian actor friend had told me about Koodiyatum, Keralan theatre old as Greek tragedy, and the Koodiyatum company called Margi.

'Margi's last performance this season begins in one hour at a Shiva temple down the road. Rama Iyer will meet you there.'

It was hot, dusty, trafficky, and I hadn't a word of Malayalam. I walked outside old walls beside racing lorries. There was more than one Shiva temple; mine was in a back-street beside a twilit tank of ghostly egrets. Straw stars hung in the vestibule, frogs chirruped outside, sky darkened.

The stage was bare, with wood drums and a lamp with three flames. A musician saluted the drums. A tall, gentle man with a pitted face folded himself on the floor beside me. 'Rama Iyer,' he whispered. Actors with green painted faces entered, touching the ground as they came. Their eyeballs were scarlet.

'They make them red by sliding eggplant flower seeds under the lids.'

The hero was a god in a forest. He saw a beautiful girl, and the god of desire shot an arrow at him. The drama was the god's emotions as he described different parts of this girl; not in words, just with body and face. His eyes rolled. Muscles flexed in his cheeks, in places I never dreamed you had muscles.

'Eyes right means surprise. Eyes up, anger. Eyes whirling like a Catherine wheel, desire.'

We got through her eyes, hands, throat, breasts. To rolling drumbeats, the actor told his muscle-by-muscle story of intolerable desire while I tried to be objective. Look – the Hindu god of desire had bow and arrows, just like Greek Eros. On the plane, I had read a magazine article about the biochemistry of attachment. It said Cupid's arrows were anointed with oxytocin, the bonding hormone produced in the hypothalamus in response to stimulation. When nipples or cervix are stimulated in birth, breastfeeding or sex, the brain releases oxytocin.

'He's describing his beloved's navel,' whispered Rama.

Strange: the love god was universal and might shoot anyone but once he shot, the only body you wanted was the one he had singled out for you. Donne's poem of the lost beloved still haunted me:

> oft did we grow
> To be two Chaoses, when we did show
> Care to aught else . . .

Thousands of miles lay between Kerala and London. We were in different parts of the forest.

'How someone touches us', the article explained, 'affects how we think.' Oxytocin is the physical key to emotional bonding. Doctors drip-feed it to mothers in labour. In Greek, *oxytocin* means 'swift birth'.

The actor was cataloguing her hips.

'Both men's and women's brains produce oxytocin, but women produce more. Men have another hormone, vasopressin, which works the same way, secreted during sexual arousal to promote bonding. Both chemicals have a dramatic effect on sexual and maternal bonding.'

Two chemicals, two brains, and receptors. Was that *it*?

'Even in mammals known to be antisocial, oxytocin can calm a difficult individual into positive social behaviour.'

Tigresses must be awash with the stuff, looking after cubs for two years, defending them against a male tiger killing them, accepting him when he does. Oxytocin was a *terrible* idea.

'Its release can be conditioned. Oxytocin makes us feel good about the person who, by touching you, causes you to produce it in your brain. After repeatedly having sex with one person, just seeing them releases more oxytocin, making you want to be with them all the more.'

The actor had got to her thighs.

'I have to leave,' I whispered.

Oxytocin means 'swift birth', I thought in my room, because it means 'swift bow'. Artemis, Greek goddess of hunting, chastity, birth and the moon, carried a bow. Birth pangs were her arrows. The best-known Indian deity to ride a tiger also carries a bow: the goddess Durga. Ayappa is a celibate hero worshipped by men. No women of fertile years are allowed near his shrine. But like Artemis, Durga protects women and is untouchable, 'beyond reach'. Armed separation of the sexes – was that the message from gods who rode tigers? The gods of desire also carried bows and arrows. If divine tiger-riders promoted sexual separation but used the same artillery as gods of desire, what did that say about tigers and how people saw them?

Two nights later, the Trivandrum bus-station was packed with prone people and bundles. I sat on the kerb; the bus left at three and rolled south through sleeping villages. Saris now – how did Indian women pee on an eight-hour journey? I didn't plan to. You could smell the urinals from the bus. Most men just used hoardings. I could not see toilets for women.

In early light we came through sloping hills covered with clumpy emerald sea anemones: tea plantations. We passed an orange tiger face on a board. India has roughly seventy-five national parks and five hundred wildlife sanctuaries. National parks are supposed to be inviolate: no human activity in them except tourism. (In fact very few have no villages in them.) In sanctuaries, people have rights of taking things like fallen wood, but not animals. There are twenty-seven tiger reserves; most are a mix of national park and sanctuary. Each is administered through the forest service of the state they are in and funded by Project Tiger, a federal advisory unit within the Ministry of Environment and Forests. This was its logo. I was entering my first tiger forest.

Periyar is in the Western Ghats. In 1895 the British built a dam where the Maharajah of Travancore had a hunting reserve. He agreed: he knew game would cluster at the lake edge. So they do now. This lake is the heart of the sanctuary. I boarded a boat in silver mist and saw drowned trees with cormorants on them, and white-breasted kingfishers with dazzling turquoise wings. Brown-black snakebirds with long ripply necks were fishing too. You would see one dive and have no idea where its spear beak would pop up.

Otters were playing in the water, swishing out to run in an undulating canter and slip in further up. The guide pointed to elephant shapes among trees below the skyline. Shafts of light lit brown-grey backs.

'Bison!'

Again, if you hadn't been looking, you'd never have seen it. Tiger prey, the enormous wild ox called Indian bison: gaur. He was chestnut-black, almost maroon. Massy shoulders, heavy-looped dewlap. Pale horns, pale nose, white socks over his knees.

I got out at a lakeside bungalow surrounded on three sides by jungle. It had been the maharajah's hunting lodge. I was nervous about my Visa card credit but the guidebook said it was the best place for animals. Protecting us from them, and them from us, was a deep trench that sambar leaped at night. The grass was covered with deer slots. Sambar! I knew them from *The Jungle Book*.

'That's why the flowerbeds are empty,' said the lugubrious manager.

Animals sleep at midday. I had a four-poster bed, violet carpet, cheval glass. He would approve. But I had left him behind.

I woke just before twilight and stepped straight out to the empty flowerbeds. Opposite, on the trench lip, was a wild boar. I stood stock still. She snorted, then started rooting earth. A jungle crow flew down. She sighed, sat, flopped flat like a dog after a walk. The crow hopped round and pecked at her belly, her parasites. He tugged at a long leech, pulling grey tummy skin into a peak like whipped egg-white. She raised her head in protest. The crow jumped back, a fat black darning needle waving in his beak. Her head dropped to earth again.

I walked to the boundary. It was forbidden to cross the log bridge over the trench but beyond, in denser forest, stood a watchtower. You could book a night in one of these, take food and blankets, watch animals.

'Can I try the watchtower?'

'It will be free in two nights' time,' said the manager.

That night there were thudding scuffles on my roof. What would it be like hearing them alone in a watchtower?

Next morning other guests went on the lake. I walked the trench perimeter. Was I brave enough for the tower? There was a rustle on the bank. A snake moved away. Dark brown; long but not skinny.

A waiter came up.

'Elephant,' he said, excited. They swam the lake with two babies, got out on the far side of the trench and browsed slowly around our perimeter. We saw them closest by the bridge. One turned and looked at us, flapping her ears threateningly. She could be over the logs in a flash – but they moved off, adults ringing the babies.

'Have you seen tigers recently?' There were supposed to be thirty-five in Periyar.

'One swam across the lake last week.'

I sat by the lake watching sambar on the far side, the size of red deer, but grey-brown: eating weed, flinging up heads to check the forest edge.

'What sort of snake did I see?' I asked the manager that night.

'Did it move fast or slow?'

'Slow.' I did not know, then, that non-poisonous snakes in India move much faster. Poisonous ones, except the king cobra which eats other snakes, do not need speed except to strike.

'Well, rat snakes go near the watchtower because people hang food from the roof, rats come for the food, they come for the rats. If it moved slow, it was probably a cobra. I saw two mating last week. They danced and twined an hour by the lake, till dholes chased them away.'

Dholes are the 'red dog' of *The Jungle Book*. Even the tiger, says

Kipling, turns aside for the dhole. Then, they travelled in large numbers. Today packs are small, but still ferocious.

Not knowing rat snakes from cobras I decided on a jungle trek, not a watchtower. The manager brought canvas drawstring bags to go over my socks. It had rained recently: rain brings out leeches. My father used to take us on Lake District mountain walks as children; I hated stiff tough boots. But last year I had taken my own daughter to Club Med Tunisia at Easter. It was cold, rainy, no one swam and she refused to try the disco.

'Let's go into the Sahara on camels,' I said.

'You'd have to have trainers.'

From the Club Med shop I bought black suede lace-ups.

'They're not really *trainers*,' she said, but we had a lovely time in the Sahara. I had not worn them since, but here they were in case I got to a forest. I put them on, over the leech socks.

'I am tribal man, madam,' said the guide. I hired binoculars at the Forest Centre; we walked in among tall trees. Rustle, dapple, slanting light. Secrecy, hush, stillness: where I had always wanted to be. A holy moment, the only one since St Lucy's Day that I had felt alive.

'*Bino*,' whispered the guide. A chestnut Malabar squirrel, langur monkeys, a hornbill. We went fast past the place where a sloth bear had savaged a friend of his the week before. Sloth bears, I thought scornfully. Some small dozy animal I'd never heard of.

I was so ignorant.

A thin turquoise snake under a fallen log. He kept me well away from that. I whispered about tigers; he had never seen one. In lake mud a leopard's pugmarks converged on those of boar: there was a drag-trail where the leopard had removed his kill. I was a long way from the leopards under which I had cut away my old life.

What about poaching?

'Not in Kerala, madam,' he said proudly. But I had seen the figures on the Net, a photo of dead Periyar elephants, bleeding and tuskless. There is poaching everywhere: Kerala has been so hammered by poachers that no one sees tuskers now at Periyar.

He showed me roots of wild turmeric, then indicated, with his eyes, a herd of gaur between the trees.

*

'What does it matter if wild tigers die out?' someone asked before I left. 'There are loads in zoos.' Yes, there are. Too many. Tigers breed well in captivity. There are more in cages in Texas than wild in Asia. Tigers will never be extinct, they're too popular. Cubs are sold on the Internet. Why does it matter that *wild* tigers are still loose in the world?

'What a joy to know,' says W. H. Auden's poem 'Address to the Beasts',

> even when we can't see or hear you,
> that you are around.

But that was sentiment; I needed arguments. The sky was white scatter in a thousand pieces. Here below it was dim. I was anxious about being close on foot to those gaur, but if I was going to ask, 'Why save wild tigers?' watching their largest prey was a good place to do it.

Tigers need prey, water, cover. If they have all they need, everything else in the forest is all right too. The ungulates they eat are OK if they have the right plants to eat. Trees are fine if pollinated by monkeys, civets, birds, insects. Myriad other creatures, small carnivores, birds, reptiles, nest in them, feed off them, sustained by still smaller animals. Everything depends on everything else: the tiger is top of all. If you save tigers, you save the whole thing.

A wild animal, I thought, watching the gaur, is not just the biological thing, as in a zoo. It has particular knowledge, the relation to the landscape for which it evolved. All the plants and creatures here were related to its thirty-five tigers. A wild tigress knows every rock, bush and animal in her territory, and teaches them to her cubs. Does that not have a value beyond the utilitarian? It seemed to me to be wildness itself.

I looked at my feet. My Tunisian trainers were alive with half-inch squiggles. While I stood on one foot brushing them off, ten more charged on to the other, galloping into seams like sperm to the egg, sensing warmth. Leeches hate light. They hide under plants, but are ultra-sensitive to vibration. If they feel a blood-pulse they get excited and reach out. The guide had a hole in his leech sock. When we left the forest his toe was bright red.

'Thanks for the leech socks,' I said, when I got back.

The manager smiled. 'Last year the American ambassador stayed with his sons and bodyguards. He trekked here through jungle after the monsoon, worst leech time. They arrived with four-inch leeches hanging from their ears. The terrace was slopping with blood.'

That night I read up on why save wild tigers. As thumps began on the roof I opened a book by a biologist called Ullas Karanth.

Because wild tigers only flourish if everything else, from ungulates to plants, is OK, they are the sign of a healthy forest. Asian forests not only regulate rainfall and reduce the greenhouse effect, they hold Asia together; they are watersheds of the river systems. They regulate water-flow after monsoons, stop soil eroding. If they were to disappear, the great monsoon-fed rivers, Ganges, Brahmaputra, Mekong, Irrawaddy, would rampage like demons, like flame. With no roots to hold slippy banks, crops would disappear, millions would die of famine and flood.

Forest and river are interdependent. People, as well as tigers, need them both. Protecting what tigers need means protecting what people, on a vast scale, need too. Wild tigers are the best sign that bio-diversity works as it should. Because everything is interrelated, any loss has dangerously unpredictable consequences.

Imagine a forest where a wild pig co-exists with a species of frog, a microbial parasite, a monkey, a mango, a leafcutter ant, a lizard, a wasp and an owl. The pig roots on riverbanks creating puddles. Mosquitoes and frogs breed in them. The mosquito carries a parasite that gives monkeys a disease, but few die because tadpoles eat mosquito larvae in puddles. The monkeys love mangoes and spread mango seed in fertilizing scat. The ant is a specialist: it depends on the mango tree and only lives there. The lizard eats ants, and also some wasps which build nests in holes made by woodpeckers, which the owl nests in too. Nine species living in balance.

Then men kill off the pig. No more puddles. The frog, who evolved as a specialist (specialists are vulnerable because they cannot adapt), becomes extinct: it can only lay its eggs in those puddles. Mosquitoes lie in rainwater and multiply, uneaten by tadpoles. More mosquitoes bite monkeys, which men have reduced by hunting. Monkeys die out from disease. Mosquitoes bite smaller mammals instead. The mango dies with no monkeys to spread its seeds. The leafcutter ant dies, with no more mangoes, so there are fewer lizards. Wasps increase because fewer lizards eat them, and fill all woodpecker holes. The owl cannot breed, and becomes extinct.

By destroying the pig, men leave only mosquitoes, wasps and a parasite that will now threaten them more. Welcome to 'trophic cascade'. Take one piece away, and everything collapses like a house of cards, threatening, among other things, us. But tigers, because they need everything in the forest to work, show it is healthy. Their disappearance is a warning, an oil light coming on in a car, said Ullas Karanth.

'The eco-system is like an aeroplane. We're all in it. We can go on taking away the rivets that hold it together and keep the plane up, for a while. No one rivet will decide when and where we crash. But ultimately, one rivet too many will bring us down.'

I looked at the cheval glass. Any loss disrupts links – between predators and prey, flowers and pollinators, fruits and dispersers of seeds. All have to be saved together, even leeches, *in the wild*. Zoos won't stop the loss cascade. Losing the way they interact means losing the earth.

The *Mahabharata* said something similar in 400 BC:

Do not cut down the forest with its tigers, do not banish tigers
from the forest. The tiger perishes without the forest and the
forest perishes without its tigers. The tiger should stand guard
over the forest; the forest should protect all its tigers.

There was a coughing bark outside. Deer, dhole, *tiger*? I turned out the light. The tiger *is* the wild. If it goes, part of us goes with it: our sense that something out there is stronger, more beautiful; something not us. Outer wildness affects our inner landscape in ways we do not control. The tiger is its epitome: elusive, with its own concerns, nothing to do with us, from its point of view. But for us the extreme image of the wild.

I did not know this forest belonged to Kerala's tiger rider. The first person I talked to was Ayappa the poet; the first forest I walked in was

Ayappa's too. I was twenty-five kilometres from his biggest shrine. I
would have had to ask special permission to visit. Being female, I
would get nowhere near. But every November hundreds of thousands
of pilgrims bathe in the Pampa river, waiting to see, on 14 January, a
light flicker opposite the shrine, and the shrine display Ayappa's
statue. Every high point – pile of coconuts, tree, vehicle – is covered
with people craning to see. After the light there is a rush for the shrine.
That year a stampede had started: a rope snapped, people slipped,
the stay wire of an electric post broke, a bus fell; fifty-three people
died. I did not know. The survivors were going home as I sat by the
lake in blue half-light before the boat left, saying goodbye to the buried
valley of Periyar.

I hoped to catch a flash of what I had come for. I also told myself I
was burying love there. But you don't do that soon, not after five years.

Light grew. There were red-brown animals at the lake edge. I
hoped . . . Or were they dhole? No: sambar, prey of both dhole and tiger.
Drinking, holding out wide ears. On the watch, like me, for predators.

I gave back the binoculars. Next time, I must take my own. Next
time? Was I going to do this again? Apparently I was. But next time I
must meet experts.

Back in Kovalam, a cab driver showed me temples. Ayappa rode his
tiger on the roof of a temple swirling with traffic. I bought a poster of
Durgha. Heel on her knee, she brandished eight hands holding bow
and arrows, sabre, lotus, trident, as if conducting an orchestra. Her
tiger had a ruff of white cirrhus, a *bindi*. Forest water winked behind
them like ice in a martini.

I squatted to have my fortune read. A woman looked at my palm.

'Your child is well,' the cab driver interpreted. I had not been so
long away from my daughter before.

'A man has feelings for you.'

Not so good. I'd need all the divine aid I could get, Durga *and* St
Lucy. I bought a poster of Ayappa too, mounted on a tigress in a
jostling herd of her cubs. Long live sexual separation. Down with oxytocin. All tiger riders welcome.

2

JUNGLE OF *THE JUNGLE BOOK*

'Tigers in the *loo*?'

My daughter came home from school one afternoon to find tiger pictures Blu-tacked everywhere – Durga and Ayappa in the kitchen; on the stairs a famous picture of a tiger family, which first proved males spent time with their cubs. She laughed and made a tiger desktop for my computer. The face filled the screen. Citrine eyes stared into mine whenever I turned it on. There was a tiny rubbed patch on the edge of one eye where white-grey skin showed through. The *vibrissae*, the whiskers, were white with black roots. I now knew they grow in a capsule of blood. When they touch or approach anything, the disturbed air stirs this blood, sending messages to the brain. Why did I know this? Why was reading tigers, writing tigers, all I wanted to do?

I rang a friend of his to check his medical tests were OK. They were. Another friend saw him at a party. She said he looked terrible. 'He wasn't bobbing about the room as usual. He whispered if I knew you'd split up. He said you were such a trooper.'

'A *trooper*?'

'I think he saw in my face it was not the ideal image.'

But what is? Our first Valentine's Day, he made a card from a painting of the Belle Dame sans Merci on a white horse beguiling a lovestruck knight. Was that his image of me? But I made images too. One poem, to my surprise, saw him as a Sumatran tiger with a predator's lonely vulnerability, fulfilling desires without regard for other people.

I needed money. The charity for which I had done that Christmas commission. Again my work was not used, the fee did not materialize. A few weeks ago there had been warmth and trust. Now . . .

'I don't know how he can live with himself,' said a friend. Maybe, I thought, he manages not to. He was left-handed as a child. His mother made him use the right. Like his Greekness and left-handedness, the part of him I loved had gone underground. Maybe he had lost touch with it himself.

I got a job saying poems at the Globe Theatre.

'Fifteen hundred people will be staring at you. You must harness the energy of this space,' said the voice coach, 'like riding the tiger. Otherwise it will turn and rend you; like the tiger.'

'What's the tiger?'

'Anxiety.'

What did it mean for tigers that they symbolized so much?

Western images of tigers came from travellers' tales. Their keynote was ferocity. The tiger was crueller than the lion and laid waste the country he inhabited. So said early encyclopedias. William Blake added beauty and awe. By the nineteenth century, tigers were gorgeous danger. 'God invented the cat', said Victor Hugo, 'so man could touch the tiger.' Today they are wild energy. The tiger on cereal packets is the crackle your body has with wheat inside. Esso tells us to put a tiger in our tank. The Kellogs-and-Esso approach to tigers says – Grab that power and energy for yourself.

And the sexiness too. Men are tigers in bed. (Lions are only royal.) Women are tigresses in defence of children, but also as lovers. In Puccini's opera *Edgar*, 'Tigrana' tells a man he must be hers or die. Elinor Glyn's 1907 novel *Three Weeks* described an affair consummated on tiger skins, commemorated in the song about sinning with Glyn on a tiger skin. Betty May, a model in London's pre-war Café Royal, nicknamed herself Tiger, lapped saucers of brandy on all fours, and called her 1929 autobiography *Tiger Woman*. Soft-toy tigers are safe-sex ferocity: they proliferate on toyshop shelves as wild tiger numbers fall. Tigger in *Winnie-the-Pooh* is bouncy but harmless; as Anthony Blanche in Evelyn Waugh's *Brideshead Revisited* says, of the hero's jungle paintings, 'Creamy English charm, playing tigers'. A recent poll says tigers are the whole world's 'favourite animal'.

Images of tropical jungle, fertilized by the forests of European fairytale, came to the West from books and travellers' tales. Even Darwin began with books. Before the *Beagle* he wrote to his sister, 'My head is running about the Tropics. I go and gaze at palm trees in the hothouse, come home and read Humboldt's *Personal Narrative*. I can hardly sit still in my chair. Gloomy, silent forests are uppermost in my mind.' The first time he saw real tropical forest he was afraid of disappointment. But, 'How utterly vain such fear is, none can tell but those who have experienced what I today have. It has been for me a glorious day, like giving to a blind man eyes.' Forty years later he told a friend he most felt the presence of the sublime in the forests. Did my delight in Periyar come from a similar leap from page to wilderness?

The garden of my grandparents' house, Boswells, was my first meltable-into forest. You walked out of the door through tangled yews to an old tinkers' caravan, climbed trees in the orchard, followed a hazel path to a blue gate opening on hills and woods. Indoors there were Chinese ceramics, T'ang horses and camels with green saddles collected by my grandfather. The children's room had ancient toys, a saggy sofa for reading, and books everywhere. Here I read the books on which my mother grew up: animal stories, naturalists' tales. My heroes were the Winnipeg wolf in Ernest Thompson Seton, Bambi, the half-wolf of *White Fang*. I was not a fan of human life. I found a poem, 'Disillusionment of Ten o'Clock', that seemed not to be, either. It thought people who were not 'strange', did not 'dream of baboons and periwinkles', as boring as I did. Only one person in this poem had an interesting time: a drunk old sailor on the street, dreaming 'of catching tigers in red weather'. Tigers meant getting away from people who thought *you* strange, for not wanting to behave like them. Like me, I thought, aged seven.

Or else like Mowgli, for *The Jungle Book* was my Bible. Bagheera was hero of heroes: bold as the wild buffalo, reckless as the wounded elephant, skin like watered silk, voice like wild honey dripping from the trees. I wanted to be, or to marry, Bagheera. The tiger was the villain; yet he brought Mowgli to the jungle. A tiger's jaws, or being drunk on the street; such things seemed necessary to arriving at where you wanted to be.

The snag about animals was death. It was everywhere in animal stories. I disliked that bit. I wrecked a first edition of *Tarka the Otter* by adding my own ending. Tarka kills the hound who killed his mother and his mate but he too is dying, swimming out to sea. The last words taper to his last breath:

> There was a third bubble in the sea-going
> waters and nothing
> more.

'Tarka had gone back,' I have written firmly beneath. 'Back to White Tip. But he had his revenge on the hounds. THE END.' I shut my eyes to what I did not want to know.

When animal heroes ran out I turned to naturalists. Dr Dolittle talked to animals and journeyed to far-off places. Jim Corbett *had* to shoot tigers who killed people, but he wrote with such sympathy for them, such passionate knowledge of jungle, I felt I belonged there. Then there was Darwin. I did not read him, of course, or connect him with animals properly, but he was everywhere at Boswells. The whole place was about him and, like Dr Dolittle, he began with a voyage. My granny was his granddaughter. She edited his memoir and letters.

At home, from my favourite *Book of a Thousand Poems*, I knew by heart the Creatures Great and Small section. It began, of course, with a tiger. I cannot separate how I see 'The Tyger' now with what it did to me then. It is one of Blake's *Songs of Experience* answering *Songs of Innocence*. Its darkness ('dread', 'terror', 'deadly', 'tears') challenges the lamblike joy which innocence takes in the created world. It speaks to every-thing I shut my eyes to in animal stories: violence and death. It says wherever there is creating there is also danger and pain. But I did then feel, though I would have shied away if you had said so, that there *were* wild, beautiful things out there, very different from the human-ness I found so difficult. Forests, colour, a secret different life: they were there if I could find them. But they came at a cost. I knew that. I could not shut out pain entirely.

*

These books made me, but their images were Western. Ayappa and Durga were on my walls now. Surely the deepest symbolism of an animal came from people who share its home?

'All over India, even in cities,' said my friend Alak, born in Bombay, 'people talk of the tiger as water, moonlight, danger, dream. It is Durga's mount but also a wild sight by moonlight, gone in a flash. A shadow, feared and revered, drinking from the forest pool. At full moon they say to each other, maybe you'll see the *tiger!*'

One book by Valmik Thapar was on tiger cults. He said the tiger was the soul of Asia, bound in to all three great Asian religions, Hindu, Muslim, Buddhist. Traditional reverence protected it, but now that is fading. There were pictures of people selling tiger bones and penises, like orange salami, for aphrodisiacs, and tiger skins. This trade is illegal, but everywhere. CITES, the Convention on International Trade in Endangered Species of Wild Fauna and Flora, is an international agreement which took effect in 1973. States join voluntarily, but then are legally bound to implement it in their laws. Of countries who have tigers, or trade in tiger parts, Nepal, India and Pakistan signed early, 1975 and 1976; Malaysia and Indonesia, 1978 and 1979; Japan, China, Thailand and Singapore between 1980 and 1988. Korea signed in 1993, Vietnam in 1994, Myanmar and Cambodia in 1997, Bhutan in 2002, Laos in 2004. Traditional medicine is still the primary health care in many South-East Asian countries. Over a fifth of the world's population believes that swallowing ground tiger bone cures muscle pain, epilepsy, piles. Kelloggs-and-Esso symbolism, Asian style. East and West know tigers differently but both try and internalize the tiger's power. Tigers pay a heavy price for their role in human fantasy. They are a casualty of symbolism.

For real tigers, I bought wildlife videos. *Tigers, Land of the Tiger*, again by Valmik Thapar.

'You must meet Sarah Christie,' said a zoological friend. 'She lives in a flat in London Zoo, runs its carnivore conservation, oversees 21st-Century Tiger, which does tiger conservation, knows the breeding lines of all captive Siberian and Sumatran tigers. She's fantastic.'

Sarah had edited a book of scientific papers on tiger conservation. What could I say to a busy international tiger co-ordinator? My interest in tigers was trivial compared to conservation. We met for a drink. She came into the bar in black shirt, black jeans, beautiful and uncompromising – pointed chin, wide, perfect eyebrows, pale skin, dark curly hair. Probably thinking, Here we go, another tiger-struck sentimentalist. I had no idea what to ask. But we got on.

'Go and see what Raghu Chundawat is doing in Panna,' she said. 'Tiger numbers are going up there.' She walked away in the dark towards Regent's Park, to keep the captive tiger stud book up to date.

'Come to the Nehru Centre,' said Alak. 'The director is a playwright from Karnataka, next to Kerala. He's written plays about Indian myths. You'd love him. There's a talk on tigers.'

Wet London night in Mayfair, a white and gold house. Girish, who would become one of my closest friends, tall and smiling. 'Come,' he said. 'And come up to my flat afterwards, to meet Ullas.'

The talk was by Ullas Karanth, whose book I had read that night at Periyar.

Ullas's father was a Karnataka poet who wrote in Kannada, like Girish. In Karnataka, Ullas worked for an American organization, the Wildlife Conservation Society. I had no idea how grateful I would become to its scientists, how much the world owed it. I cared about the slides: a tigress Ullas tracked for years, tigers' diets deduced from kills and droppings. All over that state, Ullas had trained local volunteers and increased public support for enforcing tiger protection.

He had a small moustache, pursed mouth, dazzling smile, and grew up near Girish. They swapped stories of Karnataka forty years before. 'I remember tigers at night,' said Girish, 'in the headlights. Lying in the road like cows.'

With Ullas was Amanda Bright, a solicitor who used to live in India and now administered the charity Global Tiger Patrol, which funded tiger conservation in India, partnering 21st-Century Tiger for tiger conservation outside it.

All these people would become vital, and dear, to me. I had met nearly everyone who would steer my tiger journey. There was one to come.

'If you're going tigering again,' said a friend, 'look up Valu. I met him on my honeymoon in Ranthambhore. Valmik Thapar. Have you heard of him? Here's his email.'

'Meet me at Panna's back gate,' Valmik emailed. My daughter would be fine for two weeks with her father. He came every weekend anyway; now he would live in. I left in early morning. The dog watched sadly as I checked my bag. Tunisian trainers, malaria pills, books on Indian birds. And one more thing from an old drawer, a gift from my other granny, my father's mother, when I was ten: opera glasses, with mother-of-pearl round the lenses. I took them to theatres occasionally; children loved them. Now they would look at the wild.

Panna sanctuary lay beside a diamond mine that had mashed the land to ashy mountains. Mining is one of the worst threats to tigers and forests. It disturbs wild animals, pollutes rivers, and brings strangers so poachers are not noticed.

Panna was a newish reserve, Project Tiger's twenty-second; the fifth in Madhya Pradesh, the tiger state. Tiger numbers were rising for two reasons, an excellent outgoing director and Chundawat's research. A resident scientist means eyes on the forest, which makes things harder for poachers. Raghu had radio-collared and followed three generations of tigresses. All over the world, radio-collaring has transformed research on animals that are hard to see or dangerous. The more you know about an animal scientifically, the better you can protect it, but you do not want to intrude on it. Radio-collars let you learn without disturbing it; except that moment of fitting the collar. The radio sends signals; you follow from afar with headphones, plotting its movements. Before radio-telemetry, no one knew the scale and pattern of tiger movement. Raghu found Indian male tigers travel further at night than anyone had realized. The back gate of Panna was the cutting edge of tiger science.

Guards were preparing a ceremony in a garden. A trestle on a lawn, white cloth with engraved copper plates, plastic chairs in rows, more behind the table. They put me on one of these, beside a cameraman from Bristol, where most BBC wildlife films are produced. For months on end, though, he lived at Ranthambhore. Wildlife films are an art that lies to tell a truth. The truth is the tiger's life. It looks easy; just stroll into the jungle and there the tigers are. But twenty minutes of TV may take two years of filming. This man was filming with Valmik and Raghu, but they had found no tigers yet. He had also shot my *Tigers* video, in Kanha.

'I'm going there next.'

'You'll love it. Beautiful place.'

This was a ceremony honouring guards for distinguished service. The cameraman identified people coming in. First, the reserve director. A director stays three years, this new one seemed good too so far, keen on conserving animals rather than – as many do – enriching himself. (I did not realize how crucial this is.) Dr Malik, the wildlife vet. Then a man who grew up here shooting tigers, descended from the maharajah who donated the reserve. Like many parks, Panna is intact forest only because it was once a hunting precinct. Then Raghu the scientist, tall, slender, bearded, with his wife Joanna, a photographer. Raghu looked at me, I thought, suspiciously. I had told Valmik I might finance my trip by journalism. Naively, I thought Raghu would be pleased. Finally Valmik himself, recognizable from his film. Huge, burly, black-bearded, radiating energy.

The guards stood up, Valmik strode to the table, addressed them passionately in Hindi, held out a copper plaque. A little man with a white beard and a stick came forward, scars on cheek, neck and arm. He was crippled, his shin zipped with raised flesh. He had been nearly killed by a sloth bear. 'Worst-tempered beast in the jungle,' said the cameraman.

And I had dismissed them so lightly in Periyar.

Valmik gave a plaque to a young guard arching his back in pride.

'He stopped poachers killing a deer. Valmik's saying they are the front line of the battle to save tigers. The world and the tiger depend on *them*.'

Forest guards are paid very little. Fifty are killed every year by poachers, another hundred mutilated, protecting not just animals but trees against illegal loggers. My first view of Valmik: giving awards to forest guards.

A small, shiny-haired man called Vinny kept a camp nearby. Valmik had other people to attend to. 'Stay with Vinny,' he said. 'See you tomorrow.'

I got into Vinny's jeep. Vinny loved Panna's forest but came from the Himalayan foothills Jim Corbett had written about, near Corbett Reserve (named after him). It is hard to see tigers there. I had decided on Madhya Pradesh, but longed to hear about Corbett. We came at dusk to a winding track through woods.

'Here's your tent, but why not see the sun set now, from a boat?'

On the water's face, a huge owl swooped down and caught a fish. Fretted tree silhouettes and their reflections were a black frill above and below the far bank. 'We have tried so hard to de-exoticize India,' Alak told me once, but de-exoticizing is hard when you are sitting at sunset on a wide black-and-silver river sleeved in jungle, with jackals calling and crocodiles round the next bend.

Vinny had built an enormous *machan*, a platform in a vast tree by the Ken river, which flowed through the reserve. Up the ladder; out above the shining river, by the barred marmalade glow of an iron brazier. Logs forked through the bars, charring to silver. Nine years before, this river had swept away platform and camp in a monsoon. All of Vinny's capital, twenty years' work. The only thing left was a fridge in the fork of a tree. Vinny still used it.

'They'll wake you at four. Then we'll go to the forest.'

My tent had a platform bed, level with tree-tops. I went to sleep with rustlings all round me and dreamed of tigers in a school I was not ready for, full of layers of glittering cloth. Young tigers in beautiful colours followed me like looming dogs.

Someone woke me with tea sweetened with ginger. It was freezing cold, pitch dark. I put on all the clothes I had and got into Vinny's jeep. As we waited in the dark for the reserve gate to open, a hair-thin silver saucer lit the black sky: an egg-cup holding an invisible egg. The moon as I'd never seen it.

Panna is dry deciduous teak forest. We drove in on a rutted track. Dark was darker here, indigo sky laced with black leaves. At first it looked like Western forest: I could see dimly between the trees. But everything was much taller. Teak leaves were two feet long and brown. Some still clung to branches, others were drifting down to make a crackly floor where you'd think no one, even a tiger, could move silently.

'Sambar.' Vinny pointed. Favourite tiger prey: I was picking up where I had left off in Periyar. Dawn came, olive and gold. 'Nilgai.' A tall slate-blue humped shape, trotting away. Different forests have different prey. Nilgai, India's largest antelope, shy and solitary, live alone or in pairs, not herds; they were the tiger's largest wild prey here, though tigers for some reason kill them least. Now an open area of scorched grass with small trees: grass had been burned near the track to keep down the view-lines, so visitors can see the animals. Little beige antelopes, chinkhara, leaped away; they liked open ground and were eating the new grass shoots. A dun flash in undergrowth: four-horn antelope, very rare, *very* shy. What about snakes? But this was February, they were hibernating. 'In the rains you can't walk without treading on them.' Vinny spoke of the whole forest with such love.

A langur barked from a tree, like a dog. Vinny braked. 'Alarm call!' This langur, sentinel for his group, glared disapprovingly up the slope. He could see a predator moving. More alarm calls came up the hill, each different. Sambar, barking deer, everyone saw the predator going up the slope. Alarm calls track a predator's movements. But we saw nothing. Then came a sandy track: my first pugmarks.

'Fresh. Within the hour. A young tigress.'

They say male paws are rounded, female slender with more ovate pads. We followed till she turned off the path. I stepped out illegally (this was a *tiger* reserve, no getting out *at all*) and put my hand in her print. It was warm. The young sun, surely. My hand was small in her paw.

Hours later, I sat with Valmik under an umbrella in the glare. It was boiling hot, I had stripped off two pairs of trousers, I was feverish, shivering and sweating. No one had found a tiger. They wanted to film Raghu radio-collaring. Everyone was dustily dispirited.

'I have failed to save the tiger,' said Valmik. He was fiery, passionate, telling more than I could take in.

'Tigers occupy India's richest resource. *Everybody* wants a slice of the forests. You can't catch all poachers or stop all illegal logging. Everything is too big, people are too poor. The only thing that can save tigers now is reforming the forest service and the institutions funding it.'

It took time to get my aching head round the system. India's tiger reserves are all administered only by the forest service. Anything that happens in them, all research, filming, monitoring, can be done only with the permission of the officer running that particular forest. So who are *they* accountable to? You'd think a central scientifically knowledgeable figure, a Ph.D. in zoology at least, must control all forest officers – who are, in the end, responsible for the tiger's future. Not at all. Neither the top forest officer (Director General of Forests, second most senior officer in the Ministry of Environment and Forests), nor the Director of Project Tiger has any control over the eight thousand civil servants running India's forests. They are answerable only to the state in which they happen to work.

India has thirty-one states and six 'union territories'. Some have no tiger reserve, some several. Graduating foresters are asked which state they want to go to. They say their own but rarely get it, and are sent to some other: Madhya Pradesh, say, or Kerala. From then on, throughout their career, their boss is that state's government: politicians and bureaucrats who may know and care nothing about wildlife, for whom conservation is probably the last priority. Trees and tigers have no vote.

'*Kenya* has a federalized wildlife service! Its director *commands all officers* in all national parks. India needs, India's tigers need, a *centralized national park service!*'

The only power the top central figures in the forest service have is allocating money. The Planning Commission allocates planned budets to every sector. Each gets a five-year plan of allocation of money. A state with a tiger reserve pays staff salaries, uniforms, running costs; other expenses are paid from federal funds through Project Tiger, whose director, a senior forest officer, has about four million dollars a year for the twenty-seven reserves. His advisory steering committee of experts meets every six months, but he has the final say. He allocates money, considers budget requests, sends funds where he wants.

This system makes forest officers all too vulnerable to pressure from state politicians who want to milk the forests. Corruption happens from the top. Money sent to the state's exchequer gets re-allocated to different departments: states divert conservation money into, say, health. The state's chief minister decides his own priorities. Parks will need fire-fighting equipment in dry months and road repairs after the monsoon. Money for that is eaten by something else and arrives six months late. Politicians are bribed to agree illicit encroachment on forest land, or grant illegal licences for mining and tree-felling. This violates laws protecting the park but guards are pressurized, bribed and compromised into saying nothing. (If they don't play ball they may be beaten up or killed.) Park administrations, on the other hand, can make extra money by doing unnecessary and potentially harmful work in the forest and then claiming they used more labourers than they did. Everybody makes something. The forest pays. One of the best *sal* forests in the world is (or was) in Jarkhand in the Saranda forest division, centre of the steel industry. Because of mining that should never have been allowed in a haphazard way, it is degraded, black. Some forest officers and state politicians can also work together to siphon off money. If Project Tiger's director knows a forest officer is corrupt he can do nothing. Well, he could allocate fewer funds. But that hardly helps tigers.

I sat, shivered, sweated, listened. In the federal ministry, said Valmik, we should separate Forests from Environment, which deals with things like car emissions. Within the forest service we must create a centralized wildlife service to run wildlife parks and sanctuaries, and insist on really good anti-poaching patrols, which make no money for the state or forest officers, so they often cut them. Three months before, he had seen an enormous cache of poached tiger and leopard skins in north India, animals trapped by their feet, clubbed on the head to leave the skins intact. The scale of poaching was now ten times worse than he had feared.

'I had tears in my eyes. In twenty years' tiger-watching I've hardly seen a leopard. They're *much* more elusive. But there were so many!'

'*Bagh!*' shouted a man. Tiger! Everyone rushed to the jeep. But not me. I had mentioned journalism, and they were going to tranquillize a tiger. If the dosage misfired, or the tiger fell somewhere that injured him, Raghu's research could be in jeopardy: the forest officer could cancel his permit. Tiger deaths are a sensitive issue. They drove away without me.

Two years later I saw the film they made, *Tigers of the Emerald Forest*.

It included footage Raghu took. Some shots were on night drives when he also watched for the poachers, who are always around, and removed their snares. One wonderful shot was of a young tigress with tiny cubs at sunrise, her red tongue twice as wide as their dark heads.

I had no idea, then, how politically delicate research is (and filming); nor what a minefield relations with the Forest Service are for conservationists and scientists who need their permission to work in the forest.

After I left, the park administration cut eleven hundred teak trees in the park. To create grassland, they said. To make viewing-lines for tourists, they destroyed *nyctanthes* bushes browsed by sambar (so tiger prey declined.) They also quarried stone from the supposedly inviolate riverbed for construction work, burned forest and grasslands, and stopped the park's radio centre working at night.

Raghu queried all this. And so, though poachers drove in constantly, easily, every night (leaving gunmen with the night guards but hey, the radio centre was closed, there are no records of that), guards were ordered to stop Raghu working at night and arrest him for trespass when he did. Raghu was criminalized with a Preliminary Offence Report and his jeep was seized. While tigers died (that mother was snared, her cubs disappeared; by the time I saw this film all tigers in it were dead), he suspended Raghu's research permit. Research that mattered to the whole world terminated. Films, science, any outside attention can all create jealousy. Eyes on the forest are eyes on foresters, too.

In late afternoon, Vinny's young assistant, Anil, drove me back, asking about British wildlife. Jackals, wolves, bears? Oh, Anil, we had them, we did; once. Not jackals, but wolves and bears. All gone. Predators show the wealth of your bio-diversity because to survive they need other animals. Rich predator life is an index of a landscape's health. But we did have wildcats in Scotland. And rivers were less polluted, otters were reviving . . .

'How many species?'

'One.'

Anil was politely silent. Here there were three. *And* rusty-spotted cat, caracal, wolf, leopard. India has so much more to play for. The stakes are still so high.

By a pool where Anil had seen a tigress with cubs, we stopped and listened to forest stillness. A rustle on the bank. Two animals on the dry watercourse rattled teak leaves: two shaggy otters, who saw us and vanished. Trees thinned out round a village on the riverbank. Villages in tiger reserves disturb and lessen both wildlife and habitat. These people had agreed to move. On the bank was an ancient carved stone commemorating a wife who had burned on her husband's pyre. Moon and tree on one side, man and woman holding hands on the other.

Suttee had been my image for ending my own relationship. Here, I was ashamed of that. It was an easy image for a Westerner, but the real thing is alive and violent. Emperor Akbar, the British, and the Indian government have all struggled to forbid it, but in Panna district six months before, in a remote hamlet called Tamoli, two thousand villagers watched a widow die on her husband's pyre. Those villagers live by growing betel leaf. Female literacy is nineteen per cent. No running water, little electricity. They lit incense and fed the widow betel leaves as she cradled his head on the unlit pyre. Some say her sons tried to stop her; others, that *they* struck the match. They would get her land; suttee is followed by donations. People stoned two policemen who tried to stop it. She keeled over in flames: everyone shouted, '*Suttee mata ki ji.*' Long live suttee, our mother! They were proud of their tradition, which this suttee stone marked. Now the gods would send rain, stop the betel crop failing. The pyre was lit by the gods.

A tiger had been collared and filmed: a large very yellow male. Joanna showed me digital photos.

'Dr Malik was wonderful,' said Valmik. 'He calculated the dosage and the tiger's weight at sight. He shot very carefully. The last male's collar came off. Let's see what Raghu learns from this one.'

The cameraman had ricked his back, getting on to the elephant from the jeep.

'Never got on an elephant so fast in my life,' he said.

I stayed more days in the rust-brown forest; saw crested serpent eagles, nesting vultures, pugmarks, but no tigers. My throat was on fire. In the evenings, I learned from Anil and Vinny about tigers and forests. My last night, Vinny talked to the film crew, the director, Valmik, Raghu. Happy with their success, they started worrying about me.

'She hasn't seen a tiger!' said the director. Maybe he was still a good director, then. 'Let's arrange an elephant for her.'

'She's ill and sleeping,' said Vinny. 'She'll see tigers in Kanha.'

'I want her to see a tiger from *Panna*,' said Panna's director. But they didn't wake me. Instead, the suttee stone got to me, though it mixed things up. I dreamed the man I left needed an injection. He shied off: he never faced things if he could help it. Then, like an animal in trouble, he came and I cradled his head as they slammed the needle in. He asked me to make the sign of the cross. I thumbed a stubby one between his eyes.

I was crossing the river where Bagheera drank! Shivering with fever, but thrilled. The lodge had pink battlements, imitation tigerskin arm-chairs and a small muffled man waiting for me, so cold he wore his woolly hat indoors: another Anil, the resident naturalist and camp manager. I was the only guest. Tourism even at Kanha was down, nuclear war with Pakistan threatened, Brits had been told not to travel to India. Under stars like luminous pepper, we wound past dark bun-galows, disturbing a chital deer that floated away in the dark. The last bungalow had a snarling plaster tiger head over the door. I mentioned Kipling.

'Kipling never saw Kanha. He heard about the wolf-child here and made the forest up. Someone will wake you at four thirty. Dress warm.'

In bed, I saw on the wall a spider larger than a pugmark. I called Reception.

'I can send someone to kill it if you like,' Anil said sleepily.

'No, no.' I hadn't come to Kanha to kill. 'But – there aren't any *poi-sonous* spiders in India, are there Anil?'

'No.'

In the morning the spider was gone.

'This is Hoon,' said Anil. His Chinese girlfriend from Singapore. Hoon jumped up and down to keep warm. We were all freezing.

'I've been here a week,' she said, 'but still haven't seen a tiger!'

Despite nuclear threat, there was a long line of jeeps at the gate. Then we were in a misty valley: a thousand square kilometres, ninety odd tigers. Kanha, softer and greener than Panna, is moist deciduous forest. There was green spindrift of bamboo, shadows of close dark *sal* trees like giant spindly elm, silvery flow of banyan trees. In open grassland grazed herds of spotted deer, chital, and swamp deer, the rare barasingha, whose numbers rose here from seventy in 1972 to four hundred. Stags clashed antlers in the mist. It was mating time.

Dawn came, mists dissolved, birds sang. Anil had binoculars and a bird book. He focused his camera on an Indian roller perched on a post. Hoon moved. The bird flew off. Anil glared at her affectionately. Her Chinese family were against him, and what would an Indian naturalist do in Singapore? I liked them enormously.

Jackals, peacocks in tangly grass, a beige-pink glistening young Indian python. A herd of gaur: the calves were on the track and the enormous bull thought he might challenge us, then thought he wouldn't and eased off into undergrowth. So huge, so silent. In grassland, a blackbuck skittered away. Blackbuck are rare; most grassland has disappeared. The Mughals hunted them with another grassland animal now extinct in India, the cheetah.

The morning got warmer. No alarm calls, no pugmarks, but wonders everywhere. At eleven all jeeps converged on an information centre. We stripped off, put on sunhats, drank tea, watched wild peacocks flaunt on a red termite mound, saw an exhibition about Kanha's grasses. These grasslands are crucial: deer eat grass, tigers eat deer. One tiger needs fifty deer-shaped animals a year. 'More the grass,' said the exhibition, 'more the tiger.'

Kanha's elephants go out early, calling into the centre if they see a tiger. A jeep takes tourists to the elephant, which takes them to see the tiger. This is called 'tiger show'. Days passed. I was getting better, learning the jungle by day, reading at night the naturalist's library collected by Anil. It was here, in the sixties, that the American zoologist George Schaller did his epoch-making study of tigers in relation to their prey, *The Deer and the Tiger*, insisting that you can't study one species in isolation. Prey and predator belong together. I read that, too.

We were in the forest morning and evening, but no tiger shows. One morning a leopard killed a dog by the reserve gate: the guards heard yowls before we turned up. That evening we came into a marbled tangerine sunset in the buffer zone, a thousand square kilometres of forest around the core area. 'Zoning' reserves is a complicated business; the legal status of different areas varies. Villagers whose all-too-sacred cows compete for grazing with wild ungulates (passing on diseases) are compensated if predators kill cattle in buffer zones but not in the core area, where cows are forbidden. Wild animals used this buffer zone, however, and here in the sun's last rays was a family of dholes: four cubs spinning a plastic water bottle, chasing each other. A wild red circus watched by their parents and a wary peacock.

I asked Anil about relations with local villagers. Many were moved from the forest when Kanha became a reserve. People outside the reserve could not graze cattle or gather fuel in what was once their forest.

Treasures of your own earth create powerful feelings. Local people resent an unfairly richer outside world valuing what their soil contains, coming to look, going away. In the seventies, studying at Knossos in Crete, I watched the ruined palace changing the living village. When people digging foundations for a house found ancient walls, the Archaeological Service stopped them building. They resented that. But they could open cafés, souvenir shops. That village is not quiet now, but when I first went there no one had hot water or TV. Now they all do; they live well off the world's interest in their earth. But that palace does not threaten them, does not leap its enclosure at night to eat cows, dogs, children. Wildlife is different. I could see no locals benefiting from tourism. My hotel's owner lived in Delhi. We drove to the reserve past hopelessly poor people who ate only rice.

'They are shy. They wouldn't know what foreigners would like. How to talk to them.'

Anil got them to make things he could sell. They waved and smiled as he passed. But here was this pink hotel: fake tigerskin chairs, credit cards, cinema, swimming-pool. No wonder there were attacks on the reserve from people whom some called Communists.

The air smelt of hay and crème brûlée. As at Panna, they were burning grass, so the tigers retreated to deeper jungle, following deer, which hate flames. Each two-foot grass stem was laddered black and gold in running stitch. Why did it burn two-tone like that? Anil plucked one. The protective leaf round each nodule was burnt charcoal, but the stem to the next growth-point was still blond where the flame leaped to the next. It was tiger-striped all the way up.

Some sixth sense made him look up. 'Leopard!'

Seeing leopards is rare. *They* are not so rare, but they are much more elusive than tigers. Ours was sitting thinking in open forest, inspecting chital in grassland below. My opera glasses brought it closer. Flaring honey-gold, stippled black. Without glasses those rosettes, so bright in a zoo, faded into dappled leaf background. We watched for fifteen minutes. Then it squatted under a tree, scraped its back legs and disappeared. All I could see through the glasses was a little black pile.

'Well,' I told Hoon, 'we haven't seen a tiger but we've seen something much rarer. We've watched a leopard shit.'

But by midday I was standing on the back of the jeep beside an elephant in dense *sal* forest. A sudden 'tiger show', just for me and Hoon. I swarmed up to a wooden seat with squished sacks beneath: an upturned coffee-table padded with dough. The elephant's skin was studded with orange-brown mud. She was hairy and unknowable. I patted her. If she felt it, she didn't say.

Stillness. Never mind that Kipling never came here: this was the jungle he wrote and I was going to see a tiger in it. Hoon and I sat back to back each side of the elephant's spine, our feet on slats slung from the coffee-table by chains, like a foot-rest to a mountain chair-lift. A thin wire hook belted me in. To my right, over the elephant's neck, was the mahout. He had searched for tigers since misty pre-dawn. He knew each tiger's territory, but the jungle is thick, full of boulders and dips. Tigers cover a huge area and don't consider tourists when they choose where to lie up.

We left the path and walked straight into dense forest. Mature *sal* were eighty foot high with dark growth crusted close to their trunks all the way up, but this was a patch of younger trees, horribly close together. Leaves flapped in our faces. As the elephant pushed her head between them I felt like singing out, 'No! We'll never make it. Leave me out of this. You can't get through there. Maybe your head can, but what about the rest of you? What about *us*? Those thin trunks could easily lodge' – I looked down as we squeezed through twangy boughs – 'between elephant flank and foot-rest. What happens then? They zip off the saddle, and us with it.'

But we couldn't say a thing. We had no language in common with the mahout and were going to see *a tiger*. Not just one: three. A tigress with two grown cubs. We had to be totally silent.

Sixteen feet up in the forest, moving inexorably forward, you understand what it means to be so big. Tramp tramp, down go the little trees before you. Tramp tramp, never mind if big trees are in the way, squidge lower boughs aside with your trunk, get your head through and the flanks look after themselves. We turned aside to thicker, smaller saplings, even closer together. Dark shiny leaves clustered lower, lower, nearly to the ground. The elephant stopped. 'Tiger,' whispered the mahout. Down to the left among layering leaves, six feet from my side of the elephant, was a gold and white blur. The mother. I couldn't see her head. I was looking at tummy. She had hiccoughs. I saw the belly, where orange fur faded to white, jump. Everything else was still.

She knew we were there. Of course. She was lying up in the middle of the day. Tigers have hair-trigger hearing. They can hear you breathe, hear you put your hand into your pocket. Every time you see a tiger it has already seen, heard and sensed you twenty times.

But tigers in Kanha have grown up protected. Tiger shooting stopped in India in 1970. Generations of tigers have lived, died and never heard a gun. So this is the deal: when they are resting, a few of them, *if* they feel like it, allow mahouts to take elephants close enough that visitors can look. When a relaxed tiger does not want to move, it may let itself be seen.

Leaving the tigress to her hiccoughs, the elephant backed through flappy springy boughs and went on. Where we stopped next, the undergrowth was thicker. The daughter was further off, maybe twelve feet. Again the leaves hid a lot of her. We saw her nose, the inside of her mouth; white carnassials when she yawned. A pink flash in her green bedroom. A tiger tongue, so close.

We came out from trees to a riverbed of bluish rock. The elephant walked down the ten-foot bank and stopped, front feet in shallow

water, at the bottom. A kingfisher streaked upstream. The opposite
bank was a single rock. On its silvery top was a space where nothing
grew, then dense undergrowth behind. To the left, in holly-green
leaves, was a gold blur. Sun rays spotlit patches of orange. The male.
The living shrine.

Hoon's Singapore camera had stuck. 'Take photos, Ruth,' she whispered, as if we were in church. I had a pathetic camera. There was
nothing to photograph, and it wasn't what I'd come for. I was trying to
focus my opera glasses on the orange. Then the young tiger took
charge. He walked into the open towards us, right in front of us at the
boulder's edge, eyes level with ours. The elephant was standing in the
stream sloping down, I was tipped against the mahout's back. I felt his
shoulders tense.

Taking tourists on an elephant to see a tiger depends on the co-
operation of both animals: on the wild tiger's willingness to be
watched; on the elephant, trained to go closer than it wants to the
jungle's top predator. Asian animals, unlike many African ones,
evolved in dense cover. They like camouflage, want not to be seen.
Tigers hate flies but can watch you for hours without betraying their
presence by the twitch of a whisker. But on reserves, most animals
come to feel it is not absolutely the end of the world to be seen, at a distance, by people in a jeep or on an elephant. People on foot are another
matter.

The night before, Anil had told me what had happened in Kanha
last year. A mahout had taken several elephant-loads of visitors to see
a tiger. Cameras buzzed like hornets. It was an unusually good sighting. The tiger put up with it all morning. When the tourists left for the
two o'clock closing, the mahout rang his family on the mobile, loaded
the coffee-table saddle with people, put his little son before him on the
elephant's neck. Wanting them to see really well, he urged the elephant closer than either elephant or tiger thought was right. The tiger
charged.

It may have been a mock charge, when a tiger just tells a lesser
being to clear out. But the elephant turned tail and lumped off at speed
through the trees. The boy fell off. The tiger killed him. You have to
respect a tiger's space.

I have told this story to many people. Two friends startled me by saying, 'Of course, the animal had to be killed. It had killed and eaten a human being.'

No. Well, it ate a shoulder, but had not killed for that. It was seeing off intruders. Tigers are territorial. Man-eaters are a different matter, but this was a tiger at home, getting rid of unwelcome visitors as my daughter's spaniel snaps at a pestering dog. There were no guns at Kanha. It is a *tiger reserve*: for tigers, not humans. But accidents happen. At another Madhya Pradesh reserve, Bandavgarh, currently the one where you see tigers most easily, a well-known tigress recently charged a jeep and mauled two tourists. She had been hit by another jeep. (I once saw a photo of a tiger trying to cross a track there, looking for a gap between tourist jeeps.) She had a broken jaw and missing teeth, was starving, too weak to hunt, disorientated by pain. No one died, though presumably she did: a casualty of tourism. Tiger reserves are not a hundred per cent safe. But every animal in them is precious. At Kanha, the one who disobeyed rules was the mahout. The rules of the reserve respect the tiger's own rules.

As we watched our tiger, and he watched back, I wondered what 'too close' meant. Suppose this young tiger had his own rules? He was as big as an adult but less solid. He was nearly two, when tigers leave their mother, and can kill for themselves.

He walked to the outer lip of his boulder. Young males are the most volatile members of all species, not just ours. What were the chances of surviving the return route at speed if the elephant fled? The tiger was above the stream, staring with round cinnamon eyes. Over the left was a worm of black flame. He was extraordinarily big. His withers were bony and pointed. When he stepped, the whole muscly strength of each foreleg surged up his shoulder. Everything, jungle, sky, trees, elephant, was as still as the boulder on which he stood.

Not taking his unreadable eyes off us, he lowered his haunches. I felt the mahout's shoulders relax. The tiger sat, then lay down crossing enormous forepaws – with a touch, I felt, of golden provocation: how a blonde secret agent in a sixties film might cross silk legs. What was closest now were the knuckled front feet. A blow from that foot, even without claws, can smash your skull. I remembered fitting my hand inside the Panna pugmark.

'Photo,' hissed the mahout.

Those were the words of his trade. Tiger. Photo.

Hoon's camera unstuck. The elephant stood in ripples. The tiger watched, under blue sky where the canopy parted to follow the stream. Then the elephant backed, turned; we left. I twisted round. He was watching us go like a cat speeding guests from a windowsill. He knew his power. He had learned it, in twenty months of round-the-clock education. He was conserving energy, as tigers do, watching his own power work. We were leaving his space.

I had tears in my eyes. I felt I'd taken a major sacrament and would never be the same again.

'We're blessed,' whispered Hoon as the elephant threaded back through lashing *sal*. 'Ruth. We've been blessed.'

3

HOW DO YOU COUNT ANIMALS
YOU CAN'T SEE?

'It's me.'

'Aren't you dying of penury?'

His first words since my lips against his ear. Since I had learned what he could do to me at a distance.

'How's your heart?'

'Look,' I said, 'I loved you for five years, you can't expect me to—'

'Thanks for putting it in the past.'

I sat down, muddling the phone line. Why do they twist like that?

'I wanted to make it OK to meet. We'll bump into each other soon.'

'Thank you. *Thank* you.' Pause. 'How are you?'

'Fine. I'm fine. But—'

'Yes?' What did he want me to say? People kept saying he was not himself, not going out. I didn't want to meet in public without talking first. Did he want me to *tell* him what he wrote in that letter? 'You didn't trust me. I broke it off for *you*.'

'Stop saying you're fine.'

'That mad . . .' No. No blame. I wanted us to recover, as friends, the selves we'd enjoyed being with each other for so long. I did not realize, then, his only way into that was oxytocin. Start again. 'That letter of yours—'

'Let's not talk about it.'

'What do you think it made me feel?'

'Don't know. I *don't know*.'

I had never heard him at a loss for words. He sounded utterly blank, but very miserable.

Next morning I heard from Athens that my beloved friend Kay had died. No more fat sparkling laughing letters in her large round hand. Kay had raged against being ill, against the oxygen line to her nose, the closing in of her generous life. I rang her husband Nikos. They had been together fifty years. I had known and loved them both for half of that time. He had nursed her these horrible last years. Been proud of her, fought with her, adored her. Now, as he said, *finito*. Someone came into the room; I heard him tell them to move a chair and then burst into tears.

I put down the phone and wrote to my own ex-lover. He'd sounded so hurt. I hated what he'd done, but the habit of wanting him to feel OK was ingrained. I didn't want him to feel I wasn't hurting; it wouldn't be true. My friend had died; I'd just heard a man I loved as a father weep. I felt open, gentle, appalled. Of course I turned to him – as he had to me, when his mother died. I wrote things that are clichés but you say them anyway. That I hurt too, but time did heal. I didn't miss him every second now, only every other second. Let's have lunch, lay it to rest gently. I said Kay had died: he knew how I loved her. I talked of Nikos and Kay, their fifty years. You have to value, I said, what people were to you. You have to honour love.

He did not answer. It took me weeks to realize he never would. Then I dreamed tigers again. I saw a tigress stalking, the arrested lifting of each enormous paw. She leaped: her prey was a man, she bit his spine till he flopped. I was hiding, afraid. I woke, I opened my eyes on the calm apple tree outside. Why violence and death? Kay? Or another death: him not answering a letter so written from the heart, so true to what we had been?

I would go on with tigers. In fortnight bites, because of my daughter. Her father would stay, they both enjoyed that, but he could not manage longer and anyway she was my centre and I hers, these last teenage years.

I had little idea what my tiger journey meant. Remembering the tigress, her teeth on that spine, I thought of things I'd shut my eyes to. Predation. The young tigress's carnassial yawn. Things in this man I had stopped myself looking at. St Lucy won't let you get away with not seeing. She had presided over our ending, now she was opening my eyes to what I had always wanted not to know. It was not an innocent thing I was doing, finding out about tigers. Blake's tyger is his answer to what the wilfully blind and innocent refuse to see.

I knew, now, you could never guarantee seeing a tiger. So how did people know how many wild tigers there are? In Panna, Valmik had given me a rough estimate: 3000 in India, 400 each in Sumatra and Russia; 350 all told in Nepal and Bhutan. South-East Asian countries and Malaysia, maybe one or two hundred each. Maybe five thousand overall. But how do we *know*? What were the figures based on? I was not in this to *see* tigers, wonderful though that was. I wanted to see the larger picture. Where they lived, what was happening, different forests and threats. Who protected them, and how? This was about survival. Mine, perhaps; but more importantly the wild tiger's. An institution that funded artists working with scientists gave me a grant to share with Ullas. Eventually, I would see his Karnataka work. But elsewhere? Travel costs were impossible. Magically, a publisher appeared. I could not pretend to science, but I could offer an amateur's overall view of representative tiger forests and their protectors.

First stop Delhi. The World Wildlife Fund in March. Marble floors, open-plan office, the desk of a burly ex-brigadier. Suddenly I saw Dr Malik too, the wildlife vet who had tranquillized the tiger at Panna. Animal medicine is vital to tigers and their prey. In Kerala gaur had been nearly wiped out by rindpest. He smiled, came over. We all drank tea.

'How do you know how many tigers there are?' I did not yet realize what dynamite this was. Tigers leave other signs of their presence, territory-markings, droppings, kills, but the traditional totem of tiger lore is the pugmark. Jim Corbett was brilliant at telling a tiger's sex, age and identity from pugmarks, but not everyone has that expertise. Someone once put two tigers in a compound for eight hours, then asked experts how many there had been. Some said five, others twenty. Estimating numbers from pugmarks is fallible; yet India's annual tiger census is based on them. Forest guards trace and take plaster-casts. Forest officers deduce the numbers from data and announce the figures. Software is being developed to analyse pug-mark dimensions and characteristics, and incorporate other signs of tiger (and deer), to say how many tigers use a forest.

But software cannot banish human error, the tendency to see more variation in pugmarks and deduce more tigers than there are. Nor incentives to overestimate. When park administrations say they have lots of tigers, this makes the forest service feel secure, boosts a director's career, stops scientists or other outsiders looking closer, interfering. *Tigers went up when I was there* is a boast, and pleases the boss.

I did not know this, but I had grown up among scientists. Accuracy was dinned into us. Pugmarks seemed dodgy to me.

'Pugmark counting is completely reliable,' said the brigadier. Dr Malik said there were better ways.

I changed the subject. What about villagers, moved outside reserves? Those at Kanha were terribly poor, but got nothing from international visitors streaming through. The brigadier said they had been ade-quately compensated at the time. They had been relocated thirty years ago. Communists were stirring them up against the reserve.

Dr Malik said people needed education, money, food, work, and no benefit came to them from tiger reserves. 'I come from those people myself,' he said. 'We won't get anywhere unless we take them into account.' I thought he was wonderful. But I was the brigadier's guest. So I asked another question. Reserves are islands, separated by villages and cities, so how about inbreeding? Won't genes weaken in isolated tiger populations? The brigadier looked pleased and brought out maps. WWF would buy land to make corridors between some reserves, so tigers could meet. I wondered if this would happen. I fan-cied Dr Malik wondered too. But we parted friends.

Valmik's study in Delhi, a hub of tiger conservation in India, glowed like Byzantium. Burnished bindings of old books by the tiger hunters who began tiger observation; bright books by modern zoolo-gists; tiger paintings, photos, hangings, sculptures. Valmik, bushy, courteous and intense, in a leather chair. I would never see all the tigers, watch their tragedies and comedies, the families, nuances, per-sonalities, which he had known intimately in thirty years of tiger watching; had described, loved, filmed. But I was now going to where Valmik himself had first seen tigers. He had told me where to stay.

Valmik went to Ranthambhore in 1976, three years after Project Tiger began. With its director Fateh Singh Rathore, he recorded tiger family life as humans had never known it. Ranthambhore is open forest, easier to see in than many. They saw tigers moving in daylight now the guns were gone. Saw them hunt, kill, eat, mate, suckle; saw male tigers share food with families. But Valmik also watched villagers moved out of the reserve. They were offered more land, and things they did not have: a temple, school, playground. But it was very emotional. One evening in April 1977, a village refused to go. At midnight, after hours of agonized argument, they consented.

Valmik felt tigers survived at Ranthambhore only because of the villagers' sacrifice. He bought land there and set up a foundation to benefit villagers in the tiger's name. In arid land he planted native trees, organized seed collection of forest trees that they could plant, a mobile health unit, art school, women's handicraft collective to bring in money, a farm to breed cows to give better milk. Let the people see tigers giving to them, not just monopolizing the forest.

Feathery acacia trees in half-dark; blond dunes under silver crusted stars; smell of burning dung. Thin parched cows, empty stony fields, dull gold grass dotted with Mughal tombs. Tall haughty camels, leggy ghosts with Roman-emperor noses, tatty chocolate flanks stippled with henna hieroglyphs. Welcome to Rajasthan, the hottest, driest place where tigers still live; deciduous thorn-forest far drier than it should have been. The rains had failed for three years. There was a terrible drought.

We drove up a rocky ravine beside a thin stream. I looked up a sheer cliff, longing to see a leopard peering down. Leopards like high places. We passed through an ancient stone gate – a royal entrance, with precious water splashing from a marble bull's head to a pool – to the outer zone of Ranthambhore. At the checkpoint to the inner zone, tourist jeeps queued for the number-plates that assign you one of the trails. Ranthambhore restricts jeeps to fifteen in the park at a time. Jeeps are often booked six months in advance and follow a few set trails. Canters (open trucks carrying twenty people) use only two. I knew none of this, but two people staying at my camp had offered me a place in their jeep.

We were in. There were pugmarks. A tigress had come to the guard-post in the night and turned back; someone had ringed the pugmarks with his finger. Now trees were thicker, the rocky track steep. Round a corner, over palm-tree heads and thorn bushes, past ancient peepal trees and banyan trees writhing like water, came high clifftop with crenellations nibbling the grey-pink, just-before-morning sky. The Ranthambhore fort, at dawn.

From the seventh century, Rajasthan was dominated by Rajputs, a warrior caste. Mughal invaders left Ranthambhore alone till 1301, when the Rajput women watched their men die in battle and burned themselves in a group suttee called *jauhar*. But the Mughals did not conquer here properly until 1569.

Past the fort was a valley granulated with low bushy hills. I had seen photos of it green and lush, lakes full of tinsel-pink lotus. Now there was only the dry silver of parching tree trunks, dry gold of dead grass, lakes shrunk to almost nothing. They should have been a centre of animal life: herds of sambar in water, as at Periyar, munching lotus; crocodiles stalking them from below, tigers above. We saw two does in a puddle, ears sideways like radar. Among trees a chital stag looked at us, russet flank helter-skelter with white spots, a milk-dribble white line edging his tummy. Outlined in early sun, the velvet U of his antlers shone silver. An enormous bird, a king vulture, humpy with shocking-pink wattles, was examining something on the dry forest floor, shaking untidy wings. A sambar stag, up to his belly in a muddy wallow, stretched his throat to suck water from the mud with new light beaming red through his ears: we could see every blood vessel. An owlet looked down coldly from a branch. Wild boar trotted busily away from us. A mongoose nosed a dead monitor lizard. Morning had come.

You need to like the people you go to the forest with. Lee and Stephen had saved me from the canter. I liked them very much indeed. They were thirtyish, passionate about wildlife, slung with cameras. Lee, slender with shiny, shoulder-length brown hair, was in television; Stephen, thin with broad, bony shoulders, in computers. They had an expert guide: Vipul Jain, a big, kind-looking man with soft full face and lips. Terry the camp manager came with us. He was from Zimbabwe; this was his first week in India. He had not seen a tiger. 'Please point out birds, Mr Jain,' he said. 'I do like my birds.'

We stopped to listen for alarm calls. I loved being completely still in the forest, listening. A rattle or rustle could mean anything; the world was waiting for you to learn. The jeep ticked softly, hot metal quietening. I felt the vegetation straining to pull sap into itself, conserve all the moisture it could. Here were the animals, looking for food, living their lives, but the forest had its back to the wall. Everyone was suffering. Then a nilgai strolled by, almost as big as a moose but far more elegant; a leggy cow with sloping shoulders. This was a male with shimmery blue coat. Nilgai are lucky. The human desire to show off with animal parts has decimated the animal world, but no hunter wants to display the nilgai's little horns. Also they are called 'blue cow' in India. Cows are sacred; Hindus leave nilgai alone. Apart from poachers, nilgai have only one thing to fear. Here, as at Panna, they were the tiger's tallest prey.

Terry was used to enthusing tourists. 'What a beautiful animal!' We were silent. Stephen took a photo, the nilgai just walked. Calm, purposeful, taking no notice of anybody, not like the nilgai in Panna who cantered away.

We drove across a dried-out lake. Pale mud zigzag cracks, dead trees which all their lives had roots in water. Thorn bushes; then up a little hill – and Vipul stopped the driver. 'Caracal,' he whispered, awestruck, looking back through binoculars at the dry lake. A small animal walked away. Through opera glasses it looked rose-pink, with long ears. A caracal is a rare, secretive cat with the same long ear tufts as the lynx. Ancient hunters in India and Persia used it to chase small deer and birds. In pictures I'd seen, they were pale amber, with slender, pointed, rather severe caramel faces: the pursed mouth of a disapproving science teacher. I never dreamed I'd see one. Normally they hunt at night. But their behaviour was changing in the drought. We saw it again two days later: it must have been living in the bushes on the hill. Now it looked back from the dry lake bottom and disappeared. It was no big antelope, no confident top predator. Caracal keep a low profile.

Other jeeps zoomed up to see what we were looking at. I never got the jeep trails clear but they overlapped. If another saw binoculars flash, you suddenly had a whole flock beside you, straining to see and take photos. The human desire to record: that's the basis of wildlife tourism. The jeeps were full of expensive hardware. Wildlife holidays are about photography as much as animals. Like a hunter, you take something home. One man had a whole jeep to himself and his camera. His lens was balanced longways from back to windscreen like a missile-launcher. He sat with one hand resting on its shaft.

But the guides in these jeeps were dispirited. No tigers had been seen for a week. Prey and tigers had withdrawn from the lakes. Ranthambhore was letting people down.

In the sixties, it was still OK everywhere to shoot tigers and leopards. Leopardskin was chic. Jackie Kennedy wore it. In 1964, East Africa alone exported fifty thousand leopard skins. The maharajah's guests, including the Queen and the Duke of Edinburgh, shot tigers in Ranthambhore. Then the world woke up. There were fewer than two thousand tigers in all India! In the sixty square miles of Ranthambhore, maybe only twelve. World opinion began to change. In 1973 CITES took effect and Project Tiger created reserves all over India. Ranthambhore was its flagship. With no villages and no hunting, tigers stopped bothering about being seen. They strolled through Mughal cupolas, unfazed by cameras. By 1989, there were nearly fifty. Ranthambhore was *the* place for tigers. People from nearby Sawai Madhopur became guides, hoteliers, drivers. It was a golden age. Tiger censuses were high. The government was proud of Project Tiger.

Then came rumours of poaching. Familiar tigers vanished from Chitwan in Nepal too. Fateh Singh was no longer director but he knew that tigers he had watched at Ranthambhore were disappearing. Meanwhile, at a conference in Minnesota, Ullas shocked everyone by saying there simply was not the prey to support the tiger numbers the forest service said there were. A tigress feeding cubs has to kill seventy large deer-shaped animals a year. If not a big one, sambar or gaur, then more smaller ones, chital, wild boar. A muntjac every two or three days instead of a sambar every ten. They were simply not available in India. Prey and tiger numbers did not add up.

This was a spearhead moment. Science had entered the counting game, upsetting the political handling of tigers. All over the world, field biologists were developing objective ways of counting unseeable animals. One was the long-term study of representative areas of forest. You study the same line, a 'transect', or same square 'plot' regularly, in depth, long-term, recording all animal signs in it. From this you estimate animal *density*. Instead of a subjective guess (how many tigers altogether?) you get an objective estimate of how many tigers (*and* what they depend on, prey animals) use it per square mile. You also put cameras on trails. When animals pass they flash, recording time and date. You can add that data too, *and* sophisticated conceptual tools from statistics, then run all the data, cameras, plots and transects through mathematical models to estimate numbers of tigers and prey using the forest. This is a complex process, painfully different from the political-bureaucratic approach to animal numbers. In all countries, politicians and civil servants like science when it backs them up, and hate it challenging how they do things.

In 1991, the new Ranthambhore director said tigers were currently hard to see because they were in hills because of heavy rain. The 1992 census said forty-five tigers. Fateh Singh denounced it. He was sure there were no more than twenty. Valmik, invited to help with the next tiger census, found signs of only seventeen. The warden rubbished his findings. Then a forest guard who had seemed to know too much about poaching was found murdered, and police caught someone with freshly killed skin and bones. A chain of confessions began. Over fifteen tigers had been killed in two years. A massacre, said Fateh Singh. 'They were shot point-blank, innocently looking at the man with a gun. I taught them not to fear people!' All those cubs, hardworking mothers, tiger personalities whom he and Valmik had watched and learned from: gone. Other gangs were at work in other parks. In Uttar Pradesh, tiger expert Billy Arjan Singh thought there were twenty tigers, instead of a hundred, at his Tiger Haven. Reports of skins and skeletons came in from everywhere. Valmik estimated a hundred and twenty tigers were known to be lost, and many times that had been poached unknown.

The forest department announced that poaching on such a large scale was impossible. But the impossible had happened. Ranthambhore was where the world first realized, in 1992, the rise in ruthlessly organized poaching.

Now tiger numbers here had crept back to about thirty. But recently four hundred villagers invaded the park with sticks, muzzle-loaders, swords, and four thousand cows. They demanded grazing, camped in the territory of a tigress raising four cubs, poisoned her and two of the cubs. Two former members of the local assembly were accused of egging them on for votes, fanning resentful memories of relocation. Fodder areas outside the park were barren; others were occupied by industry, which lowered the water table. Ranthambhore is a small forest, squeezed all round by grazing and wood-collecting. The drought made headlines everywhere; a police chief who tried to stop the invasion was transferred away. Finally, the director went out at the head of his guards to confront the crowd. They threw stones, three guards were dangerously hurt, but the men did leave. Luckily no one died; except the tigers.

'I carry a gun in Africa,' said Terry. 'My tourists come first.'

He had always wanted to be a ranger, a guide. But he had strong views on India's elusive leopards. 'They are fifty years behind ours.'

In African savannah leopards climb trees to get away from lions, ignoring tourist jeeps beneath. Asian leopards are different. They live in dense cover. They climb rocks and cliffs to get away from tigers *and* people. I did not think they would change. Africa was clearly different. I tried to imagine someone turning up at Ranthambhore with a gun.

We were sitting under a full moon in a garden visited by leopards. Woodsmoke drifted across the glade. This was a luxury camp. My tent had sherry-coloured matting, a snow-white coverlet spotted with tangerine tigers. Here were chairs round a fire, tables sparkling in the flambeaux, enough drink and glasses for a ball. Terry talked of Africa, elephants charging jeeps, hippos charging canoes, a wounded giraffe that stepped on a land mine.

'Did you put it out of its misery with your gun?' I asked.

'I took the tourists to their camp, went back and shot it.'

'You let it suffer all those hours?'

'Tourists come first. They might have been upset by killing. My responsibility was to them.'

I felt animals came first, in the wild that was their home. Not upsetting tourists came way down my list. Maybe that was the difference between someone in the eco-tourist business like Terry, and a conservationist or old-fashioned animal-lover like me.

'What do you think "wild" means, Terry?'

'Free. Untouched by man.'

'In Britain, the New Forest holds an annual wild-pony round-up. They corral them, worm them, brand them. But they are wild, not domestic ponies, won't look you in the eye. Huffing, kicking. *Wild* animals.'

'If they're branded,' said Terry, firmly, 'they're not wild.'

I went to sleep reading a WWF pamphlet for forest guards. *Tracking Tigers* said, in Hindi and English, 'Come, let us track and count tigers and leopards. The tiger's right and left feet are like our hands. On your right hand the third finger from right is longest. On your left, the third finger from left is longest. Same with the tiger.' Thick dust offers the best pugmarks. 'Come, let us lay tracks.' Diagrams showed how to make a sandy patch for prints, how to make a cast, to distinguish back from front and measure stride.

'I'm sure she's here somewhere,' said Vipul. 'Let's go up this track.'

We felt we were looking for a tiger in a haystack, but Vipul knew what he was doing. He had chosen a trail into steep, rocky forest. A greeny-brown jungle cat, sleek and military, big as a spaniel, stopped on neat paws and looked at us with dirty yellow eyes. Two sambar stags fought like boys bullying off in hockey, watched by a doe in grass-stalks high as her nose. We stopped for coffee and sandwiches at a forest guard outpost. From the platform I looked into a cauldron of greens and browns, wondering what secrets the undergrowth held. Snakes, rodents, predators: what was it like to live here months on end? What were the nights? Vipul gave our spare sandwiches to the guards, four thin, middle-aged men whittling sticks; they had not seen the tigress recently, but knew she had cubs close by. Vipul drew me a rough map showing the territories of three tigresses. We were after the youngest, furthest from the lakes.

'Tigresses like the water-holes. They are used to jeeps. It's rare to see a male; they stay on the heights.'

We drove into thicker forest, leaves like lily-pads, dappled thin grey trunks. When we stopped, a brigade of tree-pies, chestnut magpies with tails of two-tone grey, hopped on the ground cocking black-helmet heads. We had waited ages; no alarm calls, no tigers. Stephen tossed the remains of his sandwich on to the ground. Fifty tree-pies buzzed down. Like all crows they were opportunistic, daring when they thought they could get away with it. There were many more than we had realized. One landed on my hat and stood shifting its feet; another on Lee's bare arm.

'His claws tickle,' she whispered. Suddenly we heard a low soft boom. *Aooom!* Vipul looked at the driver, who started the engine and wheeled round. The tree-pies flew crossly up to their trees. We hurtled back the way we had come; swung left; stopped when Vipul raised his hand. Again we heard it, through hot forest. Nearer. *Aooom*. Pause. *Aooom*. A bass clarinet, *pianissimo*. If a drum could moan, that was how it would sound.

She was calling her cubs. But we were in very dense forest. We waited in silence, but that was all the tiger we got that day. The first time, though, that I had heard this wild private noise, loose and close in the jungle. I was thrilled.

Tigers have a wide repertoire of sounds. Growls, grunts; a gruff hiccough labelled 'pooking', which advertises their presence to other tigers and wards off potentially violent meetings – a little like a sambar alarm call but, says George Schaller, flatter in tone. Tigresses gargle to young cubs in birdlike chirrups; family members express pleasure in each other's company with intimate noises like breathy, puffy panting and raspberry-like blowing (*hello, I know you, I like you*), known as 'chuffing' or, in German, *prusten*. There is also woofing, moaning, hissing; and the coughing roar of serious attack.

Recent researchers have found tiger calls also have low-frequency acoustic energy. The hearing response in the brains of anaesthetized zoo tigers is best at around five hundred hertz. (People respond best at one thousand.) Low-frequency sounds carry better than high, less distorted by humidity and ground cover; so they are vital for forest animals. Even tiger sounds we *can* hear have subharmonic elements we cannot. The tiger's inner ear suggests it is built for infrasound. (Though if they hear it, it is not infrasound to them, of course.) This infrasound must be part of the tiger social system: warning intruders, attracting mates, calling cubs. It may affect creatures like us who cannot get the pitch but react to the vibrations.

These researchers believe that sounds made by individual tigers may carry an acoustic fingerprint. If you could identify tigers acoustically, could you count tigers in a forest with well-placed microphones? Field scientists are sceptical. Even zoo-keepers recognize different tigers by their sounds, but could you identify them by voice-print consistently enough, especially with all the other jungle sounds as background, to count them?

As we left I wondered if we, especially Vipul who had spent years doing this, had registered the tigress's subacoustic frequencies all morning without knowing it. Those tree-pies must have known exactly where she was, but cared more about Stephen's sandwich.

We had to drive fast to reach the gate before it closed. There were penalties for Vipul and the driver otherwise. But suddenly Vipul stopped us. 'Kingfisher,' he said, raising binoculars, 'with snake.' Over a stream stood a pied kingfisher with something dangling from its beak. Quick – opera glasses – yes, a snake, silhouetted against the sun. My eyes dazzled; I couldn't see patterns. Vipul could. 'Krait,' he said. A *krait*! Mythic figures I had read about as a child were springing up in front of me. In Kipling's 'Rikki Tikki Tavi', the mongoose hero saves a child from a krait that says from the dust, 'I am death.' Here, death was a thrashing, helpless piece of string.

I had an old book by a British military doctor on Indian snake poisons. In his pages, people and dogs bitten by kraits died in an hour; with vomiting, frothy mucus, salivation, kidney congestion, oedematous lungs, convulsions, dilated pupils, coagulating blood. All that from one small puncture. But here was the kingfisher – the halcyon, associated in the West with tranquillity – catching one for lunch.

They dropped me at Fateh Singh's house. He possessed, apparently, an uncanny understanding of where tigers go, how they behave. I was early and he was having a shower. I waited in a small courtyard by a little statue of Ganesh reclining on a bird bath. It was a shrine to tigers. On the walls were watercolours: nineteenth-century tiger shoots. Chairs were tiger-pattern fabric. Fateh Singh appeared in a tiger-stripe silk scarf. 'Sorry to keep you waiting. Been out all morning in the park.'

He was older, more gnarled than when he had welcomed Valmik to Ranthambhore in his Stetson. But there was stylish braggadocio still. A sophisticated, old-fashioned exquisite.

'Any tigers?' No guide had seen any all week.

'Falling over them. Couldn't move for tigers.' The Father of Ranthambhore is not bound by tourist rules. I asked about the villagers' invasion.

'They'll learn they shouldn't listen to politicians.'

He was an optimist. About Ranthambhore, about the tiger.

'Tigers live in the hottest and coldest places, Siberia, Ranthambhore. They are adaptable. They breed well. All they need is prey, water, forest. They're going to be all right.'

His son Goverdhan was a doctor who had worked with Valmik and the Ranthambhore Foundation on a mobile health unit here for years. His wife managed the camp. Now they had set up a hospital and school here to show villagers that tigers, and the outside world's interest in them, benefited their lives. His wife showed me the hospital vestibule painted with a forestless desert: what happens if you keep cutting trees for fuel. Gleaming equipment. A beautiful white building. The school, too, was beautiful, curving like a wing round an immaculate lawn.

'We have some scholarships for poor children but can't afford many. It's hard to get teachers to come here. We don't keep them long; they cost a lot. It's expensive to run. But we are trying to expand.'

She led me past posters, through classrooms, corridors, a library. I thought of run-down primary schools in London, leaky roofs, no books, enormous classes. My daughter's state primary school was nothing like this. The whole vision, education and health aimed at helping the tiger via helping people, brought tears to my eyes. So careful, so detailed. Tropical disease, the fear and pain. But did it achieve its larger aim? Did one school with few scholarships stop lots of hungry people taking fuel from the forest?

'You're smart,' Lee said.'Where's the tie?'

'I don't do ties,'said Terry.

Dinner in a candlelit marquee. Goverdhan dined with medical colleagues: they had seen patients all day. Four army officers dined in a corner guarded by men in sunglasses. Tiger reserves are status. VIPs, the army, politicians and their friends all take a precious jeep but are too grand to pay.

Terry saw me to my tent in the dark. A new tent, because new VIPs were coming. They wanted six tents together for them and their security men. We still had not seen a tiger, either of us.

'It's odd. In Africa at night, you really know the animals are out there. It's jumping with sound. Here it's all quiet.'

'I think Asian animals are more secretive.'

'I think I talk about Africa too much.'

Next morning this man who didn't do ties was nestling at the back of a jeep behind VIPs. All the guides believed a tigress had hidden cubs in an area of groundcover. Stephen, Lee and I kept meeting Terry's party around it. Vipul asked our driver to stop. We listened. Suddenly a guide on another jeep put his hand to his mouth. '*Aoom!*'

'That's a bad thing to do,' whispered Vipul. 'They're not supposed to call the cubs. It makes them break their mother's rules.'

The cubs had been hiding, motionless. Now one got up to see if Mother really was coming. There was a small orange flash in green; then stillness. People stood on jeep seats with binoculars, but the cub had realized its mistake and frozen. Immobility is the first skill of every newborn wild animal. Small cubs are utterly obedient, hiding when Mother says. Their lives depend on it. Anything could eat them: jackal, dhole, bear, snake, eagle, leopard.

'But they're *there*,' breathed Lee.

'Poor Terry,' I said. 'We've seen a tiger.'

'Hardly a tiger,' said Stephen.

'Don't tell them,' said Lee, fiercely. She was lovely; generous, passionate about animals, wildly against any smidgen of VIPness. 'They'd come and pester them. They'd worry the mother.'

Vipul took us to the fort's gatehouse, used by the forest guards. They had adopted an orphaned nilgai calf, chestnut, high as a pony, with dark eyes and a Nefertiti line of kohl to her muzzle, graciously fond of titbits. Langurs watched jealously from red ramparts, like the crows in *The Birds*, their silk outlined silver by the afternoon light. The minute we left the jeep they jumped in and started turning over the picnic basket. The driver shooed them off.

We walked up steep passages where Akbar had ridden in over wet blood on a war elephant. At the top was a crumbling arch, and sky like a stirrup-shaped mouthful of blue held in by dentures of pale stone. Through these stone teeth you could see how the lakes had shrunk. They were puddles, far inside where lake edges had once been. Here on top was a shrine where thousands of pilgrims came for a festival. A tiger had once charged their line and killed a boy in his way, accidentally. He had just wanted to get across.

The temple was to Ganesh. Stephen did not approve of religion and stayed outside. Lee and I came out behind a small boy holding a paper twist of seeds, who was instantly mugged by a young langur. It was an expert bit of work. At one moment a toddler was negotiating jagged stone steps; at the next he was rolling in dust, howling, and the langur had his seeds. Then he lost out, too. Like something out of *Crouching Tiger, Hidden Dragon* the boss langur, big, solid, taller than the toddler, leaped down and grabbed the paper.

'Hey!' said Stephen, and stood up. Like Lee, he hated VIPness: this bully embodied it. The langur squared up to him, flexing silver-brown biceps, clenching black fists, baring yellow teeth. Contemptuous eyes in a black mask face glittered like mica. *Cark!* he spat.

'No!' said Vipul. 'Careful! Langurs give a very nasty bite.'

Men ran at the langur, who sprang away to the roof and sat there, cursing Stephen, eating the seeds. The child went on crying.

Vipul took me into the guardhouse to talk to the forest guards. I sat on a chair in a small stone room; the nilgai peered in from outside. Vipul brought guards to sit by me, translating what they said. A transistor played Hindi songs, other guards stood round listening. They knew the forest as they knew their bodies; how it changed, felt, sounded, smelt, day and night, monsoon and drought. There were ninety permanent guards, who got clothes, shoes, a pension, medicine; and two hundred cattle guards.

Mr Dubay, a small wiry man with a torn grey woolly cap, came first.

What was their worst problem? Everyone debated. Not getting rations on time, they said. No salt, flour, vegetables, chilli, oil.

What weapons did they have against animals or poachers? Only sticks. Did he think they should have guns? It was not a fair question, but I wondered what he would say. He licked his lips, did not take his eyes off mine, said he didn't know. Mr Chitarmal Sani took his place: born in 1963, he didn't know when he had started his job, but had earned two rupees a day at first. Last year he met head-on a tigress with three cubs. He didn't see her because she was below, in a riverbed. She charged him three times. Last month he watched a tiger chasing a bear. But people were the main danger. He had caught poachers several times: tribal people, gypsies, who mainly hunted partridges and deer.

Mr Phalchand was older, broader, with a ripped, scarred cheek. They all looked frail and undernourished. He had worked here since 1979. He had joined because he liked wildlife. 'Poachers are very dangerous. They use motorbikes and jeeps. They have guns, traps, small bombs for wild boar. They poach for meat, poison their kills for tiger. Now, we do more patrolling at night.'

Did he miss his family? Well, he had five days' holiday a month and could be with them then. It was a good job, a government job. Last year he had had to find out why a cub had died. The tigress had had four; one was vomiting. He had to collect the vomit, to know what was wrong. The mother charged from behind. Luckily when the other guard shouted she went away. The funniest thing he had seen was Genghis, top tiger round the lakes for one season in the boom years, famous for hunting deer in water. He stole deer from crocodiles, lugged them ashore leaving furious reptiles lashing the water with their tails. The sloth bear was the most dangerous animal, always ready to attack.

'One evening, I came down from the fort and a bear attacked. I beat trees with my stick and it stopped. But then it came back.'

I had seen a sloth bear on video now, a large black shape with a pale, bare snout, loose hair rolling around its head, scarily jerky and quick. Was that when he got his scar?

'No, that was in 1983. I was in the forest in early morning. A mother bear with cubs attacked.'

Listeners broke in: that bear then sent another guard up a tree on the fort wall and kept him there, blood pouring from his head – bears always go for the head – till enough people had mustered to chase her away.

I wished I knew Hindi. These men were the tiger's front line of defence. But so frail, in this small quiet guardroom which had once surrendered to Akbar.

At the archway out of the park a large brown fish owl, sitting on the bull's head, studying the pool below with enormous topaz eyes, raised ear-like tufts on his head, spread shadowy wings and drifted away, a perfectly silent brown angel at dusk, over the stream.

The deputy assistant field director said he had a pugmark on his back. 'I went to a village where a tiger mauled a villager. It leaped out, clawed my back, broke three ribs. I was in hospital for three months. Thirty-three stitches. After I came out, I tried to get a wildlife posting.'

I was in the park's head office. After guards, the administrators: men running Ranthambhore. A low building, courtyards and corridors blowing with dead leaves. Everyone begins the forest service the same way. Later you can do an optional course in wildlife management but there is no guarantee you will ever get a wildlife post. You may be sent to logging operations, desert development, a dairy project in Delhi. There is no money in wildlife. If anyone is passionate about it and wants to make a difference, they can't. It is pure luck if a concerned knowledgeable person is appointed to a tiger place.

'That should have put you *off* wildlife!'

'The tiger saved me. It could have killed me, but went away.'

In the director's office, sunbeams straggled through faded curtains over bundles of papers with fabric carefully tucked under the binding to protect the paper. A big hardworking room. Its owner, Mr Reddy, a quick-faced, rumpled man in pale grey, unpinned a paper from a baize noticeboard and showed me Kipling's poem 'If'. Tigers were flourishing under him. He focused on conservation despite threats to the land. Even in good times the core zone here is invaded by illegal grazing. He was one of the few forest officers interested in biology. He had done the wildlife course but then it took him seven years to get a wildlife post. After this posting he was going to do a Ph.D. on sabbatical under Ullas. I asked what was Ranthambhore's biggest problem.

'Fuel. Tourists use it up. Villagers demand wood. Felling is allowed in the buffer zone, which is very degraded. Immediately, of course, water. We're going to have to fill waterholes by tanker soon.'

I asked what had happened after the invasion. The poisoned tigress had had four seven-month cubs: they were letting the two survivors fend for themselves, tossing them goats. 'We mustn't go near them – that would unfit them for life in the wild. They still have milk teeth. We don't know if they'll survive.'

He had thirty-seven tigers now, according to the last census: double the number of 1992. But what about defending guards against poachers? They got hurt, faced death: couldn't they be armed?

'They'd have to prove they acted in self-protection. It'd be very difficult for them legally. It would be impossible if they all had guns.'

He needed rangers for four different things: looking after four hundred tourists a day; checking how many people the canters carried, how far apart the jeeps were; patrolling the forest; a flying squad for emergency attacks and surprise raids.

'It's a hard job. Every day it becomes more complicated. They're educated to twelfth year, class five. They stay in the park all their life. Thirty years without their families. Their prime of life, dedicated to this.'

'*They* said their biggest problem was getting rations on time.'

He smiled sadly. 'They were shy. The real problem is not being with wives and families. The job's great drawback. They become guards because government service means tenure. We train them, meet their problems, try to be sympathetic. But for the last fifteen years there's been no recruitment.' The average age of his guards was forty-five to fifty. The forest service is top-heavy, but to save money the central Finance Department has banned recruitment from the bottom. Ageing, underpaid, a hundred guards die or are mutilated every year by poachers. Reddy desperately needed young staff. Here he was, running the best-known tiger reserve in the world, coping with *people* all the time: tourists, a massive illiterate desperate population, poachers, and vulnerable guards. When I looked back he was pinning 'If' on his noticeboard again.

So he should. Later, he will cross Rajasthan's forest minister by insisting on the 'no shops' law for the shrine at the fort during festival-time. The minister (pressured, presumably, by stall-holders) will try to insist on shops. When he fails, eighteen inquiries will be launched into false allegations of Reddy's wrongdoing, which will plague Reddy's final year here. Rajasthan authorities will even sit round analysing a

BBC film with Valmik and Reddy in it (made, of course, with forest office permission) to see how many technical violations of trespass they can spot.

Tigers are territorial. So are those in charge of them.

Reddy did a wonderful job there. Tiger numbers really did go up. He kept the sanctuary inviolate, even against the pressure of his bosses. A successful Ranthambhore director should be posted afterwards to other key tiger areas: instead he is tied to this state for his working life. Reddy's successor will not have his guts. In future, getting cattle out of Ranthambhore will need orders from the Supreme Court, letters to the Chief Secretary of Rajasthan to call police to move them. In 2004 a Supreme Court committee will even have to request Rajasthan to replace thirty guards withdrawn from the core area (which resulted in widespread woodcutting). By March 2005 Ranthambhore will have lost so many tigers, it will be put on red alert.

If carries a lot of weight.

On the road into town, men squatted in shelters propped on poles, women cooked on thousands of tiny fires. The china-blue feathers of the forest's burning viscera wafted past children playing on rubbish heaps. In a dry bare field was a tumble of sand-coloured buildings; a deserted cement factory where a leopard once went to ground after eating a child. It chased a goat that ran into a shed, so instead took a baby lying on the ground. They tracked it to the abandoned factory.

'I was with them when they went to tranquillize,' said Vipul. 'They planned to take him far into the forest. Everyone was frightened. He was in the boiler-room. They shot, but weren't sure they got him. He growled behind the boiler. Some people ran away. They shot tranquil-lizer again.'

A dim cramped boiler-room, a desperate animal, terrified men. Growls, designed to intimidate, succeeding. A leopard is much smaller than a tiger but can pull down a nilgai.

'They put him on a truck, but he died on the way. They had not given the correct amount.'

We drove into the old town through narrow streets full of black goats, thin men with thick moustaches, columns of flip-flops hanging like onion strings, to the Kala Gura Bharro temple built into a cliff. One arch was made of two stone elephants whose forefeet were load-bearing columns holding a colonnaded balcony; their trunks met to make the arch. The temple steps were guarded by two tigers facing each other. I put my sandals at their feet.

Walking barefoot through paired animals like these, human beings enter the world of gods. For Hindus, the whole world is the abode of god, but the temple is a god's home, where you talk to him or her. Visiting is a spiritual pilgimage, embodied here in a series of stair-cases up the cliff. The first level had a row of statues of Nanda, Shiva's bull.

'Look,' said Vipul. 'A tiger face.'

Carved into the side of the bull's head, slung sideways, was a cat mask. I had to take Vipul's word for it, as tiger. Up another level, past Durga on her tiger, were red pillars with white sixteenth-century cap-itals, one carved with the curved body, springy haunches, waving tail and head of a tiger. There were tigers at every level of this temple, part of its ancient fabric. This area was not famous for tiger cults. Tigers were just here in the temple, a normal part of secular and religious life.

As he dropped me at camp Vipul handed me a small white alabaster tigress, with two cubs, carved on a rough pedestal with a hole at one end for a biro. A tiger pen-holder. Thank you, Vipul . . .

'Look at the cubs.'

One cub was suckling; the tigress carried the other in her mouth. Oh! They were not tigers at all. The cubs were tiny adult lions, with manes.

'The carver didn't know the difference. It is the same word in Hindi. He had never seen either. He made the cubs little lions.'

4

LADY OF THE LAKE

Moss, lichen, dead wood. The sun was not up. Our route today went round the lakes through Arthur Rackham forest, underwater green. Through early-morning mist, tissue paper lifting from a page, were antlers of grazing deer. The shrunk lake was clingfilm, creeping inwards.

Lee was fresh and pretty in pale blue blouse, white trousers.

'How do you keep so clean? I just *look* at the dust and I'm dusty.'

She laughed. 'We're going to be lucky. We'll see the Lady of the Lake. Machli. She was in a TV film I saw about Ranthambhore. She fought her mother to get lakeside territory. But she'll be Lady of the Puddle now.'

Different parts of the forest were different colours. Green fuzz; silver and gold laced with amber. In open patches the stone ground was moon pale with violet backdrop folds of further forest. On a blue stony shore, once the bottom of a lake, were three male peacocks. Fire-blue, fire-green, curvy chests and throats reflected in pewter water. Three above, three below: sapphire, serpentine and emerald. With a flap-ping like someone hanging out washing, a heron landed with wide wings, legs scoring the water's skin. Behind all was a stone pavilion, soft yellow arches, columns and dome all rosy in rays of rising sun.

We got away from other jeeps and stopped alone on a hill among wide-spaced trees. The forest floor was silver-brown leaves. Everything here was platinum, ice-grey, dun. We waited, as we had all week, for alarm calls. The only sound was the cooling engine. I closed my eyes, thinking of my daughter, about to disperse like a tiger cub. The laughter and enormous teenage feet of her friends trooping downstairs, trying to be quiet at three in the morning, would stop. My daughter: what I had learned from her. And that other matter: my unanswered letter. Blank chill from someone I once loved for his warmth.

I half opened my eyes. Suddenly, where I happened to be facing, I saw among ghost-grey trees in the valley that lovely grave silhouette, head down as if its specific gravity was heavier than any animal's. Focusing on ground in front of her; on a pattern of fallen leaves. For a split second, I had the magic to myself. A secret unseen by anyone but me.

Ever after, that would be my vision of tiger privacy. Living her life, walking her path through trees.

'*Tiger!* I mean – there she is!' Lee, Stephen and the driver turned. Lee gasped. Binoculars went up. Vipul let out a chital bark. I knew he had to. He was a deeply fair man. Guides, drivers and tourists had been waiting for this all week. He was letting other guides know where she was. It did not harm the tiger. You cannot do a human shout. Whatever you say long distance has to be said in chital. But her head whipped towards us. Alarm calls matter as much to her. They say, 'Can't hunt here, I've *seen* you! ' Her face, intelligent gold-vermilion, turned full on us. She realized it was only a jeep and moved calmly on. But among the other jeeps hell broke loose. Vipul had been sitting relaxed, elbow over the side. Now he sat down hard, and told the driver to U-turn. It was a question of getting to where she would emerge on the track.

More than anything in the world, I longed to stay where we were, quiet, not disturbing her. Watch as she walked, in her forest. But tourists want photographs of tigers. Guides had been mollifying disappointed visitors all week.

We raced along the hill, down a ridge, up and down a slope where we fell in behind a line of five excited jeeps. Five more came behind. A canter came, a big carrier. Cameras out, shouting, whispering, running out of film; whirring and shushing. The tigress, indifferent to all of us, came through the trees. Everyone fell silent. Like the nilgai, she walked at an angle to us, calmly crossed the track in front, scent-marked. I saw her tail go up, spray shoot back and drench a bush. This was her territory whether fifty humans were watching her or not.

She was so close. Her bright shoulders moved loosely in a film-star slouch. So red and extraordinary, black stripes moving over shifting copper. So oddly shiny. Cameras clicked like an audience at the Vatican.

This was the end result of what Valmik and Fateh Singh had watched happening through the eighties. Tigers who grew up not worrying about jeeps. Whose mothers taught them other things, but not to bother about humans. Was this wild? That argument with Terry. But if we got out . . . There are different ways of being wild.

She walked towards a knoll. Her ears, white spotted on the backs, swivelled forward. She stood with her back to us. The stripes on the backs of her haunches were rivery whirls on burnt umber, parting round the hanging bony tail. She sat, looking through ivory saplings and a floss of grass dried so pale it was white, down into the valley and up a further hill. She was concentrating, ignoring us. Maybe she had not yet got herself and the cubs a meal.

'She's doing the shopping,' Lee whispered.

The tiger stood up slowly and moved off into a cloud of gold and silver saplings with small buttery leaves. Far off, she was a spot of split-conker, fading to misty beige. The audience was over. Going, and gone.

The film crew I met in Panna had made the film Lee saw. This was the tigress they had called Machli, a name the guards originally gave to her mother. They filmed this tigress standing up to that mother for this very territory, shaking before the confrontation. (The mother afterwards moved to neighbouring territory.) They made a second film, showing a male courting this successful daughter, hoping to film the cubs growing up. But the male disappeared. A male's reign is short. One Chitwan male fathered fifty-one cubs in a reign of six years; but the average is thirty-two months. Genghis ruled a year. A quarter of males die fighting others. Life is tough at the top.

His disappearance put Machli in the worst tigress position. He had been her protector. When other males found his scent fading they would move in. With her hunting-ground, she was a valuable acquisition. Prime territory, resident tigress. They would kill her cubs to get her. The candidates were Chips, five and in his prime; a tiger aged eight with distant territory, and young Nick who had recently left his mother. The crew would now film the story of whether she could keep the cubs. Could she hold off the males? There was no fighting, possibly because tigers here are closely related. They filmed Machli flirting with Nick, rubbing him, leading him into bushes. Not for proper sex: she had not come into heat. Maybe he was too inexperienced to know the real thing. Her seduction was not gentle: I have watched it. She came on to him, then turned and swiped. He sheathed his claws, tried to smother her blows, but she split his pad. He limped off to wait till it healed. Two and a half months later the cubs left, Machli came into heat properly and mated with Nick for real. But what had been happening before?

Valmik was presenting the film. Raghu had seen something similar at Panna. They decided that Machli was deliberately confusing Nick, fooling him into thinking her cubs were his so he would not kill them. With a hint of sex and violence she was buying them time to grow up. Oxytocin was working in her for the cubs, not him.

That is one interpretation. If you go by results, it worked: the cubs survived. The film also showed a moment when they were seventeen months, as big as her. For one last time, she lay down to suckle them, though her milk was completely dry.

Now she must be hunting for her next litter. A tigress's work is never done. In her lifetime, fifteen years if she is lucky, she may bring twelve cubs to maturity.

I said goodbye to Lee, Stephen and Vipul, hugged them, thanked them. We were all stunned. On Sawai Madhopur platform for the Delhi train, a European girl came up. 'Are you Ruth? Valmik told me to look out for you.'

WWF's tiger representative, checking tiger reserves all over Asia. We slept on the train; I woke in the gloom, said a hurried goodbye, got off on the outskirts of Delhi and took an auto-rickshaw to Valmik's house.

'You left your bag on the train,' he said. 'I'm having it sent round.'

I had left passport, tickets, everything, on my bunk; the European girl had rescued them. Before flying off to Malaysia she had dined with P. K. Sen, ex-director of Project Tiger, who had rung Valmik. My Tesco plastic bag was coming through Delhi in a car. Valmik passed to more important things. 'George Schaller's here!'

A tiger and George Schaller in one day? This was like meeting Bagheera *and* Dr Dolittle. I had a new set of heroes now, though I still think Dr Dolittle was a pretty good one. Compassionate, tough, adventurous; dedicated to knowledge and wildlife; brilliant linguist; passionately curious, scientific. But top of my new list was George Schaller.

I had first met him, too, in a book, Peter Matthiesson's *The Snow Leopard*. In the seventies, Schaller had written his tiger books, and another on lions in the Serengeti. Then he planned to observe blue sheep, the snow leopard's prey in the Himalayas, and invited Matthiesson to join him. Matthiesson describes him as a lean young man who outwalked everyone on the toughest mountains, wrote haiku in a rain-lashed tent, scooped up snow-leopard shit on a rock-ledge that Matthiesson traversed on hands and knees. Who said, at a moment when they knew a snow leopard was near, because the sheep were frightened, 'We've seen so much, maybe it's better if there are some things we *don't* see.'

Today Schaller oversaw the Asia programme of the Wildlife Conservation Society, which Ullas worked for. Here he was in Valmik's study, long-legged, quick-eyed and, yes, lean. Valmik suggested he tour Indian reserves.

'But there are scientists here.' Schaller had been in the ex-Soviet Union where there are few structures for protecting people, let alone wildlife. 'There are places that need help and have no scientists.'

He had seen into the abyss, and now went where he could do most good. In 1977 he wrote,

> Man is modifying the world so fast and so drastically that most
> animals cannot adapt to the new conditions. In the Himalaya as
> elsewhere there is a great dying, one infinitely sadder than the
> Pleistocene extinctions, for man now has the knowledge and
> the need to save these remnants of his past.

For twenty-five years he had watched that dying, doing as much about it as he could, encouraging others, advancing knowledge because knowledge helps you to help animals who cannot adapt to the destruction of their home.

They asked what I had seen. How could I mention a tigress that I and fifty other tourists had seen to *these men*? There are other great tiger-watchers and tiger scientists, but these two between them had spent more hours and years watching wild tigers than anyone in the world. They had changed our thinking about them. It was like being asked to sing a nursery rhyme to famous opera singers. Instead I mentioned Terry, who had shocked me with talk of an experiment to bring tigers to Africa.

Valmik snorted. 'Ridiculous. They've never been there.'

But George Schaller, along with that vision into a dying world, appeared to have a vein of mischief. 'A lot of the habitat would be OK. It may be only accident that they never came across the Bering Straits in the Ice Age. The skeleton's pretty much the same as the lion. Only a little larger.'

I was not going to tangle with the Bering Straits. They were one key to the spread of species between continents, but complicated.

'We saw a caracal. And a kingfisher eating a krait.'

'How do you know it was a krait?' said Valmik instantly.

I didn't, of course. My opera glasses had shown a kingfisher and a snake. Vipul, with better glasses, had said it was a krait. But I did not care. Everyone has circles of ignorance, places where you can enjoy not knowing. To me, the amazing thing was that it could have been a krait. Valmik's *Land of the Tiger* shows a peacock pecking a large cobra, dancing on it with sharp claws. The snake's poison could dispatch the bird in seconds, but it looks as worried as a cobra can look, and is sliding away into a hole. Unlike the kingfisher, the peacock does not want to eat the snake. He is policing his patch. It is a basic principle of being a peacock that where you are is better without cobras.

What fascinated me was the power relation. Like the game of scissors, paper, stone, everything wins out over something. A fragile bird, vulnerable to practically everything, attacks one of the great poisoners.

If a tiger had been involved it would have been very different. I would have cared about exactness. A scientist cares all the time. Still, if I met that snake on the path I would care a great deal.

When Schaller left, Valmik and I had one more drink.

'Revenge killings and loss of forest are the worst. Tigers leave forest to find food. They kill livestock, villagers poison the carcass, the tiger returns and dies. We've found tiger bodies just left lying.'

I was silent.

'What do you want, Ruth? You can't go on like this.'

I wasn't sure what 'like this' was. An innocent in Asia leaving vital documents on trains? Or saying I saw a krait when all I saw was a snake? Or a woman on her own, not settling down? He didn't know my life; he was just being nice. He had invited me to stay, was my initiator into tigers, looked after me long distance in Ranthambhore. His shelves, with all the books on tigers ever written, were generously open to me. I asked him to sign his new book.

Next day on the plane to Calcutta I thought, Valmik is right. Poetry or science, what matters is saying it how you see it. Saying precisely what and how you saw, and no more. In science, poetry, or describing a journey, accuracy is all you can do. Saying it as you saw.

5

CROCODILES AND MAN-EATERS

'Kali temple!' The driver lifted both hands off the wheel. Through bucketing rain he pointed at red lights below the midnight fly-over. There were no windscreen-wipers. He was drunk or high, or both. 'See now?'

'No! *Mission*. Please!'

The road from Calcutta airport. I was staying at the Ramakrishna Mission, I hoped. A car shot past, brushed our front mudguard, slammed the barrier and bounced back at full speed. I shut my eyes. No bang. We looked back. It stood facing us, headlights glaring. My driver leaned out to smear an oily rag over the glass while swinging into a street of roadworks. Now we were the only car in the right-hand lane, facing oncoming traffic.

'Wrong side!' He nodded, swerved between bollards, slithered over tramlines. Calcutta: where Durga is Kali the Destroyer. Thin beggar-shapes on drenched streets. Wet maze of hell with a mindblown driver. Forget sloth bears and kraits: Kali deals in human beings.

Scholars stay at the Ramakrishna Mission. Over chilli omelette next day I asked an elderly woman beside me what she worked on. 'Universal values,' she said. The *Calcutta Statesman* said a cyclone was coming. Cyclones are frequent at the top of the Bay of Bengal, though not common in March. It also said local hospitals were in trouble. Rats in one morgue had gnawed a patient to pieces. In another, a cat had stolen a baby from Intensive Care. Nurses told his mother, who had rescued him, not to fuss about the bites on his throat or they would not look after him. If she kept quiet, they would treat the bites for nothing.

The courtyard pelted with rain. In my room I looked through notes on my next tiger terrain. The rain was apt: the Sundarbans are mostly water. You visit them by boat: the world's largest tidal mangrove forest, just south of the Tropic of Cancer, a delta of soil swept from the Himalayas and deposited by the Ganges and Brahmaputra. A forest that breathes like a lung, up and down twice a day with the tide.

Under the British it was all part of India. From the late eighteenth century to the 1930s, the British tried to 'reclaim' it for agriculture while exploiting it for timber, make it yield as much money as possible but stay as a buffer against cyclones and tidal waves. In 1947, two-thirds (about 5770 square kilometres, including 1750 square kilometres of water) became part of East Pakistan, separated from Pakistan by India. In 1971 it belonged to Bangladesh.

I was going first to the three or four thousand square kilometres on the Indian side of the Sundarbans. Within that is the Project Tiger reserve, where felling and hunting are illegal, though poaching is rampant. The land is carved by thousands of creeks into islands. Large ones where crops grow (water is saltier on the Indian side, crops poorer), tiny ones covered at high tide. People go between islands by boat; wild animals swim. The largest mammals, wild buffalo, gaur, barasingha, hog deer, rhino, have been extinct since 1900. No leopards, but chital, boar, rhesus macaque monkeys and, at the top of the muddy, slippery tangle, the tiger.

It was ten in the morning but dark as night, drumming with rain. Outside my window, women in red and green saris ran across the road with umbrellas, sloshing to the ankles. Armed guards before a jewellery shop dripped in its iron-gated vestibule. Sand-coloured pie-dogs with curly tails and sores shivered under ancient cars sheathed in private waterfalls. Tomorrow I would be out in this on a boat.

A tenth of all the world's tropical cyclones happen here. Like a huge funnel, the Bay of Bengal whips up tidal waves. Sometimes they fall on the coast of Orissa below Bengal, but mostly they rush straight up, attacking the Sundarbans. In 1972 a cyclone killed over two hundred thousand people in Bangladesh in two days. In 1988 even more hundreds of thousands died. With them went precious trees, and tigers.

Sundarbans tigers, uniquely, treat human beings as natural prey. Official figures say tigers killed 544 people in the Bangladesh

Sundarbans between 1975 and 1999: over twenty a year. In the Indian Sundarbans, it has been 1500 in the last twenty years: seventy-five a year. But these figures leave out people mauled who then die in hospital, or deaths not attributed to tigers because they happened where the man had no permit to be, so no one said it was tiger. Unofficially the deaths are probably twice as high.

Tippoo Sultan, the 'Tiger of Mysore', loathed the British, loved tigers, and decorated his palace with murals of British soldiers killed by tigers. At the siege of Mysore in 1799, British troops took from him a mechanical organ (now in London's Victoria and Albert Museum) shaped as a tiger. It stands on a redcoat soldier, biting his throat. When the handle is wound, the man calls and lifts an arm, the tiger roars. Some people think it was inspired by a Sundarbans story of a tiger that killed and ate a young British officer while his companions watched helplessly from another island. It was written up in the *Gentleman's Magazine* of 1793, just after Tippoo's palace was ransacked.

No one knows why Sundarbans tigers behave like this. Elsewhere man-eating is the exception not the rule. In the seventies, a researcher suggested it was because these tigers drank salt water. All Sundarbans water is salty; all animals (and people) drink it. There was no scientific underpinning to this idea but any was better than none. On the Indian side 'sweet-water' ponds were dug to give tigers a low-salt diet.

In fact, there must be many reasons. First, there is a lot less other prey than there used to be. The tigers also take fish and crabs, but these are not filling. The great wild-animal principle (not that different from human economy) is getting the maximum amount of fuel for the least expense of energy. In those terms fish are costly, humans are cheap.

There are also many vulnerable people in their forest. Man-eating is worst where people are most, in the north Sundarbans. People are in the forest all the time, honey- and wood-collecting, gathering thatch; often squatting, which makes them look more like animal prey; or fishing from open boats in narrow creeks. There are staring masks to wear on the back of the head, supposed to put off tigers attacking from behind, but most people are too poor, too unconnected, to get these. And no one knows if they work.

How many tigers? The Sundarbans is a tough place for research.

You have to use a boat; the mud is full of mangrove spikes, the tide covers tracks twice a day; border areas are sensitive. One secretive civil service is bad enough; the Sundarbans has two. WWF figures in 1999 gave the whole Sundarbans four hundred tigers. The last census on the Indian side was 271. Ullas, using camera traps there, found less than one tiger per hundred square kilometres, a much lower density than any pugmark estimate. 'They find a pugmark,' said one friend, 'trace it, feed that into a computer, and the computer says two hundred tigers! It's a *computer fairy tale!*' Scientists and conservationists who know the place say the real figure on the Indian side is fewer than a hundred, more like seventy or eighty. But the state Forest Department can make research or conservation permits impossible for anyone who reveals how few tigers there are, and how much poaching. In 1998 P. K. Sen, then director of Project Tiger which oversees the tiger census, announced publicly that India lost a tiger a day to poachers. There was civil service uproar. When P.K. left, his successor announced that he had been wrong.

My phone rang. Amanda, at the front desk! I had first met her in London. The charity she directed, Global Tiger Patrol, funded an NGO, a non-governmental organization, in the worst man-eating zone. She was now visiting its work, and had kindly invited me too, on the boat GTP had donated to this project. We would board it on the east of the Indian Sundarbans, go south along the border, the Kalindi river, and wind west into the Bay of Bengal.

Raindrops slowed in the courtyard, darkness rolled from the sky. No more cyclone. The flowerbeds glittered. There was blonde Carole, a GTP trustee, and Amanda in her elf cap of grey hair. Both laughing, waving, in floaty rose-and-cream Indian dresses and leggings, beside a stocky man with a navy-blue shirt and a kind, heavy, anxious face: Mrinal Chatterjee, who took us out into the suddenly hot streets to get permits for the forest.

He was a remarkable man. When young, already interested in wildlife, he had worked in a plywood factory and was devastated by timber coming in from Indian forests to be sold overseas. He visited conservation projects in Australia, then launched one here. His day job was insurance, but he worked tirelessly, unpaid, for an environmentalist NGO, running Project Lifeline Sundarbans. With the motto 'Serving People to Save Tigers', he set up a school for children whose fathers had been taken by tigers, and a clinic. The same idea as Valmik's: protect tigers by helping the people who live with them. If people see medical care, education and support coming in the tiger's name, they will be less likely to kill one.

Next day we drove south over flat land full of brick factories and market gardens, stocking up on cauliflowers for the voyage. The boat was small, neat, white, with a scarlet deck. We crossed over a red and white ladder to a sheltered platform covered in paisley. Here we would eat and watch the banks, maybe tigers too, go by. Downstairs was a cupboard bunk where I would sleep, a crimson and primrose dining area, blue door to the engine room and sky-blue kitchen quarters with bunks for the crew of five. A gypsy-caravan, primary colours world. The dining room had photos on the walls: a tiger drinking from a bank, honey-gatherers with anti-tiger masks on the backs of their heads, five fishermen in a boat. I looked more closely. Four squatted; the fifth lay on his bare stomach, blood on his hair. One man held his wrist, another his leg. He had been attacked by a tiger. He later died.

'I saw two tigers on the bank when I was here two years ago,' said Amanda. 'Just sitting there watching the river.'

'Waiting for lunch,' said Carole.

The land was flat, the banks a horizontal smudge of liver-brown mud. Above, since this was low tide, were paler brown mangrove roots, then a green canopy: dozens of different subtropical evergreens. Close up, the banks were glossy molten toffee bristling with up-ended pencils. This mud is non-aerobic, with no oxygen, so trees breathe through special spikes, pneumatophores. Every mangrove species has a different type of spike, some blunt, some narrow and pliant, all pushing up through gleaming mud. Darting through them were tiny crabs and six-inch silver carrots with bulbous eyes, wriggling, leaping, swarming up trunks: mud skippers, amphibious fish whose pectoral fins are modified to jump and climb; they store water in gill chambers so their gills stay moist in air. They are all over the

Sundarbans, in and out of water, in mud sometimes covered by the tide, sometimes not. The banks quivered with little moving things. I lifted my glasses.

'What are *those*?' said Amanda.

'Opera glasses. My granny gave them to me. I find them easier than binoculars. But you can't see as well.'

Amanda and Carole burst out laughing.

'There,' said the pilot suddenly, pointing to a large crocodile, sunning. Presumably armour-plated enough not to worry about spikes. When he saw us he threw up his head and cantered into the water. These crocodiles are estuarine; unfortunately for people living here, they too are aggressive and short of their natural food, which is being fished away from them. So they eat people if they can. The argument for crocodile conservation is even harder to run past local inhabitants than it is for tigers.

We stopped at a forest outpost set up for tourists, and walked ashore past a yellow-and-black-striped dinghy with a pugmark on its flag, into a green mesh cage-walk. The Indian side hangs this mesh everywhere to stop tigers eating guests. Mrinal introduced the new range officer, a twenty-something man with a cheery face.

'He's a bachelor. People's expectations of him are very high. His is the area with the worst political problems.'

We walked on brick-column stepping-stones set in mud heaving with crabs. Crabs with turquoise and indigo legs; mud crabs who skittled sideways up mangrove trunks. I liked the fiddler crabs best. Each had a large salmon-pink front claw, which it waved like the bow-arm of a gypsy violinist or drew tight over large yellow eyes, as if embarrassed.

'Oh, no,' I said to Carole. 'Look!'

A very large mud crab had grabbed a small fiddler crab by its fiddle and was starting to eat it. We peered through my glasses aghast. Every now and then the fiddler crab slowly tried to disengage itself and failed. The mud crab munched.

'Red in tooth *and* claw,' said Carole.

From a lookout tower, the officer pointed to pugmarks in the mud. 'Several *different* tigers. Different sizes.'

One had walked the length of the mesh.

'Looking for way in.' He beamed. 'Last night.'

The pugmarks were deeper, splashier than others I had seen. These tigers must spend ages cleaning non-aerobic mud from between their toes. Further off was a sweet-water pond: the banks held the slots of many deer. Twenty-two ponds had been dug in the seventies in case salt water caused tiger aggression. Only eight are manned properly – there is no manpower for more – so the rest are an open invitation to poachers to shoot deer, tigers, anything that comes to drink. Here there were egrets, herons, curlews, four chital lying down, and a fawn learning to skitter between pneumatophores.

Before we left we stopped at the shrine on the bank. An altar, with small flower offerings, to Banabibi, Lady of the Forest.

On both sides of the Sundarbans, Hindu and Muslim, the forest has two opposed deities: Banabibi or Bonbibi the protector, and Dakshin Rai the cruel king, god of tigers. Banabibi once fought Dakshin Rai to save a honey-gatherer named Dukhey. Everyone worships her, asks her permission before entering the forest, prays she will save them from tigers. This shrine was a little bright hutch, like a Nativity. Banabibi rode an orange tiger with red tongue, white teeth, black Gucci eyelashes, white patches above the eyes. The painter knew tigers all too well. Banabibi, in a gold headdress, held the shoulder of a young man in blue Louis Quinze court dress. A little woman in black stood by the tiger's paw, about to tear her robe: the mother, unaware Dukhey was safe. All glistened with lacquer. Incense sticks stood in a vase; a little flame waved. Like St Lucy, Banabibi, Saviour of the Forest, was light in a dark place.

'Decorated hope,' said Carole, looking at the glittering headdress.

A boat full of tourists was docking. Hindi songs echoed from loudspeakers. Everyone was shouting. Any tiger would be as far away as possible.

'They insist on television and loud music,' Mrinal said.

'But they'll never see anything! This is a *nature reserve*. It needs quiet!'

First off the boat were stout men in neat slacks and suits, holding the hands of women in bright green, yellow and blue saris, whose edges lifted and glittered gold, flower-gardens against the brown river as they teetered, anxious, laughing, calling, over the gangplank. Hundreds of faces watched us curiously, not altogether friendly.

'They want their day out. Conservation education,' said Mrinal gently, 'has a long way to go here. They're saying, "Foreigners spend money like water." What can I say? I told them, 'This is their boat. They gave money for tigers for this boat.'"

Our pilot steered close to the bank towards pugmarks where a swimming tiger had scrambled out into molasses mud. It was a study in shining browns: the river's cappuccino ripples against slimy bank; mud like toffee; the dark walls of the pawprints; pale breathing-pencils. Tiger signs are different in every place. But there.

We crossed to the other bank where it had entered the water. It had walked along the water-side then jumped – you could see the powerful hind feet pushing – into the water. I pictured its head as it crossed. I longed to see a tiger swimming. Instead, a pied kingfisher fluttered off a branch and flew up the creek, calling.

Last time Amanda was here she met a forest ranger who had survived an attack in a rowboat. He went to the prow to answer, he said elegantly, a call of nature, and saw a tiger sitting on the bank *waiting* for them. The man behind, poling, did not see and propelled them straight into the tiger's jaws. Amanda's friend just had time to get a stick into the tiger's mouth along with his head. He spiked the tiger's throat, the other man pummelled it with his paddle, and the tiger ran off. Twelve hours later, he reached medical help, fearfully clawed round the middle. But he did survive.

This journey was all the same but different every hour. Mrinal hailed a fishing-boat, a long narrow oval with a ragged sleeping cover at one end. No protection against a hungry tiger. The woman stood up very straight, hollowing her back in a red-gold sari, to meet whatever came. She looked up at us, then back at her man. He was very dark, with a dun cloth round his loins, poling the boat in close. She had a gold stud in her nose and seemed defiantly afraid. They thought we might take their fish and not pay for it, as officials sometimes do.

Mrinal called down and the couple swung alongside. Our cook climbed down barefoot, lifted sacking off a hole and held up different fish, chatting. Mrinal told them not to worry, we would pay for their fish. They had seen a tiger in this inlet that morning. The cook picked the fish he wanted, the fisherman closed his fish-hole and sealed it with mud. When I looked back, I saw him dancing on it to press it down again.

The sun sank; the world changed. No more silver-dazzle surface, brown waves, dun mangrove trunks, racing-green canopy: all the colours that had been in our eyes all day. Instead a sun-trail: orange feathers on ruffled copper, from a rose-edged pearl pulsing in sepia-washed sky flushing different every minute. Tangerine, pewter, violet.

'But look,' said Amanda. 'The rival show!'

On the other side, the just-risen moon: nearly full, a pure white airy circlet above the bank. Its reflected trail was subtler than the sun's, a faintly pink exclamation mark, a candle laid on grey. There was eerie calm everywhere: flat banks, huge darkening sky, two competing points of light. We moored midstream to sleep, because of tigers.

'But I don't think you will sleep on deck,' said Mrinal. 'The moon is full, but the dew's heavy and cold.'

Before we went to bed the tallest, oldest man in the crew, a start-lingly good-looking very dark Cary Grant, about forty-five with a white moustache, came to the prow and put sticks of incense into a jar below the front. He lit them and knelt in his loincloth. Prayers at the prow to Ganga. A *puja* to keep us safe for the night.

Someone had drawn mosquito-netting round my shelf-bed: it zipped to meet an undersheet. I crawled in and zipped. Waking in the night, I switched on my torch to look out at the water. Nearly at surface level I saw dark ripples but no tiger-face swimming towards me. Beside me, where I had left my clothes, outside the net but still on my shelf-bed, were the biggest cockroaches I had ever seen. One waved antennae from the cup of my bra, froze as the light touched it, and scuttled away.

At dawn the deck was thick with dew. Mist everywhere. I peered at the bank, opera glasses close just in case. Cowled in cloth against the chill, we drank Nescafé and I asked about running a tiger charity. Global Tiger Patrol works mostly in India, but partners the Zoological Society's 21st-Century Tiger which funds projects in Sumatra and Siberia.

'It started out of Ranthambhore,' said Amanda, curled on the lolling-platform. Like Mrinal, she got no salary from the charity she ran. She and Carole paid for their own trips. Tigers need all the help, and integrity, they can get. GTP began by supporting Valmik's

Ranthambhore Foundation, but other places, not so well known, needed help too. Now they chose projects with expert advice to get maximum impact for tigers for the money, often small, urgent, specific needs: as when the forest guards at Sariska, another Rajasthan reserve, needed uniforms. They did not even have jackets. The state government decides when uniforms are needed. These guards, the all-important tiger front line, were freezing cold.

'Carole and I scoured Delhi, found two hundred and twenty uniforms and balaclavas, and took them down. Surprisingly heavy, two hundred and twenty uniforms! Boots were more of a problem. That was a targeted need. We did it ourselves on the spot.'

They also funded Raghu's first research at Panna. When he found his first male walking longer distances than expected, he needed a motorbike. He chose it, Amanda bought it at the shop and he rode after his tiger.

'That's the level at which small vital things are best done. *Not* big companies with offices, overheads, time-lags and plans that are impressive on paper. With large projects, money often gets siphoned away by middle-men.'

'But I hope big companies give you money too.'

'Yes, but they often want to fund a big project which looks good on paper but isn't the most helpful thing on the ground.'

The vital thing is anti-poaching: equipment, jeeps, training and paying men. If a company wanted one big thing to sponsor, to be proud of, how about funding anti-poaching for, say, five years?

'That would be *perfect*! But there are loads of other things. Last month we funded a video workshop to show how you can make an impact in the courts, and on the media. Explaining why a mine polluting a reserve should be closed, for instance. There are hundreds of good projects. We just have to pick very carefully.'

The light grew stronger. Fishermen's boats, a few chital, egrets, herons; a ruffled curlew after a bath. It had not quite got its feathers in order and was running along the bank, flapping, changing its mind about which way to go, like someone trying exciting new clothes all at once. A man fishing with a little girl was on the bank, untangling nets in early morning, prime tiger time. He was *not* supposed to be out alone. Or on the bank.

'If the father is taken,' said Mrinal, 'what will the little girl do?'

The forest department compensates the widow for a tiger death, *if* her husband had a permit to be there and was in the boat. But, of course, they untangle nets on the bank. That is where tigers usually get them. The family says the tiger jumped into the boat. A few months back a tiger killed an eleven-year-old girl in a village near the Bangladesh border. Next day it visited the village again. Project Tiger officials caught it and released it in deep forest. Six weeks later, it entered another village. Again forest officials caught it. They found, as Corbett often did with man-eaters, it could not catch normal prey: it had broken teeth. They took it to Calcutta Zoo.

The forest service captures and relocates 'straying' tigers but had not, so far, allowed radio-collaring in the Sunderbans. After my visit, West Bengal would announce a scheme to radio-collar six tigers here and track them by satellite. The forest service has no experience in radio-collaring, but has not invited scientists to help. India has some of the finest minds in the world; and a system which stops them helping tigers.

'We have fifty thousand people on our island,' said Mrinal, watching the father get back into his boat, uneaten. It was clearly a deep feeling for justice that drove him. 'The children are the worst off. They are neglected. Men abandon families. Especially girls are neglected. Our island is at the edge of the reserve, worst man-eating area. We support victims' families.'

Men are not allowed to enter the forest without a compulsory insurance policy of fifteen rupees. If a tiger kills them, the widow should get thirty thousand rupees from a Calcutta insurance company, but often ends up with twenty-five thousand because she cannot read, does not know how to get the claim form, and has to file it in one month. Middle-men charge five thousand rupees, just to get the form. Mrinal helps widows, which infuriates the middle-men who say it is not his business: they make money from it. Even a forest officer warned him to be careful about the middle-men.

'But how can a widow who can't read, with young children, get a form from Calcutta while crying for her husband?'

Helping widows had not been Mrinal's original brief. But he was in insurance himself and could not help seeing what was wrong and doing something about it. Other charities had come in now. One Western girl had registered a charity in her country to help tiger widows. But she kept disappearing.

'The villagers say, "Why is she here? She talks to us then goes away and has not helped us."'

'That's terrible,' said Amanda. 'It gives aid workers a bad name.'

The island's official name was Hamilton Abad Island, named after an early Scottish governor. The village was Anpur, but the villagers say they live on Satjelia No. 13. The British divided the Sundarbans into lots and many are still known by their numbers.

On the bank by Lot 13 was a shrine to Banabibi. Along the bank was anti-tiger mesh. This was top man-eating territory. Recently many hungry tigers had 'strayed' into the villages. Over twenty last year. Deer were being badly poached, so the tigers turned in desperation to the villages. At the landing-stage people stood smiling to welcome Mrinal, Amanda and Carole. The last time Amanda and Carole had been there, two years before, the foundations had just been laid for a clinic funded by the Irish government.

We passed into the mesh walkway, high above the mud shore. In this shrine bare wood figures were lit by stripes of white sun; flowers withered at Banabibi's feet. A large crocodile had been seen, and we looked back at the water round our boat. The tide was going out. A little black kid bleated from mud below the walkway. Its mother, cruelly unconcerned, grazed on top of the eight-foot drop.

'That'll fetch the crocodile,' said Amanda. 'Or a tiger.'

Escorted by curly-tailed pie-dogs, we went into the enclosure. A plaque in Bengali said the Irish ambassador had unveiled it to mark the opening of the new clinic. He and his wife were due next week; everyone was getting ready, hammering, scurrying round the half-built clinic. Children were sitting in rows with filled plates. Not only tiger orphans; others who needed help too, all tackling the post-school evening meal.

Volunteer doctors used to come twice a month, travelling a day each way. They had nowhere to stay, no toilet, little food. Mrinal had changed that. He had first come in 1989, in a boat that took eight hours. He hired boats, stayed in villages. In the monsoon it was very difficult. That was why GTP had given his NGO this boat. The government requisitions it sometimes for MPs, ministers, VIPs, the census. It *is* a lovely boat. One government guest was so enamoured of it he took the sheets when he left.

We sat on the lawn. Mrinal had arranged for Amanda, head of the charity, to present tiger widows and their children with saris, biscuits, pencils. We would watch a Banabibi play. Men were building a stage with poles. Musicians rehearsed.

'What's that tune?' asked Carole.

'The Irish national anthem,' said Mrinal, rather anxiously.

'Charming,' said Amanda firmly. She had lived for years in Delhi in the diplomatic world.

Mrinal's assistant had the saris and biscuits on a table. On one wall a cotton banner showed a merry yellow tiger, on another, there was a photo of a tiger's head. Watching us give saris to women was the animal that had wrecked their lives. One delicate girl of nineteen in dark green had lost her husband just after she was married, four years ago. Another widow was blind, led with a stick held by an elderly woman in white. A woman in orange and black came forward with burning eyes on me and spoke urgently to Mrinal. 'She says one of you must be the Western woman who promised to help her when her husband was killed by a tiger, and then went away. She wants the help this woman promised.'

We had tears in our eyes. The other widows watched. They had been through this too.

'Tell her,' Amanda said, 'we will discuss with you. We all look the same to her. It could have been any European woman waltzing in promising things, then fading out again. It's very bad.'

The Western girl had been here when that woman's husband was killed, so it had made an impact on her.

'Many of the others are much worse off. This woman has grown-up sons. She is just the most recent.'

Thirty children, aged three to fourteen, came up one by one, with wide dark eyes. Many were tribal, some Hindu; some tiny. Girls in bright ruffled dresses, beads and bows. Proud boys in coloured T-shirts. One girl, in a much-too-big green dress and shaved head, ran round giggling. A girl of nine in a ruffled yellow dress, who was going to play Banabibi, sang a song from the play. All were much better nourished, Amanda said, than they had been two years ago, now that Mrinal provided an evening meal.

Dusk fell. The actors were made up. The yellow girl was hung with red, orange, gold; in pink garlands and bangles. A woman painted white tiger whiskers on the villain's cheeks. Insects danced round bulbs.

'We have few opportunities to do something like this.'

The company had started going round other islands performing plays taken from a traditional local cycle on the Banabibi story. They would perform for the opening ceremony of the clinic, and had coached a few children in supporting roles. We were to see the dress rehearsal.

'Ruth,' said Amanda suddenly, 'you have got your opera glasses, haven't you?'

The stage was wooden poles and sacking, the roof was sacks lit by a bare electric bulb. At one side sat a boy with brass cymbals and a musician in a wool turban moving a squeeze-box back and forth. Children crouched near, as if they felt safe in the music. On the other side sat an anxious man with glasses, the director-prompter. We were privileged guests on white plastic chairs. The rest of the audience was banks of children and mothers. Tiger orphans, tiger widows, watching the story of Dukhey who survived the tiger.

We began with Banabibi's childhood. A father in a red crown abandoned his pregnant wife in the forest. She gave birth to a girl and a boy, left them there and returned to the husband whom she berated for leaving her, like the riven family histories we heard that afternoon. Fathers abandoning wives, mothers abandoning children. Economic necessity; in the village, on the stage.

Banabibi, in the scarlet apron and headdress of a Venetian carnival queen, grew up in the forest with her brother. The musician sang softly along with the children but they kept perfect time. Little Dukhey came, parted from his tearful mother, went to the forest with honey-gatherers. They were given their honeycomb permit, crossed the water in a boat with fat boatmen – who were comic and the audience laughed – then fell asleep in the forest. Wicked Dakshin Rai entered in electric pink and gold, rolling his eyes like the Koodiyatum actors in Kerala. White whiskers gleamed on each cheek. 'He's a slender young man really,' whispered Mrinal, 'with two toes missing. Attacked by a crocodile.'

Dakshin Rai was in the honey-gatherer's dream. He promised him honey if he abandoned Dukhey on the island; and hung a honeycomb on a pole. The honey-gatherer woke, took the honey, and left the sleeping boy. A tiger appeared in a wasp-rippled jumpsuit and ferocious carved head. Banabibi rushed in and walloped the tiger, who shrank away like a smacked puppy. The children laughed. But Dakshin Rai challenged her. She called her brother: they fought with paper swords while Banabibi's animal champion, the crocodile, in a green jumpsuit and another beautifully carved head, fought the tiger with boxing-glove paws.

'Like Valmik's film,' whispered Amanda. At Ranthambhore Valmik's nephew had filmed a tigress attacking a crocodile who tried to take her kill. Like Tippoo's tiger, she jumped on the crocodile's back lengthwise, biting its neck. The crocodile later died of its wounds. But here the crocodile won, driving back the tiger as Banabibi's brother drove back Dakshin Rai. Banabibi blindfolded Dukhey so he would not be scared; the crocodile took him home to his grieving mother.

The play ended. We walked back to the boat under the moon. The black kid had gone.

The dream journey went on, south and west to broader waters, away from areas protected by Project Tiger into the Matla, the 'drunk' river. It was placid now, but often stormy. People die there every year. They have no radios to hear warnings. Amanda was in a storm there once and heard rain coming over the water like an army before it hit the boat. The lightning was bright as day. The boat was crashing against the steps, so they chugged out to midwater, rolling.

'I got an inkling then of what it's like. Many fishermen were drowned that night. But Mrinal said it was nothing.'

'People here are vulnerable in *everything* they do,' said Carole.

'Last year,' said Mrinal, 'a man mauled by a tiger was waylaid by dacoits in a water ambulance on the way to hospital and killed.'

This was a bad pirate area. We saw boats everywhere now. Any could be pirates. As we neared the Bay of Bengal there were more and bigger boats. Sailing boats from the open sea; deep-sea trawlers. Black dolphin fins dipped through the waves. We stuck on a sandbank: the tide was going out; we had hoped to get through while it was still high, but had to go back and round by a different channel. The banks now had opened out into sea. I looked at the pilot in his little cabin.

'Can I have a go?' I steered us into the Bay of Bengal. We started to roll. I panicked. 'No problem,' said the pilot, and left me there till he took the wheel to head back into the Sundarbans. Our last mooring was at an outpost run by the forest department outside the Project Tiger reserve. Mrinal said he would sleep in the station. At eleven a frightful smell drifted to us. It stayed all night. A rubbish boat. Even rubbish has to go by boat here.

Next morning Mrinal waved goodbye to the men in the station. They were supposed to patrol against poaching but both their boats, rowboat and speedboat, needed repair. Ten dollars would do it. Appalled, we pulled out our purses.

'No. The forest office hasn't sanctioned it. There's no point. There should be seven men here. There are only two.'

At Namkhana port we docked among hundreds of boats. Faded reds, blues, pistachios. Fish hanging on clothes-lines; a latrine at each stern surrounded by sacking. Yellow plastic sacks of fertilizer, pale green fishing nets, black umbrellas against the sun. All boats had the same little altar with sticks of incense and flowers, where prayers were said to the terrifying river. As each left, heading out on to that treacherous water whose calm could turn so quickly to chaos, someone did *puja* to Ganga – to keep them safe.

6

THE LORD OF MUD AND TIDE

'Welcome to the Sundarbans.' Mowgli poured coconut water. 'The name's from sundari trees. They say it means Beautiful Forest.'

'Are those sundari? They're much taller than trees on the Indian side.'

'Most sundari are here in the east. The Indian side's too salty. Our side has twenty-six mangrove species. *And* hundreds of mangrove associates, which behave like mangroves, throwing up breathing-spikes.'

His real name was Rubaiyat. My brother and I were on a boat called *Bonbibi*, in the Bangladesh side of the Sundarbans.

A tiger could have jumped off Mrinal's boat and swum across. I went back to Calcutta, met my brother and drove to Bangladesh by road through paddy-fields and an avenue of ancient tamarinds (each so wide three people could have stretched round and not touched) whose black boughs (meeting above bicycles, ox-carts and cycle-rickshaws with wicker baskets of chickens and goats) bristled with strange green manes. Orchids, thousands of them! In April they would glow yellow and white for miles in the road's long perspective V. The tamarind trunks beneath were studded with dimpled gingernut biscuits in geometric patterns: cow dung cakes, sold for fuel, corrugated with prints of the hands that had slapped them there.

For centuries these giant trees had supported life, spread shade, and withstood the sea roaring up this tragic flat land. So much drought where I had been. But Bangladesh's fear, and medium, is water.

The border was traffic, lorries, tea-stalls. 'Where's Bangladesh?' A boy pointed to a building full of soldiers. We came out to dazzling dust in an even more chaotic place. Cycle-rickshaws, saddles brilliantly painted with turquoise Paisley squiggles; then Bob Marley, shaking my hand. Erudite, wiry, very alive, passionate about the Sundarbans, Mowgli drove us through more flat country, full of mosques now, and men in long white robes. Then wider water, tropical fenland frothing with pale purple water-hyacinth, patched with ailing shrimp farms. Big companies have encouraged farmers to fill their paddy with salt water and farm shrimp caught – along with a lot of other fish fry which they threw away – from the Sundarbans. There are now far fewer wild shrimp and other fish. When the farmers' stocks weaken, companies pull out. Farmers are left with fields that grow nothing because of the salt. They turn to illegal fishing, of fish they helped to deplete, attacked by crocodiles who have fewer fish too.

We came to a village called Bachachra, Tiger Scratch, and a wide river. Red-wattled lapwings in neat black bibs gazed at their own reflections at the water's edge. In open water was a double-decked boat. We rowed up to it, climbed on board, the engine started, lapwings rose in a cloud and a butterfly blew into the dining area, opening blue and chocolate wings on the window-frame.

On the Bangladesh side, the delta runs into the Bay of Bengal in three peninsulas, the western Satkhira range, the Khulna range and the Sarankhala range in the east where our furthest target lay. We would go south, then meander east through creeks.

Mowgli, about thirty-eight, grew up in Dhaka through the bloody struggle for independence. In 1970 this was East Pakistan, forced to speak Urdu. When a cyclone killed half a million people, foreign aid poured in; West Pakistan did little. By March 1971 the Pakistan army was killing students in Dhaka. By December, the country of Bangla-speakers was born. Mowgli grew up through the 1973 famine, the murder of the man who led independence, martial law, through President Zia re-establishing democracy in 1979 and his assassination in 1981. Martial law returned in 1992. Corruption, nepotism, assassination and flood were the background to any protection for Bangladesh tigers. In 2000, the Asian Development Bank gave the

Bangladesh government eighty-two million dollars for a Sundarbans conservation project. A naturalist friend told me the project saw only seventeen million; no one knows what happened to the other sixty-five. Out of that seventeen, twelve more vanished. Everyone, politicians, civil servants, wants a slice of such a big pie: one reason small, targeted conservation aid, like Amanda's, is better than large dollops. In the end, only five million dollars of the original eighty-two million was used, most of it badly. A proper tiger study was never done, though some Bangladeshi scientists wrote a good report on fish.

Mowgli and my brother talked trees. Sundari had flanged buttresses; keora were the tallest, with the most thin, soft, pointed pneumatophores, here called shulas. Deer love keora forest because there's not much undergrowth and they can see what's coming. As we talked, thousands of wagtails shot across lead-coloured water, streaked red in setting sun. The boat slowed, the bell clanged, the engine stopped for sunset prayers. These were Muslim boatmen.

I woke in the dark. My brother was playing Bach on the foredeck. He lives in Orissa, which he has known for twenty-five years, has studied ancient Indian tampura in Benares and carries a violin on most journeys. I went out. Dew was everywhere, the river layered in muslin mist. His blue shirt sash glimmered in the half-dark. He smiled hello and switched to an early-morning *raga*. I went to the stern where a young man in purple was praying in a rowboat.

'Take your coffee,' said Mowgli.

The young man rowed us out into hushed, pale mother-of-pearl. I curled my hands round my mug to keep them warm. The sun was not up, but the water knew it was coming: the surface swarmed with apricot triangles, little waves catching beams we could not see. We had moored at a confluence where the river met an inlet. Three black curves leaped through the waves – Irrawaddy dolphins, which congregate at confluences where there are fish and deep water. They belong to Burma's main river but live here too, often in threes, a mother and two young. Mowgli had often watched them hitching rides in front of the boat, pushed by the water, like boys on bikes behind a lorry, fighting for the best place in the middle.

'The top dolphin wins, and can be quite fierce about it. Sometimes at night in the south, phosphorescent plankton come in with the tide. You don't realize till dolphins break the surface, darting with sparky trails in moonlight, like lightning.'

On the far bank were adjutant storks: tall, hunched, black and white, increasingly endangered, hunted for meat. The near shore was specked with sandpipers and wagtails. A kingfisher streaked away, calling; egrets rose from tall trees behind, white wings soaring over forest canopy.

'Black-capped kingfisher! It shouts, "Man!" to all animals on the river.'

The bank was covered with shulas bigger, stouter and denser than those on the Indian side: black wizards' hats with no room between, even where there were no trees. Mangrove roots pushed a long way under mud to come up here. How did tigers manage, with their soft paws?

'Tigresses teach cubs where shulas are hard and soft. They learn. I've seen tigers cantering over shulas.'

Sun rose, a red globe through blue rag clouds. We rounded a tongue of mud into an inlet between branches weeping to the surface. From a fringe of trees came a sudden hollow boom. *Aoom!*

'My God! You're very special, you two. All my years I've heard tigers vocalize very few times. It's *fantastically* rare here.'

The tiger called again. Five, six times more, then coughed. From our low boat, level with spikes and mud, we stared at the biggest chital herd I had seen since Kanha. In the Indian Sundarbans I had seen few deer, only groups of two or three. These were under trees whose trunks were red as deer in the sun's first rays. A few grazed, but most turned anxiously to the trees. A jungle fowl called in alarm.

'If we're even luckier we might see a hunt. This boatman saw a tiger chase a deer last week. Both rushed across right in front of him.'

I was not sure the tiger would boom if it was hunting. Or, at least, not hunting deer. *I* could not dash across hobnailed mud. Those stories about Sundarbans tigers taking fishermen from boats . . . But the deer dropped their heads to graze.

In other terrain, tigers update scent marks all the time or they fade away. Here, territories stretch over islands that appear and disappear with the tide. Territory marking must be different, territory behaviour may be too. Some trails get covered twice a day, others are submerged once a month at high tide. You can see territory scratches, but not sprays, because of the tides. Everyone swims. Tiger, deer, boar, leopard cat, civets: they all know the tides.

We poled on slowly, watching for anything russet-gold like those chital. Crabs and monitor lizards climbed branches, rhesus macaques peered at us with ruddy coats, pinker rubbery faces, red bottoms. And it was heron heaven: small, large, white, grey, purple, graceful, wavy; long legs, snake-necks, crests. They posed like catwalk models till we were nearly on them, flew up, then coasted behind, heads bunching back on their necks to see what fish we had disturbed. And kingfishers! Black-capped, bronze (with iridescent bottom), stork-billed, pied, white-throated, ruddy, brown-winged, gaudy. In the south-east, where the water was sweeter, there were Eurasian ones too. This unique intermingling of sweet and salt: that is why there is such diversity. Everything finds a niche.

'I must swim,' said my brother.

'We used to have rock pythons, but they've been so hunted for their skin they're very rare now. King cobras, quite a lot. Longest I've seen was twelve foot. Other cobras, three kraits, and golden flying snake. You rarely see them – snake-charmers catch them. They're easy to handle and there are a lot of myths about them. All the snakes and monitors are poached for their skins. If you see a snake swimming it'll be a land snake. We have lots of sea snakes but they swim deeper. They're very venomous but don't bite much. Their teeth are too far back.'

'I think,' I said to my brother, 'I'd prefer it if you didn't swim.' Once an older sister, always an older sister.

'I swim,' said Mowgli, 'but only to my waist. I stay close to the edge. It isn't the snakes, or even the sharks—'

'Sharks!'

'It's crocs that are really dangerous.'

The creek got narrower, trees leaned into light above it, getting away from others crowding the bank. Branches brushing the water forced us to the middle; then they met in the middle. We ducked. The stream became a puddle. We did a three-point turn. The bottom scraped on shulas. All was hot, secret, still. We were stuck in the densest, slimiest jungle possible. Kraits, tigers, king cobras ... We might stay here till the tide turned.

Mowgli sprang into mud and heaved us round. He touched a dead tree frosted with little purple flowers like Judas blossom. Orchids. As we came back to the river the egrets flew up. We were back in the world of sky, open water, low boats with little blue plastic shelters. Slight men crouching in them stared as we passed.

Bonbibi chugged south-west. A brahminy kite with russet wings landed like a lord on the rail, then flew off as we got into the dinghy to free an illegal fisherman's catch. Bobbing in the water was a wicker hurdle, sausaged up into a tube. He had caught them, then left them wet, alive. We were deep in the sanctuary, where fishing was forbidden. Mowgli grabbed the basket and tried to lift up an end so the fish inside could swim out, but it was too heavy. We bashed a hole in it and let them exit that way. The fisherman would have paid for a permit *outside* the sanctuary, then paid more secretly to get inside. But as all sorts of other people had to be bribed for that, he had to take many more fish to make it worth his while.

How the system works: people in the office make money above their salary, the fisherman gets fish *in* the sanctuary, the fish and their predators dwindle.

We headed for a watchtower near a survey place run by the forest office. We had to take forest guards with us. They were on board, but out of sight: Mowgli did not want his wildlife tours to look like a military expedition.

'We used not to have them. But once, filming with a Scottish cameraman, we got into trouble. A hotelier in Khulna built a boat, filled it with Bangladeshi businessmen and they went down the river shouting, drinking, throwing plastic bottles into the water. We came along behind picking up the bottles. Mike wanted to confront them. He said, "This is a sanctuary! You've thrown plastic in the water!" The hotelier shouted, "No, they haven't, it's not from our boat!" An hour later they got drunk and came in a speedboat with *hockey sticks*! Who'd take hockey sticks on a nature trip? They had guns too, and boarded us like pirates. The crew were terrified. I sent them up to the roof. He held a gun to my head – my neck was dislocated for weeks – yelling, "Who

are you to tell me I can't throw plastic in the water? Plastic is GOOD!"
We complained to the tourist board. He lost his licence. Luckily we had
a British witness. Ever since, we've taken armed guards. And the
dacoiti don't bother us.'

The forest guards appeared, with guns. One gave me an umbrella
against the sun. The boat nosed into mud; Mowgli jumped out barefoot.

'I'm going barefoot too,' said my brother.

I stuck to trainers and socks. 'Stuck' was the word. I sank up to my
ankles. The mud was surprisingly smelly when you broke through
the green crust. 'Yuk!' Mowgli laughed. 'It's called "love-mud"
because it clings.'

'That's one definition of love.'

'It's supposed to be very good for you. You rub it all over you.'

It was as unpleasant walking through shulas as I had thought it
must be, though these were only thin soft ones. You had to fit your foot
between, while looking ahead to see the pattern in which they grew.
There were millions of mudskippers and fiddler crabs. I followed
Mowgli to a waterhole. One guard had picked me to protect. He followed, gun over his shoulder like Dick Whittington with his stick.
There were thousands of chital tracks. We walked round looking for
pugmarks. Meanwhile my brother and the guard protecting him
walked to the watchtower. He wanted to go up.

'Watch for snakes,' said Mowgli. 'Last time I saw a king cobra there.
They like sleeping in the sun.'

After lunch, we cut through the western peninsula towards the
Khulna range. At first I sat on the foredeck with the others but it was
too hot and I went to the lower deck. I began by looking ahead, to try
to spot an animal on the bank before the boat startled it. Then I stared
at the side trying to see inside bushes, leaves, branches. Suddenly I
spotted a gold body half hidden. Chital, surely, but ruddier than most.
I looked through the opera glasses. It walked forward. I could not see
a head but there was a long gold tail, bony sloping quarters, a fine pair
of dark grey balls. Body longer than a deer's, and *striped*.

He was sideways on to me, then moved gently into undergrowth.
My first thought was, had I dreamed it? There was nothing there now.
Somewhere in the Bible God says, 'Thou shalt see my back parts but

my face shall not be seen.' I had not seen his paws – tigers on Mowgli's camera-trap photos had mud to their knees – but what matters is the reproductive end.

I raced up. 'Terribly sorry, didn't have time to call, gone in a second but – Jesus – I've just seen a tiger's bottom!'

The banks became taller, more tropical: a Rousseau jungle now, palm fingers sprouting out of the earth, lianas gurgling down over their own reflections, monitor lizards with pink tails, shiny russet dragonflies on the tips of tall shulas, making little forays out and back over the water. A thousand different species of plant in one eye-blink; behind them a thousand thousand secret animal lives. Most visible, scattering songs and calls everywhere, were the birds.

'If birds didn't exist,' I grumbled, trying to memorize the legs of different egrets, 'trainspotters obsessed with taxonomy would have had to invent them.'

'If birds didn't exist,' my brother replied, 'nor would this forest.'

Mowgli pointed to an overhanging knot. 'That was the nest of a masked finfoot. It's only recorded in four places. No one knows its breeding habits. We watched one on this nest.' The brown head of an otter swam away, a fish owl staring from a mossy bough, chital browsed. Along one bank the lower edge of foliage was cut neatly as if a gardener had chopped it with a strimmer.

Mowgli laughed.

'Can't you guess? That's the nibble-line. As high as a chital can reach on hind legs. There are grasslands here in the south. No man-eating down here because there's so much prey. People seldom come here – no shrimp-collecting or honey-gathering – so tigers don't take them.'

On one grassy bank something red was half hidden in long grass at the water's edge. Tiger cubs? No, macaques, a mother and two babies. Then gulls over open sea.

'Mowgli,' I said in disgust, by the map, 'we're near something called *Putney Island*!'

'*Pootni*, Ruth. It means "great-great-granddaughter". Brits called it the Isle of No Return.'

The sun went down; we moored at Katka on the eastern peninsula, the other side from Tiger Point. The stars came out; my brother played an evening *raga*. Gorgeous. But I had, finally, to ask about poaching.

It was everywhere, all the time, and increasing. Cobra skins were sold in Dhaka hotels; tiger skins opposite the Sheraton; crocodile handbags in the Sonargon Hotel. All illegal, all critically endangered; the laws were not enforced. An investigative journalist got a tanner to say he'd do a tiger for him: his boss called him off the story. Skins were done for army officers, exported to Hong Kong, China, Taiwan. There were links with Burma, Thailand, Singapore, Saudi Arabia, Dubai, Kuwait, Qatar, the United Arab Emirates, Oman, even Hungary and Poland. Here, poaching was mainly for skins. Display, not Chinese medicine. Only a few poachers knew the demand for tiger bone. Hunting was illegal, but increasingly popular with amateurs as well as poachers. Chital were hunted constantly.

'They snare them, or put sleeping pills in bananas and catch them asleep. Deer meat fetches high prices. For tigers, it's usually poison.'

Half-moon, stars in black velvet, soft slap of water, rippling violin – he played so beautifully, it was heartbreaking – and all this. The poaching was part of a rising crime rate. This place is impossible to police. Thirty thousand fishermen get permits to work in this forest. Unarmed in small boats, they are robbed by people backed by the big fish traders, who bail the robbers before trial. An article in the *Bangladesh Daily Star* described a 2003 clean-up operation code-named, optimistically, Operation Golden Tiger. With the navy, police and Village Defence Party, the poor forest service organized six hundred people to comb the waterways for robbers and illegal loggers. Their men had Second World War rifles, ancient bullets. The criminals had new ones.

'It's pointless,' a forest official was reported saying. 'The robbers went to ground and will return. Unless we get modern arms and ammunition, criminals will always rule the forest. They fire when we see them. Our guns won't fire until we've tried twelve times.'

A well-known robber, Razzak Dakat, told the deputy forest officer of the Sharankhola range that if they tried to stop him he'd steal their weapons. If the forest department arrest someone, police give him two options: pay fortnightly tolls and continue robbing, or jail. They pay. A journalist interviewed a tiger tracker called Khasru Chowdhury, who had worked there since 1974. God knows how many tigers he had killed. *He* said the worst crime was illegal logging, that forest officers were involved.

I read the clippings. Smoke curled from Mowgli's cigarette. He listened to the haunting *ragas* and watched me read.

'How do you live with this?' I asked him.

'We do what we can; those of us who love the forest.'

My brother wiped dew off his fiddle. 'Most people poach because they're so poor,' he said.

In Orissa he lives in a mountain village where there are tribal people who, like my guide in Periyar, know the forest well. Their forest home, the only life they know, is being taken by mining, industry, agriculture. Politicians have been captured on secret camera taking bribes to grant mining leases. My brother had watched tribal villages bulldozed to make way for an aluminium refinery. Many of his friends are activists for tribal people.

'I thought you were lost in the music.'

'My friends wouldn't agree with protecting wild animals against local people hunting for meat! What else can they do? Project Tiger has a *very* bad name in human-rights circles. It threw people out of the forest in the name of tigers and gave nothing in return. Many people *hate* tigers because of that!'

There is a deep argument in India between human-rights activists, upholding the right of traditional forest-dwellers to live in forests and use their produce, and wildlife activists who want the last fragments of India's pristine wilderness, and the animals that live in it, to be free of people. My brother and I were on opposite sides of a bitter intra-Indian conflict. Mowgli looked on amused: two of Darwin's great-great-grandchildren, clawing an Indian hot potato on a boat in Bangladesh.

'That divide shouldn't *be* there. Both have a common enemy: corruption. Greed. Everything and everyone exploiting the forests. From what I've heard, even some members of the forest service, local politicians, or NGOs who siphon off money sent for tribal people *and* wildlife. And behind them are the bigger players: the World Bank, *our* banks, foreign mining companies, dam projects. Human rights and conservationists should hang together *against* all that!'

'You can't dismiss the "people before animals" argument. Tribal people *love* the forest. They have a balanced relation with it.'

'But the world outside their world has changed that balance. People who live in forests *do* harm them now. There are more people, fewer smaller forests, fewer animals. People live longer, want more things that the outside world has. They graze cattle in the forest and change it, hunt wildlife, cut wood, want roads that give access to commercial poachers.'

I knew where he was coming from. I remembered Valmik's searing account of villagers leaving Ranthambhore. Valmik had said the tigers only recovered there because of the sacrifice those villagers made. Early relocations *were* like forced evictions. I thought of the villagers in Kanha, the Delhi brigadier, Dr Malik's defence of the poor. But I also heard Ullas saying there are a million injustices in India; and getting rid of the last surviving forests will not right them.

'If they poach all tigers, kill all deer, use up all the forest, what will they have then? They'll *still* be badly off. The extinction of wild tigers, and the forest, will have been for nothing. You can't magic all that back; and it won't make *them* better off.'

Sunrise. Orange eye in blue-veined cloud. A monitor lizard, blush-pink and silver-green, scrutinized water from a branch. Bushes hung over us as we slipped through water-hyacinth. Everything was lusher in the south. The green skeins above were studded with ferny orchids and red birds: scarlet minivets like berries in holly. How was it for tiger cubs, growing up in this sticky secrecy? Their mother would have to leave them on land that would not get covered by water. Did she drag kills to them over mud and shulas, or leave the meal where tide would not reach? An adult tiger can eat a chital in four hours. But a larger kill, in other places, lasts several days: you stash it in a safe place and come back. Here it would float away. (At full moon or new moon there is three metres' difference between high tide and low. Mid-cycle, one and a half.) It must be difficult being a Sundarbans tiger. Floating food. Mud between the toes. The first things tiger kittens catch here must be mudskippers and crabs. Apart from human poachers, not many predators. No leopards or bears, a large monitor lizard and crocodiles, near water. But there were other dangers. Mowgli pointed into milk-green water to a snake under the surface. Head out: black with a white throat, mottled white belly, eye black and bright. The body oddly flat, twisted. A black Escher ribbon, motionless.

'It's dead.'

'No, it's not. That's a cobra head, a young king cobra.' Mowgli took a photo, the snake dived and vanished. The dinghy nosed to the bank. We got out on to those wretched shulas, and then a real path through long grass to a meadow. Long time since we'd been on any land but mud.

'Chital herds come here. Tigers approach from the tangly bit we came through. They stalk, hiding in this grass and then,' we crouched, stepping through a tunnel of branches to a grassy knoll, 'drag the kill to a place never covered by water, except at really high tides. *Here!*'

I stepped up on the knoll. Dried pugmarks in red earth, old bones, fresh deer skull. Of course. If a kill might float away, drag it to high ground. We were standing on a tiger's dinner-table.

'Glad it's still being used. We can go further into the grass if you like.'

Suddenly I wasn't sure I did like. I felt like Jack at the top of his beanstalk in the giant's kitchen while the giant was away. But I had to trust Mowgli. We went on through grass that would have hidden an elephant, let alone a tiger.

'Grasscutters come here. They once saw a tiger chase a deer right through their midst. But in the seven years I've known this place, not one grasscutter has been taken. When tigers have deer they don't eat people. Most man-eating happens in the west and north, where there are most people and fewest deer.'

A second stopping-place, stickier. Shimmery mud, grey semolina, flowed down between banks held together by roots. In it were large deep tiger tracks. The animal had got out of the water and followed the flow up onto proper land. The pawmarks were deep, far apart, so fresh that no water had gathered in them. A tiger with a large stride, bounding, within the last half-hour. The mudflow tapered up to a rivulet, a sloshy furrow, hardly a path, which then became a jungly tunnel into undergrowth. There the tiger had slowed, hind paws overlapping front. Walking now, not cantering.

'Tiger trails are always fresh here. Most of this is washed twice a day by the tide. Watch how you get out.'

'We're getting out *into these tracks*?'

Wonderful, to be so hot on a trail, tread where a tiger had trodden so recently. All the same . . .

This mud was the deepest yet. The guards and I wore shoes: Mowgli and my brother again went barefoot. My Tunisian trainers had never seen anything like it. I laced them tight so they would not come off. My ankles were covered with melted chocolate. Further in was drier, with fewer spikes, almost a proper path, though we still sank in. The tiger had, too.

Or, rather, tigers. Beneath us now, as we bent under branches, were more tiger tracks, toes shinily separate; big, medium, small. Squelch, slither, whisper: we were on a tiger thoroughfare. Once a cub had taken a little private wander to the side, then rushed back to the trail and pounced. Small paws had landed close together, slipping in mud. Then they joined other feet, all going one way. Our way. This was Tiger Alley.

It grew drier. The side bushes were greener, lighter, with palm fronds. We came to an atoll five foot high, twenty-five square, where twisting roots nested into each other to raise a table of dry ground. At high tide, it would be an island. Pugmarks everywhere, up and round. One tree growing out of the table was gashed orange where a tiger had recently raked the bark. I scrambled to the top of the table. Chewed bones: a place of skulls, bigger, more secure than the first. Tiger Golgotha. The forest was very still. If a tiger was watching, we did not know. Edgy but thrilling: the banqueting hall of Sundarbans tigers. At least no skull was human. My brother climbed a tree on the far side which had more tiger scratches.

'Last time I was here, I saw a king cobra coming out of a hole in that tree,' said Mowgli thoughtfully, watching.

A keora forest, light and open; no undergrowth, soft pale shulas. Deer grazed among the trees, wild boar lifted their heads and stared.

'Tigers go along the sides. I've seen them checking here from the undergrowth.'

Returning to the boat, sloshing through mud, we saw two small men in another boat. They saw us and looked away. They were crab fishers, not supposed to be in the sanctuary. Someone in the forest department was making money by selling them illegal licences.

The next creek was overhung with trees. Kingfishers, a green heron and fish owls watched us, macaques ran along branches, jumped from one side to the other. We were stuck in the shallows.

'The boatman saw a tiger here last year. The water was very low, like this. The tiger came to drink, saw him, jumped across the water, up here and away.'

We jumped into the mud and floundered onto long grass, way over our heads. Perfect stalking grass. The sun was low; sundown was near. For all he had said about no man-eating in the south, even Mowgli started talking loudly. There are always accidents. 'You don't want to startle a tiger on foot. Give them time to hear us, get away.'

He stopped at a white-flowering bush. '*Must* photograph this. *Tamarisk indica*. Beautiful!'

The sun slipped lower. Minutes passed. I did not favour hanging around in prime stalking habitat at sundown. Mowgli was a perfectionist. A sudden rough noise, *chock chock chock*, was followed by little coughs. I jumped. 'Macaques settling down for the night,' Mowgli muttered, checking the aperture. We came out on an empty beach. Grey sea glittered. 'Now,' said my brother, 'I *am* going to swim.' He left his clothes on the stones and disappeared into the waves. Mowgli and I walked to the end of the beach. On the moist sand were labyrinths of minuscule sand pellets: ghost crabs eat mud and digest it out in little balls, walking in circles. By the last circle was a lone tiger pugmark. A few hours ago, a tiger had stood where I was now, three paws on stones, one on sand, looking out to sea.

In London, I organized more trips. There was a spate of pre-Easter parties. He avoided them, at least the ones I went to. 'Where *is* he?' I heard people say. 'I was sure he'd be here.' Afterwards, he told me, he sat in a pub with a friend imagining them. We saw each other, finally, at a gathering in an antiquarian bookshop, a long room full of map-cases. First time we'd set eyes on each other. The mix of people meant we couldn't speak. We glanced across and away. He looked dimmed and miserable.

I'd always felt *on his side*. Like houses on opposite pavements, linked by an underground passage, we'd been open to everything inside each other. It was only six months. This was unreal: he had always been my care. 'You make me feel such a hero,' he often said. I hated thinking of him in a scabby moral light. I wanted to think well of him again. Maybe poetry was the answer. Everything we had seen, argued and laughed about for years, all the lucky places we'd travelled, were only the outer things. Inside, we talked endlessly about words and songs. I emailed some Ezra Pound. To me it said, be glad we had what we had:

> Whatever comes,
> One hour was sunlit and the most high gods
> May not make boast of any better thing
> Than to have watched that hour as it passed.

Not everyone's idea of a gift perhaps, but the person I'd known would understand what I was saying. What came back, though, was auto-reply. 'I am out of the office and will not return until after Easter. I will respond to your message when I return.'

He didn't. Why had I thought he would? Ezra deserved better: a great poet, whatever his politics. We deserved better too.

7

HEART OF THE JUNGLE,
SHADOW OF TIBET

The forests are the realm of the tiger.

Epitaph from tomb of seventh-century Tibetan king

'We're going into a forest of six man-eaters *on foot*?'

'Only through the territory of one,' said Chuck.

Chuck was eighty. Small, wiry, American, accurate; and a legend. He lived between Mexico, Kathmandu and Tiger Tops, this lodge in the Royal Chitwan National Park, Nepal, where he masterminds the world's longest-running tiger study. Thirty years and still going.

Outside was indigo mist and dew so heavy it sounded like rain. In forest we instantly saw prints like a naked child's, with huge claws. Sukrun the tracker whispered, 'Sloth bear. Fresh.'

'*Very* fresh?' I now had a healthy respect for them. They are most active in half-light; this one had come to the forest edge, raked a tree far above my head and turned back the way we were going.

'Two hours.'

The light was dim and smudgy, the trees mainly *sal* and *saj* with crocodile-skin bark. People in red saris and frayed trousers appeared barefoot, heads wrapped against the chill.

'They get poorer every year,' said Chuck, crouching over a tiger's scrape by the track.

Chitwan means 'Heart of the Jungle'. It is perfect tiger habitat: water, prey, dense cover. There are as many tigers here as can squeeze in. Our track bounded the territory of two males and several females. Where territories are very close, tigers mark often. This scrape was fresh. Hind claws dug deep into earth as he kicked back half an hour ago.

'Eastern Valley,' said Chuck to Sukrun, who nodded. Chuck has seen hundreds of tigers hold kingdoms here. He names them for their territory. Eastern Valley was a big male. Sukrun showed me his spray. Drops had trickled down reddish bark, sinking in. Chuck took off his cap and sniffed. Sukrun followed, removing his ranger's cap. The peaks would have got in the way, but they did look like men whisking off hats before entering church or kissing a woman. 'Very fresh,' said Sukrun. I sniffed too, and it was. Triple X tomcat, right up the nose.

We took a side path, brushing flowers of Indian acanthus, enormous dewdrops rolling down mauve petals. Leeches here were ginger not black, on bushes not underfoot. Leaves flopped like hands; it was hard not to touch, and leeches were waiting on them, rampant, responding to our vibrations. You had to applaud their technique. All mammals must be plastered with them.

A stream trickled over the track where several tiger boundaries touched and many tracks converged. One was a tigress with nearly grown cubs. Chuck and Sukrun wanted to know how many cubs were with her and which sex. The more females the better. Dispersing males here have a fifty per cent chance of survival. The forest is hemmed on all sides by humanity. Territorial conflict between tigresses was one thing Chuck had revised his opinion about since he wrote his famous study of Chitwan tigers in the seventies, watching them at kills as they made friends and established hierarchies.

'Tigers don't take more territory or food than they need, but if I wrote that book again I'd say tigers *do* kill each other. Not as often as they might. Not nearly as often as human beings do. Their social system is designed to minimize fights. Dispersing tigers read territory signs, take care to avoid trouble and are pushed out to marginal habitat.'

Marginal habitat means less prey, less cover, closer to humans. Dispersing tigers may take cows or human beings; they keep away from stronger tigers only to be trapped, clubbed, poisoned. Tigers did not evolve to realize that if they kill cows, people kill them. Smaller predators, foxes, leopards, evolved alongside larger ones and had to be warier. Tigers, top predators, put their energy into other things.

The tracks were inconclusive; Chuck thought she still had two cubs. This tigress was the man-eater. A few months before, she had ambushed a man and his wife walking down this track. She took the woman; the husband bravely rushed at her with a stick and cooking pot. She mauled him but retreated. He lodged his dead wife under boulders and came back with other people. She was so furious at losing her kill that she chewed his stick and cooking pot to pieces. The pot was now a squashed sieve. Huge teeth had bitten and bitten. 'Tiger art,' said Chuck, showing me.

Sundarbans tigers apart, Jim Corbett thought tigers took human beings mainly when incapacitated, unable to take other prey. Chuck thinks it happens also under intense pressure of habitat. Tigers without a patch of their own, therefore no natural larder, are potential man-eaters. The following year, man-eating would increase here in the buffer zone; between December 2003 and March 2004, four tigers killed eighteen people. There are also accidents. This tigress was not a habitual man-eater. Like the boy in Kanha, it was a tragic one-off: the couple came along, she heard them; she had cubs to feed.

We started back. We had seen tracks but no tigers. That's how it goes. One person walks along a path and is taken. Another misses everything.

'Our tigers are shy. You have to work to see them. Tigers behave differently in different habitats. It's easier on energy here to hide. Tigers are great conservers of energy. In more open habitat like Ranthambhore it's harder work, hiding. They've found it's not worth it. They save their energy for hunting.'

'What do you think "wild" means, Chuck?' A rocky stream, birds calling, spokes of milky olive light falling through leaves above.

'An animal living as it always has, in the place where it evolved. Not only free. Indigenous.'

To get to Tiger Tops you bump in a jeep through shallows of the Rapti river in south Nepal, past crocodiles and herons. Langurs sit in trees outside your bedroom, a baby rhino runs round bumming food. The front lawn – Glyndebourne with rhinos, a Merchant Ivory film set with bamboo armchairs – looks over grasslands, which should be backed by the distant Himalayas. You hardly see those now, it is too polluted. Chuck once saw them daily. Now they are a bran-coloured smudge on a mother-of-pearl haze.

Meals were in a giant wooden tepee. Traditional Nepalese design?

'Only building I've seen like it was a cat-house in Acapulco,' said Chuck.

John, domestic manager and Chuck's scientific assistant, fair-haired, fair-faced and British, laughed. 'All Nepalese lodges are copying it now,' he said. 'Little do they know. A string of safari camps based on a Mexican brothel!'

A plump young visitor looked grumpily at scrambled, fried and boiled eggs, omelettes, porridge, yoghurt, fresh fruit, wholegrain toast, tomatoes, curly bacon, sausages, cereal and fruit salad, served from sparkling copper by courteous Nepalese in immaculate uniforms. A luxury breakfast anywhere; a miracle, in jungle. 'There's nothing I can eat!'

'Porridge,' said one waiter, encouragingly.

'I don't eat porridge!'

Tiger Tops struggles to balance tourism and science. There were photos on the walls: baby-faced Mick Jagger on an elephant, Beatles with pudding-basin hair, Hillary Clinton. But unlike Africa, Asia can never guarantee a glimpse of its glamour. 'There is no *tigre* here,' an Italian had written grumpily in the guest book. They used to bait tigers with live goats so tourists could tiptoe there at night to watch them feed from a viewing platform. Once a tiger got curious and moved behind in the dark to view *them*. They stampeded in high heels up the ladder, shut the gate to the platform and wouldn't open it, even to let Chuck in. But now from this platform you saw only water birds and a sign: PLEASE DO NOT GO NEAR THE WATER. MAN-EATING CROCODILE. Baiting, invented to attract tigers for shooting, was not great for goats. Animal-rights groups complained. So did other tourist lodges: it gave Tiger Tops an advantage. Everyone was chasing fewer and fewer visitors because of the Maoist insurgency which began in 1996 and was spreading. Seven thousand people had died; the British government was advising us not to go to Nepal.

Tiger Tops has a concession from the Nepalese National Park. It pays for a permit every year. Chuck works for two beers a day.

Tourism pays for the tiger protection: anti-poaching equipment, paying informers about poachers.

As at Ranthambhore and Panna, this forest was preserved because of tiger hunting. Some of the largest tiger shoots ever happened in Nepal. Over eleven days in 1911, George V killed thirty-nine tigers, eighteen rhinos. Seven hundred elephants went out. Somehow the fair-play British thought seven hundred elephants encircling one tiger was sporting. The longest recorded shoot, twelve weeks in 1938–9, killed 120 tigers. The Nepalese prime minister's guests shot 433 tigers here between 1933 and 1940. But if they had not, tiger habitat and tigers would not be there today.

After the Second World War, forests were turned to agriculture, jeeps were easier to get, poachers spotlit tigers at night, the skin trade boomed. In 1973 protection was introduced. Poaching seemed over. But here too it rushed back in the nineties. By 1991, 253,000 people lived round the 932 square kilometres of Chitwan Park. Their numbers increased daily. They were very poor. Only fifteen per cent of homes have electricity here, average life expectancy is fifty-eight, twelve per cent of children die before they are five. Tigers are a fortune on four legs. But Chitwan tigers have it easier than some: an even more valuable animal shares their land. Tiger Tops lies between grassland and forest. Rare one-horned rhinos live in the grasses and horn is even more valuable than tiger bone. A gram that costs ten dollars in Nepal costs four times more in the West. Rhino horn, the myth of unicorn horn, is really just hair and skin, but robbers break into European zoos (and German castles with rhino heads on the wall) to hack it off. Tiger bone is big magic, rhino horn even bigger. Chuck had photos of a rhino killed by poachers, collapsed on flung-forward knees, its nose a bloody splodge. Symbolism can be a force for good, but also a terrible force for bad.

'Like a king,' said Chuck. 'With a good one, a brilliant system. With a bad, the worst.'

In Nepal, the army protects the parks. In Indian courts, tiger crimes take ages to filter through and fines are not high, but in Nepal the chief warden of the Royal National Park can sentence poachers to jail. And soldiers shot twelve poachers here last year. So the risks are high.

But because of the Maoists fewer troops were now protecting the forest, at fewer patrol posts. As soon as the troops retracted, poaching increased. Tiger numbers reflect political instability instantly, like ripples round a flung stone. Apart from poaching, there is constant conflict over wood, grass, grazing: cutting timber or grass lessens the area of the animals' home and disturbs them. From the lawn we saw peacefully chomping rhinos throw their valuable noses in the air and move off as villagers cut grass. Illegally. Who can tell a barefoot man it is in his grandchildren's interest that he does not cut wood for cooking, or grass for his cows? If he doesn't, there may not *be* any grandchildren.

The mailbag came from Kathmandu. Chuck and John examined new camera-trap photos. It is an expensive business. Each camera needs eight batteries, which are costly and hard to get; Maoists want them too. Hundreds of photos are wasted, triggered by wild boar, people, a falling branch. In some reserves animals destroy cameras. Different tiger populations react differently to the flash. Chuck had photos of inquisitive cubs looking into the camera, nose and eyes up close, out of focus. Cubs chewed one transmitter to pieces.

'Most tigers are camera shy. Ours'd go mad if we set them as Ullas sets his. But he never gets tigers younger than a year. We get lots of cubs. Is that a bulge under the tail?'

Through a magnifying glass, yes, it was. The man-eater, alas, had two male cubs. On his laptop John showed photos (taken from an elephant) of Eastern Valley. He used to mock-charge elephants and jeeps. Older now, more confident, he just sat there or rolled. In a serious charge a tiger's ears are forward, eyes locked on its prey. A mock-charge is done to frighten. Unless you are used to it you cannot tell the difference. A lot of bravura is involved in mock-charges, for both tigers and tiger watchers.

In a jeep we checked the cameras. Nepalese soldiers searched the vehicle and scanned our permits. No smiles. They were bored, scared, young. Each camera was hidden on one side of the track, its transmitter on the other. Stepping into the beam between the two sets off the flash: the animal takes its own portrait. We stopped. John deactivated the beam, we drove through, he checked the film and reset it.

'I met a leopard here last year,' said Chuck, 'staring from a few feet, there on the track. Didn't run off. Later he started attacking people, trying to take them from jeeps.'

A female protecting cubs? No. Leopards round here are male. Females keep cubs above the tiger habitat.

'Just a mad leopard.'

We saw a jackal family, parents curled in sunlight, two cubs moving restlessly. They turned narrow muzzles to watch us, ears pricked.

'Is that the Indian jackal?' I whispered to Ramdin, the naturalist.

'*No!* No Indian jackals here! We have Nepal jackal.'

I looked it up later. The golden jackal, *Canis aureus*, lives in both places. I remembered Ramdin later when I came across different nations calling *their* tiger the symbol of their country.

An elephant platform. No scrambling from jeep-backs here: Tiger Tops did things properly. 'Left or right?' asked Chuck, courteously, and settled beside me. John stood barefoot on the elephant's rump looking high over grasses to see them sway as hidden animals moved.

'Don't worry if the mahout taps the elephant's head with his stick,' said Ramdin, to visitors on other elephants. 'Elephant and mahout know each other. Elephants need to be controlled.'

Ours was a female, Sita Kali. Her mahout sat on her neck; she curled her trunk up to him as we splashed across the river, passing the rare, highly endangered gharials: lightweight crocodilians, slender snouts slanting up like spears. They avoid the heavier marsh crocodiles, or muggers, but there were only three males left. Here the Rapti river joins the larger Narayani, which flows into India, and the Ganges. Last year many gharials were swept by monsoon floods into India, to places where they were unprotected and killed for meat.

In the river were egrets, black storks, and flocks of bright ducks: plump, conker-coloured, duck-headed cushions. Ruddy shelducks, migrants from Siberia. A gold flash came, as we heaved on to the bank – a black-capped oriole.

'Now the black-hooded oriole.' We entered grassland Chuck has known intimately, and its birds, for thirty years. I had met this renaming

of birds elsewhere. The blossom-headed parakeet is now flame-headed.
I had visions of men waving bird-books, tinkering with names while
species die.

The grasses were extraordinary. They are highest after the monsoon, but even now, even on elephants, their plumes were way above
our heads: purple and pale rose, blushing fluffily above soaked blades.
Then silky white heads etched on tan sunrise. A wet green world of
reeds, nodding candy-floss, rustling silence.

'Golden silk-spinning spider.' Chuck pointed to a huge translucent
amber spider in a web between coarse blades. Dawn rays lit pearls of
dew along the strands. The mahout dropped his stick. Sita Kali
stopped. The spider shot out of its web and hid. Sita Kali's trunk tip
moved among grass-roots and snaked up with the stick. We were all
on edge. Swish of wet grasses, parting before elephant feet. To the
sides, little runs through grass where small animals could disappear.
You saw nothing till you were on it. A good place for a tiger to lie in
wait; but surely still too wet and cold for fur. Eastern Valley would
only want to roll here when the sun had warmed it.

Suddenly grasses swayed violently beside us, plumes dashed up
and down, there was loud rustling, a snort. A rhino, huge, upset, very
close. I'd never felt compassion for a rhino before I saw Chuck's
photos. Now I watched the mobile ears twitch, the folds Dürer had
drawn.

'They're very stupid,' whispered John. 'Prehistoric, really.'

But stupid, weighing a ton *and* armed with a sharp horn. One book
by someone who had worked here said how easily startled they were,
how indignant. If they treed you they stayed around for hours. This
one lolloped off. On elephant is very different from on foot.

'My friend Dave was badly gored,' said Chuck. 'Nearly died. He
pushed his son up a tree. A helicopter got him to Kathmandu just in
time.'

The day before, tourists had seen two tigers, probably mother and
cub, leaving a dead rhino calf. Chuck wanted to know if it was a kill.
If so, the tiger would still be near. Like all babies, rhino calves are vulnerable. Despite the one-ton mothers, Eastern Valley specialized in
killing them. In a patch of trees we saw the dead calf half-eaten,
clumsy head sideways under flies, white bones sticking from magenta

flesh, the spine a dark thin line. My first view of a kill. I had read about them in Jim Corbett. It seemed so lonely. The elephants stood in a semi-circle, swinging their trunks.

Tigers usually start eating from the back. The little rhino's hindquarters were missing. How had it died? Park officials thought it was a kill. Chuck and John thought it had died of disease. Eastern Valley would never have left it. Some tigers had been at it but there were none here now. When we went back next day, villagers had taken the meat. Everyone competes for resources here, even a three-days-dead rhino.

As we rode back I watched the mahout with Sita Kali, the relationship that drove relations between humans and tigers on the subcontinent. The British and the maharajahs would never have shot so many tigers without elephants. Today the elephant, once the tiger's nemesis, is the best way to see it. When we got down I went to the elephant lines. A dozen elephants, each picketed in a shelter, were dusting grass on their knees before eating, their eyes dark panda splodges as if they'd been crying. Anti-fly lotion, apparently. A small one, Sharshota Kali, kept lunging for contact, shaking her head. She wanted to work but was only nine and too young. It takes years to train an elephant. Tiger Tops buys them trained – all except one bull who was born there. They had not known his mother was pregnant.

'That afternoon she went out with the rest. In the night, they were all calling. We went to see. Another female, this one,' Ramdin pointed to a steadily eating elephant, 'had broken her picket, gone to the mother and was supporting her side. All were trumpeting. Then the baby was born.'

It was now a huge bull with massive tusks. When he was old enough, they had sent him away for training. Now he was back. Both bulls had fences. Until you are close you don't realize how vast they are. In zoos everywhere, elephant keepers have the highest mortality. In London recently, a keeper was killed by an elephant he had loved for thirteen years. My daughter and I had watched him scrubbing her, brushing her teeth, climbing on to her when she lay on her side. One day he was in her cage alone, against the rules. Suddenly irritated, she pushed him against the bars and squeezed him to death. Males in musth are also very dangerous. A Keralan cab driver showed me where a bull had run amok, killing people, trampling cars. This bull had killed someone when he first came into musth.

'You read the signs. We lessen food to make him weaker till it's over. But that was his first time. It started too soon.'

Each has its own mahout and is jealous if he rides another. How *did* you ride them?

'Why don't we teach you?' said Ramdin.

I was barefoot on a brown-sugar riverbed. Soft, if I fell. Sita Kali swayed her trunk. 'Her name means Brave,' said Ramdin. They made her sit, then lie down. She was still enormous. I wanted to ask her permission to scramble up her naked hairy legs, bottom, spine. I was rock-climbing warm grey leather; she was naked but for a rope round her neck. I put my legs behind her ears, she lurched forward, tipped back. Back legs up, front legs. Terror, as she got to her feet. With a horse there is a neck in front of you, a mane. With an elephant, everything is below. I tucked my toes into slits in the rope behind her ears and grabbed the rope.

'Don't hold!' Ramdin shouted. 'Arms like a T.' It was all in the balance, in getting used to her movements. 'Now kick her ears!' Would she mind? Did she know I really, really admired her? What about the elephant that butted a loved keeper to death? *I* wouldn't like being kicked behind the ears. But I kicked, and Sita Kali moved. Her slow walk felt like a gallop.

Control came from your toes. Kick right ear, go left. Kick left ear, turn right. Draw both heels sharp back: stop. Trained elephants know hundreds of verbal cues; I was learning the basics. We did a figure-of-eight. She walked slower, slower, knowing I was hopeless. 'Make her go faster. Kick harder!' Her mahout was watching and felt discipline was slipping. They wanted to teach me more but after a few turns up the river I felt I'd be pushing it. I didn't fancy going back to Kathmandu with a broken leg. I gave the order. She lurched down. The sand felt wonderful.

'Thank you, Sita Kali.' I found her incomprehensible. With dogs, I can usually tell how they are feeling or thinking. With horses, sometimes. This was different. But I saw that communication was intense:

mahout and elephant were closely linked even while I was on her. She was teasing him by being slow with me. A power game. There was knowing mischief in this bulk.

Back in the lines, I gave her an elephant sandwich, leaves bound with grass, filled with grain. The little one, Sharshota Kali, watched and clamoured for one too. So did the bull. A close community, these elephants.

It was John's birthday. His party that night was in the elephant lines. We drank in the dark, danced to Ramdin's tape-recorder watched by panda eyes from the shadows, big shapes swaying, foot to foot. Then Ramdin led up Sharshota Kali with 'Happy Birthday John' painted in white on her side, surrounded by hearts and flowers. Her mahout brandished a cake with lit candles. Sharshota Kali had a job at last, as a greetings card.

On my last morning I woke in half-light to elephants trumpeting. The air was grey with mist; dew drumming on leaves. A langur hunched on the balustrade so near I could have touched him, facing silver-fogged grassland like someone watching a play. He saw me through the mosquito mesh, said, '*Kock!*' and vanished. I slept again, dreaming there were tigers in Chuck's camera.

Saying goodbye, I gave Sita Kali an apple. She flapped the rubbery, lingerie-pink and black-blotched ears I'd kicked. Their tatty frills wobbled.

I told Chuck my dream.

'That would make things all too easy,' he said.

The jeep to Kathmandu sloshed through the Rapti, past the rapier noses of two gharials. Night mists were rising, horizontal rays pasted the surface with diamond. A wallowing rhino floundered out and trotted into giant grass. The mountains rose higher. Their terracing was corduroy, wrapping contours in stripes of a hundred greens: lime, olive, pistachio, emerald. As the day wore on, this smudged into denim shadows. There were nose-to-tail lorries moving south to the Indian border, filling the air with exhaust. No wonder Chuck could not see the Himalayas now. One burned-out bus, full of passengers, had been bombed by the Maoists. This was the road where police had found some of the worst hauls of tiger skins; lorries like these heading the other way, to Tibet, to China, whose desire for tiger bone shadows wherever tigers live.

Kathmandu distressed me. The hotel was fine. It was built like a cold-climate pagoda: curly eaves, black and red bulgy-eyed caryatids, mustachioed demons with erect penises, tiny black demons clinging (like monkeys) to the penis shafts. They were supposed to drive off evil spirits. But the English-language paper said the king had just repealed the law by which Parliament fixed his exchequer. He would decide his own exchequer from now on. I did not think apotropaic phalluses were much help against injustice like that. The poor got poorer every day. The king, apparently, got richer.

From twilit streets I saw mountains beyond. Nepalese legend says mountains were winged, once, but the raingod wanted to give Nepal water so he cut off the wings. The mountains sank to earth and their wings became the clouds that still cling to them. That is how mountains and rivers came to Nepal. My guidebook said Nepal was the watershed of Asia. But no – 'Tibet's snowy mountains are head of everything: source of uncountable rivers, centre of the gods' sphere,' says an ancient Tibetan hymn. Tibet is Asia's furthest watershed. It still has a few tigers leaving pugmarks in southern snows, eating yaks or wild goats. People feel their presence – the wind on Everest's South Col, said Tenzing, roared like a thousand tigers – as Nepal feels the weight of Tibet itself.

The divine favour that created Nepal's rivers had shot its bolt for now. Kathmandu was a tourist city without tourists. After years of political corruption, poverty, inequality, in a 1990 revolution inspired by Tiananmen Square, Nepal had become a democracy with a royal family. But the rich bent politics and poverty continued. The Maoist revolt began six years later. When the crown prince killed himself and his family in 2001, the Nepalis were devastated. They loved their royal family. People I talked to felt the current king, who had escaped the massacre, had been behind it. Everyone was insecure and out of business. Rugs, mandalas, climbing boots, carpets: and no buyers. Stall-holders were frantic. Unsold T-shirts embroidered with cannabis leaves swung unsold, some carrying the refusals repeated by vanished tourists: 'NO rickshaw, NO rupees, NO tiger balm.'

'Tourist tiger balm isn't real, of course,' said Tenzing.

Drawn in by a tiger rug, escaping desperate stall-holders, I was in the back room of his antique shop. He was a second-generation Tibetan refugee, thirty-five, relaxed and hospitable. He had antique chests, rolled-up rugs and a rose-coloured tapestry, a museum piece with a pale animal in the centre. (My first mythical, Tibetan Buddhist snow lion. I would meet them *en masse* in Bhutan.) Tenzing was not desperate, his family sold to international collectors. I might be able to afford a modern tiger rug. He spread two. 'Choose which you like. If you like.' He smiled. 'Real tiger balm is very expensive. Tibetan clinics here say it cures arthritis, joints, knees, rheumatism. It *is* here, for those who know.'

Thirty years ago, at Pokhara, Dervla Murphy worked with Tibetan refugees. The camps are still there. The Tibetans wanted to stay, keeping alive their culture and language. They refused permanent homes in Nepal, opting for permanent transit till they got back to Tibet. They had woven the modern rugs.

I had begun to realize that Tibet was the backstage presence everywhere, in religion, history, geography, art. Tenzing opened a book about Tibetan freedom-fighters at a photo of men with guns. 'My father. He killed the most Chinese people.'

When the Dalai Lama left Tibet in 1959, and the Chinese occupation turned genocidal, Tenzing's family escaped to Nepal. Many Western hippies who came in the sixties were still there: now rich, he said, from buying and selling things the refugees brought with them.

I gave him my money but he was closing for a Tibetan festival. 'I'll wrap it for you tomorrow.' He wrote a receipt while I opened other books. One, *Parables of Sri Ramakrishna*, said, 'Illusion lingers even after attaining knowledge. A man dreamed of a tiger and woke up. The dream had gone but his heart continued to palpitate. It is hard to get rid of an illusion.' *We The Tibetans* said, 'The true journey is within.' I closed both. I was on a tiger journey. I had illusions and a vanished dream to get rid of too, but was dealing with them the true journey? Tigers were what mattered. Inner journeys ought to know their place, not shout at you from back rooms of antique shops.

But one book was about tiger rugs. Could I borrow it for the night? It was precious and out of print.

Tenzing hesitated. 'We'll have to trust each other. You have my book, I have your dollars. Come in the morning. We'll have tea.'

*

Tiger rugs are all about Tibet, and the influences that have poured in and out of it for centuries from India and China. Antique originals are rare: only two hundred are known. The West first saw them in 1979, when an American museum bought one. Scholars guess at what they symbolized by looking at the tiger's role in ancient Tibetan culture and countries around. The heart of their tiger symbolism is, of course, power. In the seventh century AD, when Tibet was strong in Nepal and Bhutan, sitting on a tiger skin represented power over the wildest possible nature. Tiger skins covered kings' thrones, judges' seats. Rich travellers spread them as saddle-blankets, over luggage: they shouted money and status.

In Hinduism, a tiger skin signified divine power too. Shiva wore one because the sages of the Deodar Forest, jealous of his influence on their wives, tried to kill him by hiding a tiger in the forest. He killed it and took its skin. In Buddhism, tiger skins had protective power, warding off scorpions or evil spirits, tiger masks repelled demons, tigers were an image of luck. Tigers and tiger skins appear on *thangkas*, in initiation ceremonies and New Year dances. Stripe marks on the legs, 'as of a tiger', are a sign of the Dalai Lama's incarnation. Gods and holy men ride tigers. Hinduism and Buddhism, India and China, religion and human hierarchy all meet in the art of the tiger rug.

But the underlying point of the rug was control, especially self-control: power over your own wildness. A sage sitting on a tiger skin signified spiritual victory over impulses. A *swami* who once tamed real tigers told a disciple, 'There are many kinds of tiger. Some roam the jungle of human desires. You must conquer the ones within.'

Tiger rugs owned by the ancient Tibetan élite were beautiful fluent metaphors of power, woven to suggest, rather than substitute for, real tigers. Sages sat on them too, to meditate and control inner impulses. Taming wildness has erotic overtones. Some antique rugs were indelibly stained, probably with semen, the 'stain of meditation'. Sex always gets into tiger symbolism somewhere. Such meditation dealt with unruly impulses by celebrating rather than repressing them, especially in Tantra, which emerged in Bengal and Bihar in the seventh century. Orthodox Hinduism and Buddhism shunned sex; Tantra said any path to enlightenment was just fine.

There were three traditional types of tiger rug. Semi-naturalistic

'Flayed Tigers' portrayed a skin with hanging paws and face. I hated
them. They began in the late nineteenth century, as a substitute: tiger
shooting was already diminishing India's tigers and real skins were
getting scarcer. The largest group was of abstract rugs. They alluded to
tigers, and seemed to me about the basic concept of stripes: stripes like
paired lips, eyes, smiles, waves, mountain terracing; lone stripes
writhing across a weave of pale rose-honey ginger. Some added delicate nostrils, muscle whorls, or skeleton effects round an S-shaped
spine. Most were pure, brilliant abstraction. Those were the most
admired, but the ones I loved were representational. Tigers on their
own, stalking through mountains, stiff-legged as a guard dog on a
doormat. 'Happy Tiger Walking through Bamboo', a Chinese motif,
was surrounded by narrow leaves. There were tiger pairs too, male
and female supposedly. I had bought one of those from Tenzing. My
tigers stood back to back on a red ground, merry and fierce with fat
grey eyebrows, rolling blue eyes and lashing tails. Their heads, separated by blue lotus, twisted over their shoulders. They did not look at
each other but their energy came from mutuality, awareness of each
other.

Like us, he said in my head. No wonder you want it for the bedroom.

Get out, I said back. My journey is getting rid of illusions.

Next morning I walked in fog beside Buddhist stupas. Small black
sacred cows nosed rubbish; glossy despite their diet, fatter than the
people. I passed an old sheet, then realized I was skirting not rubbish
but a wrapped corpse, with candles at head and feet. Women kissed a
leafless tree plastered with red wax; children in woolly hats waited
with offerings of marigolds. The morning *puja*, but little stone Buddhas
were also splashed with scarlet paste. The Buddha, born in Nepal,
reached enlightenment in north India. Buddhism and Hinduism were
balanced in medieval Nepal. Today it is the world's only Hindu kingdom, but Buddhism is big too. Everything is mixed in Nepal.

The wooden houses, dusky *sal* wood carving spotlit in dawn rays,
were built in the fourteenth and fifteenth centuries, Nepal's opulent
period when city states competed for Tibetan trade. The Terai, the

lowlands where Chitwan lies, look south to India. The mountains look north. A fourteenth-century Nepali architect taught China to build pagodas. The frisky roofs and guardian lions said 'China'; but China transmuted. This was my first exposure to Himalayan alchemy. South to north, Nepal and Bhutan run from subtropical lowland to the highest peaks in the world. They created their own cultures out of the two great ancient tiger countries. They are squeezed between India and Tibet; and, beyond Tibet, China.

In the nineteenth century, India meant the British. Nepal tried to keep the missionaries out. 'First the Bible, then the trading station, then the cannon,' one king said. Dead right. By 1815 the British forced Nepal to surrender the Terai. Eventually they signed a peace treaty and invited Nepalis into the Indian Army as Gurkhas. Later, grateful for Nepalese help in the Mutiny, they gave back the Terai.

Durbar Square, heart of the old city, was palaces and temples. Under a sign saying 'Dental Clinic', and parsnips spread for sale in plastic washing-bowls, a young man asked to show me round. I hadn't much money left. He told me I could give him as much as I wanted, then showed me temples, garlanded wood doors, medieval pagoda pageantry. I gave him all the notes I had. He wanted to give me half back for a cycle rickshaw. I said I'd walk. It is true, as someone who lives in Kathmandu tartly said to me afterwards, there are poorer places in the world. But I felt such panic here, and loss. Nepal has always had corruption and injustice, but it did have the outside world. Now, shopkeepers strike when Maoists command. Most visitors on whom Nepal depended have gone, leaving the useless flotsam made to please them.

Someone from a tour company with his three-year-old daughter took me to the plane. What did he feel about the country? Many tour companies had gone bust. He was on half pay.

'It can't go on like this. There'll be . . .'

'A conflagration?'

'Yes. And I, too, must join the fire.'

Neither of us knew that in February 2005 the king would sack his government, dismantle civil liberties, and cut Kathmandu off from the outside world in a headlong confrontation with the Maoists: giving India and the West the choice of siding either with revolutionaries or with a suddenly refeudalized monarchy brutally supported by an army; and creating worse problems for Nepal's impoverished citizens and threatened tigers.

The plane was delayed for seven hours, average for Nepal Airlines. Waiting, I tried to connect the desperation I felt here with Chitwan's tigers. A miracle that Nepal, caught between king, Maoists and rapacious politicians, protected tigers at all. A stable tiger population depends on a stable system of people intelligent and generous enough to think long-term, who can control the need and greed of humans at every level, from grass-cutting to politics. This army protecting tigers was responsible to a king now refixing his own exchequer. If the Maoists got rid of him, what would happen to the tigers and forest?

'You'll love Bhutan. Seventy-five per cent is forest,' Chuck had said. He had written its new tiger conservation programme. 'Thirty-five per cent, protected.'

Paro airport was a temple to earth colours, rust, ochre, blue, rose, silver-grey, spacious archways spooling with garlands, demon faces, lotus buds.

'The tiger is one of the four power animals,' said a card on the plane. 'It makes its way through the jungle with quiet confidence and unlimited energy, representing the dignity that comes from meekness.'

We load the tiger with sexiness, power and status. But – meekness?

'The snow lion is the joyful, energized mind. The garuda, a man's head and hands and powerful wings. It embodies mind far away from normal reality. The dragon is powerful but beneficent, filling the world with its voice.'

Bhutan is Druk Yul, Land of the Thunder Dragon. Druk Air, the national airline, is the only one that flies into this tiny airport ringed with mountains. And only when the wind drops does the cloud lift. You have to be a bit of a dragon to fly in and out of Paro.

'Tiger, snow lion, garuda, dragon embody qualities the spiritual hero cultivates: courage, strength, luck, wisdom, melodious voice of great renown.' Tigers had brought me to Narnia, a cut-off world where religious symbolism was rampant, citizens were spiritual heroes, and even the buildings wore national dress.

Karma Tshering had done the tiger study and written the tiger conservation programme with Chuck. His brother Hishey met me: a big, ebullient man in a navy-and-red tartan garment patterned with tiny squares. People wore national dress, at least in public. Men had the *gho*, a knee-length dressing-gown with wide white cuffs. It pouched above the belt to make a repository for everything: a pocket, briefcase, tool-kit, safe. You assess manhood and style from the way men wear it. Colours were sober: dark red, green, navy. Very smart *ghos* were grey. Hishey, optimistic for his country and its conservation, ran an eco-tourism company. Tourists come for trekking, botany, rafting, ornithology. He pointed to a sewage plant favoured by rare water birds. 'I'm the only operator who starts his guests off at a sewage works.'

We drove through mountains, past painted farmhouses whose woodwork was the gypsy pink and blue of the airport. On their white walls Himalayan tigers pranced, fierce and playful as those on my rug, all rolling eyes and lashing tails, accompanied by the other power animals: lofty dragons, man-headed garudas carrying snakes, and snow lions like my daughter's spaniel, enthusiastic clouds of bouncy fluff.

Just now Bhutan has the stablest government among the tiger countries. When China invaded Bhutan's ancient neighbour Tibet, Bhutanese policies slowly began to modernize and look west. The current king, film-star handsome, intelligent, self-disciplined, adored, succeeded as a teenager; tourism began under him in 1974. His four queens are sisters. One is passionate about conservation. He is canny about bringing Bhutan into the modern world. Many people want to help but he is choosy. He says Gross National Happiness matters more than Gross National Product.

'Some people complain we are too conservationist,' said Hishey. 'Unemployment is rising. But . . .'

The national animal, the takin, is a goat-antelope in a taxonomic class of its own. George Schaller called it a bee-stung moose. Some takin live in Myanmar and China; otherwise they live wild only here. They like it rugged. Some inhabited an enclosure outside Thimphu in what used to be a zoo: lanky, shaggy six-foot cows crossed with a moody elk, head like a dustbin, heavy swept-back horns. Feeling they shouldn't keep animals in cages, the Bhutanese disbanded the zoo, but the takin kept coming back, disrupting the town. Now the tourist board pays for their upkeep.

In Bhutanese legend, takin were created by Bhutan's favourite saint Drukpa Kunley, the Divine Madman. He came to Bhutan from Tibet in the fifteenth century, knocked out demons' teeth with thunderbolts, hung his bow on sunbeams, and said women should thrust their pelvis as high as possible in sex. Rigid piety, he said, stopped you learning true Buddhism. Bulbous phalluses, tied with a bow, were painted on some walls. They protected the house, encouraged fertility, and belonged to Drukpa Kunley. When his followers asked for a miracle he ordered a whole cow and goat for lunch, stuck the goat's head on the cow's body and told it to get up and walk. That's the takin.

I offered one a banana skin. It drew it through the mesh with surprisingly graceful chocolate lips, then wanted more. When there wasn't any, I got an impatient threatening movement of horns. In the wild, takin are disturbed by other animals. Yak herders keep off the slopes when they see them.

Bhutan has no traffic lights. At Thimphu's central crossroads an official in national dress waved from a circular russet and blue-flowered booth. Every building in Bhutan, monasteries, petrol stations, traffic booths, checkpoints, must be painted like this. The streets were full of stray dogs, black, sandy, dirty white, tails curled over backs like small wiry huskies. Hungry, wary, some with hair falling out, covered with sores, crippled. It is a sin to take life. Dogs are a major problem everywhere. Hishey had emailed me to bring ear-plugs. I had forgotten.

The national sport is archery; Hishey took me to a tournament. When anyone hit gold, his team put their arms over each other's shoulders and kicked their legs in the black-necked crane dance. There are six thousand black-necked cranes in the world and they winter in Bhutanese valleys. Their arrival is a major festival. The national sport spotlights endangered wildlife; a tournament takes all day because of this dance. People were selling juice to men in *ghos* and women in the *kira*, an ankle-length dress with a silk jacket over it: cherry red, dark green, dull sheeny blue. Many women folded their sleeves back into winged cuffs. Cuffs were important here. This place cared about detail.

The archery green is the only bit of flat ground in the country apart from the airport. Most of Bhutan is mountain. Forked threads of snow came down peaks behind the town; pythons of white cloud lolled between. Everything was bright and cold. Opposite the green were houses whose high-arched, cloister-shaped windows had the now familiar garlands of soft ginger and white-stippled blue snow lions, garudas, dragons, tigers. The market had fruit, brass bells and tiger rugs: flayed tigers and a naturalistic tiger walking through pale blue mountains and green leaves; 'Happy Tiger in Bamboo', made in Darjeeling. Bhutan gets nearly everything from India. Leeks, potatoes, bananas, cabbages and chillies were heaped on the ground. Men in ghos fingered arrows and knives. A girl with a purple jumper over her kira sold boxes painted with tigers.

'What are those strings of white squares?'

'Yak cheese. It breaks teeth! You chew for hours till it goes soft.'

Even little boys wore the *gho*. One toddler holding his mother's hand wore a dark red *gho* with a Mickey Mouse satchel. Another said daringly to me, 'Hello please?' His friends collapsed in laughter. Hishey looked anxious.

'We have to watch it. Today it's "hello" to foreigners. Tomorrow, will they have their hands out? Our society is poised for change. We are getting mobile phones next year. But unemployment is growing. How will change affect our children?'

His brother Karma, small, dark, with a narrow head, sweet, watchful smile and the springy family energy, was in a restaurant above the green drinking Red Panda beer with the maroon mask of a Himalayan panda on the label. The national dish was melted cheese with hot chillies; I opted for a cheese omelette. Outside came cheers as a team danced the crane dance.

'We came to conservation late,' said Karma. 'Entering the global community slowly, we learn from our neighbours, above all not to treat people living in national parks as a threat, but as part of the park.'

Bhutan is an amazingly varied ecosystem in amazingly little space; a hundred and fifty metres above sea level in the south, seven thousand in the north. Forty-nine kinds of rhododendron, six hundred orchids, forest corridors between parks so tigers are in touch with each other. Tigers live at all heights up to four thousand metres. Bhutan does not have problems on India's scale, vast expanding population, complex entrenched civil service. Even so this culture, cut off for centuries, was grappling as in a test tube with issues everyone faces. There are many villages in the national parks; they depend on forest resources. Traditionally, villagers slashed and burned, cultivated patches and moved on. The forest recovered as secondary not pristine forest. *But* Bhutan had political stability and the political will to keep tigers safe. The government was trying to offer these villages alternative ways of living. As embodied by these brothers, Bhutan seemed in love with conservation, and poised to implement that love.

'We have better healthcare now. No more infant mortality so the population's going up fast. Hence more cows. Cattle graze in forest and prefer some leaves to others, reducing growth in trees they like, changing the balance of vegetation in the forest. Our worst problem is tigers killing livestock.'

There are not many sambar here. I kept being told that Bhutanese tigers do not eat wild boar: a pity, if true, as well as a waste, for the boar were a pest, villagers were not compensated for crops they ruined, and fencing was expensive. In high mountains tigers took takin, but everywhere they supplemented wild prey with livestock like domestic yaks, which moved up in March, down in autumn. In folk-tales tigers constantly attack yak herds; they still do.

The Bhutanese government had started compensation (funded by WWF) for an animal killed by a tiger or snow leopard, but not by a leopard or wild dog. The government was breeding cows that gave more milk for less feed (so people could own fewer) and offering Swiss hybrids at bargain prices. But if your cow is a beautiful Swiss hybrid, losing it to a tiger is worse. Leopards, apparently, mainly killed ponies. In Nepal, villagers got half the value of a cow killed by a tiger. In Kanha they got money for a cow outside the protected zone, nothing for one killed inside. But at least they were compensated for leopard kills. I now felt strongly that if you lived by or in a tiger reserve you should be compensated for harm done by *any* animal – crops eaten by tiger prey, animals killed by anything – since the whole system, including leopards and wild dogs, supports the tiger. But governments dislike paying compensation. Sarah Christie also thought blanket compensation was the answer, because protected areas could not be sustainable.

'There *is* money in the world. People want to give money for tigers. So make that the source of compensation.'

But managing compensation is difficult. Villagers may make false claims, or punish tigers if they do not get paid – and sometimes if they do, once a tiger has advertised its valuable presence.

Chuck and Karma guessed 115 to 150 tigers lived in Bhutan, maybe more. They did not see them. They based the figures on tiger traces. Unlike Chitwan, this is not great habitat. Prey is sparse and spread out; tigers go long distances to eat. What matters in a tiger population is how many breeding adults there are. Saving the tiger does not mean protecting one forest here, a few tigers there, but protecting a genetically viable population: breeding tigers in contact with each other. In Bhutan they can be, but they have to travel higher and further for it than most. Tiger society will be different from that in Chitwan or Ranthambhore, where males can rule thirty square kilometres with several females.

Territory also varies across Bhutan. In Royal Manas Park – southern subtropical lowlands, like Chitwan – two adult tigers may have territory in a hundred square kilometres. Higher up, a hundred square kilometres may be half of a tiger's territory. He will go up and down constantly: his territory is vertical. Like yaks and takin, Bhutan's tigers go down in winter, up in summer, following prey. Some go up into snow. In 1998, Chuck and Karma found fresh tracks in snow at 3000 metres, 10,000 feet.

But even Narnia knows sin. Dealers come from China, Tibet, north India. Poachers exploit political unrest on both borders. Sometimes rangers find a dead tiger and villagers say they were trapping boar when really they trapped the tiger to sell to dealers. Isn't it a sin to take life?

'If you kill animals,' said Karma, 'your way ahead will be unclear. You'll meet demons in your next life. Some people take that risk.'

'We try to educate people to conserve animals,' said Hishey. 'We run education programmes. We all grew up like them, in villages where predators threatened livestock. But it's hard. I remember once, when I was young, I threw a stone at a leopard cat. It couldn't have hurt me, it was too small. I'm ashamed of that now.'

Leopard cats, the size of a domestic cat, are endangered too.

'That was instinct, Hishey.'

'That's what I'm ashamed of. The *instinct* was bad. That's what we want to change in the villages.'

Buddhism is full of self-scrutiny. By my hotel bed I had seen *The Teaching of the Buddha* in English and Dzongkha. Bhutan is the only Buddhist kingdom left in the world. Its religion is very, very alive.

Karma's assistant, Sharap, came in, a tall, dark young man with narrow face, pursed mouth, wide, innocent dark eyes. He was in charge of implementing the tiger programme and would drive me east.

'You won't see tigers, none of us has. We've got one camera-trap photo; tiger tracks are two days' trek from any road. But you'll see how we protect tigers, the forests they use. Sharap's buying provisions for your journey. What food do you like?'

If I'd known this was the only market, only fruit, and in some places the only food, for ten days, I would have thought harder.

'Bananas? Tangerines? Eggs?'

'And chillies,' said Sharap and Karma, simultaneously.

8

INNER JOURNEY, HIDDEN TREASURE

The journey began with a flat tyre. I came to breakfast early, for the Thimphu dogs started barking at five. They barked through the night, but five was maximum volume. At dawn they went to sleep. I never saw any Bhutanese pavement without its mosaic of sleeping dogs like furry cup-cakes. Long ago the gods, horrified at our human greed, removed our food. Dogs pleaded for us. Now we eat what the gods gave back to us – because the dogs asked. Dogs help in the after-life too, leading us through the dark with lights on their tails. Bhutanese strays are inviolate.

Sharap turned up as the young waiter wrote my receipt beside his copy of *Reader's Digest*, open at an article titled 'Sex and the Healthy Male'. To get a new tyre levered on to the hub, our first stop was a workshop in Thimphu's Sunday back-streets: *ghos* on washing-lines, incapacitated jeep filled with wicker baskets of bananas, tangerines, eggs, chillies; boys in jeans (you can wear them in private) playing billiards on a board over a barrel. They did not look at me. Not looking at strangers is a mark of respect.

If I had known how crucial tyres would be, I'd have watched the new one go on. Instead I watched a black goat beat delicate front feet in the air while nibbling willow boughs. A young man with a shy soft face, wearing green forest uniform like Sharap (because today he was on official business) was accompanying us as far as Thrumshingla. They had done conservation training together. Sangay had the same keenness to communicate but less English. 'Hi,' he said carefully.

Cloud was low: there would be no views. Candy-floss mist tumbled down steep valleys as the one road rose. Then we were in real cloud, with forest at the road edge. Wild magnolias, white butterflies against the brown-green of oak and hemlock coming into leaf. Rhododendrons a hundred feet high breaking into blood-red blossom. At a checkpoint tiny women, Tibetan refugees in yellow and red, sold yak cheese oblongs dangling from white strings, and thin men in ragged cotton scrutinized my visa, our travel permits, car documents. Bhutan vets every detail. This was its only hard-top road.

At three thousand metres, Deche La, my first mountain pass, our breathing changed, ears popped. Did tiger ears pop too? A 'pass' in Dzongkha is *la*. In mountain country, passes are holy things. This whole vertical landscape had a spiritual as well as a physical reality: every pass had a shrine. In another intonation (a higher tone according to Sharap, but I could never hear it), *la* was a mark of respect, which is also crucial in Bhutan. Sharap put it on the end of words when talking to strangers. He even said it when he picked up a phone. *La*: a little word with two big uses.

Over the pass were strings of prayer flags glowing red, green and blue, through the mist, hanging from poles around a *chorten*, a monument where a sacred relic is buried. You go clockwise round a *chorten*, even in a lorry, because it clears your sins – but this can create problems on a one-track road over a ten-thousand-foot drop. We got out, for the view I could not see, and stared into rifting silk mist. The freezing air was sweet with early blossom. Occasionally the cloud-wad shifted like a dream fading, revealing blue sky, forested slopes, snow peaks. We were driving through the world's most beautiful mountains, unable to see them.

I looked at a green flag. The power animals were in the corners surrounding squiggly Dzongkha prayers: dragon and garuda on top, with winged clouds; below, the snow lion pranced among mountains, the tiger walked on earth, round-pawed as Tigger in old illustrations of *Winnie-the-Pooh*. Tiger is where you start. You move up the mountains for the snow lion, into the sky for the others. In the centre was a windhorse, from whose saddle sprang a plume: the Flaming Jewel, which fulfils wishes. A windhorse is power, energy, your vehicle on your life journey. Your windhorse is high or low depending on how far you have gained spiritual warriorhood. Its energy fulfils your desires, carries you on the path to enlightenment. It reminded me of Tenzing's books: that inner journey, getting rid of illusion to find the reality beyond. For me, this reality had to be the tiger. I had come to a place where everyone accepted that life was a spiritual journey, where prayers were blown to the highest mountains in the world.

As we came down, a blue whistling thrush flew out in front of us, dark purple freckled with iridescent blue spots as if someone had scattered him with cobalt. Then another, and a third. No other bird behaved like this. As we crawled for hours, up, down, round corners, these thrushes watched from boulders, waited till the last moment, then flew in front. Where cloud lifted, there were denim triangles of sky, forested mountains, blushing nipples of wild peach.

'When the wild peach blooms, they say it is time to sow wheat.'

I loved talking to Sharap, watching his dark, severe young profile, with Sangay leaning forward from behind, not so confident but just as alert. Bhutan's conservation was in enthusiastic hands. Macaques peered round tree trunks. On a bend were two chestnut animals, big as dogs. Tiger colour – but these were muntjac, barking deer, the nearest to what tigers eat that I could expect to see, but for me the least exotic Asian animal. They were common round Boswells, even in the garden, when I was small. Nineteenth-century English deer parks loved Asian imports, especially muntjac with their glossy coats. Muntjac escaped, went feral and now live in British woodland.

'People in my village say they eat snakes,' said Sharap. 'One man saw with his own eyes a muntjac with a snake hanging out of its mouth.'

The rare traffic on this precipitous highway was very generous. Behind lorries, Sharap sounded his horn. They pulled over gently without danger to any of us, despite the drop on one side and a sharp water gully on the other. Except for a Dutch contractor, who came fast round a corner without hooting. He slewed to a stop an inch from the edge.

'Hello, Piet. You should have blown your horn.'

'You're in my lane,' said Piet. There was only one lane.

'There'll be more of this,' I said. 'You have five thousand tourists a year now. When you get fifteen there'll be more accidents, more Westerners driving at fifty round blind corners.'

Bhutan is all water as well as all mountain. Water gallops down slopes and would destroy the road without the gully, which is constantly cleared by small Indian women, gold in their nostrils, shawls over heads to keep out the cold. Many nursed babies as they worked. Children sat by the edge guarding lunch parcels. Some lunches had an umbrella over them. On one stretch a long frieze of tipped-up umbrellas stood out against mist. These workers are sometimes washed away in rains and landslides, but it is considered a good job, with security.

The Lobesa valley was warmer: prickly pear, spiky yellow laburnum, grey langurs in trees below, their sentinel on a rock at the road edge. A yellow-billed blue magpie, pale violet wings and long tail, flew up calling. Altitude changed so fast, even at twenty miles an hour, that vegetation and animals did too. Tigers adapt to them all. Farmers, plaiting bamboo fencing, had laid fronds on the only flat place, the road. Sharap drove over as many as he could to flatten them. Over the next pass was Rukybji, a bleak moorland valley where potatoes grew. Yaks grazed a slope of dwarf bamboo. A tiger had been seen there recently, attracted by the yaks, which were mainly piebald, to my surprise; glossy, fluffy, wide pink nostrils. A yak calf skittered down, looked at us, shot away. Even yaks play. Sharap turned on the radio to a request programme of English and Irish pop, then Dzongkha songs with plucking strings.

'They are love songs. This is about two passes, Deche La and Tue La. She'll wait for him behind one, then the other. If he really loves her, he'll find her.'

In English, the DJ had an Irish accent.

'Is that Irish? He must have trained in Ireland.'

Irish accent, Irish songs, potatoes, bleak mist on a dark-honey moor: this was Connemara with tigers and yaks. I was back driving round real Connemara. Travelling, we were most together. I met him at Dublin airport and drove him west. In misty moorland just like this he got out of my car by a lake to discover what it felt like. Rain came back in with him. We put on the heater and drove off singing Irish songs. We both loved singing. At the next town, crossing the road, he grabbed my arm. He said he had learned from films how to seem to cherish women. 'I realized it impresses girls from the boy singing "I'll Take Care of You" in *The Sound of Music*.'

'In the next scene he betrays her to the Nazis.'
We laughed.

At dusk we approached Trongsa, a stretch where Sharap had seen
leopards. This mix of alpine cold and leopards felt like an odd blurring
of boundaries, for this is where Himalayan species (black bear, say)
overlap Indo-Malay species like leopards. A black leopard had been
seen here recently: Bhutanese panthers have melanistic genes. I peered
into darkness, longing for my first love, Bagheera.

Trongsa, a chilly crossroads town, smelt of juniper smoke. Outside
the hotel an orange lorry had Buddha eyes on its bonnet, a tiger head
on its petrol cap. Inside was supper: melted cheese with chillies and
fern fronds.

I woke to fog, and a wet pigeon cooing moodily outside my
window. I imagined soaked panther cubs, shivering. This cloud was no
Kanha mist, which burns off so that fur can dry. When it shifted I saw
the yellow roofs of Trongsa Dzong. Since medieval times Bhutan has
been organized into districts governed by a *dzong*. This one was a
fortress stretching over many ridges, dominating the valley.

Trongsa National Park is central to Bhutan's forest corridors. It runs
from alpine to tropical habitat and contains twenty per cent of Bhutan's
tigers. The forest office had yellow silk frills over the doors and tiger
distribution maps on the wall. Everywhere, said the director, there
was a constant tussle between agriculture and conservation, and many
retribution killings when tigers took cattle. The park had a compensation scheme, but also offered the indirect benefits of living with
protected tigers, which Karma had mentioned: better grass seed, and
cows that give more milk so the villagers do not need so many. In a
protected area, villagers cannot fish, snare animals, cut wood. The
director asks what they want instead. Their list always starts with a
vehicle. 'We say what we give must contribute to conservation.
Vehicles don't. We steer them to things they need that benefit the park.
Those Swiss hybrids really have reduced grazing pressure on the
forest.'

The ever-winding road rose sharply again. Sharap had seen little
yellow foxes here above Trongsa. Wolves were rare now; wild dogs

had been poisoned almost to extinction but when the wild boar population exploded, villagers realized they needed them. Now wild dogs were returning, and boar were under control. Farmers have to choose between wild ungulates and wild predators, crops or livestock. In one region last year, a bear killed twenty sheep; the villagers killed it. Bhutan has black and sloth bears.

'Black is worse than sloth bear,' said Sangay. 'Much larger. You have to stay still and not breathe.' A friend of his pretended to be dead; the bear sniffed him all over then left him alone. But Sharap's grandfather was attacked by one in forest where Thimphu's archery ground is now. He had the scar on his skull. I hoped both bears were still hibernating.

Sharap pulled to the cliff edge for a cavalcade led by a black limousine with a little boy inside, the reincarnation of a lama.

'How do they know he's a reincarnation?'

'Sometimes he talks about his previous life. Sometimes the parallels simply reveal themselves.'

As we came into a valley, luckily near the bottom, our spare wheel – held on only, we discovered later, by a single screw beneath the jeep – fell off and rolled away. Sharap and Sangay raced after it. I looked at farmhouses painted with Drukpa Kunley's erections. They were in pairs at either side of the door, like ceremonial swords. The orange balls were boots pointing opposite ways, coming together under a segmented tan phallus. The Divine Madman had tiger-coloured tackle.

A *chorten* outside Bumthang contained the head of a seventeenth-century Tibetan general who had attacked the town in vain. A signpost on a striped stone like a circus tiger's tub said, 'Trashigang 284 km'. Beyond Trashigang lay Sakteng, the world's only yeti reserve. Yetis, *migoi*, go much higher than tigers. Bhutanese ones can make themselves invisible so there are not many sightings. When visible, they are covered in red-brown hair. Their feet point backwards, so they are hard to track, but an Oxford University expedition, fostered by Bhutan's royal family, discovered a hair follicle there. Its DNA is being tested in an Oxford lab.

This was one of the most important crossroads in the country. The only traffic was a bull, bellowing. A soft moo answered. Dogs barked: he shook his horns at them and disappeared. Behind him was a single-storey building hung with banners. DO NOT POLLUTE WATER: IT MIGHT POLLUTE US IN RETURN. THE TALISMAN OF GOOD FORTUNE: LATEST BOOK BY BHUTANESE AUTHOR SOLD HERE. Bumthang may have got its name from *thang*, 'flat place', and *bumpa*, 'vessel for holy water': the valley is shaped like a cup. Or from its women: *bum* means 'girl'. But it was also the only town I saw with traffic bumps. I bought an umbrella from a shop selling saws, prayer flags, yak cheese and Johnson's Baby Lotion. As we left, Sangay said he knew of a tiger monastery nearby.

Buddhism officially came to Bhutan from Tibet in the early seventh century. A thousand years before that Tibetan general attacked Bumthang, the Tibetan king Songtsen Gampo was building temples in Bhutan. They say he built a hundred and eight in one day. But Buddhism really got going here in the eighth century with Guru Rinpoche, a saint who emerged to the world in Pakistan as an eight-year-old boy in the form of a blue lotus. He meditated in Tibet and Nepal; in Bhutan he also hid his teachings as treasure, to be unearthed by treasure-discoverers, the *tertons*. He came to Bhutan on a flying pregnant tigress, whose condition spoke of Buddhism's future growth. They landed above Paro (where the airport is today) on the mountain ledge where Tiger's Nest monastery now stands.

'But he came here too,' Sangay said, 'and his tigress followed.'

The rocky track wound up beside the tiger-coloured Tang river. Even its fish were yellow. Dzongkha for tiger is *ta*, *tak*, *tag* or *tang*: this was Tiger Valley. We passed a turn to Burning Lake, connected with a treasure-discoverer born there in the fifteenth century, Pema Lingpa, who discovered holy objects and texts in fairy script, where one word stands for a thousand and each has a deeper meaning than the last. He found and deciphered them in caves, lakes and dreams. Sceptics accused him of duplicity. He waved a lamp, shouting, 'If I am a true revealer of treasure may I return with my lamp still burning,' leaped into this lake and emerged with his lamp still alight.

These *tertons*, discoverers of treasure hidden eight centuries before by Guru Rinpoche, seemed characteristic of Bhutan's longing to find deeper meaning on the path to enlightenment, and dig ever deeper for treasure buried in the earth – or in the heart, for Pema Lingpa found fairy texts in dreams as well as caves. Everything held secrets, treasure, deeper meanings. Like my Keralan dream of lost treasure, Bhutan specialized in hiddenness. These beautiful mountains I could not see because of cloud. Bhutan's tigers, the most elusive in the world.

This was the most remote of Bhutan's valleys. Like the path to enlightenment, the track was rough and rocky. It would be treacle in monsoons. At three thousand metres, a barefoot girl with chapped cheeks walked along spinning wool, herding cows with a tiny boy. There are many stories of tigers attacking cows. Herders still see tigers; children are the main herders. Yet there are no stories of man-eating in Bhutan.

The monastery was on a cliff striped orange and black. An old man revealed frescos of Guru Rinpoche with frowning gold face. The tigress who carried him and Buddhism to Bhutan was a striped magenta sow. She had left her cubs in Tiger's Nest and flew here to join the guru. When she got back, her cubs did not believe she had been there, so she returned and rubbed against these stripy cliffs to prove it.

In front of the monastery were a male and female garuda disguised as two boulders. Climbing the male guaranteed eternal life. Sharap and Sangay looked at it longingly, but there was no time. Behind a *chorten* was a rock where Guru Rinpoche knelt, and the goddess of the place entered him. One of his tasks was converting earlier local deities.

'It's a pugmark,' I said, putting my hand in it. 'The tigress, landing.' But Sharap said it was Guru Rinpoche's knee.

Coming down we heard a radio song: a snow lion longs for snow on the mountain but it melts before he gets there. Then an ancient song, 'Tapa Sita', 'Tiger Skin Leopard Skin', about a lama's throne covered with skins. Then Bhutanese rap.

'He observes a lady from behind. She is very sexy, very stylish. But when he sees her face she is an old woman with no teeth.'

Good old misogyny driving rap even here, with a Bhutanese spin about hidden meaning. Only when you look back do you see the truth.

I looked back too. What happened with my work was one revelation. When he did not answer a letter I wrote to the hurt in his voice –

longing, like the snow lion yearning for snow, to see our healing rap-
port work for each other one last time – that was another. How, I asked
the mountains, do you look back with good memories at someone
who, I could not help feeling now, dishonoured his own love?

This was no good. I had to forgive him for poisoning things. Get rid
of my contempt.

We passed a man driving a mechanized tiller with children in the
back. Sharap stopped and spoke; a boy jumped out and ran back. The
man had dropped his starting-handle.

'I saw it up the mountain. He won't be able to start without it. I
thought of picking it up then. But if I hadn't caught him, he'd never
have got it back.'

Much later, further down, Sharap said, 'I hope he found it.'

9

THE ROAD TO TIGER'S NEST

'Villagers here respect the tiger,' said Sangay. He was a ranger in Thrumshingla National Park; we would sleep in his mountain hut. 'They say, "The tiger used to visit us, the tiger is good fortune for us." They also say, "We rarely see now." I tell them snow lion, garuda, dragon and tiger are protectors of Buddhism. The other three used to exist, only the tiger is left. We must protect it.'

This was red panda country: spruce, juniper, bamboo, and lichen flopping off trees like pale green boas. Sharap had seen pandas here but they are shy, and hunted for their pelt. They look like otters bundled in rusty fur with white-masked faces. They eat bamboo like giant pandas, but their closest relations are racoons. They are active at night. By day they sleep in trees. Cushions of furry moss kept seeming to be pandas on branches, and then not.

'Yaks eat the lichen. I saw one once that died doing it. It had its hoof on the tree, slipped, and caught its neck in a V between two branches.'

Sunset behind black lollipops of cloud, misty air turning pewter, then black. We heard a clucking double echo from slopes above: the highly endangered Monal pheasant. They live only here; hunters take them for their iridescent feathers. We saw a dog in the headlights.

'He'll be leopard food tonight,' said Sharap. 'I've often seen leopards on this stretch.'

A tiny hut, four thousand metres up a mountain. Plank walls full of cracks. Sangay chopped wood for the small stove, Sharap boiled a tin of curry sauce and chopped chillies. We heard squeakings. Were those . . . inside?

'No, no,' said Sangay.

'They go to the forest in summer,' said Sharap soothingly.

Protectors of the wild live alone in remote places. Dealings with the nearest human beings are difficult, since they threaten the forest and animals. Mr Reddy's guards were too shy to say they missed their families; Sangay 's wife was currently having a baby but he had to get back here. Bhutanese national parks have two wardens, one for research, anti-poaching and monitoring wildlife (as Sharap had done in another park, Tintibi, before he joined the tiger programme) the other to work with local communities on conservation education: to advise, warn, and impose fines for infringements. Here the big problem was over-grazing. Traditional grazing rights, *tsamdrogs*, are important household possessions passed down to your heirs, but grazing is one of the biggest threats to bio-diversity. Sangay had produced Bhutan's one camera-trap photo of a tiger. In the year the park opened, 2000, he walked miles up the mountain to check the cameras, developed the film and delighted the Bhutanese conservation service with the sight of one of their own tigers, walking through forest at night.

Thrumshingla has 770 square kilometres. A 2001 survey estimated five or six tigers here, but two months afterwards a tigress with cubs was killed. This was before compensation: she had killed three hybrid cows, worth twenty thousand *nu* each. Their owners received only three hundred. They tried cable wire, then summoned a hunter from a remote village. They skinned her. Sangay found the bones, and had to fine them.

Thrumshingla also has clouded leopards. I had seen only pictures of them: kohl-black lace over a dun coat like netted bubbles. This camouflage for dappled leaves is, unfortunately, extraordinarily pretty; they are hunted hotly for their skins. They are smaller than ordinary leopards – their ancestors diverged from the *Panthera* tribe millions of years ago – and they live mostly in trees. I had not known they lived so far north.

'I've never seen them this far up,' said Sangay. 'They like oak forests lower down. I often see ordinary leopards. Ten kilometres from here, I followed a sambar trail and saw a leopard following the deer.'

I was dying to see a leopard. Any sort. Also dying to walk *in* forest, rather than drive past it. I knew we couldn't go high enough for tiger tracks but we might see *something*. So we got up at four. The stove had gone out. Sangay stayed in bed: he had a day's work ahead. Sharap, a guard who knew the terrain and I drove up to the snow line through pelting snow. Black air was greying; snow caps loomed. Any animal would be mentally defective to be out in this – but no, the animals who lived here had *chosen* this climate, evolved for it. As Fateh Singh had said in his bright courtyard, tigers live in some of the hottest and coldest places in the world.

We slithered down through tall bamboo into rhododendron forest so steep I would never have dreamed we could walk here. They plunged, I followed. It wasn't *completely* vertical. You could hang on to flesh-pink peeling trunks of rhododendrons whose leaves were coming out a hundred feet above our heads, but any dead wood came away in your hand. This was mulch untouched since the Ice Age, thousands of centuries of pure *wood*, looped in lichen like a wedding table. The light was dim green-brown. Every branch swathed in moss could have been, but was not, a panda.

Sharap found sambar droppings. Droppings are everything when you cannot see the animals themselves. How could a tall, antlered deer get through this macaroni of trunks on a slope the angle of someone leaning against a wall? Fresh droppings of serow, goat-antelope. (There are twenty-six goat-antelope species, several in Bhutan.) It had sheltered in a shallow scoop of cliff where we, too, stopped to breathe. It was lighter down here, bamboo grew, rays filtered through its pale green blades. A squirrel chewed moss on a high branch, stopping to check for danger. Thrumshingla has nine kinds of squirrel. This one was small, with stripes. Sweet: but all this – my breathing was slowing a little – *for one squirrel*? The roads were bad and long: we didn't have time to camp the three days necessary to get to tiger tracks, but could we not go somewhere more – tropical?

'We'll go south,' whispered Sharap, 'to broadleaf forest.'

I respected altitude now as never before. We climbed up a soft, wet, laddery tunnel. My lungs tried to fill the space between crotch and throat, hammering at the heart to help. Every few yards I had to stop and gulp. I had never done fitness training, these rasping breaths would never stop, my heart was exploding, thigh-muscles tearing. Then we stopped, for a sausage of red panda shit. Sharap broke it open. Inside were bamboo-tips like the fern fronds in melted cheese at Trongsa.

Ura, a thousand metres below, was a valley village surrounded by mountains and pouring with rain. I wanted to find the parents of Karma Phuntso, a theology student at Oxford. The Bhutanese writer Karma Ura had been born there. He wrote a novel about a famous civil servant, also born there, in 1928, who was recognized as a lama reincarnation at the age of four, became secretary to successive kings through Bhutan's modernizing period, and designed Bhutan's flag. Things had changed sharply in his lifetime. Government servants were no longer caned on their bare rumps in public, there were now roads, not just mule tracks, and at Ura a health unit, a phone. But fewer tigers. And it is harder now to protect crops from the wild boar that Bhutanese tigers mysteriously refuse to eat; perhaps because they stay on the heights while the pigs come down for the crops.

Puddles shone in the mud round the monastery, which was crowded because today was an auspicious day. Walking round the walls, twirling burgundy-and-gold-painted prayer wheels in bucketing hail, we met Karma's small, white-haired mother. She smiled radiantly through falling ice, and gave directions to her house.

The monastery had wall-paintings of saints and demons with tigers beneath, and a lama's throne covered, as in the song, with a real tiger skin, carefully patched. Then we ran through the rain to Karma's house, and climbed two thick wooden ladders into the dark. Bhutanese farmhouses use the ground floor for animals, the second for grain, the third for people. Karma's parents welcomed us into a dark, chill, beautiful wooden room. We sat cross-legged round a stove, drinking butter tea and *arak*. A young woman with toddler strapped on her back made buckwheat pancakes while Karma's father talked – and Sharap translated – about tigers. People here thought tigers were bad until a passing guru explained they brought luck. They now believe they will have good crops if a tiger is around. Which is true: it will keep deer away. Karma's father had often seen tigers while cattle-herding. They killed cows but never men. People said long ago a tiger *did* kill a man. Karma's father did not believe it.

The young woman sat down and unwound the toddler. All women carried their babies on their backs: small, crop-haired women, bent nearly double, did everything with little bare feet dangling behind them. The babies never cried. Awake, they rested their heads calmly against their carrier's nape. I never saw a fretful toddler in Bhutan. I thought of my restless daughter. Before she was one she would grab a wooden snake for ballast and practise walking, hour after hour. She would have been a nightmare at that age with this stove, these ladders. *And* she woke in the night. Maybe the Bhutanese were brilliant at conservation not only because of Buddhism but because they began life in a sling.

The *arak* went round. I wondered if I could get safely down the ladders barefoot. Karma's father told old tiger tales. Donkey was the only animal Tiger was afraid of. He once plucked Tiger's hairs, stuck them between his teeth and said he ate tigers. Tiger demanded a swimming competition. 'If I win, I eat you. If you win, you eat me.' Donkey couldn't swim but a fish flopped into his mouth. He got on to the bank saying he was so hungry he had had to catch a fish. Donkey yawned, a bird flew into his mouth and he explained he was still hungry. Tiger wanted a race over ice and galloped off; Donkey just made marks on the ice with his hoof. Tiger couldn't read: Donkey said he was writing that he was so hungry he must now eat a tiger. Tiger ran away. Another time they agreed to paint each other. Donkey painted Tiger beautifully, even little stripes by his paws. That was how Tiger got his stripes. Tiger thought Donkey would never see, so he painted only one stripe down Donkey's back. He did the hoofs, which Donkey *could* see; Donkey was so delighted he brayed, which terrified Tiger. Guilty because he had skimped the rest, Tiger ran away – and has been afraid of Donkey ever since.

Arak and buckwheat, crossed legs on boards round a stove: these stories had been told, in this language, in homes like this with tigers outside, over food like this, for a thousand years.

We said goodbye, climbed down, and went to masked dances in a sleet-filled monastery yard. Masked dances have been part of Buddhist teaching here for centuries. Like everything in Bhutan, they have layers of meaning. The masks are elaborate art forms that reveal truth about morality, enlightenment, life after death. You can be delivered from cycles of suffering by seeing the dance. A tiger in such a dance represents the wild. You need to know wild animals. If you don't see them in life, you will meet and fear them more after death.

'The tiger mask teaches,' said Sharap. 'It is good luck to see a tiger. Better to see it alive than face it first in the after-life.'

But on these dancers the masks were upstaged by tall red and yellow wizard hats. We sheltered from driving ice in a doorway. Children's cheeks were chapped and red. Many dancers were barefoot and slipped in mud as they pirouetted. There were child clowns in grotesque masks, bashing tambourines. I was relieved to see them showing off, taking advantage of their masks to hit others with their staffs. Even Buddhism cannot make instant angels out of little boys.

'The dance is to drive away demons,' whispered Sharap. Other rangers from the conservation office had exchanged green uniforms for *ghos*. Their little sons, also in *ghos*, stood holding their hands. Mud and sleet were normal. This was an auspicious day. The *ghos* did it honour.

We drove back to Bumthang, stopped for a puncture and called on a princess. Kunzang Choden, born there in 1952, was related to one of the previous king's wives. She was also a writer. She collected folk tales she had heard as a child, when Bhutan was beginning to shed its isolation from the world, and pioneered interest in folk tradition just at the time it might have been lost with modernization. I had two of her books, tales of animals and yetis.

'Hope she hasn't got a dog,' said Sharap, as we entered the garden. I stared. We had been knee-deep in dogs wherever we went. But he was right: guardians are different from strays. A gigantic mastiff, shaggy and vexed, came rapidly over the lawn. I got to the front door; Sharap stepped back. The mastiff's teeth met in his jacket.

'Don't step back,' said the princess, too late. 'He won't hurt you.' Small, graceful, apple-cheeked, she rescued Sharap, took us in, gave us tea. Another dog, small, white and woolly, profoundly interested in biscuits, lay under the table. The watcher at the gate was a tiger; here was the more privileged snow lion.

I told her a Frog and Tiger story in her book was exactly like the Ura

Donkey story, except that Frog stuck tiger hairs in his arse not his teeth.

'Different valleys say different things. It was a frog where I grew up. But we always spoke of tigers with respect. We said "Big Animal", not to say its real name. Mostly we called it "Parent".'

We were on the road at five next day. Radio began at seven. There was only one station: it opened with trumpets, the national anthem and prayers to the Tantric goddess. Sharap joined in as he drove. Then there was talk in Dzongkha. Bhutan does not often have programmes in English. We were going south, there would soon be some in Hindi. Was this news? What was happening in Iraq? No – this was the astrology report for the day. It was not an auspicious day to move house or saddle a mule, but a good one to get your hair cut.

'Do you think the mule thing means *any* travel?' We pretended to forget the new tyre. We did not trust it. There would no *Kuensel*, Bhutan's only newspaper, till Saturday.

As we went down it grew warmer, not because the mountains were lower but because the valleys were deeper in the Himalayas' descent to the Bay of Bengal. We were moving into a climate familiar from India: ferns, white lily trumpets, the kind grown indoors in England; hoopoes, scarlet minivets, and my favourite black drongos. Softer, tanglier, lusher with every mile. We were at the top of the Mangde river valley: the river runs over the border to Assam and is the only place in the world inhabited by golden langurs. We saw them in a flowering tree, three thousand metres above a gorge. Shimmering monkeys, milky-ginger and tangerine, eating buds like a god eating lotus. The babies were bitter-orange dolls, clinging to mother. All had a black face-mask with tufts like feathery ears, orange button eyes, and a gold-silk bell-pull tail. They became known to science only in the twentieth century. Unconcerned about their rarity, they hung upside-down over the abyss nibbling buds like children eating sweetcorn.

We were heading for Zhemgang district, a village called Tintibi where Sharap had been warden; where he had met his wife. Zhemgang was absorbed into Bhutan in the seventeenth century, but only administered by a *dzong* in 1963. Its inhabitants, the Kheng, are supposed to be the original Bhutanese. Across the border in Assam the Bodo Liberation Tigers, wanting independence from India, hide in Bhutan's

southern jungle, Royal Manas Park, whose terrain is like Chitwan –
elephants, grassland, tigers – but closed to foreigners. The year before,
the Tigers had blown up a green Bhutanese forest lorry. Indian police
lorries are also green. Three rangers survived out of ten. Sharap would
have been on it if he had not changed jobs.

There were always cows on the verge, looking for food. Young
calves, unused to vehicles, skittered headlong nearly over the
precipice. In Incholin village, a chicken clucked round the car. Sharap
had driven for six hours. He eased on gently. I watched a little boy carrying a puppy, a crow hopping under slow-moving cows; it had
spotted a tick in a cow's elbow. Suddenly there was a squawk. Sharap
negotiated the next sharp rut, got out and looked.

'I killed the chicken,' he said. This was a sin. I knew he was upset.

'Think how many dogs, cows and chickens you *haven't* killed that
wouldn't get out of the way! You're a hero.'

He had darted a leopard here once, in the ground floor of a house
where chickens were kept. They had barricaded the doors so it couldn't
get out. Sharap tranquillized him, drove forty kilometres, laid him under
a bush, waited four hours and left. He was afraid he had overestimated
the dose. But when he came back the leopard had woken and gone.

'He had ticks all over him, even his tail. I pulled them out.'

At a village with a phone, we stopped to call ahead to Tintibi. I
tried to stretch my legs and found I couldn't. The rhododendron forest
had left my thighs screaming. The guidebook said trekking in Bhutan
strains the quadriceps muscle at the front of the thighs. At least I knew
which bit was agony.

Sharap could not get through: the Tintibi phone used solar energy
and there was no sun. We went two thousand metres down through
cloud and pouring rain: a narrow track, crumbling, slipping, anxious.
A lorry had gone over the cliff outside Trongsa the night before. We
gave a lift to an old man from a village called Ta Ma, Mother Tiger,
who remembered wild elephants there when he was eight. The elephants were no more, but tigers still visited. Sharap's friend had seen
a tiger recently on this road, crossing at four in the morning.

'In 2000 we saw pugmarks here. Villagers said there were two
tigers, probably a mother and cub. One cow was killed, another
injured.'

This happens when a tigress is teaching a cub to kill. Not good for the cow, but cubs must learn. The instinct is there, but killing is a technique that must be taught.

I stared at the twilit road. A black leopard had often been seen around here. A bat zigzagged in front of us in the beam; a drenched mouse rushed across. If we did see a leopard, it would be a very wet one.

Sharap's brother-in-law was caretaker of the Tintibi electric plant: I could stay at its guest-house. We waited for the gatekeeper by an arch painted with Bhutanese florettes. The pillar bases were striped orange, yellow and black. Tigers were everywhere, from village names to power-plant gates. I slept there alone and woke to the croak of a hornbill. A guard was walking round the building swinging incense, chanting. Even power plants need divine protection. On the terrace outside were red lilies – and suddenly, completely clear skies. I could see the mountains at last. There were banana leaves and jungle all round.

Wonderful. Surely tigers liked it better here too? Chuck had found tigers breeding at 3000 metres, tracks at 4000. People have seen tracks on a Tibetan pass at 5000 metres, 16,500 feet. But those tigers would not stay there in winter; they would follow prey below the snow line. Tigers vary from place to place. But I bet that if they knew about this warmth and lushness, they would come. Alpine ranges are marginal habitat for tigers, with sparse, spread-out prey. Further south still, in Manas, there were fewer villagers, more prey, denser forest and more tigers. But also more poachers, who take advantage of political unrest. Maybe the alpine tigers were better off where they were.

The hornbill croaked again from a tall tree. A sound like tearing silk: two hornbills landed together, tipping up vast yellow beaks like children pretending to be haughty. They would never get away quietly from a hunter.

Tsaung, Sharap's successor down here, had an oval, haggard face and spiky hair. He had survived the Tigers' bomb. We walked along the river under blue glass sky. Cormorants dotted rocks in little rapids; a serpent eagle soared over bare cliffs frequented by goral, another goat-antelope. The forest was an aviary of gentian blue flycatchers, bulbuls, chestnut mynah birds. Once Sharap had found tiger scat on this path. But Tsaung had seen a black leopard there two days before so tigers were unlikely today; leopards keep clear of tigers. He said the nearest recent tiger signs were two days' walk away in mountains.

Pied hornbills clattered and croaked; so did a dark red hornbill, the rufous, which lives only there.

'We say "Don't be a hornbill," to a husband who does everything his wife says,' said Sharap. Female hornbills are cemented into a hole in a tree to incubate the eggs. The males pass food to them.

'We say "henpecked". I suppose a female hornbill can't peck, walled into a tree.'

Crossing a stile we met women with baskets on their backs. Sharap and Tsaung peered into the baskets. The women met no one's eyes. Nobody spoke. They were allowed to collect fallen wood but there were things they were not supposed to take. As we went on up, Tsaung made a long speech in Dzongkha, throwing his hands about. His voice echoed through trees: no chance of black leopards now.

'He's having a bad time with these villagers. He's from north Bhutan, this language is difficult; they resent him saying not to use the forest.'

Conservation needs diplomacy as well as science. Sharap had learned this language, married into it. Tsaung was awkwardly placed, and upset by the bomb.

'It looks calm now,' said Sharap, staring at the river's lazy gold. 'I used to swim here. But once I had to cross it after the monsoon because poachers were gathering caterpillar fungus, which is very valuable, on the other side. I was nearly swept away.'

We crossed a fallow field full of tall weeds – no, wait . . .

'Yes. Cannabis. It grows wild everywhere here.'

'My daughter's friends would pay the earth for this in London. Do they smoke it?'

Sharap looked horrified. 'Isn't that very bad for your *mind*? They give it to pigs, it makes them sleepy. Pigs are aggressive and this makes them easier to deal with.'

'In Britain it goes to teenagers. Don't they boil it with milk, like they do in India?'

'No. Our villagers are very innocent. It's a sin to offer someone something that will harm them.'

'We want to do eco-tourism here,' said Tsaung. 'The government is relaxing rules for foreigners. We want to open this trail to them.'

There was cannabis as far as I could see. Dealing with the contaminating West, Bhutan had chosen the opposite path from Nepal. No wonder Hishey worried that increasing contact would harm their children.

When Sharap worked here, he had constant trouble with this village. 'I once caught them fishing on an auspicious day, when fines are double. They denied they had fish, but I got them to show me the pool where they'd hidden them. I put the fish back, made them sign something saying they wouldn't do it again, and let them go with a caution. It's *very* hard to fine poor people. We set up a fish farm but they still used the river because people pay more for river fish. When I left, I was so happy not to have to deal with this village again.'

We drank mineral water in the shade of a pepper tree.

'We have two peppers, a tall one and a shrub. This tall one is *very* hot.'

If he said it was hot, it was. I could not eat the chillies he ate at every meal. A brown bird sang in it, a firebird, which seemed right for a pepper tree. Sharap dropped the plastic bottle on the ground for the villagers to find and fill with oil. Then we set off for the paper factory called Tagma, Mother Tiger. She was painted over the lintel among green *Sound of Music* mountains, with her cub.

Paper-making is one of thirteen arts, including bamboo work, weaving and iron-casting, set up by the treasure-discoverer Pema Lingpa. All have strict traditional rules of pattern and technique. The point is detail, reverence and tradition, not self-expression. This tiny shed of four people, power-house for an ancient art, was courted by some of Japan's most famous paper houses. Sharap showed me gluey vats and explained how they made paper from daphne bushes in the forest. But unless it is harvested carefully, this too threatens the forest.

'People are greedy. Japan has used all its own daphne. A Japanese firm in Thimphu uses a machine. Here they do it by hand, one of the last places in the world. But we have to watch how much they harvest.'

Every night we went for a drive to Ta Ma on roads where people often saw leopards and occasionally tigers. The last night we turned back after an hour. There, trotting along the verge, was a little leopard cat! She skipped sideways and over the edge into the forest. We crept to the place where she had vanished. All was still: forest, black sky, stars. Frogs trilled, a nightjar called, rainwater ran down a gully. We peered over. There she was, four feet below, wet leaves round her soft tail. My torchlight caught the black freckling on the pointed blond face looking up, afraid; a look I had seen in photos of leopard cats at Bangkok's infamous wildlife market. There are various sub-species, all endangered, all hunted for their skins.

'I think she's pregnant. Moving slowly. Usually they run away fast.' She disappeared into undertangle. 'Now we're lucky, maybe we see the big one. The spots are the same. This is where they see the black panther.'

We hoped round every dark bend. But Bagheera was hunting elsewhere.

Back in Thimphu, American eco-tourism experts, who had worked out with Karma a scheme to let in ten thousand more tourists a year and open new treks, were putting their joint proposal to the government that day.

'We'll bring good things but also bad,' said one, who loved Bhutan. 'Eco-tourism's the only way to balance conservation and expansion. But it's got to be done well.'

'It must have been exciting,' said the other to me, kindly, 'seeing red panda droppings. What did they look like?'

'Like a small dog,' I said. 'Same bore.'

The civil-service area was criss-crossed with one-storey pagoda-like offices. The people caring for Bhutan at its moment of change walked through grass corridors between: men in *ghos* with snowy cuffs, women in silk jackets of magenta and indigo. Sharap's office had maps of different categories of forest: Already Lost. Renewable. Proposed Core Area. Evidence of Less Important Wildlife. Key Evidence of Wildlife. Degraded Habitat. Next door were Data Management, Administration, Accounts. After mapping your reserve, you must pay for it. Everything comes down to accounts in the end.

All for 150 tigers. But protecting them means protecting not only the forest but this country's traditional way of life. I had seen how the tiger was knitted into people's minds. Sharap worked for the social-forestry section of the forest service. That 'social' was crucial. As Karma said, Bhutan learned from its neighbours' mistakes and was making people in forests integral to their conservation. You cannot save wild tigers if you do not respect people's as well as tigers' needs. This was why the divide in India between human and animal rights, which my brother and I had argued about in Bangladesh, was so sad.

Sharap's boss, Dr Sangay Wangchuck, a big man in a red tartan *gho*, said, like Hishey, that this generation of civil servants grew up in villages. 'So we understand their problems. But the tiger is a non-negotiable species. We have committed to protect it, and we will. We have legislation.'

'Our position here is different from that in other countries,' said the WWF officer, Chadho Tensin, over a WWF mug of Nescafé. The WWF funds more than the compensation scheme. In Thrumshingla they do anti-poaching training, fund fish farms and orchards to make villagers less dependent on forest produce; fund guard posts, watchtowers, waterholes, houses for park workers, road patrols. Every jeep, every patrol motorbike. The WWF did not work here as an NGO; Bhutan had not yet passed an NGO bill. They were donors and advisers, but their work was easier here because the government was so keen on conservation. Elsewhere WWF has to lobby governments constantly, and conservation policy shifts when governments change.

The WWF's strength, he said, was its network. If they thought a policy was in the interests of a particular country, they made a financial commitment and other donors followed. Here, they had said, 'Why not have different parks, representing your different eco-systems?' Hence the protected areas I had seen. They suggested corridors, the government implemented them.

'Once this government sees a policy is useful it says, "OK, show us how, give us money." We got those corridors for forty thousand dollars. In other countries we'd have had to reconstitute. Here we had forests already.'

I was bothered about prey. These tigers depended on livestock. We had seen wild prey droppings but not many. Bhutan has not yet estimated its prey. Chadho Tensin, to my disappointment, saw compensation for dead cows as a short-term strategy till they 'thought of something better'. (What? So much has been tried elsewhere, and has failed.) I could not imagine anything more likely to put people against tigers than a farmer losing cows and not getting anything back. By now I felt strongly that if the rich world wants wild tigers to exist, the least it can do is pay for animals tigers take from the poor. But the idea here was to encourage fewer, more productive cows. Instead of compensation, which might make villagers keep more cows, the policy was to subsidize better cows and seed for better cow fodder. They had to tread carefully. Because of the religion they cannot order a cull of useless cows. And at Thrumshingla over sixty per cent of the land belonged in those traditional grazing rights. A villager who does not use his rents it out. Grazing rights are an important source of income.

Still, the tiger programme was new, the government was feeling its way and religion helped. Tigers in temples, tigers bringing luck. Parent Tiger.

'The present king began as a teenager. People wanted us to catch up with our neighbours. *He* saw that our strength is in our nature, culture and religion, not our military or economic potential. The question is how to relate everything, culture, environment, conservation, to the people's needs.'

'I bring my mother here every year,' said Sharap, in Thimphu's Institute of Indigenous Medicine, a hospital of traditional healing. 'She has a bad leg. They always make her better.'

In a courtyard of low, painted buildings a doctor with a white coat over his *gho* popped out of a door and handed a woman a prescription. I thought of my local hospital. Eight hours on plastic chairs, grimy walls, overworked nurses. Here, patients waited in a garden beside eight-foot prayer wheels. When you turned a prayer wheel its bell rang: gold hieroglyphic prayers went out into the world to work on your behalf. The courtyard was gently full of bell-tones. There were modern wheelchairs, but otherwise everything was ancient, calm, light. A hot herb smell surged from the steam bath. Hippocrates' surgery might have felt like this.

'The authorities here asked us for tiger bone. I got a letter yesterday.'

'What for?'

'I rang the man. He wanted it as a reference so he'd know if anyone brought something fraudulent, like dog bone.'

In the hospital museum, everything was labelled in English and Dzongkha. Wall charts of the nervous system, plants with Latin names. Precious substances used in treatment included Chinese ink, pearl, oyster shells, camphor. Also bear gall.

'That shouldn't be here,' I said. Poaching bears for gall is one of the worst wildlife crimes. Wild animal parts belong in the traditional medicine of Bhutan, too. Blood from a takin's heart maintains good memory. Its horn gives 'heat' to the body and helps women giving birth. In a glass case I saw on the bottom shelf a large round bone like a skull without eyes. 'What's that?' A piece of pelvis from a big animal. Unlike other items, it was labelled only in Dzongkha. Sharap knelt beside me. 'Tag.'

We looked at each other.

'So they *have* got some.'

The custodian said the medical department asked her for it recently.

I thought that request was dodgy. They might have had legitimate reasons – but why worry if people bring him dog bones calling them tiger unless they *know* he buys tiger?

'These shouldn't be on display, or be here at all. Not tiger bone or bear gall. They *must* be using it. It is against CITES, which Bhutan has signed. How *dare* they approach you for it?' I felt incredibly upset.

Sharap looked worried. He thought they must have got them from the police. Even in gentle, Buddhist, self-scrutinizing Bhutan, firing on all conservationist cylinders, respecting the tiger as protector of Buddhism, bringer of Buddhism, as Mother, as Parent, even here I seemed to have come up against the substance which is threatening wild tigers more than anything except logging.

It will always be a struggle. In the wild, between tigers and villagers, poachers and wardens. In cities, between people making a lot of money from wild animals and people trying to protect them. In very poor people, deeply and innocently religious (I remembered the cannabis), for whom it is sin to take life, the battle is between conscience, reverence and sudden economic chance. In every conservationist, living uncomfortably alone in remote places, it is between despair and day-to-day hope.

'It takes two hours,' said Sharap. In a plastic bag he had a butter lamp, a pious offering. We looked up between oak and pine at yellow roofs twinkling on a crag against burning blue sky: Taktseng monastery. Tiger's Nest, where the tigress and Guru Rinpoche landed. One of Buddhism's holiest sites, 2600 metres above sea-level. In 1998 it burned down. It was twelve hundred years old. Rocks crashed round charred timbers. The caretaker was never found. Rebuilding began in 2000 with funds from Japan, America, everywhere that cares for Buddhism. Now it was nearly finished. Elderly Japanese were being helped on to mules with no bridles. We were going to walk up the mountain.

Again the feeling that your lungs stretch from collarbone to crotch, or if they don't they should. That your heart is the knocking heard by the porter in *Macbeth*. Sometimes we had to stand back to let mules trot down, picking a path on neat hoofs over pointed rocks, tree roots, boulders. Some saddles had faded pink cloths embroidered with a snow lion. The joyous heart, making its way to the snows.

Leopard scat. It had dined on pony, wild boar and chillies apparently. This was partly forest, partly open path with sun beating down. We took a perpendicular short-cut and had to turn down, defeated by tangle, losing height we had sweated to gain. Among oak and pine were tall flaky rhododendrons. Sharap picked a chunk of pink bark. 'When we consecrate a building, we do a big *puja* to keep away demons. People dance with masks, and ignite their torches with this. We crumble it and throw it on flames to make the fire bloom.'

He tossed a leaf on to a wayside cairn covered with flowers: prayers for getting safely to the top. Buddhism's image of the Way evolved in high altitudes. The steep track, remoteness, effort.

A shrine on a ledge: Sharap turned the prayer wheel. The bell rang over cliff and green peaks beyond. What prayer should I ask it to take into the wind? Suddenly an old woman spoke from the ground like the guardian of an oracle. She was sitting against a rock covered with scarlet splashes of betel juice. Singay was angry, she said. Every monastery had a local deity who helped humans in life. The monastery had burned because Singay, god of this valley who rode a snow lion, was angry.

Further up there were mossy, twisted trees, and on every branch the green-bronze mop-head of fern orchids. Up further, at the cliff edge, was a guard. We were on the same level now as Taktseng. We could see it over a chasm. There was a rope bridge. But I was a foreigner: I needed a permit, only available in Thimphu. Sharap was worried. I said I would wait for him here. 'It's the most beautiful place in the world. Say a prayer for me.'

I sat with my legs over the cliff edge. Workmen were restoring the last bit of Tiger's Nest. The roof was on, but mostly unpainted. The sky was blue silk. Pine trees clung to thin soil, cables groaned over my head, carrying building materials, clouds threw shadows on fir slopes below. A Bhutanese pilgrim let out a Dzongkha yodel. Cliffs flung back the echoes. There was fierce wind, but workmen walked on that roof painting it gold. No one but a mountain goat or a prophet would have built a temple here. It was enormous but looked, on that precipice, so small. The white foundations seemed to melt into the rocks they impossibly stood on. In this land of hidden meaning, it was a symbol of human determination – to find a hold in nature at its ruggedest, raise human nature high as it can go. You go up to your goal but sometimes, on the way, you lose the elevation you struggled for, and go on up again. If a sacred place burns, you rebuild it.

Watching the rebuilding, I remembered the Italian architect Renzo Piano talking of what happens when things go wrong with a design. You need what he called the lucidity to see where it went wrong. If you are blocked, you stay in the dark.

'Sometimes,' he said, 'you must accept to suffer. Gradually you see through the dark to the right solution.'

I started on this road because a light went out. The opposite of the Buddhist goal enlightenment. From St Lucy to lucidity. I too needed that, to get through this dark despising of someone I had loved. That should be my prayer. Not to give in to despair: either about tiger bone, or about the nature of someone I had been close to. Let the contempt I did not want to feel blow away in Singay's racing wind, chased by his radiant snow lion. Pray, through Sharap's butter flame, to leave contempt behind.

There went Sharap with his plastic bag, pulling up the top part of his *gho* to be formal. Snow-white cuffs over the swaying bridge, the chasm. He turned at the gate. I waved, and he waved back. Sometimes you have to trust other people to light the lamp for you.

Back in London, a low ceiling, purple walls, parquet floor. People milling. He was there. He had recovered his party habitat. The first face-to-face conversation.

'Do you like my new suit? Look at the *label.*'

He flashed stitching on the cuff, a shiny gold lining. He mentioned a new novel, not yet out, which he had read and expected me not to have. The note was one-upmanship. I had reviewed that book, but didn't say so. I felt bombarded with a savage competitiveness. I had forgotten it. Or maybe it had never come into play like this with me.

It was very noisy. We had to stand close. He had to bend to hear.

'This reminds me of other situations we've been in. Your black hair, tickling my cheek . . .'

I was listening to a stranger. Or he was talking to someone else.

My hair is brown. Always was. He had known it for years. I had forgotten how captive he was to fantasy: it swept everything away, even reality standing beside him. He had lived so long in my heart and never known me. Or had changed me into someone very different.

I remembered how aggrieved he used to feel when women asked him to do things he had promised to do. Prized assistants, secretaries, relations. When they complained that he had let them down, they suddenly became frightening, as if his own guilt came beaming back at him, as the Furies. The turnaround was oddly sudden and savage. Now he had done the same to me. Nothing like feeling guilty towards someone for turning you against them. Why hadn't I foreseen that?

According to Jim Corbett, a hunter on foot has only one advantage over a man-eating tiger: tigers do not know that we have no sense of smell, so they treat people as they treat wild prey, approaching upwind or lying in wait downwind. Your strength lies in knowing he doesn't know there is something you cannot do.

Well, we both felt vulnerable. He attacked because he felt on the defensive. There was no hunter or victim. My advantage, if I had to have one, was that now I knew he could no longer see me as I was.

Still, he liked to see himself respecting the rules a chap should play by. That was how he had learned to be English. How to treat waiters, the boss, the beloved of the moment. Surely a chap also answers letters from someone he had loved. Why hadn't he?

'It was a ghastly idea, meeting for lunch as if to bury it.'

I was silent.

'I couldn't. It was too sad.'

Still silent.

'I didn't want to collude with you.'

Never mind being Greek: he knew what *collude* meant. But he always did use words for how they sounded.

That night I dreamed my beloved dog Jenny was still alive, sitting beside me on a train. I had my arm round her. We went into a tunnel; when we came out she was gone. In her place was a skunk. We got off the train. I sat in a meadow, looking at him. He was OK as skunks go, flashy black and white, grubbing in long grass for insects. But he was, indisputably, a skunk.

I was supposed to have stopped despising him. My psyche had not caught up with Tiger's Nest.

PART II

EAST

Russia, Korea, China

Amur (or Siberian) and South China Tigers

10

CLAWMARKS AND PAWMARKS AT
THE ANTLER VELVET FARM

'Sikhachi Alyan means Boar Shape Hill. Boris and I *love* the Nanaian settlement there.' Irena, in red headscarf patterned with white hearts, a breezy twenty-five-year-old working for an American company in Moscow, was back home in the east for the summer to marry Boris, who was driving us north from Khabarovsk through a green and purple plain to one of the oldest representations of tigers in the world, the petroglyphs of Sikhachi Alyan. Nikolai came with us: director of the Museum for Indigenous Cultures of the Amur, all black eyebrows and tense hazel eyes. The forest closed in. The world's seventh-longest river glittered behind.

The Amur is an innocent river compared to the Kolyma, but its banks hold the bones of millions murdered by Stalin. Two hundred kilometres north was Komsomolsk-on-Amur, Stalin's City of the Dawn. In 1932, idealists had barely started building it when it became a labour camp. A hundred thousand prisoners died there, then thousands of Japanese prisoners-of-war. The even worse gulags were a thousand kilometres north in Kolyma, where winter temperatures are twice as cold, and where the poet Mandelstam was being taken when he died in a transit camp outside Vladivostock.

The Amur bounds the largest continuous area where wild tigers live. It has given the world's largest tiger the name most tiger experts use: Amur tiger. The popular Western name is 'Siberian'. But this area is hardly Siberia: it is the Russian Far East. Below Khabarovsk, the Amur meets the Ussuri. I was in Ussuriland. Locals say Amursky or

Ussuri tiger. When it crosses the Amur, it is the North-East Chinese tiger. The last count, winter 1995–6, estimated 330–70 adult tigers here, and a hundred young. In the 1930s they were nearly extinct. But the war that devastated Russia saved its tigers. Men died at the front; with no guns at home (and no men capturing cubs) tigers and deer increased. In 1947 Russia became the first country to ban tiger shooting. The numbers rose, and bounded up again after 1954, when laws controlled the capture of cubs. But the tigers had been through a genetic bottleneck, which can make for low reproduction and survival rates and vulnerability to disease, so there is little variation between them.

They live on a completely different scale from subcontinental tigers. Russia is the opposite of the subcontinent. In India, reserves are islands; here, forest is continuous. In Nepal, a tigress might hold twenty square kilometres; here she has five hundred. Only eight or ten per cent of tigers live in the *zapovedniks*, reserves, but they are the key to conserving all tigers, the core and back-up for tigers outside. Tigers reproduce more successfully inside but even inside, half are poached. Outside, no one knows; it is probably over seventy per cent. The tiger population is fairly stable, but hunting, trapping, fur and meat are vital to the rural economy. Everywhere, except the reserves, is open to hunting. It is illegal to shoot tigers but not deer, so tigers lose out. And with the economic desperation, the temptation to sell tiger bones to Chinese dealers is strong.

There are tiger rehabilitation centres here for cubs whose mothers have been shot, and for tigers found mutilated. One centre replaced a tigress's broken tooth with gold. Irena said Ussuriland is proud of its tigers. 'Bengal tigers fear elephants. *Ours* are afraid of nothing!'

Nikolai led us, through grasses fizzing with dragonflies and purple hornets, to a tin speedboat on a swollen, willow-hung river, wide as the Mississippi. Here, in the eleventh century BC, a hundred and fifty petroglyphs were incised, over five kilometres, on massive boulders. Tigers appear on five-thousand-year-old seals made in the Indus Valley: these petroglyphs are not as old as that. But they are very, very ancient and mysterious.

We stopped at a tumble of smooth grey boulders and scrambled up to an incised human face: a staring mask with whirling eyes. Then earlier carvings, an upside-down deer, whorls on shoulders and hips, a horse whose belly carried a backwards swastika. The river had shaped the boulders, but incising them with stone tools must have been hard work. The spirals were perfect. Nikolai splashed the carvings to darken them, and talked passionately about their symbolism. He thought the swastika and whorls represented the sun; that the people who made these were sun-worshippers.

The tiger petroglyph was the last of a skirt of rocks engraved with little labyrinths, but the river was too high, and this tiger, like so many, was not to be seen. I jumped to the furthest rock. Twigs whirlpooled round the hidden boulder, waves whipped over it as they had over a tiger engraved here before the Russian language was formed. But I had missed it – unless I dived. Irena let me off. 'Is photo in museum.'

Russia colonized Ussuriland, the wild east, while America colonized its wild west. A satellite photo from the 1860s would have shown two streams of people trekking across the globe towards each other on different continents, displacing native inhabitants. Here, too, there had been a gold rush. But this was bitter-cold forest, and its real wealth was 'soft gold'. Animal furs. Not tigers: the new Russians made money from furs in large numbers, sable, bear, squirrel. The indigenous tribes, whose descendants now lived in little settlements like these, never killed tigers. These Nanaians were linked with north China and Manchuria.

The great celebrator of this area was the Russian naturalist and writer Vladimir Arsenev. He wrote up his expeditions in the best-selling books on which Kurosawa based his film *Dersu Uzala*. His hero, the native tracker Dersu, piloted Arsenev through the *taiga*. Chinese ginseng seekers, trappers and dealers had bound native settlements in a spiral of debt, poverty and opium; there were hundreds of pits of dying deer. Even in 1902 they thought wildlife would be gone in ten years: 'In their own country the Chinese have long exterminated almost every living thing. The Pri-Amur country, so rich in forest and wildlife, waits the same fate.'

Nikolai showed us modern Nanaian houses, heated by hot air blown under benches that ran round the walls. In winter, this lush terrain was a snowscape. Dog sleds stood by the woodpile. Were they very big dogs? Nikolai answered impatiently.

'Big, is not important,' translated Irena. 'Strong, is important.'

The central building had a carving of the mythical Fish-Dog, which shows Nanaian hunters where to fish. Fish was everything here: Boris had caught some, a Nanaian woman was making soup. Fish from the Amur! I was still amazed I was here.

Nikolai spoke of Tigrovy Dom, Tiger House, the most northerly point tigers go. Where, he said, they went to mate. I had heard beliefs like this before, like the island in Korea where tigers went to give birth; as if tigers, like people, had special places for special events. No tiger lived in Tigrovy Dom, but the tribes there worshipped the tiger. 'They call it Amba.'

That was what Dersu called it too: Amba, guardian of the forest. It was bad luck to see him but, like the tiger god in the Sundarbans with honey in his gift, he protected this forest's most valuable product: ginseng.

Arsenev had first met the tiger in a prayer, in the hut of a Chinese ginseng-hunter. 'To Lord Tiger who dwells in Forest and Mountains. He saved the state in ancient days. His Spirit brings happiness to man.' Arsenev nearly met the real thing in dense rainy forest when, going back for a lost pipe, he saw pugmarks with no rain yet in them, superimposed on his footsteps. The tiger had followed, listened, jumped off the path. It was terribly close. Arsenev was terrified; Dersu asked Amba loudly why he was following. The *taiga*, the dense Russian forest, had room for them all. Later, hunting deer, they heard a growl like a crack of thunder. To Arsenev's astonishment Dersu stood up unarmed like a courtier greeting his king. He apologized, begged Amba not to be angry, said they would leave now they knew this place was his. Russian Arsenev watched in awe as Dersu dropped to his knees and prayed, then strode away, saying Amba would not attack. If Arsenev tried to shoot Amba he would disown him. As Valmik had said, traditional reverence protected the tiger. But that was in 1902.

Nikolai's museum had a photo of the tiger petroglyph, a stripy beast with a pointed nose, upsettingly like a bandicoot; and relics of native cultures like Dersu's. Fish-skin clothes, tiger faces in red cloth ('The wisdom of centuries discovered that design,' said Nikolai), and shaman artefacts, for this was shamanism's ancient home. There were shaman headdresses and dachshund-shaped wooden tigers, for the spirit that entered a shaman came on the back of a winged tiger: Jaga, sea-god, most terrifying tiger in the world, who flew like a bird and swam like a fish. One had a lizard carved along his spine, another had detachable stripy wings, snakes along his cheeks, a human head at the end of his tail. Another had spots like black bubbles on his body, and a striped snarly face.

Two cities administer the Amur tigers' homeland: Khabarovsk, capital of Khabarovsky Kraij (pronounced *cry*), and Vladivostock, twelve hours' drive south, capital of Primorye, the maritime region. Khabarovsk, so vital for the world's tigers, began as a fur-trade garrison. Its coat of arms is a tiger and bear shaking hands. An international tiger conference was to be held there the next month. On the surface, there was restoration everywhere. Tree-lined boulevards, tall buildings repainted, a blue and white church, onion domes (one, stripped to be remade, showed sky through its ribbony skeleton), a lake studded with swan boats, and a park full of beer tents where people made ice sculptures in winter. China was a few miles west, Japan a few hundred east, but mostly this city looked like Budapest or Prague: handsome frontages, nineteenth-century colonial statements in an Oriental land. There were fitness centres, pedigree dogs, shops selling Gucci, sushi restaurants. The Japanese, four-fifths of Khabarovsk's tourists, own most of the big hotels. But the cross-streets were unlit and muddy: small dilapidated wood houses, peeling apartment blocks. I watched an elderly man bend to a pump and step back to swill clothes in a bucket while a girl with a baby stepped forward. Others waited behind. That pump was all the water there was for the block, and only available at this hour. Most faces looked at me stonily, though older ones broke into sweet smiles when I asked for the railway station.

I looked into the darkening plain. Fifty kilometres south lay the Khor river. Legends say two birds flying north and south collided here and dropped the seeds they were carrying, which is why this area has unique botany: northern and southern forest meet and merge. As tiger and bear shake hands on Khabarovsk's arms, so temperate rainforest mingles with pine and birch; lianas trail over walnut. I was taking the overnight train to Vladivostock, end of the Trans-Siberian Railway but the beginning of my journey back south – which would end, like that of the original tigers, in Java. No water, not even in lavatories. I longed for an Indian train. When I began, India was daunting. From here it felt like home.

Before I left London we had our first lunch: the first time we had been alone since St Lucy's Day, facing each other again over a table. This time in a tapas bar whose wood chair-backs were fret-sawn into hearts.

'I told other people we'd bust up,' he said. 'I felt dumped.'

This was so far from any truth I was embarrassed for him. I ordered red and yellow peppers. I asked what he was working on. We used to be delighted to give each other ideas. One of his charities was showing films: he was writing their programme notes for them, focusing on shots of liquid dripping down surfaces.

'I call it the semiotics of trickle.'

He used to bring round favourite films to watch with me. One ended with blood trickling down the screen. Now, to be helpful, to show interest, I mentioned that. He looked – heavens, he looked furious.

'Oh! Well, of course, I'd have got there in the end.'

A conference was coming up in another town. We'd both be there. He had changed his hotel to mine. I had no idea how he knew.

'You looked after me,' he said. 'I've never felt so looked after.'

I thought of the Gaviscon, not used by anyone now, which kept falling out of my bathroom cabinet. All I knew about Gaviscon before I met him had come from a poet with a job in a police station. The canteen had separate bowls of Gaviscon and sugar. Heartburned policemen took Gaviscon with their morning tea. I learned to keep it at home for him. Heartburn had struck him once in a borrowed flat; I drove out into the streets at two a.m. to find some. I hated him being in pain. Ending our five-year idyll for him was Gaviscon too. He was in trouble, I delivered the cure.

'We can't get back together,' he said, half asking me to say we could. In that letter he wrote after Christmas, I had seen his soul. Now he

wanted me to re-spin the magic, like the Belle Dame sans Merci of his
first Valentine.

'O what can ail thee, knight at arms?' asks Keats's poem. The knight
explains he has met someone:

> 'She found me roots of relish sweet,
>   And honey wild and manna dew,
>   And sure in language strange she said –
> "I love thee true!"'

He fell asleep in her arms and discovered, in a dream, that she was the
Belle Dame sans Merci and she had him in thrall. That poem, I realized
as I looked at food I couldn't eat, was all about men suspecting
women. What he saw in me now was his own desire that I'd *want* to
enchant him.

'Better watch out at that hotel,' he said. 'Might get drunk and
proposition you. Make you an offer you can't refuse.'

I asked a waiter to wrap up my peppers, so I could take them home.
My daughter would love them. Holding them horizontal so the oil
wouldn't spill, I said, 'You couldn't possibly.'

Now I was sharing a carriage with Roman, a young Russian businessman, and Piet, a Dutch Russianist researching Chekhov's visit to
Sakhalin Island in 1890. We drank vodka; I asked Roman about tigers,
poaching, Chinese dealers. He said people in the *taiga* had no idea of
tiger bone's value. They were very poor and got two hundred dollars
a carcass. Piet talked of Chekhov in Khabarovsk thirty years after it
was founded, sixteen before Arsenev came; Chekhov lancing a child's
abscess, recording indigenous tribes. Suddenly Piet slapped his own
hip.

'My money belt! I left it in the *toilette*! Credit card, passport, everything! Five hundred dollars.'

He rushed out to find the conductress. After thirty minutes he came
back. 'The thief agreed to give me my documents, if *she* kept the
money.'

Roman said nothing. I looked at the conductress, at people outside.

The faces were blank, a Hitchcock cast of shut expressions, refusing shared humanity, watching what we would do as if watching spiders trapped in a basin. The conductress in the next carriage knew the thief but would not tell Piet her name, just pushed him in to negotiate. The woman waved his money in his face, saying, 'I'll keep this,' and asked how much his documents were worth. She said other people might have thrown them away.

'That's true.' Piet was a fair man. Then he yelped again. His air ticket to Amsterdam! I said I'd go back with him, pretend I was a journalist. The thief was in her thirties: black Adidas tracksuit, loose, dyed-blonde hair. Piet talked Russian, I took notes, people listened in the corridor. She said she hadn't got it. She flicked his dollars in his face and replaced them in her pocket. Big, is not important. Strong, is important. What hope had tigers against economic despair?

Back in our cabin Piet absently put his hand in his pocket and brought out his ticket. The blonde walked past, tossing Russian over her shoulder.

'She said had I found my ticket?' said Piet, even more surprised.

I poured us all vodka. We had angered them by showing we had money they did not. We were stupid to lose it: we had rubbed their noses in injustice.

'Is people,' Roman said. 'This happened to me too, twice. In my car outside Khabarovsk at night two men burst the tyres with guns. They said give them my money and I could keep my documents.'

'Do they hate us? I feel they do.'

'They hate Japanese more. They think you are American. British, Dutch, is no matter. They think you have endless dollars. Much money is spent in Khabarovsk but the people have nothing. So yes, they hate you.'

My hotel was a Chinese casino facing the sea on Tiger Hill, where Russian colonists first saw a tiger. Gambling was forbidden in China; the Chinese came here to do it. SARS had closed the border, but now it was open, and Chinese men stood over shiny bags in the lobby, escorted by Russian redheads. I wondered how much tiger bone was in those bags. Or tiger clavicle bones, for good luck at cards.

Vladivostock, Lord of the East, built in 1860 by Chinese and Korean labourers, was the ultimate colonial city. The tiger rules supreme on its arms: no shaking hands with bears down here. In 1890 Nicholas II blessed the Trans-Siberian Railway which linked it to Moscow, confirming Russia's hold on the Far East. In living memory, this home to Russia's Pacific Fleet was one of the most secret places on the planet. The last foreign consulate left in 1948. In 1958 the city closed even to other Russians. It reopened in 1991. Today Chinatown was full of boutiques, but the new-painted arches led to broken courtyards of decaying brick. I imagined knives glinting through opium smoke in the new Byzantium of 1905, as imperial, Orthodox, maritime and secretive as the old.

From here, since 1992, the Wildlife Conservation Society has run one of the world's most important tiger-conservation programmes, combining education, anti-poaching, surveys and training with hard science; making top-level research stimulate conservation and political action. Difficult, when some people most actively involved in poaching are the police.

Russia is the only tiger country with a government-run (though foreign-funded) tiger protection team. In 1994 the Ministry of Environment created a new department, 'Inspection Tiger'. The economy had changed, people were turning to the forest for income, the frontier was open, plants and animals were vanishing illegally into China: above all, ginseng, bears, tiger bone.

'Even jellyfish! You'd never get *me* to eat them, even at gunpoint,' said Sergei Zubtsov, Inspection Tiger's head, a big fleshy man with very black hair, moustache and shirt. He was responsible for protecting tigers outside *zapovedniks*, which do their own anti-poaching: Inspection Tiger cannot enter one without its director's approval. Sergei had a team in Khabarovsk as well as Vladivostock but no funds, these days, to visit them often. He monitored wildlife smuggling and poaching, forest protection and fire-fighting (one way to get a logging licence is by setting fire to forest and applying for a permit to tidy the results), and above all the unique Conflict Team, for 'problem tigers' that attack livestock or people. He showed me earlier photos of dead tigers slumped on snow, but now they do not shoot a problem tiger: they catch it with help from specialists on the WCS team, check its health, radio-collar and relocate it far away. Only if it attacks livestock again do they kill it.

Different Russian forests are protected differently. Poorly paid guards protect state reserves; hunting societies have reserves and pay their own guards; the naval fleet pays guards for its hunting reserve. Guards live in cabins and do little except stop people looting these cabins. These organizations do not work together. It sounds a mess. It is. But the human population is not increasing, so if commercial hunting and poaching are controlled, the tigers should be safe. But poaching is constant. One Russian reserve is called Kaplanov after a Russian biologist who pioneered tiger research there, arguing for a tiger-trapping ban. Poachers killed him in 1943. Protecting tigers is dangerous. But not because of tigers.

Today's poaching groups are highly educated and organized. Policemen join them. When Sergei broke a poaching ring in 1999, one of its members was a police sub-lieutenant. Each man in an anti-poaching team has a pistol. If they know they are tackling a well-armed group they invite the militia.

'But we have to keep the law! Our constitution says the highest value is human life. We can't shoot poachers unless they threaten people. But *their* law is money! What do people in England think of Russia now? Crime. Mafias. We're in a transitional period. But we'll get on top of crime in the end.'

'On the waterfront, opposite Hocus Pocus floating casino.' Those were my directions for the Phoenix Fund, which channels international monies into the Tiger Team and runs conservation programmes of its own. It was scorchingly hot. I walked through a gold arch down broken steps to the Pacific Fleet rusting in the harbour. Phoenix's director, another Sergei, gave me Nescafé above that so-long-secret view.

One of Phoenix's main roles is co-ordination. They work with both the WCS and the government – on, for instance, anti-poaching. Anyone proved to have killed a big cat gets five years in jail. Not only tigers: Primorye has Amur leopards too. Not snow leopards, but long-furred like them, and heart-stoppingly beautiful. I had seen camera-trap photos taken in winter south of Vladivostock: a male padding along a snowy river, turning his head at the flash. Cream-ivory, silver-spotted-blue. Occasionally a large tiger, gold instead of silver, used his trail.

There are three protected territories in leopard habitat. Shooting leopards was prohibited in 1956, but poachers kill them constantly with guns or cage traps baited with live dogs. Five in 2002. Two in 2003. There are supposedly thirty left. In leopard territory Phoenix was buying up the villagers' rifles, which they were not supposed to possess. One poacher had even killed a leopard in a cage.

'We found it trapped, it was recovering, and he shot it! Did him no good. And one leopard fewer.'

Thanks to his school visits, every child in south-west Primorye knows the Amur leopard's height and weight. But the prognosis is bad: extinct within five years.

With the WCS, Phoenix helped the Tiger Team and tackled problems the other Sergei also handled: fires, wildlife smuggling. Last year they found eighteen live bear cubs heading for China. They also pay compensation for livestock killed by tigers and leopards. No arguments here about the principle: people get anything up to three hundred dollars per animal.

While Sergei was talking, a tall man in a striped T-shirt walked in. Wide shoulders, curiously pale face with wire glasses; he could have been twenty-five or forty. This was Michiel, a Dutch environmentalist who came to Vladivostock having taught himself Russian on the Trans-Siberian Railway. He set up the Tigris Foundation and now fundraised for tiger and leopard conservation, working with Phoenix, the WCS and the government. 'But they've changed the name of the ministry we work with. It was Environment. Now it's *Sustainable Use of Resources*! That says it all. Environment is now something to *use*.' He radiated impatience. 'One needs to study the *people*, that's desperately important: how tigers affect *them*. In the end, the tiger's fate depends on the people.'

Blind eyes are easily turned: important people like to go hunting.

'What you see, Ruth, is not the reality. Russia is run by big-business clans. *Everything* is controlled by mafias.'

He described a plan to put in an oil line to supply China and Japan. For Japan, it would come out in a bay, but the governor had no financial contacts in any suitable bay. Bank managers in towns that did have oil infrastructures wouldn't play ball. With no chance of making money there, the governor proposed a port town he *did* have contacts in, right next to a *zapovednik*: a spill would wreck beaches where Russians go for holidays, and the pipe-line to it would bisect leopard habitat. China has offered to meet the costs, and there is not enough oil for Japan. But the Primorye administration is still pushing for that port.

Wasn't it dangerous, what Michiel knew? Contract killings of rival-rous businessmen were currently two a month.

'I don't *think* they'd kill a foreigner. At least, not straight away. The first thing'd be my apartment bombed when I wasn't there. One bank manager ignored warnings: car bombed, family threatened, flat bombed when he was out. After that, they got him.'

But Michiel loved the Russians. 'They love nature! They go into the *taiga* constantly to walk, gather mushrooms, just enjoy it! The Chinese are afraid of it. They don't want to *enter* nature at all.'

Current hot news was conflict on a deer farm: a cat had killed four deer. If it were a tiger they could dart, examine and relocate it. A leop-ard needed validation from Moscow.

'If it's a leopard they shouldn't capture it,' said Michiel. 'They could do untold harm. They should be *glad* it's there and taking deer. Let it! Darting it might affect the whole population. There are *only thirty left*!'

There are different views on human–carnivore conflict.

A poetry reading, for a poetry circle called Grey Horse. Dimitri the translator, with a warm brown beard, worked in television. A thin bio-chemist in a charcoal T-shirt, one of their best young poets, worked on a building site. Young and old, they were passionate for poetry. This was the Russia I had hoped for, along with tigers. An elderly poet in a Hawaian shirt showed me a tiger-claw scar on his wrist.

'I was helping hunters. They said, "Hold his paws so we can tie them." I didn't know, I held the wrong way. He got me.'

'Tomorrow,' said Dimitri, 'you'll be on a food programme, *The Silver Fork*. A typical Englishwoman cooking a typical English breakfast.'

'I can't. Please tell your producer I'm very sorry. You've been wonderfully kind but I've got a date with a tiger. Or maybe a leopard. One of the last thirty Far Eastern leopards.'

*

At last I was going into the field, to leopard habitat, and tiger too, south of Vladivostock, between the sea and China. We drove round Amursky Bay through marshland cut by little channels purple with Michaelmas daisies, and dancing with grassheads. Then we ran south over a huge plain, yellow-green under grey-silver cloud. Everything white, yellow, purple, green. After two hours we came to dense oak, alder and silver birch. It began to pour. The further we drove, the more army we met. China was very close. We passed a village pond with five white geese. If a nuclear bomb fell on North Korea that would be it for the Amur leopard, as well as the children who know its measurements.

The farm lay in bare green hills. We passed a high outer gate of rusty mesh; the rain slowed to drizzle. We saw Sika deer, spotted like *chital*. Interlocking enclosures curved round them up the slope.

There are many deer farms and they need a lot of territory. Their purpose is antler velvet for Asian medicine. Farmers get five hundred dollars a pair. They cut the antlers when the stags are still in velvet, which must be very gory: all those little veins. Venison is a by-product, but it draws tigers and leopards like a magnet.

Three tall, bare-chested men stood round a jeep, tinkering with the engine, making tea: the Conflict Tiger team. With them was John Goodrich, tanned, barefoot, tall: field director of the WCS Siberian Tiger Project.

'Nothing's happening. We're delighted to see you. A tiger killed those deer, but a leopard's been round too. It scratched a tree climbing the fence. That's how leopards get in. Tigers usually crash over, but this one scrabbled under the wire. The leopard decamped when it arrived.'

The hills held trees, long grass, bushes. The tiger might be watching now. Higher up, the leopard might be watching the tiger watch us.

'The tiger killed three deer in one week. Unusual, but it didn't finish the meal each time and came back for more. We've set snares but I think we've scared it off. We're camping where it killed two deer.'

We walked up the hill past untidy sheds and broken walls. Crows were everywhere, black against green. In head-high grass outside the perimeter, mosquitoes began. A large bite came up on my hand. Everything was buzzing, feathery, hot. How about snakes?

'Two non-poisonous, two pit vipers. One isn't aggressive, one is, quite. You see them all the time. A woman scientist I know was bitten doing field research. Bitten on her bottom while peeing at night. She was pretty sore for two days, but OK.'

Antler velvet is supposed to help arthritis and improve sporting performance. Horn? A whole industry based on symbolism?

'Well, the ever-richer Asian market doesn't care. But it can't support all these farms. The Soviets subsidized them; now they're struggling. This guy says he'll go under in five years. He has fourteen workers, his vehicle is pre-war. I don't know what he'll do.'

An alder overhung the enclosure. John had coiled his snare and smoothed earth over between two roots, where he had found pug-marks. 'The tiger ran along here, where we set more snares by the fence. It could have watched us from long grass as we worked. Funny it tried to dig under. Tigers don't usually do that.'

'Maybe it's young, and remembers being small.'

John looked at me indulgently. 'There's a mosquito on your throat,' he said. 'Here are the leopard's clawmarks, where it climbed.'

Deep pink scratches, high in pale bark. I touched them.

Everywhere else leopards do better than tigers. Not here. They never went as far north either. They don't fare as well as tigers in deep snow, and maybe there are fewer prey animals further north of the size they need. At the edge of any animal's range many factors limit their survival, decide where they go. The Amur leopards' northern bound-ary probably shifted according to hard or easy winters. Where did they have cubs?

'Rocky outcrops, high up. So do tigers, here in the south. We found one place where the tigress suckled cubs outside a cave she couldn't enter herself, sending them back in to hide. The cubs' main predators are bears; anywhere a tigress could go, a bear could too.'

Other predators here are lynx (in the north), brown and black bears. Once there were dhole in the south, last seen in the 1980s, and wolves in the mountains. When tigers came back in the 1960s the wolves declined. (Tigers are expert dog-killers.) The tigers ate Sika deer, musk deer, red deer, moose and boar. Not livestock often, except dogs.

'One tiger up north specialized in dogs. Kolya here, one of the team, darted him. We radio-collared and moved him, called him Fedya. He came back, circled the village – we saw his tracks – and out of five thousand homes he chose Kolya's dog! Lovely dog, called Dick. Kolya's wife phoned crying, "Fedya has eaten Kolya's Dick!" I had to laugh. But she was very upset.'

'Can you scare tigers off?'

'Fedya ended his dog-eating days finally when Kolya let off a rocket as he was stalking a dog. He ran three hundred yards and never returned! It's important to find ways of scaring them off; but not at a deer farm. Can't put them off their natural prey. In winter they mainly take dogs. One winter a tigress in very poor condition, starving, came into our village up north with two six-month cubs, and killed two dogs. She left the cubs under a shed and never came back. They were very thin. WCS looked after them; they went to zoos. It must happen in the wild. A tigress goes hunting, is hurt, and cannot get back.'

John felt that if they could control poachers, tigers here had enough wild prey. They bred well, the population was stable at 450. As everywhere, it was dispersing males who were mainly killed. One farmer saw pugmarks in snow leading into his barn and not coming out. Instead of calling the team, he got an old blunderbuss and went into the dark barn knowing there was a tiger there. It charged out: he fired, but it came on and got past. He killed it running away. A young male in perfect health who just made a mistake and went to sleep in a barn.

Tigers normally attack prey from the side or behind. They vary, showing their individuality in the hunting technique they evolve over years, as Valmik recorded at Ranthambhore. A tiger will try to knock over large prey like a sambar at speed and grip the shoulder or neck. Those Gothic teeth find a killing-spot by feel, like a burglar snicking a key into a lock. If this fails, a strong animal can get away. A tiger depends on surprise and gets no second chance. It has two options. The nape grip kills by crushing or displacing vertebrae, severing or displacing the spinal cord. The smaller the animal, the easier. With a big animal the tiger works by leverage, turning the beast's weight against itself; a throttle grip is best, closing the windpipe, keeping the tiger's own soft parts away from backwards-threshing antlers, though it is still threatened by razor-slashing feet. If it gets that grip at once, throttling can be a curiously peaceful business, seen from outside: the deer's head thrown back like a worshipper gazing at the sky, black lips parted, grey tongue hanging. In a really expert charge, deer die with scarcely a mark, except on the throat. And it is very quick. Killing is precise, not frenzied. Choice of charge and bite is geometric, depending on angle. Victorian hunters said a tiger's first act was to suck its victim's blood: a misreading of the throttle grip. A tiger cannot suck. Cubs, yes; but an adult's mouth is made for dismembering and slicing.

We splashed through streams up towards this tiger's recent kill. He had dragged it away and eaten the hindquarters. It lay on grass, head twisted back. Crows had eaten the eyes. In gravel was a pawprint, my first trace of an Amur tiger, now maybe watching tetchily as humans disturbed his nice new source of food. Rain had stopped. The hills were dappled with cloud-shadow.

'The bare spaces are from fires. Poachers start fires at the *zapovednik* edge. When fire-fighting teams are busy they go in and take animals.'

I looked down again at the pugmark.

'Nine and a half centimetres. Pretty small for a Siberian. Must be a female, or young adult.'

'There you are – it remembers being small till quite recently.'

He smiled.

11

ATTENTION! TIGERS CROSSING

Four glasses of rose-hip Cognac sparkled. Sunset in the *taiga*, fifteen hours north of Vladivostock. Olga had kidnapped me. I was with her friends in a forest cabin outside Terney.

Yevgeny says, 'To a good path through the forest.'

We had left Vladivostock at dawn with a driver called Leonid, a former submarine pilot, past a suburb where tigers were seen in the 1970s. (Nowadays, the Tiger Team would relocate them.) Then came the north–south mix of lianas, pine, silver birch, red vine: green woods just about to turn, splashed with yellow. The town of Arsenev, named for the great man. A statue of him stood on a boulder carved with copies of Sikachi-Alyan petroglyphs, commemorating native people like Dersu. Up to the territory of Arsenev's 1906 expedition, the Sikhote-Alin mountain range, which generates ten per cent of the world's plant oxygen and is the hub of Amur tiger life. Trees everywhere to the spiky horizon: a green, undulating sea. What Europe was before we destroyed our forests. Close up, you saw hundreds of different trees, pine, oak, maple, larch. Creamy silver birches drooped like overcooked asparagus over the road: last winter, a metre and a half of snow fell in one day. They never recovered. Timber lorries passed, loaded high with long logs. One had capsized.

'We export logs to Japan,' said Olga. 'People hate seeing them go. They say, "These are *our* trees".' I remembered Mrinal in Calcutta: 'Timber from *our* forests.'

Settlements were wood bungalows limed pale blue: faded pistachio shutters, iron roofs, rotting fences, cabbages, maize. On one hillside I saw a stone tiger's face round a spring, and red ribbons tied in trees behind. Water trickled through a crack in its jaw: a bottomless plastic bottle was wedged to guide it. Buddhists loved this place; and it was good luck to drink, so we did.

Christianity was the latecomer. Koreans and Chinese were here long before Russians. Arsenev thought many of Dersu's tribe were Buddhist. Elsewhere, tigers are Buddhist, Hindu, Muslim, animist. Russian tigers regularly see the sign of the cross. But only for the last hundred years.

'These towns once had the names Arsenev used. Now Russian names. I like the old ones. More eastern.'

On this mountain pass in 1906, Arsenev looked east towards the coastal region, having struggled up through *taiga* on foot, and realized that the Sikhote-Alin ridge separated two quite different climates. He looked into a sea of fog; we, under a kingfisher-blue sky, saw mountains thick-clothed in one of the best tiger forests in the world.

Leonid had a shrunken fallen eye and took great care of his old jeep. When we stopped for bortsch, he rubbed it down. When we reached the Pacific again, his face crinkled in smiles. Here it was, the Sea of Japan where Arsenev, also in late August, watched sea-lions play. One winter Olga took visitors with a poodle to that beach. Coming back, she saw a tiger's tracks overlapping hers in the snow. It had followed them, hoping for poodle, but turned away into the forest.

Outside Terney, where the WCS field station was, we met a sign slung between silver birches, showing a tiger scampering over a road. ATTTENTION! TIGERS CROSSING! The mud lanes were jammed with smooth brown cows who ignored cars and stood imperious in the middle. Then came a white dust track through thick forest, sea on our right like a mirage, and in through a gate to a log cabin, enormous woodpile and a shelter open like a nativity set. Chained dogs barked under apple trees. Tamara, statuesque, round-faced, red-cheeked, in her fifties, with long glossy loose black hair, smiled. Yevgeny, naked to the waist, woodsman, maker of honey and forest liqueurs, welcomed us to a trestle table.

Yevgeny was born far inland. He had read Arsenev on military service, fallen in love with Ussuriland, and come here to find work to take him into nature. A co-worker in a factory had taught him bee-keeping. He and Tamara had a house in Terney where I would stay tomorrow. Yevgeny stayed in the forest as much as he could.

'In winter,' said Olga, 'they have everything here. Meat in forest, fish in river. Vegetables under the snow. But Tamara prefers Terney.'

Well she might. Cooking every day on a stove open to the wind in a metre of snow must be wearing. Now there were insects, not ice. Arsenev said biting flies were the curse of the *taiga*. Ticks and mosquitoes bite all mammals but give encephalitis only to humans. Insects would be worse in the humid months, May to July; now there were only flies, midges, wasps and hornets. I flinched. Yevgeny looked at me reprovingly. All his own movements were calm.

'Wolf bee,' said Olga. 'They try to eat Yevgeny's bees.'

When you visit a bee-keeper, you say hello to his hives. Yevgeny held up a copper jug of glowing coals, squeezed concertina'd leather at the back, and smoke puffed through the spout. Olga and I put on bee-veils. I hung back. My business was tigers, not bees.

'He says, you must love bees. Do not make sudden movement. It frightens them.'

Yevgeny puffed into the hive, trod on a wolf bee trying to sneak in, and lifted the top. Dark gold bees rose round our veils. Yevgeny pulled out vertical trays trickling with bees. We stood over a seething brown-gold mass. Thousands of tiny wings glinted in the sun.

While Tamara cooked, we tried different forest liqueurs. A jeep came and three men in green jumped out: the tiger team, back from Vladivostock. The leader's jacket hung open. He had a certificate from Omaha for immobilizing tigers. Now he carried a gun and a bowl of rubies. Mel Gibson with red bilberries.

After supper I suggested Russian songs. In a dark bass, Yevgeny began a melancholy tune with many verses. Olga joined in. 'Mountain ash loves an oak tree, other side of road. They are fated always to be distant.' Everyone seemed very cheerful about it. As they sang, a crescent moon came over the trees.

'Love is a gold boat, a miracle. But when you travel in it, it may be only wood.'

'Just as well. Gold sinks.'

After each song, we toasted the forest, the bilberries, the tiger, in a whole rainbow of liqueurs. Finally they sang 'Kalinka', which even I knew. An owl called, mosquitoes bit, and I went to my hut in the dark.

My room was at the end, nearest the forest. The chained dogs would warn of tigers and bears. I dreamed I was sitting with friends at a long table. He was on his own at the end. He hated being alone; I invited him closer. Someone asked how he was. Not well: he had moved house when I left, and spent the first month cleaning a baby's cradle.

'There are vents in a cradle,' he said. 'The baby gets fond of them. When you grow up, all that is left of those vents is a book.' He opened and shut his hands like wings. 'A book is an image of loss.'

There was a howl or a roar outside; I woke in the dark, appalled. Never mind the predators: *I was feeling sorry for him in my sleep.*

Breakfast was river trout, bilberries to sprinkle on them, herbal liqueurs. Yevgeny ate sweets in coloured wrappers, which I had seen loose on shop counters. Russian men seemed to like them. My daughter's boyfriend had asked me to bring back Russian sweets; I realized he knew something I didn't. We were going to walk where Yevgeny had a hunting permit, just outside the *zapovednik*, but it was still too wet. Yevgeny had an oboe of spiralled birch-bark: a deer trumpet, the 'stag's challenge'. Rutting was beginning. Soon the forest would echo with hormonal stags, and hunters trying to shoot them. Yevgeny blew a blast, which swelled and fell. I tried and got the same.

'If another stag hears, is very angry. He comes looking for the stag who challenges. Then, you shoot him.' Olga sprayed me against ticks. 'They are on trees and want to get in your skin. Very dangerous.'

For his date with the forest, Yevgeny was kitted like an Edwardian squire in fawn jacket, tan trousers, boots like polished oak, pale peaked cap, a knife in his belt. He was showing the *taiga* respect; I felt ashamed of my Club Med trainers.

We walked through chest-high grasses and wildflowers under vines beaded with berries. Yevgeny held up a stick like a conductor's baton and made a speech. There were rules for walking in wilderness. If I followed them I'd be safe. Walk three metres behind him. Touch no plants:

some were poisonous or thorny. Make no sound. The forest was in balance; human noise was not balance. The front person's stick had to move things like spiders aside. He plucked berries, lifted leaves to show hazelnuts forming, pointed out lemonberry vine, grapevine with red leaves, two different maples, purple flowers we absolutely must not touch. Arsenev, I remembered, was full of names. But what Olga loved were the hundreds of mushrooms, green, red, orange, yellow, white.

Slippery rocks underfoot, trees pressing all round. The first mammal trace was where wild boar rooted. Then a bear scratch, high on a tree, and lynx. Yevgeny said he had killed many lynxes. I flinched. What did I think was the main problem, asked Yevgeny, for tigers?

'Hunting,' I said sadly, embarrassed.

'Wrong. Logging is the main problem.'

Fresh bear scat, badger tracks, deer hair on tree trunks, and at last a fresh tiger scrape. A tiger, here on this path, an hour before.

In a boggy patch surrounded by Manchurian lilac and hazel, hunters had buried salt in mud so deer would dig for it. There were deer tracks but no tiger. Trees were higher here: fir, spruce, larch, cedar, oak and one with spongy pale bark, the velvet tree, or Amur cork tree. Then thick bushes, grasses furious with insects, ash, lime, walnut, pine, and a silver birch eighty foot high with iron steps up ghost-white skin. Yevgeny pointed critically to where the bark had been stripped in a spiral. Amateur work: that strip was too wide for a good trumpet. He climbed to the hide from which hunters shot deer licking salt, and brought down a forgotten axe.

'In Soviet era no one killed tiger. If they met tiger they ran. Now they kill it because they are poor. It is big money. They sell to Chinese.'

The forest kept changing. We stepped round fallen cedars, past bushes blazing with currants. Yevgeny smiled.

'Beautiful,' whispered Olga. 'For us, the forest is very philosophical.'

When we got back I found a black tick running inside my T-shirt, brushed it off, tried to stamp on it and failed. I took off all my clothes, checking every inch of skin in case another was embedded. I had thought they were slow. The only ticks I had seen before were bloated white bubbles; these were quick and wriggly.

Tamara came with us to Terney. I looked at the dog chained at the gate. Dogs here were chained all the time.

'They want to talk to us. Dogs need relationships.'

'They are *dogs*,' said Olga, firmly.

Terney, a settlement of four thousand people, had wooden bungalows, faded blue and green, fenced by rusty orange metal. Tamara's had red steps to the kitchen door. The garden was stained-glass bright: plums, red and yellow apples, scarlet dahlias in urns of silver-painted old tyres, gold nasturtiums, white daisies, crimson hollyhocks against a white outhouse; blue cabbages big as turkeys, yellow marrow flowers, sunflowers round fluffy asparagus. A beautiful blond boy of six, Tamara's grandson Victor, ran out. I remembered a children's book at Boswells. Milly-Molly-Mandy, with Father, Mother, Uncle, Aunty, Grandma and Grandpa, lived in a house and garden like this.

The outside toilet was a cabin with a diamond cut in the door. The *banya*, to wash, was through a gate to the woodshed and past two chained huskies.

'Hot like sauna, ' said Olga. 'You'll love it.'

'Do tigers come here often?' I was worrying about dogs again. If you're chained, you don't have a chance. Terney was where Fedya had eaten Dick.

Tamara said a tiger had looked over this fence when a neighbour staked a pig in her garden. It put its paws on the fence, jumped in and walked round the pig, but didn't touch it.

My bedroom, through the kitchen, had gold velour curtains, an iridescent picture of mallards on a snowy river, floor-to-ceiling books, and a knitted patchwork coverlet. Out of the window I could see the fairy-tale garden, blue-washed houses, wooded hills, clouds glowing pink and beige. A child's room, overlooking a fence a tiger had jumped. I imagined it looking at me, paws on those white slats, then leaping into the garden. A cottage paradise, with tiger.

As Tamara piled Olga's and my plates with salmon dumplings, red caviar, sour cream, Dale knocked, took off his shoes and came into the kitchen in beige shorts and turquoise shirt: a stocky dark man with a kind, fleshy face, welcoming me to Terney. Could I radio-track a tigress with young cubs next day?

When he left, I got the gossip. He had married a Terney woman.

'When Dale came nine years ago he wasn't big and beautiful like now. Then he married. Now, is beautiful.'

They admired fullness, presence, energy. Strong is important, and strong was what Dale needed to be, standing between Amur tigers and all the political and other forces here, threatening extinction.

Breakfast was more red caviar, glistening like redcurrants. I had modestly hoped for coffee and fresh plums; Tamara ladled fried potatoes, onions, pancakes, baroque bulges of sour cream. 'Eat up! Yevgeny says if you want to be in harmony with nature you should eat a big breakfast.'

Victor was in a dazzling white shirt; his dandelion-silk head shone. This was his first day at school. Dale was at the door.

'Your job today is finding Lidya with her new litter, two months old. We want to know where they are. You'll be with Sasha, who works for the WCS, and his girlfriend Katya from my Vladivostock office. Her father's a great tiger biologist. She knows as much about tigers as anyone.'

Olga sprayed me. 'Tuck T-shirt in your jeans. Dale, don't let her get eaten by tigers.'

'I won't be there,' Dale said. I got into his car and asked about the iron fences. Dale laughed. 'Metal airstrip brought from the US in 1941. You never throw anything away in Terney.' We stopped for the cows; Dale waited for a yellow calf to finish standing still. 'People back home say at least you don't have rush-hour. I tell them we do! Cows, going out at morning, coming home at night.'

Shining woods, sea, headlands, river mouth. Terney Bay was put on Western maps in 1787 by a French explorer, Jean François Comte de la Perouse. Then came an English discoverer, William Broughton, in 1797. After that, this coastline sparkled alone to itself, visited only by Chinese trappers, till Russians mapped it in 1874. One local historian had searched nineteenth-century newspapers for what Russian settlers thought about tigers. There were lots of tigers: they thought them the forest's nastiest inhabitants, who came into villages to eat cows and men. These days tiger attacks fluctuated. There had been none for three years, although one person was injured. Someone died in Terney in the 1980s from a heart-attack, just seeing a tiger.

'But there was a decade when someone was killed every year. In 1996, tigers killed five people in Primorye.'

Katya, pale and skinny, came out of Sasha's bungalow and spouted breathless Russian. Sasha laced his boots behind her. What was going on?

'Well, it is a little scary. Last week she found a tick embedded over her ribs and had a panic attack. They don't only carry encephalitis. It's Lyme's disease and other things people don't much know about. They're worst in May and June. But check yourself every hour. And all over at the end.'

'I had my T-shirt outside my jeans that day,' said Katya, tucking hers in, her hair in a scarf. 'I'm not immunized.'

'Even when you are,' said Dale, 'it doesn't entirely protect.'

Our tigress held prime territory, the best they had – prey, water, cover – but a road went through it.

'Lot of good that TIGERS CROSSING sign did. We've had young tigers killed there, and the road means poachers. Roads always do.'

They collared their first tigress here in June 1992. She gave birth in September and was killed in November. They caught her four cubs: two died, but they sent the others to US zoos. The second tigress survived two years, had a cub which disappeared, and then was poached. Lidya was the first collared tigress who had managed to raise cubs here.

'I hope you *don't* see her! With young cubs is the most dangerous time. The point of radio-tracking is *not* seeing them, but hearing them without spooking them. Get as close as you can. Pinpoint her. Good luck.'

We stopped at the shop for food. An old man looked through the window and made a scolding speech.

'He's from another reserve,' Katya said. 'He knows my father. He says I'm too nervous of ticks. I *am* too nervous.'

Did ticks bite tigers?

'If they're healthy, you don't find many when you tranquillize them.'

Smartly dressed women walked with flowers in one hand and small, clean children in the other. The first day of school was important. At Terney's shop, a cement-floored barn, Sasha bought sausage, crackers, cherry pop, toilet paper, water.

'Never forget those last two in the forest.'

We drove sixty kilometres to get Lidya's signal. The radio can pick up signals at six kilometres. From the air it can do fifty. It gives angle but not distance. Sasha would get one position, go further, take another and triangulate the two. The transmitter crackled with static, the signal would be a pulse beneath that noise. They had eight tigers collared just now. We might pick up five here, depending on where they were. When the tiger moves the pulse is faster, indicating activity. Tigers are always moving, unless they are asleep. If one stays in one place several days, it has a kill or young cubs, or is ill. Here, they slept mainly from midnight to four a.m., and were most active in the early morning, or from evening until midnight. Males walk many kilometres, mostly at night. Dale has found they usually travel about twelve kilometres in twenty-four hours. They can move further, but deep snow must slow them down compared to, say, males at Panna. They scent-mark, check their territory, maybe visit one of their families and spend time with the cubs. In India, cubs have been seen to run to fathers affectionately.

Dale's collared tigers currently included Volodia, father of Lidya's new cubs, who moved in when her first mate died. They collared him two years ago. He was seven, and this was Lidya's third litter with him. They had no idea where he was. Sasha once saw him very far off, in mountains. Then there were Lidya's last two cubs. The male, Vasya, had left her; Galya the daughter was still in Lidya's range. There was also Vera, young daughter of Nellie, Lidya's radio-collared neighbour.

Dale was waiting to see what happened between Lidya and Galya. At Chitwan, tigresses have moved up for daughters. At Ranthambhore, traumatic mother–daughter negotiations suggest this relationship can be a see-saw between power and affection. And, oh, my own daughter, just now abroad alone for the first time, in Amsterdam with friends: did I leave *her* enough space?

'Sasha's picked up Lidya. He's wonderful at hearing the signal.'

We strained to hear the pulse. Sasha drove, stopped, lost the pulse and tuned to other tigers. Suddenly there really was a pulse. *Tick, tick, tick.* White dust floated down, stirred by our tyres, and the sea shone below: we were eavesdropping on sound from a tiger's throat! Galya, walking fast. Sasha checked her position on a map. She had not moved much for some months. She was twenty-six months old, trying out adult life, and had left her mother in May.

'She's over there.' Katya pointed at a wooded headland across the bay. We drove down to sea level along a rutted track fringed with stunted oaks and Michaelmas daisies, to dunes spotted with crows and gulls. The waves were high, creamy, empty. Surfing had not arrived in Primorye. Everyone was busy making a living and the Sea of Japan is achingly cold.

There were rocks here where seals lay. Roma, a young male tiger, caught seals there last winter, stacked them in threes and ate the heads. He came back later and ate the rest. They collared him young, but Volodia ruled this territory, so Roma had left. Young males without territory pass through what they know belongs to a breeding male. If they're feeling feisty they may challenge him, try to take over. Otherwise they stop when his spray-mark hits them and head the other way. No one knew what had happened to Roma: he had pulled off his collar. But John Goodrich had seen him just here.

'Our tigers like beaches. Deer too. They go into the sea to eat seaweed.'

These cliffs could have been Cornwall or west Scotland, but with unbroken forest and a young tigress adjusting to a solitary life. Galya's signal said she was on a very far mountain. We would try Lidya again. Sasha swung into an overgrown forest track. We bucked through saplings so close together I didn't think any car *could* drive between them, and left the truck where brushwood was stuffed between two trees, making a little tunnel; they had tried to set a camera trap here for lynx.

It was rough, trackless going: moss, loose stones, dense bracken. Often I couldn't see my feet. *Two sorts of pit viper, one quite aggressive; we see them all the time.* Waiting for Sasha to get Lidya's signal I flicked a tick off my chest. A woodpecker drilled; a large yellow toad rustled at my feet. We crossed dark rivers on slippery rotting logs.

'Elk fly,' said Katya, holding a small black insect. 'We call the big deer elk. Dale said they are really red deer, but we still say "elk fly". It looks like the tick, but not dangerous.'

After two hours we found a real trail. There were tracks and droppings of red deer, sika, roe, racoon-dog, badger. Lidya was on a slope of dark, dense pines, half a kilometre away. This was *her* trail. Large purple flowers, four feet high, were broken where a large animal had brushed them. On one tree at hip-height, caught between flaking bark and trunk, were gold and white hairs. I pictured her coming towards us, big as a pony but longer, orange as autumn. We were walking towards her.

'Sasha says it's not dangerous,' Katya whispered. 'A hundred and fifty metres is dangerous. We are half a kilometre.'

Tigresses are passionate, dedicated mothers. Medieval fantasists used to say the best way to catch one was with a convex mirror. She sees her reflection diminished and stops, thinking it's her cub: then you fling a net round her. Lidya would feed them, kill for them, defend them, teach them to hunt, teach this territory till they knew it so intimately they could walk it blind and never roll a stone. Her twenty-four/seven job is the basis of tiger culture. We went on towards her, up the mossy, rocky trail. It would be impossible to run: you would fall. Which trees were climbable?

'Lidya's in there. Sasha says we must be quiet.'

We were on a steep slope in a tangle of shoulder-high bracken. Opposite, Lidya's slope ran upward, with dark trees, thick undergrowth. Sasha went forward with his aerial. Katya did not.

'I really don't want to go further,' whispered this girl who knew so much about tigers. Standing in high bracken was very different from sitting on an elephant or in a jeep. How reliable was Sasha's instrument? Suppose Lidya charged out, defending her cubs?

'And this is a tick.' On Katya's finger, a small frilly black spider. 'A juvenile. But they are hungry, we are tasty . . . I want to go back.'

I was not sure if the tiger or the tick bothered Katya more, but I, too, could have done with a bit less closeness to both. Beside us was a dead tree with semicircular growths like upside-down cups: cup mushrooms, which kill the host tree.

'Useful to get up, when the tiger is near,' said Katya, echoing my thought.

'You're safe!' said Olga. 'You're very late.'

'What did you eat?' asked Tamara.

*

Next morning John, back from the deer farm, phoned to see if I'd like to go up in the telemetry helicopter. Would I see a tiger? No. In winter I might. The governor of Kamchatka and his councillors had just died in a helicopter crash; I went instead to the *zapovednik* headquarters. *Zapovednik* directors are answerable to a separate division for protected areas in the Ministry of Natural Resources in Moscow. There is no direct link between the forest department and *zapovednik* management. Many *zapovednik* directors have scientific backgrounds and begin work as staff biologists on *zapovedniks*, for Russia has a strong traditional respect for science. All *zapovedniks* have scientific staff, responsible for monitoring within the protected area. This one had about thirty tigers. Its director talked chillingly of trained, well-equipped poachers taking tigers on commission from Chinese dealers. Of how little he could pay forest guards: four times less than other work, no use to a man supporting a family. And of the worst threat to tigers: logging. If only Primorye could *stop* depending on the timber industry, make the bulk of its money from sea resources. But logging taxes and licences provided most of the state budget. Once a timber company leases a place it can do what it likes: even build villages for workers, and roads. Once roads exist, hunters use them. You can never, he said, close roads.

In fact, the WCS has managed it, but it is hard. If you use a gate, you must pay a guard, build a cabin. If you replant trees, people cut them down. Farmers want the access. The WCS have dug up roads twice: people put them back the first time, so the WCS bulldozed again. Logging companies claim they need roads to fight fires, but fires are started by people who would not be there if there were no roads. Further north, administrators sick of poaching have *asked* the WCS to close logging roads. Others want the access, or just not to be isolated.

I walked down the corridor from the bleakness of politics to the passion of science: Yevgeny Smirnov, tiger biologist in his fifties, stocky and intense. His walls held charts from joint projects with Dale as well as his own. A graph of all tigers radio-collared. Over half ended 'signal lost' or 'poached'.

The world's first reserve was Yellowstone, in 1872. Primorye's first was established in 1916. This one began in 1935, when tigers were at their lowest: it then had twelve. They increased to twenty-five, but people were still allowed to capture cubs. Scientists got that stopped in 1954.

'One study of tigers was written in 1915 – *that*'s how old Russian tiger science is. They say we're crazy because we work for low salaries. But look at this!'

Two aerial photos. One of unbroken forest, the other patchworked fields. Russia and China, two sides of the Ussuri border.

'*We* still have forest, because of us crazies! Here, *scientists* brought the laws and *zapovedniks* into existence.'

Like Dersu, Smirnov preferred *not* to see tigers. He had worked on them for twenty years before he saw one. In 1983, he and his colleague Anatoli were crossing a stream. Anatoli had rubber boots, and sloshed through; Smirnov went over a log bridge. He heard a stone move behind and turned. A tiger was four steps away. Now he crouched on his office floor, looking up, showing me.

'Close as this! Sitting, staring. I looked into its eyes and swore! I used *very* bad words – Dale never uses bad words – and it growled.'

It disappeared; then they saw it looking at them again. Anatoli took a stick, but the tiger had gone. Smirnov had to stay in the cabin alone and found he had lost his nerve. 'If a mouse squeaked, I panicked. I thought I'd have to change my job, like a pilot afraid of flying. But after three days it was OK. I've seen more since, but never so close. I take this flare with me to frighten them.'

He held up something like a firework, labelled 'Red False Fire: For Use at Sea'.

'Even going to an outhouse at night I take it with me. The tiger's *very* dangerous.'

A fisherman friend of his, coming through the forest at evening recently with his catch, was charged by a tiger. He climbed a tree; the tiger grabbed his boot. He shook it off; the tiger fell to the ground with it. He went higher; it tried to climb but the branches were too thin. He threw his other boot at the tiger. It was young, and its mother turned up too. They ate his fish, chewed his socks, and lay under his tree. Tigers are not particularly aggressive but do not like to be crossed. Come morning, with no tigers left, he crept down and ran barefoot through the *taiga*.

Smirnov gave me a poem by a Moscow poet, Ilya Sielvinsky, who had visited Vladivostock in 1932, when tiger numbers were right down. He went hunting with a man from the Gol'd tribe (like Dersu), saw red ribbons tied on trees to honour the tiger, and shot a tiger. It staggered off with fresh red ribbons on its withers.

'I write poems too,' said Smirnov, 'but I've never dared write one about a tiger. A tiger's a very thoughtful animal, not like others. A *mysterious* animal.'

'I've had them eat out of my hand,' said John, looking at blue nuthatches in his tree. Below was the shine of Terney Bay. He had worked here for nine years, with Dale, supervising research on tigers, bears, lynxes. Dale had come earlier, as Russia was starting to focus on using all the natural resources it could. Russian forests are Europe's lungs, twenty-two per cent of the world's forest. Only the Amazon absorbs more carbon dioxide. Now the Kremlin was about to sell 843 million hectares to private companies. But because of Dale, the WCS could influence change, at least where tigers were. It takes a long time to become effective. Most local people supported the WCS. Dale worked *with* them: conservation has to be done by local people in the end.

'It's important we've been here a long time. Dale's wonderful with people. They trust him. But we have to educate them. They have no idea the *zapovedniks* don't hold all tigers, that tigers are everywhere. In schools I say, "Where are tigers?" They say "In Africa." Or "In reserves."'

Unlike tigers in India or Chitwan, these tigers cannot be observed. Dale's long-term study shows they organize their lives like Bengal tigers. Males are often poached before they lose their territory; those that survive hold territory for at least six years. But Dale had to prove everything again – for *these* tigers here. Because of language differences and Soviet isolation, Bengal and Siberian tigers had not been much compared. Many Russian biologists thought cubs stayed with mothers for three years. Most tigers are in remote areas where it is hard to follow. In winter, scientists can track them in snow.

'I once found traces of a fight. Blood and hair everywhere: two males had tumbled, fighting, down a slope. But our tigers spread out, there's less interaction than at Chitwan. We find few scars on them.'

In an eight-year study of eleven tigresses, most gave birth for the first time at four and had two cubs. Usually one died within a year. Over half of these deaths had a human cause. Less than ten per cent of cubs survived their first year. Tigresses varied according to personality and territory. Lidya kept cubs in the same place for two months, and bore these new ones in the same spot as the last. Others moved their cubs all the time; like Olga, whose range was often disturbed. Olga was their longest-running tiger, collared at eleven months, now thirteen years and with her sixth litter. No one knows how long Siberian tigers live in the wild; or go on bearing cubs. Olga may tell them. Others had all been poached.

Young males, however, were often poached at dispersal. Most went south, hit a settlement and turned back. Sometimes evidence turned up, a collar by a skull. Or someone says a tiger was killed.

'Once we found one of our collars round a bottle in a river.'

They have studied tigers only on the coast, in *zapovedniks*. They do not know what is happening inland in different habitat, or in unprotected areas where hunters take many deer and boar.

'Do you ever despair, John? Logging, poaching, roads, tigers you know well getting killed, hit by cars . . .'

'Of course! It's frustrating, heartbreaking. You start something and it's blown sky high by politics. But there are fewer people than in India, tigers are relatively stable. Things are better than in many places.'

'Will you stay for ever?'

'Ten years ago, I came for two years. I don't have a plan. I can't imagine spending the rest of my life in Russia, but I can't imagine leaving. I'm useful here. If I went home I'd do something others could do.'

This is what it takes to save tigers. A state that tries to enforce laws despite poverty, greed, corruption. A young man giving his life to a hope on the other side of the world. How were people like him trained? Science, obviously. But what about dealing with *people*?

'We need more of that sort of training. I didn't have any. But there are incredible rewards. Once, tracking Olga by sea in my kayak to know if she was travelling with cubs, my signal said she was on a cliff. The beach held tracks of racoon-dogs, otters, foxes but not tigers. I couldn't camp by the cliff, it might have disturbed her, so I paddled half a mile along the beach, roasted scallops for supper, pitched a tent, drank a beer. Olga wasn't moving, the signal was slow, I went to sleep. I woke when an animal ran on the cliff. Stones fell. There are goral there. I heard them scolding, and pointed the antenna up the hill. Olga was within a hundred yards. I thought, OK, she spooked the goral. I stared at the stars and slept. Next day, searching for firewood, the hairs on my neck stood right up. That running noise had been Olga! Her tracks were on the sand. She'd stopped fifty yards away, I guess when she saw the tent, then carried on towards me. *Ten yards* from me she turned and went up the hill. Where it was too steep to walk, she ran, which woke me.'

I was talking to a man who had slept, like the gypsy in Rousseau's painting, ten yards from a loose wild tiger.

'Then I found what I wanted, the proof. Little prints, cubs' prints, beside hers in the sand.'

'Good hot day,' Dale said. 'We're going into the reserve. Bring your swimming things.' He had friends with him: Dimitri, a tiger scientist in his sixties, who worked for the Geography Institute, and his elegant wife Olga (another Olga), in jeans. We got ready for the forest. Dimitri watched me tuck jeans inside my socks carefully – for ticks. He growled Russian at Dale.

'He thinks your pants should hang outside so if snakes strike they may not get your flesh. I said, "Don't frighten her."'

Encephalitis or pit vipers? We walked through dense Mongolian oaks, red berries, chin-high purple flowers. The trail crossed sharp rocks covered in gold moss and streams. One we jumped, stone to stone. Another had a narrow log. I heard a splash: Dimitri was in the stream. He laughed, and surged up the bank. There were hundreds of mushrooms. Pale buff ones like branching coral, bright orange ones; red, yellow, conical, flat. Dimitri and Olga stuffed them into a knapsack.

'Russians are incapable of going into forest without gathering mushrooms,' Dale said.

Suddenly there were thudding hoofs. A little roe deer galloped towards us, skidded, hesitated, zigzagged away, slender legs firm at speed in stony hollows where I watched every step. Dimitri and Olga, arguing mushrooms, had seen nothing. Was it a doe?

'Very young stag. Tiny horns.' He could read what I could not.

We came to a cabin for forest guards. Olga opened a dusty book. As the seasoned wife of a tiger scientist, she loved guards' notebooks. On the wall were paintings by Gainsborough and Goya torn from magazines, a portrait of Pushkin and the poet Marina Tsvetaeva, watercolours, sketches of the forest, the woodpile. Amur tigers are protected by the most educated guards in the world.

We rested in the hut; I heard about Dimitri's moment of tact, defending his Ph.D. in Moscow. The Moscow examiner played a recording of what he said was a tiger imitating deer. First the real deer, then the so-called tiger. He wanted someone from the east to verify it. Dimitri rubbished this idea: that sound was just another deer! Not the best thing to say before the guy judged his thesis.

But could tigers do that? I did not believe it.

'That's the myth. No one's proved it. Everyone interprets, Ruth. Scientists should be the most objective people; they often aren't. Most tiger stories are people interpreting little bits of what they saw. If you saw *all*, you'd see many more similarities between these and other tigers. Of all people, scientists should be the first to say they don't know.'

We went on through forest to dunes above the sea. Everything looked blue, bright, blowy and European.

'It keeps surprising me: tigers wandering around in *this*.'

'I know. I grew up in New England. When I first came it looked so familiar, same latitude, lots of the same trees, I had to slap myself to remember there were tigers.'

'Walking along beaches?'

'Sure. Often. Beaches are the shortest point from A to B. Tigers are very keen on finding that. They often do it at night.'

We climbed a cliff. The wind-history of little wiry trees growing out of it had gyred them into a jigsaw-tunnel. I said to Dale's boots, creeping through over loose boulders, hunched, slipping, 'I'm no field scientist. It was a *stupid* thing to do, try and see where tigers live. I'm scared of snakes, ticks and bears. But I'm *most* scared of breaking my ankle.' He chuckled among the little trees. Coming out over a precipice with dark peacock sea below, we stood on knobbly rocks and azaleas whose round leaves smelt sweet when trodden.

'I've seen a goral up here.'

'Hard to imagine it under snow,' I said, 'all this lush green and gold.'

'Come back in three months – see how long you can stand against the wind!'

The beach was deserted. This was a *zapovednik* – there was *supposed* to be no one here. Dale and Dimitri raced into the sea. The wind was a knife, the waves were ice, my ankles were incredulous, I had toothache in my feet. But Olga's shoulders went under, so mine had to too. Then we made a fire. We should be having vodka.

'Heavens, no,' said Dale. 'I've been up till three with Dimi two nights running, drinking. Very nice too, but it gets a bit wearing.'

Dimitri took out a plastic bottle and poured. All his movements, even when he fell off the log, were outsize. Tiger science, tiger people . . .

'My God, it *is* vodka,' said Dale. 'I'm not having any.'

A couple came along the beach. 'Victor!' said Dale. 'Victor used to work for the reserve. Now he's married he works for the border patrol and earns more. But he was with me when I first came. We took our first steps together.'

Going back we recrossed the streams and there, in wet sand, was a tiger's footprint. Probably Lidya's. I had seen her fur, her back door. I knew where her cubs were. Now this. I was used, now, to the way people lived with tigers. Better not see Amba, said Dersu, and most people did not. But they know Amba is there. He leaves hair, scrapes, pawprints. In the last few hours, strolling from the beach like us, a *tiger* had walked through this stream. A perfect day, with a pugmark at the end.

'It's not over yet. You're coming to supper – I forgot to tell you.'

'Can we stop at the shop? I want to take your wife some chocolates.'

People strolled in and out of the Terney shop, chatting, buying milk, sausage, thyme soap. A nice community.

'No, it isn't. I love it here, it's my home, there are a lot of great people. But the Soviet legacy is suspicion and isolation. That's still rampant. They are *not* a community. Most wouldn't help if they saw someone faint on the street. It's very sad.'

His house was high over the bay, the garden as colourful as Tamara's but more open. Bird tables, lacy stone walls, and that fantastic view. His wife Marina, blonde and glowing, came down the steps. We smiled at each other, languageless.

'She's the one who does the work,' said Dale. 'It's Marina's garden.'

They had married four years ago: a three-day wedding.

'Our Cossack neighbour insisted on building a cart to take us. He harnessed three horses to it and told me their life histories, *and* their parents'. He sure loved his horses.'

Wine, vodka, wonderful food: John, Dimitri, Dale, Marina, Olga. I wanted to ask what Dale felt about his work. What about never observing, as Valmik and Chuck do, the tigers he has given his life to?

'We can't study interaction. I'm jealous of that, of course. But we do things no one's done. This is the longest-running radio-collar study of individual tigers. We know where they pee and poop, what they eat, how often they kill and give birth. The information is slow. A trickle in eleven years. *But* we make our knowledge work to help tigers.'

His road study had *proved* roads cause tiger losses. Lidya's territory, brilliant tiger habitat with lots of prey, had a road through it. Four out of five tigresses there were poached, one every two and a half years. Of twelve cubs born there, ten died. During the same years two tigresses in roadless areas, and their cubs, survived. But when *they* moved to an area with a road, they were poached too. Cause and effect were officially accepted now. That was why the WCS could organize road closures.

'The system works in the States and Europe, where people also destroy blockades, wanting access to poaching areas. The key to long-term protection is working with the state. Gate the road. Pay gatekeepers and guards. NGOs like us are the only people doing real work here in terms of putting money in. Inspection Tiger was created by NGOs. It's run by the state but funded from outside. But there's so much bureaucracy. You have to hang on to your patience all the time. I see now why it's called a virtue. When I first started, it sometimes took all day to get a tank of gas. I learned never try to do three things in one day. You end up frustrated.'

In Russia, tiger poaching rose violently in 1992. Before that, things were regulated: there was no outside market for tiger parts. When everything was deregulated and the border opened, with Chinese dealers demanding tiger bone, hungry Russians went to the forests to make ends meet. But this was when poaching exploded everywhere else. That was the black year at Ranthambhore too. Why? What did Dale think of the idea that Chinese manufacturers of tiger-bone medicine then came to the end of a dead-tiger mountain, begun under Mao?

'I don't believe it was like that. Not a whole stockpile. It was scattered, one guy in a back-street, one tiger here, another there. People responding differently to local situations. I don't buy that line. Why *did* poaching rise like that everywhere in 1992? There must be more to it.'

In 1997, he began working with hunting groups, suggesting ways of co-existing with tigers. You have to belong to a hunting society to own a gun. Hunting societies, responsible for the areas they are licensed for, ensure their animals are protected and reproduce, keep out poachers and stop fires out of self-interest. But permits cost more now, so poor people cannot hunt legally. They poach.

Dale's work had an indirect impact too.

'A hunter friend of mine said recently he'd had Olga in his sights but did not shoot because of me. He said, "I know you; and I know *her*."'

He told me of a sick tiger that had crept under the rotting *dacha* of an elderly farmer. The family said the tiger came to them for help: Dale must *cure* it. To keep it in they had stuffed a bedspring, which a kitten could have knocked down, in the opening. Behind, Dale saw a huge tiger head. While the family bubbled on about another tiger they had seen that morning too, Dale watched the tiger, afraid it would charge out, scared and furious. He watched it blink. How sick was it? It showed no response to the noise. But if it had got in last night it could charge now. Two tigers. One inside; another, maybe an angry mother, somewhere outside. And the family behaving as if their pet was ill. He thought they were mad and shooed them away.

He could not do anything legally without one of the Tiger Team. By the time one came with a tranquillizing gun, the tiger had retreated to an inner cellar. They could not remove the bedspring and go in: it was sick but mobile. The farmer cut a hole in his floor above the cellar. They darted him from there and carried him out. A young male, completely emaciated, every rib visible, muscles like string. They took him to Terney; he died two days later. Dog distemper had wiped out half the Serengeti lion population. If it broke out here . . . The autopsy suggested it was distemper, but didn't do the culture tests to prove it, or say what kind. It was important to know if it was canine, if it had jumped species.

'They only said it was consistent with distemper. So we don't know.' Another tiger, however, had died of canine distemper since.

Dale felt passionately now that the family had been right; he was sorry he'd thought they were mad. His effectiveness, I realized, came from a generosity of spirit that people here recognized because they had it themselves. To do conservation in someone else's country, you must be in tune with the people, learn their language, love *them* as well as tigers. A sense of humour clearly helped; plus the stamina to drink till three in the morning, then be in the field all day.

Dimitri talked about China, and Chinese attitudes to conservation. He and Dale went there on projects for the tigers they shared.

'They think, Capture animals! Cage them! No *idea* of conserving wildlife *in its landscape*. The only nature left there is on mountain-tops they can't cultivate. One day the whole world'll be like that!'

'You mustn't despair,' I said.'Despair's the temptation of the devil.'

Dimitri looked at me blankly.

'Despair the temptation of the devil!' cried Dale. 'You take that one, John. She's been asking me to translate things like that all day. Tiger poops I'm fine with. Population, distemper. But *theology* . . .'

'Are there any myths here about white tigers? In England people think Siberian tigers are white because they go in snow.'

Everyone was embarrassed and silent. Someone laughed. They had given their lives to tigers. They had more important things to do for them than mess with their colour.

12

DON'T YOU UNDERSTAND?
THIS IS AMBA!

Grey apartment blocks, dusty squares, women with slumped shoulders; women sitting on the road selling tomatoes. On the road to Vladivostock, everywhere looked dreary after Terney. But beautiful Terney had no work. Logging had been stopped: they lived off their vegetable gardens. People in these towns had work. No logging means no jobs. People in Terney poached tigers using roads they had made when they worked.

We slept at Arsenev, dreariest town of the lot. That man who had hymned the *taiga* was commemorated in cement. At dinner I asked about *perestroika*. Leonid said it was very hard for ordinary people, older people.

'Before, there was system,' said Olga. 'You were taken care of. All was free. Medical care, electricity. You were guaranteed work. Now all has collapsed. News tonight said we'll have hot water in Vladivostock on a rota, two hours a day, till next summer. Hotels have their own water. Sometimes we have none at all. I keep in buckets in my flat.'

Yevgeny had invited Leonid back for deer hunting. Terney had three official hunting licences; Yevgeny's was one. Leonid said we need not worry about tigers, there were too many, his hunting patch of twelve kilometres had three: there was not food for them.

I did not believe much of this. John said people took tigers' kills so they had to kill again. I looked at Leonid's kind battered face. Dale had said hunters would decide the tiger's fate here. I was travelling with the problem.

*

We drove south and west, towards China: flat marshy land, with bul-
rushes. Lake Chanka, biggest lake of the Russian far east, on whose
shore Dersu saved Arsenev's life. Then Spassk, a derelict cement town:
broken chimneys, ruined windowless walls, once a heart of industry.

'Everyone wanted jobs here. Central government withdrew funding
overnight. Gorbachev wanted to do things slowly but . . .' Olga shook
her head. 'Who said to create we must destroy?'

'Lenin.'

'Also Yeltsin. What's the difference?'

A huge tigress walked towards us through trees. Huge paws, gold in
the undergrowth. She might have been Lidya; but there was netting
between us. Nyrka belonged to a biologist called Yudin. She had
reared several litters on this hill, which looked like all the *taiga* I'd
walked in, but had not taught them to hunt. Yudin's tigers lived as a
family here. Kuchera, the male, was a symbol of Primorye. His face
was on every brochure.

Nyrka half glanced at Yudin, then jumped into a cage beside the
enclosure, and lay three feet from us, her back towards us in not-
looking intimacy. When you never see them, you forget how large
they are. She flicked her ears; mosquitoes danced round them.
Mosquitoes evolved along with warm-blooded mammals and bother
them all, from baby owls to tigers. Loss of blood from their bites brings
down reindeer calves in buzzing Arctic summers. They give malaria
only to us.

A small face haloed in cream fluff peered out from a bush. The
female cub, big as a terrier, stood doubtfully on too-big paws. She sat
down to solve her uncertainty. The male cub behind her was torn
between wariness and curiosity. When she ran forward, he ran after
her. They came to Yudin and sucked his fingers: he had been feeding
them. The mother half turned, exaggeratedly indifferent, and closed
her eyes.

The cubs saw us. I squatted down. Again the female was more curious at first, came near, then stopped. The male hung back but was
ultimately bolder. He thought he should hiss: a soft hiss, half-hearted.
He was used to people. There were mosquitoes in his ears, too. The

roof-ridges of his small mouth were blue-grey. He saw bears move in cages behind me and spat in real fear. A mosquito bit my cheek.

'Yudin calls him Velvet. They were born four months ago. May the eighth.' Oh. My birthday too. 'Up to twenty days their eyes are blue. Now, are gold.'

A tiger's eyes are less efficient than ours at giving information about shapes, but adept at marking the slightest movement. Jungle survival depends on evaluating movement. For everyone, prey and predator, a move in the wrong place is a giveaway. In low light, Velvet's vision would be six times as efficient as mine. If you shone a torch, the centres of his eyes would glow. He had what I did not: the *tapetum lucidum*, 'bright carpet', a reflective extra layer over the receptor layer of his retina, which makes animals' eyes shine in the dark. Human eyes do not shine.

The mother poured herself back to the ground. The cubs ran up with snuffly squeaks. She licked them and moved up the slope. The audience was over, for her. But they came back. The male chewed a grass stalk as a puppy chews a stick. A red fox in another cage ran round anxiously, watching the tiger cub. Suddenly, another presence and a stage hush as the father stalked past, as big as they get. He did not relate to Yudin, as Nyrka implicitly did. He was just silently here, checking his patch, big as a bed, red-gold: how a male tiger looks as he checks his range in dense trees like these. Round topaz eyes, gigantic front paws. What Lidya depends on to keep her cubs, the world's future tigers, safe from other males.

He walked up the hill. His cubs batted dying flowerheads. A sudden flare-up in undergrowth when the parents met: a growl, a big paw flashing in air. The male disappeared, the tigress lay down. Velvet, used to such exchanges, settled his hindquarters to look at me, the movement I'd seen from the teenager at Kanha, the same 'I'm going to watch you watching me' stare. But Velvet had only been doing it for three months. Then he and his sister raced uphill into the green.

Back on Tiger Hill in Vladivostock, where I had hot water and Olga who had been born there did not, I listened to the Chinese casino and thought of the *taiga*. In 1902 Arsenev thought its fauna were being hunted to extinction. But here they were, still. I thought of roads and logging. Salt licks and hunting. Orange hairs in a tree. Failing the gods, I thought sleepily. We always have. It is what most myths, from every ancient world, are about. We never match up to what we think the gods expect of us. We defile the sacred precinct, kill guardians of holy river and forest. The gods punish people who transgress their laws or trample their shrines, but they have always brought back the world for us. Till now.

I closed my eyes and saw a tiger cub gazing at me, unsure if he should hiss. Somewhere in the gut of a large mosquito my blood was mingling with that of a small, determined Ussuri tiger, born on my birthday. But I saw him now as Lidya's cub, in bracken. *He* would hiss at me for real, and quite right too.

The casino was hotting up.'Don't you understand?' Dersu's words. 'Don't you understand? This is Amba!'

'The most a land of freedom while the most supersensitive area,' said a tour brochure in a cab from Seoul airport. 'Don't be afraid even with such unstable conditions we guarantee to bring you back safe! Exhibits include souvenirs, Freedom Bridge, war footage in 3rd Infiltration Tunnel discovered 1978.' Korea's tragedy had become a selling-point. 'The most fortified border on Earth that only Korea can offer.' One tour on offer included the Dora Observatory from which you could see into a North Korean village. 'Aren't you curious about their lives?'

Far eastern Russians love Seoul. Shops, nightclubs; consumption, not deprivation. Residents compare it to Manhattan. My cab took two hours in nose-to-tail traffic on a rainy motorway. Before the city, there were distant green hills and white mountain ridges, once the southern end of the Amur tiger's range. But there are probably none left here. North Korean biologists say there are. Dale and his Russian colleagues found no evidence, though there are reports from the demilitarized zone. But if any tigers were struggling there to maintain ranges and breed, I would not meet them on a DMZ tour.

Dale had given me contacts in Seoul, directors of research centres, a geneticist reconstructing the Korean tiger. ('He might as well try to clone the Korean dragon.') I had emailed before I came; none answered. I had a day between Vladivostock and London to find tigers here. My guidebook said Korean belonged to the Ural-Altaic family of languages but was seventy per cent Japanese borrowing, written in a fifteenth-century alphabet called *hangeul*, which tries to make its syllables look as much like Chinese characters as possible. Koreans say it is the most rational alphabet in the world. That just about summed up the problem of extracting information about the Korean tiger from the city this weekend. I had no time to go outside Seoul, to the mountains that make three-quarters of this wild, beautiful peninsula. But there were cultural tigers.

I needed the Emille Museum which contained folk art tigers. But it had moved; had closed. I walked past Top Shop, fake Burberry watches, butterfly earrings, *bulgogi* stands (bright-glazed beef, a favourite dish), labyrinthine subterranean arcades, signs written only in *hangeul*, to Insadonggil, a slanting street that defied the city's grid plan and sold ceramics of silvery blue-green celadon. There were paintings of tigers in every window. Stall-holders knew three words of English. 'Dollars' and 'Korean Tiger'. There were books on folk tales; on the old mountain religion. Mountain worship was central to the earliest Korean civilization. Even today ceremonies are held in remote gorges, and shamans light flames on sacred peaks to San-Shin, Spirit of the Mountain. His main personification is as an old man with a white beard, accompanied by a tiger. Long ago, the Chinese called Korea the 'Country That Speaks with the Tiger'. They said the Koreans worshipped mountains and performed rites for the tiger even then.

San-Shin's tigers were very varied. One curled round the old man, looking up lovingly; his hand rested on its shoulder. One was fuzzy and grey like a fluffy cat. Some were spotted not striped – again that odd confusion. A large purple tiger, a yellow tiger with a big grin, a red tiger bowing to *bullo-cho* (a herb that made you immortal). Many older tigers were abstract and Picasso-like with crossed eyes. Later ones were more realistic. It is ironic, said one author, that when tigers lived here they were painted abstractly; now they have gone, they are painted true to a life they no longer have. Some tigers *were* San-Shin. Some San-Shins rode a tiger, like Durga. One purple tiger had a chest puffed with pride like a pigeon. Some were white: Korea, at least, had white tiger myths. The White Tiger of the West was one of the four animal guardians of west, east, south and north: White Tiger, Green Dragon, Red Bird and Dark Warrior (a black turtle). Looking for a propitious site for a house you put Green Dragon on the left, White Tiger on the right. Green Dragon brought five blessings: longevity, health, virtue, wealth, and peaceful death. White Tiger warded off disaster: flood, fire and wind.

But not invasion, to which Korea, with China above and Japan in the east, has always been fatally open. In the nineteenth century, Korea tried to seal itself off; it became the Hermit Kingdom. In 1910 Japan annexed it. At the end of the Second World War Japan was out, but Russia gave North Korea weapons, China provided soldiers and America walked in. When the country was divided, the north became the most closed country in the world; the south was in ruins. Only industrialization would help.

No wonder Koreans painted White Tiger above the door. They needed to ward off everything they could.

Many paintings reflected folk stories. There were hundreds of tales about tigers, the animal most often mentioned. One woodcutter met a tiger stuck in mud. It begged him to save it. He pulled it out, but it tried to eat him. He asked an ox if this was fair. 'Eat him,' said the ox. 'Humans make us work, and when we are too old, they eat us.' The pine tree said much the same. But a magpie saved the woodcutter: he told the tiger to collect evidence for judgement by getting back into the puddle, and left him there. Ever after, magpies have nested near human homes and been an auspicious symbol in Korea. The ungrateful tiger and the clever magpie were everywhere. (Indian tree-pies flock round a tiger's kill. Maybe magpies used to do that here.) Some tigers were painted affectionately. An old tiger smoked a pipe held by a deferential rabbit. Tigers smiled big smiles, chased evil spirits. But one tiger attacked a couple in a field. The husband harvested rice while his wife screamed in the tiger's claws.

A lone tiger was often the icon of a shaman. Shamanism used to be important in this whole area, was always linked with tigers, and was part of this riven nation's identity. Spirit possession, ecstatic dance and divination were common even now. I saw photos of shamans dancing on knives and not getting hurt. The Hyatt Regency recently celebrated a twelve-million-dollar refurbishment with shaman rites. Of course Korea chose a tiger as the symbol of its 1988 Olympic Games, and journalists were hunting proof of its existence. The country still spoke with the tiger, even if real ones were no longer around. The tiger called to their beleaguered identity. This city of rainbow neon – high-rise shopping centres sheathed in video ads, underground malls echoing to computer games – pulsed with ancient shamanic practice ruled by a mountain spirit. Behind and beneath the whole thing was the tiger.

Next day on a six-lane boulevard I found a small building painted maroon, pink and gold, dark green: Seoul's nineteenth-century post office, where a rising was once planned against a corrupt regime. A post-office rising, like Dublin's, but Oriental . . . Suddenly Korea reminded me of another once-sealed mountain kingdom, where Buddhism had melded with animist belief, where mountains were sacred, traditional buildings painted in intricate earth colours. A country of masked dances where the tiger was a spiritual guardian. But, apart from Tibet, Bhutan had managed to keep the world out. Geography had been too much for Korea, what with China, Russia, Japan, America. Bhutan still has tigers; Korea does not.

We all owed Amba our own dreams of wildness and beauty. The tiger was a potent symbol throughout Asia. Khabarovsk and Vladivostock had it on their coats of arms. Here, the living tiger was lost but the symbol was still vital, along with what it stood for: mountains, wildness, spirit, magic. Every country has betrayed that magic differently, and struggles differently to keep it alive.

Back in England, I had to face that literary weekend. Where, he told me, he had changed his hotel to mine. After *taiga* on the turn autumn in England. On the first train, the hills were gold coin in cottonwool mist. I changed trains: a writer who worked in my local stationer came up. He was travelling to hear V. S. Naipaul speak. Most people in my neighbourhood were from Gujarat; he came from Kashmir. Asia was tracking me even in the Cotswolds. I was met by the woman who would whisk me on to the platform; but suddenly I no longer had my laptop. Had I left it on the train?

'I'll fill in a report,' she said. 'I'll get you on stage and come back.'

There was nothing I could do. I was working, railway offices were closed. On Saturday I dined with other people. On Sunday I breakfasted, as it happened, with the friends who thought the Kanha tiger should be shot for killing the boy. A girl with loose hair and bare feet chatted through the breakfasts of several people, looking up when anyone came in.

When he came, he spotted me instantly. After his fantasy, breakfast might seem a defeat; but the girl made up for it, joining him as if she had only just got there. He picked a table where he could meet my eyes through my friends' heads. She sat opposite, unaware of anyone else. He began talking intensely, forking up sausages, looking deep into her eyes, as we had sat at hotel breakfasts all over the world. There are deaths of relationships happening all the time like the deaths of stars. Every city, every script, *hangeul* to Dzongkha, Ussuriland to Java. On that suttee stone, the couple held hands. We had died separate deaths.

I spent four days ringing up train companies. I'd rather have lost my laptop on the Amur river. By midweek I wondered whether to complete the suicide. My chin was prickling oddly. All my half-thought work, buried in chips and wires. Why was my life bound to a sandwich of grey metal? Then the phone rang. A voice said, 'I think I've got your laptop.' Someone had picked it up the minute I left, getting off a train for his first day at university.

After I got it back, the prickling on my chin blossomed.

'*Acne?*'

'There aren't any real cures,' said the doctor. ' It's triggered by stress. You have to wait and see what it does.'

Asia saved me. The Indian chemist round the corner sold me *Agnus castus*. Chaste thorn. Five drops at night cleared it in a week. Could it also cure the pain of opened eyes, of realizing you had simply not let yourself know what someone you had loved was like, all along?

13

TIGER RAG, TIGER BONE

From one year's end to another one hears the hatchet and the
axe. The destruction of primitive forests, of which there are only
fragments in all China, progresses with unfortunate speed. They
will never be replaced.

Père Armand David, 1875

'Don't eat dog,' said my daughter, ruffling her spaniel's ears. 'And don't catch SARS.'

I had always longed to go there. My grandfather's Chinese ceramics at Boswells were the first sculpture I knew. Chinese artists painted the free-est tigers – not hunted, not divine pets, just enjoying their own wildness. Most zoologists today consider China as the cradle of tiger evolution. Until DNA was decoded, their origin was speculative: did tigers evolve, perhaps, in the Yakutsk region of northern Siberia, where some skeletal remains were found, when the climate was far milder? That would explain their love of cool forests and water . . . But in 1986 a morphological study suggested that they originated in south to east-central China.

China today, however, is the black hole pulling in all dead tigers. Tiger poaching in Asia is driven by Chinese demand for tiger bone; and, more recently, among newly affluent Chinese, for tiger skins. Traditional Chinese medicine, TCM, uses tiger bone for fortifying bones, 'pain and fear', joint pain, hypertonicity, epilepsy, piles, a prolapsed rectum. Other tiger parts, penis, eyes, whiskers, flesh, heart, brain, supposedly cure anything from impotence, foot sores, laziness, nausea, malaria and leprosy to acne. Tiger-bone medicines and tonics are officially banned in China. But illegally made tiger-bone products are exported to Asian communities in the West and sold over the counter in Japanese pharmacies or 'virility product' shops.

China's first instinct with a problem, especially a health one, is control by denial. Until 2001, Beijing denied China had Aids. For every dedicated Chinese doctor in remote provinces helping thousands infected by selling blood in an enforced government scheme, five officials were denying Aids, ten policemen chasing journalists from affected villages. A culture of control, denial and avoiding embarrassment, a developing country whose top layer is enjoying no-holds-barred capitalism, is not the ideal monitor of tiger-bone medicine, which *everyone* believes in.

Tigers are part of something bigger anyway: the whole illegal wildlife trade. Despite CITES, local wildlife laws are routinely ignored in China and South-East Asia. Endangered animals and their parts are sold openly. Bear gall is eighteen times more valuable per fluid ounce than gold. It supposedly protects the liver: you take it, live longer, drink, and do not worry about cirrhosis. In many countries it is illegal. But though TCM has seven hundred traditional herbal substitutes for it, China farms bears for it. A tube is implanted in the gall-bladder, and gall siphoned out from the bear in a squeeze cage. One bear makes seven pounds of it a year. The live Russian cubs saved by the Phoenix Fund were destined for bear farms. Or for food: in one year, Harbin's restaurants cooked four thousand pounds of bear paws. The Cantonese in the south say they eat anything with legs except a chair, anything with wings except an aeroplane. Recently a bear was found wandering Guangzhou's streets: local wildlife protection society officials were hiring bears to restaurants to attract customers. As I got my Chinese visa, eight hundred bear paws were impounded at the Russian border. That made 218 fewer wild Russian bears that I knew about, in six months. The tip of an iceberg.

SARS was caused by China's wildlife trade. Animal viruses do not normally infect human cells: the surface proteins do not match. But when there is very close contact a jump is likelier. Margaret Thatcher's government made BSE worse by denying it; China did the same with SARS. The first case known to the West died in Vietnam. When China admitted it had cases, the patients had worked in South Chinese wildlife markets or restaurants. Masked palm civets, racoon-dogs and ferret-badgers in a market carried a coronavirus similar to the SARS agent. The virus had jumped, shifting its genetic make-up to a human host. China admitted it had more cases. It slaughtered civets. The wildlife trade always flouted the law. Now 170,000 forestry officials raided 14,900 animal markets and restaurants, found 638,500 endangered animals, arrested 1428 people. They *could* crack down when they wanted to. I wondered what was happening now.

Until SARS, the luxury dish in Guangzhou's ten thousand restaurants was Dragon Tiger Phoenix Soup. Dragon is snake; phoenix, chicken; tiger, palm civet. But recently a Sino-Thai company sold a hundred tigers bred in Thailand (whose government denies farming them) to 'Sanya Love World' theme park on an island off China's south coast. 'SANYA TO ALLOW EATING TIGER MEAT OPENLY,' said headlines. Yes! said the first publicity. Tourists *will* be able to admire and eat tigers there. Have photos taken with them, feed them, eat them. After an international outcry, the manager played it down. 'It'd be impossible – unless UN protection policy changed. But we'd be well placed to benefit from change. We'll be the biggest tiger house in the world.'

China traditionally reveres the tiger as a symbol of power. The film director Ang Lee said *Crouching Tiger, Hidden Dragon* was a common phrase signifying power beneath society's surface. A *Book of Documents* of 850 BC says a responsible ruler trembles with anxiety as if treading on a tiger's tail. Black marks on a tiger's forehead are the hieroglyph for 'king'. People born in the Year of the Tiger are brave and generous.

Admire and eat? Every culture has betrayed the tiger. But I felt China had *most;* had betrayed its own feeling for it.

For SARS, I found a mask at a late-night chemist. I had seen Thai air hostesses wearing elegant ones. But mine, made in Bombay, approved for industrial use in Germany, had an ugly red plastic valve. It was hideous. Why on earth was it called 'Venus'?

'Fly trap,' said my daughter. 'You can't go to Shanghai in that.' I gave up on SARS and bird flu. Millions of Chinese were not getting them. Air France, however, said I was entering an area of *grippe du poulet*: 'Tell us if you suffer from psychosis, fever, or had contact with SARS.' Fifteen hours later I was following a girl called Eve Li, in an exquisite tweed miniskirt, through gold-plumed skyscrapers to a

Shanghai banquet. Eve's Ph.D. tutor, Endi Zhang, ran WCS in China. He was mayor of part of Shanghai, tall, fun and graceful with a Cambridge Ph.D., and a close colleague of Dale's. They monitored the same tigers across the border.

'Don't eat dishes that don't appeal to you.' Jellyfish and foot-wide mushrooms appeared on white damask, accompanied by claret.

China once had five of the nine subspecies. In Chinese Mongolia, the Caspian (Marco Polo called them striped lions); Bengal tigers in Yunnan and Tibet; Amur tigers in the north-east; Indo-Chinese north of the Indo-China border; and South China tigers, with whose DNA the Indo-Chinese has close affinities. All were always hunted.'If you won't go into the tiger's lair,' ran a 200 BC popular saying, 'how will you catch the cubs?' In 1682, sixty were killed in one area in a day. In the 1950s the thousands left became, along with China's forests, land and people, a casualty of Mao's environmental experiments. He unified a country that had suffered for centuries, but wrecked its ecology. First, urging unlimited population growth, he made farmers cut millions of trees to make charcoal for blast furnaces. Crops rotted, famine struck, innumerable wild animals were eaten. Then he made them plough up fragile grassland so that soil blew away; fell trees on hills, causing erosion; kill tigers as an agricultural pest. Over three thousand were killed in the 1950s and 1960s. Tiger-bone medicine expanded; wild South China tigers were all but eradicated. None has been seen by officials since the last was captured twenty years ago. There are twenty-one reserves in its supposed range, but no evidence that they are there. By 2000 it seemed unlikely that any could be left. Maybe thirty in forest fragments. But there were some bred in zoos. They were genetically weak, because inbred from – how many originals, I asked. Six?

'If that,' said Endi. 'Probably fewer.'

Endi had twelve Ph.D. students and ran three programmes for the WCS. One was on TCM, working with its practitioners, discussing substitutes for endangered species, explaining protection laws. Many did not know tiger bone was forbidden. After workshops, some said they *would* try substitutes. But TCM is a proud, popular, lucrative expression of the oldest continuous culture in the world, up there with

China's invention of coinage, paper, bureaucracy, silk. You must respect a culture to work with it. Tiger-bone products are sold increasingly, everywhere in the world. Many are fake, but fakes encourage belief in the real thing. Western Asian communities see TCM as a link to their culture. In 1998, fifty per cent of TCM shops, in cities with weak trade controls (like Atlanta, Los Angeles, Vancouver), were selling tiger products made in China; in New York, over eighty per cent. In London, tiger-bone products overflow the cupboards of the wildlife protection offices at New Scotland Yard.

Well, does it work? Some researchers claim tiger bone is analgesic and anti-inflammatory, though weaker than aspirin. Possibly all bone reduces pain and inflammation. Some say there *are* chemical differences between tiger and others; if so, their medical significance has not been determined. There are traditional alternatives. In the Cultural Revolution, China said, 'Use pig and cow instead.' Mole-rat bone (from the *sailong* or *zokor*, a small rodent, a real agricultural pest) is an officially recognized substitute. Sarah Christie had shown me a photo of a bottle of mole-rat-bone wine. Medically, the evidence is inconclusive. But, given human nature, the symbolism outweighs the evidence. Who wants to have their piles cured by mole rat?

Neurobiological research on the 'placebo effect' says any substance that patients believe will cure them probably will. Especially in pain relief, the main area tiger bone is used for. A top gastroenterologist says placebos relieve pain better than anything. In many areas (especially pain-killing; and anxiety, also treated with tiger) placebos cure two-thirds of patients. They work because brain circuitry modulates the transmission of pain. Imagining your hand to be warmer increases blood flow, raises its temperature. The fact that mental imagery causes physical change explains all possible effects of tiger bone. It is the ultimate placebo.

But for placebos to work, doctors as well as patients must believe they are genuine. The doctor's belief is vital. That is the catch. For placebos to work instead of tiger, even the practitioner would have to think they *are* tiger.

Apart from tiger bone, the WCS researched China's last viable tiger population in the largest tract of forest left, the north-east. After the disastrous 1950s and 1960s, the government tried to reverse things. In

1994, George Schaller said no government had accomplished so much in conservation in fifteen years, despite little money and few trained staff. China set up a new tiger reserve in the north-east and ran a local arms amnesty afterwards. Poachers there are not armed. They use wire snares. If caught they are sent to jail; dealers are never caught.

China also favours that concept Dimitri mentioned in Terney: 'conservation breeding', wild animals seen as a resource. The impulse behind many government conservation drives is captive breeding, supposedly for possible release, in the future. Pandas, for instance, were taken *out* of the wild for that. But a lot of endangered animals in cages look very like a farm. So what about farming – those Thai tigers, and other tiger-breeding establishments in China? Does farming endangered animals for medicine help their wild counterparts?

No. Since China allowed bear farming, the bear-gall market has expanded from traditional medicine to unnecessary additives in throat lozenges, even shampoo. And despite farmed gall, people pay more for illegal gall from wild bears. Wild is supposed to be *better*, so poaching increases. Farming bears makes thing worse for wild bears. Captive tigers, too, are a potential resource. People are paid to breed them.

'People think tiger meat makes you strong,' said Endi. 'Tiger-whisker toothpicks keep your teeth healthy. Health's an obsession here.' The mineral-water bottle said, 'Pure water, for your *healthy* life'.

'Men eat black sesame seeds to stop going grey!' said Eve. We were laughing. But the world cannot depend on China keeping a ban on tiger bone, tiger meat. Regulations can be changed.

'Sanya does want to produce tiger meat and bone. They slipped up on publicity. They weren't supposed to say that *then*.'

Eve had arranged visits, north and south. She said mysteriously, at parting, 'In the south, make them show you the field. *Not* architecture.'

December, midnight. Yanji's minuscule airport in Jilin province. Endi's student Leo, or Liu Yu, was there with Li Zhi Xing who ran education in the newest tiger reserve, Hunchun, hard by the Russian border.

Dongbei Hu, North-East tiger, lives in two provinces, Jilin and Heilonggyang (from *Heilong*, Chinese for 'Amur'). There are two populations. Most, based on the Sikhote-Alin, come in from Primorye and Khabarovsky Kraij; a few from south-west Primorye. Dale and Endi have proposed a joint protection system for these tiger forests, arguing that the forests *can* make money even while tigers' needs are met.

Hunchun had four regular tigers: a sub-adult, two male, one female. Recently a truck driver had seen one at night, padding along the snowy road while he drove behind hooting. Another killed a dog, left the stomach and carried the rest back to Russia. Leo, studying tiger movements for his MA, tracked a tigress for two days, eight hours behind her in snowy *taiga*. He photographed her pawmarks.

Hunchun, a long, thin territory, had a lot of human disturbance. There was a core area, an experimental zone where fifty thousand people lived and cut wood. They were hoping the government might fund people in the core area to move to the city. Tiger prey was boar, a few last musk deer, roe, red deer; but tigers also took over thirty cows a year. One man had been compensated, others wanted to be, the government was promising funds. But when boar wrecked crops there was no compensation and there were wire snares everywhere. Last winter, the WCS found over a thousand.

'Mr Li's father grew up here herding cows,' said Leo. 'They banged bamboo and lit flares to frighten tigers, but the tigers never harmed them.'

We drove to this remote northern border in a white police four-wheel drive. Villages had chestnut cows fluffy as cats, ponies with black toothbrush manes, streets of mud littered with torn plastic. No birds. What I thought was a sparrow was plastic flapping in the rubbish-filled ditch of a village that had a thousand people fifteen years ago and now had three thousand. Bare hills, timber yards everywhere; sparse stands of silver birch with red rags tied to their branches like those over the tiger spring in Russia or in that Soviet poem, 'Tiger Hunt'.

We got out in thick snow among bare trees, where Leo had cameratrapped a tigress who killed a mare. This was the last area for musk deer. All deer have scent-glands in their faces, but musk deer unfortunately have strong-smelling glands also in the skin of their stomach and under their tail: the source of 'musk'. Other animals, too, die in the snares.

The police driver stayed in his car; we walked up a frozen stream, as tigers do too, into a white-and-brown world. Bent poles on the bank: frog-hunters' huts, in which Leo slept while tracking. This was Arsenev's snowy *taiga*, frail shelters, lonely hunters. Frogs were caught by the ton. The park controlled their numbers, and poor people resented it. Russia had more frogs because Russians did not eat them.

The first inhabitants here were hunters; the tiger was their highest god, Shan Shin, Protector of the Mountain, *shan*; like San-Shin in Korea. Leo said there were many tiger temples. Oh – could we see one?

'It is very simple and in the field so it is not necessary for you to see it; just red cloths round a tree. They don't touch, they pay it worship. Any log man going into forest drops food on ground for tiger, for Shan Shin, and asks for bless. They think tigers are divine. This is why we still have tigers. If a person hurts a tiger he is cursed.'

How did this square with poaching?

'Last time anyone hunted tiger here was 1974. Now, is forbidden to kill tiger. Tiger bone is against the law. Only the West buys tiger bone.'

I said nothing. Maybe 'West' meant Japan, or South Korea. But I began to realize there were limits here to knowing things.

This was the other side of the range where we tracked Lidya: easier going now, through snow crust and the skeletons of plants that had been green and buzzing last summer. At a camera trap for deer were a few ancient roe droppings but no tracks. Tigers are all about prey. The ideal prey is hoofed animals, which the tiger evolved its teeth, skeleton, eyes, digestion to hunt and eat. Every tiger need is related to its prey. Water, because deer need water. Cover, so they can ambush deer. Tiger numbers depend on prey numbers. A grown-up tiger needs fifty deer-shaped animals a year. Mothers feeding cubs need many more. How did tigers here eat *anything*?

Up the frozen river where a trail crossed it, Leo had seen a place where a male tiger had lain to watch three trails at once. Then he leaped a bank and followed a ridge trail before plunging down to the next river and going up it. We followed his route a while: I imagined the solitary pad back to Russia, orange against snow.

The policeman had tossed out an empty bottle. I picked it up and put it into the car. He looked outraged. Leo moved it into the boot. We were going to the village nearest the core area, which lost twenty cows

to tigers last year. Only old people lived there, no children. There was
no bus to town. At first local people had been against the reserve; Mr
Li, genuine, generous and friendly, seemed the ideal person to change
this. Thin faces smiled when they saw him. They led us through mud
alleys between woodpiles and small rust-red cows. Twelve per cent of
Chinese are near starving. There was no money for pens; cows slept on
the path, vulnerable to tigers. A farmer's wife in a quilted red waistcoat sat us on a heated platform that ran three-quarters round her one
room, as in the Nanaian houses. The longer you sat, the hotter. I knelt
on my pullover, Leo shifted, Mr Li sat unflinching. The policeman
found eating hard-boiled egg with chopsticks as hard as I did. The
farmer brought out home-made liquor. We drank to Mr Li, to people
who helped preserve tigers by putting up with losing cows. I gave the
farmer's wife my scarf. Cameras came out. I presented it to her again,
both of us kneeling on the hot platform for the camera.

'Say it'll keep her warm.'

'She won't *wear* it!' said Leo. 'It is a present from an honoured guest.
It will be folded away and taken out to show people.'

Mr Li persuaded the farmer to stop pouring liquor and take us to a
Shan Shin altar. Four blue-grey trunks tied with red rags rose like fingers from a field. Over the roots were broken boards, to be mended for
Shan Shin's birthday when everyone poured him wine, put food on
the altar, and then ate it themselves. He didn't mind, apparently.

On the way back to Hunchun the sun shone, the car's heater roared,
and the only person controlling the windows was the driver. Could he
wind them down a bit?

'He won't because it's dirty outside.'

'But it isn't.'

'I know. But I can't say any more.'

'He's dissociated from nature.'

This poor policeman had become my image for all that had begun
to upset me about Chinese relations with nature. First he littered the
reserve, then he kept clean air out of his car.

'I don't want to agree with you,' said Leo, 'but I must.'

A van passed, spraying white dust.

'You see? He's right, it *is* dirty.'

For two hours we drove through sparkling air, heater full blast, windows up, while Leo asked about London fog and what English words described his feelings for Japanese who still wanted to invade his country, and I wondered what China would be like when his generation was in power: a nation composed entirely of only children.

Hunchun Forest Office, which ran the tiger reserve, was as big as a palace behind tall gates. Size bespeaks status. Everywhere the relation between forestry and wildlife is crucial. Forestry is always in charge. Trees make money, preserving wild animals does not.

Here was the reserve director, answerable to the local state's forest department. The forest administration in Beijing is the highest-level government department dealing with wildlife conservation. There is a central system for promoting and demoting government officials, so directors are always looking over their shoulders. I shook hands with chief directors of every possible department: Mushrooms, Wetlands, Wild Animals' First Aid, Anti-Poaching. There is no central directive for anti-poaching. Directors have various policies; the reserve's finances, of course, are a big factor. Some reserves have their own police team, but all police can arrest someone for killing a tiger. If there is enough evidence the court will convict and sentence him. Occasionally to death.

Finally, the Chief Director of Breeding. *Breeding*? Roe deer, said Leo, to supplement the wild population.

Oh. Where do they come from?

'Fawns that are lost.'

'How can fawns get *lost*?'

'Local people rescue and rear them. They're not supposed to, so we do.'

'Rescue': that euphemism for 'capture'. Like tigresses, deer leave babies hidden in bushes while they find food. The fawns wait, obedient. If human beings take them they are indeed lost: to their mothers, to the wild. Conservation with staff ignorant of animal science and behaviour, who are administrators not zoologists, is – difficult. How about anti-poaching? How often did they remove snares?

It took a month, apparently, to do it. The WCS funded it. It happened once a year. The farmers knew snares were wrong, but set them constantly. One year poachers killed a deer and were mauled by a tiger. The guards took them to hospital, then prosecuted them. The poachers said, 'It should have been OK. We made offerings to Shan Shin before we started.'

Mr Li said sadly, 'It needs time. We'll try our best. I keep asking myself, how can local people benefit from living with the tiger?'

No one else had put it so clearly. This *is* the question the world has to solve. He was trying to save what could be saved, while doing his best by a very poor population. The whole enormous tragic history of China weighed on everyone here. Thousands of years of exploiting peasants. Mao's errors. A man whom people evidently trusted, trying to solve the insoluble, for a region he loved.

'We will be with the tiger till the end. We try to persuade the government to fund us but this is a developing country. We have to answer that question for *this* region, *here*.'

I admired him deeply. Conservation has universal principles, but it is the local that matters, how you apply it in each place.

A technician ran a video about the reserve. We began with heaps of impounded traps, then saw a tiger lying on snow. He had put his head in a snare set for musk deer. Men lifted him on to a lorry, laid him in a cage. His own magnificent strength had severed his windpipe. He had then killed a woman but could not eat her. He had never attacked humans before. In red livid detail we watched three operations to rebuild his throat. Press, surgeons, unconscious tiger. Someone dragged him across the cage floor by his flame-coloured fur. He lurched to his feet, massive chrysanthemum head low and stiff on his stitched throat. He could not eat, he stared. I was in tears. The technician played with his mobile phone.

'The reconstruction worked,' said Leo. 'Then not.'

Another operation. Tigers are so strong. He got to his feet again.

'They injected milk into.'

After the third, he died. We watched the autopsy, huge body opened down the middle, a red pencil case, infected. To some, this film might show China doing all it can to save the tiger. But money spent reconstructing windpipes is better spent removing snares *much* more often. George Schaller's longest involvement anywhere was with China's pandas. Forest staff avoided going into the field; pandas died from snares they had not removed. Russians love nature, said Michiel, but most Chinese do not want to enter it.

Couldn't they put up posters saying 'SHAN SHIN SAYS NO SNARES'? Killing that woman when he was hurt was Shan Shin's punishment for the snare. Surely the god of the wild could enforce the protecting of wild things? How about TV ads: 'POACHING HARMS OUR LAND'?

'The people are simple, but government doesn't want to do things that *look* simple. They do ads for social things. Not conservation.'

I flew back to Shanghai, hypnotized by yellow eyes in a dying body. He had guarded his patch of the Sikhote-Alin five years. Chinese lore says that when a tiger dies its spirit sinks to earth and returns as amber. I hoped his had got through the cage cement to naked ground.

Strings of neon, floating night-clubs at the mouth of the Yangtse, zig-zagged beside Shanghai's most famous street, the Bund. Glow-in-the-dark spiders, skewed trapeziums, pink parallelograms, purple and daffodil wigwams; they all pulsed to hip-hop on a black river, one in the shape of a giant shoe. City glamour while doors were closing on China's wild nature. In the 1930s deco Old Jazz Bar, a German busi-nessman told a Chinese, 'You have to make a promotion! Make them with *rubber* handles. No one will see if you don't show!' From a menu on the bar I ordered 'Tiger Rag'. But it was a musical number, not a cocktail. Of course – Louis Armstrong. Feverish drums, pouncing scales on the piano: a tiger was among us, crackling with energy. But the real thing walked into snares on a mountain, pulling wire so tight with that same energy that he sliced his throat in two.

People clapped frenziedly. 'Tiger Rag' was the hit of the night.

At my poetry reading, a Shanghai novelist said *The Madman's Diary*, by a 1920s writer called Lu Xun who loved Darwin, was now much stud-ied in schools, and Darwin was the emblem of human progress. I walked to the old city, bewildered. Darwin had made our relation to animals central to our view of ourselves, made us see ourselves con-nected to other animals. If you take Darwin to stand for *human* progress, that connection is lost.

The Jade Garden was supposed to celebrate harmony with nature. It had blue-grey rocks, carted from another province, and arches to feel good about nature in. Pavilion for Listening to Billows. Pavilion for Enjoying Happy Fish. To me, it seemed the opposite of harmony. I loved the people at the reading, Mr Li, the conservationists, but this country was making me more and more unhappy. I suddenly hated gardens. This one confined nature, bossed it about. I thought wildly of bonsai and foot-binding. It was beautiful, but it was nature squeezed and planned, not the natural balance of animal and plant which was Darwin's great insight.

What was wrong with me? I *loved* gardens. Boswells was my first paradise. The Chinese love of nature was ancient, real, far bigger than me. 'If enjoyment of nature should end, who would understand what all this means?' said Hsieh Ling-yün, fourth-century poet. The official who helped George Schaller begin the panda conservation project was called Wang Menghu, 'Dreaming of Tigers'. Why did I feel oppressed and wretched in a culture that gave people names like that?

I found an art gallery and lovely paintings of cranes, the 'birds of heaven'; of monkeys and forested landscapes. But many crane species were severely endangered here, wetlands where they fed and bred were gone or threatened, birds and eggs eaten. Monkey brains were eaten for – what imagined benefit? Here were exuberant tigers, yawning, rolling, curling round pine trees: this was not how life was for tigers in Hunchun. Was I against art now, too?

14

DREAMING OF TIGERS

'I'm here to make big money for my company General Electric in America. Where are you going? Why didn't you take the plane?'

'I wanted to see the country.'

'There's nothing to see.'

I looked outside the train. Flatness. Every inch of land completely, minutely, *used*. Even mud shanties on town outskirts were tidy. Our sleeper had pale green satin curtains and coat-hangers, a Thermos of hot water, a soft carpet (pale green), fresh paper slippers, TV. On the toilet wall, a vase-shaped screw-in ceramic held fresh carnations. China took pains with human things. Lids on mugs made you feel cherished. Billions of people here, longing to feel looked after. For five thousand years they had not been. Now they could.

'I'm going to Yihuang.'

'I grew up in Yihuang. There's nothing there.'

But another man said, '*Hu!*' Tiger! He said more, excited.

'He says you are going to see tiger,' said the first man, reluctant to share his English conversation. 'It killed someone in Yihuang.'

Nanchang is capital of Jiangxi province. In the seventh century it was key to the north–south inland waterways when a Grand Canal linked the Yellow and Yangtse rivers. Now it had four million people. Half seemed to be at its station in rainy dawn. A small girl held a placard with my name. The interpreter's daughter, perhaps?

'Mrs Ruth? I am Mrs Wang. We find Mrs Cao.' She pounced on

another girl in a candy-striped jumper with an equally radiant smile; then a car, a driver. They were twenty-three, not twelve. My interpreters: tourism students. They did not know what 'conservation' meant, or 'reserve'.

'Where wild animals live,' I said, and drew a lugubrious stag.

'Zoo!' said Cao.

Ouch. '*Not* zoo.'

We zoomed down a pouring highway. Paddy-fields, mud; villagers in dun translucent wellingtons; water-buffalo, cement. The driver stopped for Cao to be sick. After Fuzhou the road was being made. We crawled between raw banks: tomato mud splashed our windows. The Hunchun policeman would have hated it. On misty hilltops where terracing had not reached there were a few stands of bamboo, but then a burnt hill of dead bamboo. If China was the model, wilderness really was doomed. Of the world's twenty most polluted cities, sixteen are in China.

Yihuang was mud-splashy, crowded with auto-rickshaws. We were meeting the reserve director in a playground, Wang said. We parked in the middle of the central square (ah, the playground) by a large black car. Men in suits got out with umbrellas.

'Director,' said Wang. 'We go to lunch with.'

With my interpreters holding me as if I might float away, we splashed to a banquet. Wine, dumplings, soup; twenty officers of the reserve. The director made a speech through Wang about the South China Tiger, Darwin, human progress. Wang and Cao were happy: Yihuang reminded them of their home towns. But – could we walk in the reserve now, please?

'We go now!' Reserve was Wang's new word. We got into our car with the one woman, Mrs Zhang, and followed the men's car into a misty valley. I was lacing my trainers for the field when Mrs Zhang spoke.

'We are not going to reserve,' said Wang. 'To temple.'

'Make them take you to the field,' Eve had said. But everyone was in suits and polished shoes. My interpreters had no coats. How could I insist on a rainy forest? As a field adventurer I was a fiasco. No one had the slightest intention of walking. This was a culture of control and I was its object.

Swollen paddy-fields held all the light the sky did not have. We drove through dripping hills to a valley head. Two carfuls of umbrellas blossomed among red sheds, bamboo poles. Where was the temple? Ah – it was destroyed in the 1970s: this was where it would be, when it was rebuilt. There were large new Japanese Buddhas on their sides, wrapped in plastic. The director pointed to hills. 'Hill of Flower. Hill of *Sleeping Tiger!*' Wang said. I asked the wildlife protection officer about real animals. Say, leopards? He said they had two kinds. One had been wounded very near here by a farmer; it had had black and white spots like cloud and died in a zoo. Could we go to where this clouded leopard was found?

'Too dangerous because of weather. It is rain.'

Wang and Cao were very sweet, but I was seeing everything through their excited understanding. 'South Chinese Tiger' fell happily from their lips. That was what this landscape, too dangerous to enter in rain, was all about. We drove to another banquet and finally, at evening, to the reserve headquarters in the unlit forest office. We picked our way over rubbish through dim corridors to the director's smart bright room, his own calligraphy on the walls. He gave me an article on the South China tiger and the reserve brochure, *Roar of South China Tiger*, with a snarling open-mouthed tiger. The Protecting Animals Officer showed me the reserve map. In some places it was five kilometres wide: a tiger could walk through it without blinking. No one knew how many deer it held, but wild pig sometimes spoiled crops. Did that trouble local people? 'Mostly they support.' How often did they remove snares? Wang had trouble with 'snares'; I tried 'wire'. Not regularly, he said. 'Before 2000, people set wire. Now, reserve is bigger.' I kept getting answers to questions I had not asked, logic that did not add up.

'Now we see video.' Cao must have been unbelievably cold: the unheated building was freezing, I was shivering in a winter coat, she was in her thin jumper. But she sat down with smily enthusiasm to a video about death. In 1999 two peasants went snake-hunting on a summer night, with miners' lights strapped to their heads. (No one seemed bothered about snake-catching in protected areas.) One screamed, his friend found him on the path with a gashed head and ran away. Police brought back the body next day with bite marks in the scalp. They found a thirteen-centimetre pawmark. Its owner had swiped the snake-hunter's head, where the alarming light was. This was frontal attack, no ambush for food. Tigers mostly attack from behind; it might have been an upset bear. But everyone said it was the South China Tiger. Hair and scat were found and analysed. Tiger, said the commentary.

Of course the man on the train remembered. Of course the brochure's tiger had vast teeth. A man had died. What better proof that tigers existed and were fierce?

Another video showed a chicken coop where an animal had killed fourteen hens. Footprints and hair were again 'identified as' tiger. *Chickens?* With dogs, buffalo, people everywhere? There was something wrong with this tiger. But Yihuang reserve had been enlarged because of it. I remembered something said in Shanghai. 'They are so thrilled by tiger, excited by it: it is all in their mind. They *feel* tiger bone does them good. In southern reserves they *feel* the tiger is there. They see animals mostly at night, two eyes in the dark. They say tiger, though these are tiny areas, nowhere larger than hundred square kilometres. They say, "Here's a patch of green, let there be tigers in it." They think in zoo terms and that's bigger than a zoo. You say, "But there's no prey." They say, "Well, we have goat, pigs." It is a question of belief.'

In 2001–2, a Chinese survey of eight reserves in five southern provinces said tiger prey was increasing; tigers lived in four places, including Yihuang. No tigers had attacked livestock in the last ten years but there was enough wild prey; or tigers were avoiding 'things with human flavour'. A distinguished American biologist called Ron Tilson, however, helped with the survey. What *he* saw was decreasing prey, areas too small to support tigers, massive disturbance in core areas, even new hotels in some. People cut wood there, gathered plants, trapped animals. In Yihuang, that tiger attack was unconfirmed; four hundred families lived in the core area unaware that woodcutting was forbidden. Some said they had seen a *laohu*, but that was the word for leopard, tiger or clouded leopard. People did have firearms, though they were supposedly impounded. Leg-irons for tiger and leopard were sold in local markets; one scat offered as tiger evidence was an owl pellet. Livestock grazed the reserve; villagers had lost some to predators before 1990, but there had been no recent attacks on livestock. To tiger scientists, that says it all. Tilson concluded that a few may be hanging on but the South China tiger was basically extinct in the wild.

I reread this report in my room, and turned to the director's article. He said fifty-five tigers were captured, i.e. killed, here in the 1950s, twenty-five in the 1960s, ten in the 1970s. People saw tigers in the 1990s: one was killed in 1996; in 1998 a farmer saw one eating a boar, drove it off and took the boar. (No comment that tigers should be left to eat their natural prey.) After the snake-hunter, *five* tigers were 'identified' here. Yihuang was 'the only place South China Tiger was discovered breeding'. In 2001, 'Lang Terson, director of animal preserve in Minestar America, investigated here'. (The conclusions of Ron Tilson from Minnesota were not mentioned.) In 2003, Chinese investigators found 'two tiger claws, which proved a driver saw a tiger crossing a highroad a week ago'. I turned out the light, unsure whether to laugh or cry.

Later I asked a Shanghai scientist why everyone said the killer's DNA was tiger when Tilson called it unconfirmed. A lab testing was a lab testing. Surely, hairs either were or weren't tiger DNA?

'The government cannot afford to lose face and say they have lost tigers. They are not impressed with science. They play games, they balance one NGO against another. The scientists are excellent. Reports are changed when they leave the lab.'

Now we really were going to the reserve. It was raining but not heavily. Schaller's panda research had been done in rain. South China's mountains are not green for nothing. Surely the reserve staff were used to their own weather. They were not dressed for walking, but in Russia they had told me Chinese scientists went to the field in suits. It is polite to meet guests in suits.

But no. No walking. Wang translated the explanation. 'Is danger.'

Were they worried about tigers? Because, I said, I was not.

'Is car, on road.' There was more debate. 'In rain, the animals go in their caves. They not like rain.'

I got a picture, dangerously near *Winnie-the-Pooh*, of a mountain where clouded leopard and South China tiger sat down, shook out umbrellas and complained of the weather. But if I agreed we would not actually walk, then somehow we *could* drive to the core area. The men went ahead. We followed.

'I hope,' said Wang looking round, 'Chinese tiger will come out.'

Like the sun. Like a cuckoo from a clock. Mrs Zhang waved at a clearing. 'The government pay money to protect tiger, not to cut trees. No guns. To protect Chinese tiger.' We came to Dunkou. 'South Chinese tiger's village,' said Wang. The main street was a sea of mud lined with woodyards and timber lorries. Even peeled bark was carefully shaved and stacked. Corners and streams were mounds of litter, plastic shreds, and forlornly pecking hens. Further up, the car nearly stuck in thick mud. As at Hunchun, a new road was being made, which would make things much easier for poachers. Mrs Zhang apologized for the mud. 'We have not been up here a long time.' So when, I wondered, did anyone last check for traps?

Every now and then mist shifted and we could see. A man carrying a child in a glowing field. Knobbled mountains swirling with mist. So much space, the figures in it so small. A reservoir, dam, power station; a poster advertising the reserve with a roaring tiger; Shengangg, one of two towns around the core. The Master of Shengangg was a woman. With a young chief of police she welcomed us with rice wine.

'We have lunch here,' said Wang.

'Aren't we going on?'

Impasse. They wanted a banquet, I wanted to see their reserve. We agreed to drive further and come back. With ten men now, and a photographer, we transferred to two other jeeps. One they had been going to use had broken down; someone found another at four in the morning. People had taken a lot of trouble. But there were clearly not many patrols. Jeeps were difficult. This director, it seemed, did not often leave his office and his beautiful calligraphy.

Rainy mud track, up, down, up. A tiny village, Dasan Kou, centre of the reserve. Wang was thrilled.

'Here Chinese tiger comes often. But not so often now. They have photo of cow killed five years ago. Along this road is vegetable, which Chinese tiger likes very much to eat.'

I could see my daughter raise an eyebrow-stud over her A-level biology.

'The South Chinese tiger cannot run very well in forest. But on this vegetable it runs very well. That is why it goes on road.'

Oh Wang, I could see it doing exactly what you said.

The director wanted me to see the village. I wanted to go up the mountain behind; we walked in instead. It was very poor. Outside reserves, up to thirty people live in every square kilometre here. They grow rice, sweet potato, fruit; cut bamboo shoots and herbs, transport them, with difficulty, to sell in town. Living standards are way below the national average. Most belong to the 'warmly dressed and well-fed' category. Some do not. We were warmly dressed; our third banquet in two days waited in Shengangg. The director walked us into someone's barn. A family was in one room, playing mah-jong on a red felt table. A large unconnected TV was on a chest in foam packing. There was one bed, and a poster advertising a three-piece suite. I turned over the pieces. The granny who had given me the opera glasses also taught me mah-jong.

'Green dragon?' I asked. Wang translated; that was wrong, everyone laughed. I asked if wild pig ate the woman's crops. Yes. But not many. Did she chase them off? No, there were not enough to be a problem. (Or maybe she was scared of the director.) I had no idea of the issues and relationships behind all this. Back at the jeeps, the photographer took pictures of us all. That was what this trip was for. I looked longingly up the mountain track. They saw.

'A pity cannot see mountain,' Wang translated. 'Are many herbs there which South China tiger likes to eat. He comes there very often. Are many animals if you walk that road.'

I gave it my last shot. What animals? The men from Shengangg debated.

'There are,' said Wang, finally, 'many rabbits.'

A wet dhole looked up at us. Pointed blond muzzle, deformed ear.

'Is ill,' said Cao, anxiously. She had got me to Nanchang Zoo at last. It was pouring with rain; the only animals were us, cranes and this dhole. Two tigers lay curled in cages, black fishbone spines towards us, by a signpost showing a tiger balancing on poles, for Animals-Show-Skill Hall, where tigers sometimes jumped through burning hoops.

In 1996, China News Service reported Nanchang Zoo chaining a tiger to a table and charging visitors sixty dollars to have photos taken sitting in triumphal poses on it as keepers poked it so that it lifted its head. I had seen photos taken at a zoo in Yunnan of a tiger similarly shackled: a Chinese tourist in tweed sat on its neck grinning, flushed, almost post-coital, fists waving in macho brag. Keepers stood by with iron bars. Maybe the South China tiger was better off as a chimaera.

I took Wang and Cao to lunch to thank them. They asked if I liked mushrooms and ordered from a sea of Chinese. Wang translated another article by the director: 'In Yihuang, a power station, railway and road destroyed environment. People must use people's affection for tiger to do nature tours. To improve green food industry, Forestry Bureau paid much money for trademark of South Chinese tiger.'

I saw now. Never mind animals dying in snares. Tigers must exist: it is their commercial existence, as trademark, that counts.

The mushrooms were various shapes and sizes. Wang took a large wobbly one and asked if we ate pigs' blood at home. Clearly there was more than mushrooms here. A long yellow thing knobbled like a thimble was cow's stomach. I chewed a thin small stalk without its head. Wang pressed an electronic dictionary and showed me what I was eating. Leeches.

In my sleeper to Amoy, an older man was lecturing a younger man. Wang asked him something; I saw him snub her. She tried to smile it off. 'I asked him where he was from and he would not tell me,' she said in English.

In English he said, glancing at me, 'I am from *China*.'

They started talking. Cao said, 'He says we do not know much.'

'We must teach the young generation,' he said. 'They know nothing.'

'I think they're *wonderful*!' I went out with them to the corridor. We hugged goodbye. They gave me a present.

'We wrapped,' said Cao. 'But is not very beautiful.'

'Oh Cao, it *is*!'

I unwrapped a seven-inch steel hairpin.

'For your daughter,' said Wang.

I was looking forward to this journey. It would end on the coast oppo-site Taiwan, at Xiamen, once called Amoy, which gave the South China tiger its Latin name, *Panthera tigris amoyensis*. I had no time to see the subtropical south but this twenty-four-hour ride would take me through Jiangxi and Fujian, two provinces where tigers used to flourish.

My plans had changed. From Xiamen I would have gone to a tiger breeding centre. Most tigers breed brilliantly in captivity. Not South China ones. They are very inbred with a poor sperm count. In 1995 international vets and zoologists visited Chinese zoos, teaching med-ical care, record-keeping, tiger husbandry, recommending better genetic management on the Western model, which swaps tigers inter-nationally to maximize the gene spread throughout all captive tigers. That is why there are stud books of Sumatran and Siberian tigers. But it was a hard thing to try here. Some zoos were run by the forest department, others were municipal. Power and status struggles meant zoos resisted an overall programme. One refused to put a proven male with a second tigress because he had sired so many cubs with the first. The more cubs the better, never mind the genes. But that training was a start, and since then China has had a better breeding programme.

The breeding centre I had hoped to see was Meihuasan, opened by local staff as passionate for their own region and its tiger-haunted his-tory as Mr Li in Hunchun. Two zoos donated six tigers. They hoped to teach tigers to hunt and release them in the Meihua mountains, source of Fujian's three main rivers. But Tilson had seen 3500 people living in the Meihuasan buffer zone, cattle grazing unsupervised in mountains. As at Yihuang, hundreds of people gathered forest plants and there were no patrols, few signs of prey.

I had this centre's observation notes on their six. A moody male with 'beautiful unscrupulous coat as if trimmed in a salon, boastful if people are photographing him'. A timid female, a good hunting strat-egist. A male fond of water play; a female obsessed with hygiene; a male who 'only catches prey if ladies are around'; a shy female.

Affection, pride and delight ran through these notes. But Tilson thought the southern reserve that could best support wild tigers was Hupingshan in Hunan province. It had the most varied intact forest, most prey and small carnivores (best bio-diversity, in other words) and was least encroached on by people. If Meihuasan was anything like Yihuang it would be very dangerous, to people and tigers, to release tigers there. If there is not enough wild prey, real tigers kill live-stock and people. Large carnivores who have depended on human beings for care and food are used to people. They may not be used to being nice to them, but they are not afraid. Released carnivores are more dangerous than wild ones.

These tender profiles had been emailed to me by Li Quan, who had given up a career in fashion to start a charity called Save China's Tigers. She knew Meihuasan and emailed me the reserve's phone number. They spoke no English, so Eve had kindly phoned for me to see if I could visit. She got a brush-off. 'If this person's a friend of Li Quan, why doesn't she ask us herself?' I did not want to drive for two days into winter mountains on bad roads and not get in, so I decided to skip Meihuasan and stay on an island off Amoy. They were rude, I was told later, because they did not know what might happen. If a for-eigner criticized anything, the state bureau might know about it *before them*. People in competing organizations do not trust each other. Later, Li Quan kindly got me permission to see Meihuasan, but by then it was too late; my itinerary was fixed.

I stared miserably into night over Fujian's mountains. Somewhere near here, they think, was where the first tiger evolved. Li Quan's own plan for saving the South China tiger was to take China-bred cubs to South Africa and release them in China. From the outside this seems a nice idea, but there are reasons, carefully and firmly expressed by the world's top scientists and reintroduction specialists for the World's Conservation Union, why it is not. I did not want to think about this. Li Quan had been kind. But I had to.

The tiger is an Asian animal. It never lived in Africa, but an Afrikaans myth says that it did. Seventeenth-century Dutch traders on the Cape, used to Java and its tigers, called any spotted or striped carnivore (like hyena or leopard) *tijger*. Later *tier*, the modern Afrikaans for leopard. African travellers told tiger tales. An eighteenth-century traveller said the Tygerberg mountain was 'spotted like a tiger'. That word *tier* kept the myth alive. The issue was hotly argued in the quarry at Robben Island, where Nelson Mandela was imprisoned in the 1960s. A well-informed prisoner said there were never tigers there. Then why *tier*? They argued so much that the warders handcuffed them. It is a passionate myth, as many myths about indigenous animals are. What your own earth produces matters to your soul.

In my dark carriage, filled with Chinese pop music, South China and South Africa seemed linked by the need to believe in the presence of tigers in the teeth of evidence. And also by Li Quan. Impressed by South African tourism, by a reserve where she saw leopards, and by people who taught lion cubs to hunt for films, she thought tigers could energize tourism in South China. She has taken Chinese-bred captive cubs to Africa, to be taught to hunt and eventually released in China.

One reason against this, explained to me by a wildlife vet, is the danger of infection. Immunodeficiency viruses come from Africa. It is 99 per cent certain that HIV came from SIV, the simian form. Chimps carried it. It did not bother them, they evolved with it. Humans did not: Aids developed when it jumped to us. Many lion populations in Africa have the feline equivalent, FIV. It does not develop into full-blown Aids but put it into an Asian animal like the tiger, which has not evolved with it, and they might import feline Aids to the whole Chinese environment. From anything: a tick, any parasite. You could test them when they left Africa, but they could develop Aids in China two years later. By then the parasites could have spread everywhere. And prominent South African and international conservation organizations are worried about the effect of alien tigers on indigenous African wildlife.

The World's Conservation Union's expert report said the best place to breed South China tigers for reintroduction was China, their natural habitat, as Meihuasan is doing. From a conservation perspective, the first priority is habitat; to make sure it is suitable before animals come anywhere near it. Today, South China's wild prey will not support tigers and there is little biodiversity left to support such prey. Ecologists experienced in developing habitat and re-establishing prey found that officials did not know how to look after protected areas, maintain fences, monitor wildlife, enforce wildlife laws in South

Chinese reserves. The chosen area will get a fence, protection and tourist investment, but fences will break, animals will get out, poaching around will increase. Everything needs to be ready to deal with that before any tigers arrive.

There are also the horribly inbred genetics of captive South China tigers. (Captives are the only ones available, probably the only ones left. But the latest genetic study by the US laboratory of genetic diversity shows that the DNA of one of their two lineages is indistinguishable from northern Indo-Chinese tigers, which probably infiltrated the zoo population long ago, so those in Africa may have Indo-Chinese genes anyway.) These zoo-bred tigers have all the problems, including low reproductive rates, of inbreeding. Experts urged that if some were removed and bred with each other in Africa they should be selected carefully by genetic experts, to lessen further deterioration and inbreeding in China, *and* to ensure the best possible lines for the African lot. They also said existing plans for better management of the captive population should be made to work *before* any tigers were taken out and bred for for reintroduction. This was not done.

As for 'teaching to hunt': one of the definitions of 'wild' is no contact with humans. It is vital to insulate wild carnivores and humans from each other. (The increased man-eating in the Chitwan buffer zone seems a result of more tigers and people using the same area.) Cubs taken from a mother do not learn how to be tigers. Some orphaned wild cubs do teach themselves to hunt. At Ranthambhore, the cub whose mother died learned to catch live prey: guards left live goats and kept away. In Russia, too, young wild orphans have taught themselves to hunt. But they do it in private, away from people, in dense cover.

For tigers naturally hunt secretly. Their technique is all about getting close under cover. It is the art of stillness, geometry, concealment. Tigers have great speed over short distances but are no use in a long chase. Once they get into a race with prey they have lost. Cheetahs are light on their feet; they run down the prey they evolved to hunt (in open plains as well as woodland). Tigers are heavy, and work through long grass, dense bushes, trees. It can take hours. The angle you come from is all. A hunt ends with a burst of explosive power but depends on long preparation. The fifty yards that a jungle-smart man will cover in two minutes, thinking he is quiet, may take a tiger fifteen. The tiger will really be invisible. Rather than risk the faint crackle of a dead leaf, she will slowly crush it to dust. With prey in sight, a tiger going for a sambar is like a cat after a robin. Same crouch, same just-not-wobbling stillness, low-slung between whispering grass-heads. The last seconds before the charge have an air of superstitious double-checking: she weaves her head in fractional advances and retreats, eyes confirming her final assessment of distance like a referee making up his mind on a football foul. Then she breaks cover and bursts out, her face a mask of concentration.

Li Quan's ideas were inspired by captive predators trained to hunt to camera. Wild tigers hunt alone, undercover, not in a group; very different from lions. Asian eco-tourism is not as commercial as African partly because, as that disgruntled Italian tourist found at Chitwan, it is normal *not* to see tigers, still less see a hunt. 'Rewilding' is training hand-reared animals to hunt in a way they can be filmed. Chinese tourists paying to see tigers kill goats behind a fence are nothing to do with the wild tiger or its future. China does not protect animals against cruelty. There are about thirty safari parks. They put live horses and oxen in enclosures so visitors can see tigers kill them. In March 2005 this was banned: people thought it might 'implant violent tendencies in youngsters', though they were only acquiring a taste their parents already had. Twenty-two safari park managers agreed to the ban, but it does not cover smaller animals and birds. Tigers will kill them instead, and live large animals will be given them after opening hours; viewed, presumably, by a select few. It must save on labour. No cutting carcasses up.

But Save China's Tigers' scheme *seems* glamorous. There is money and publicity in it, despite opposition from prominent South African and international conservation organizations, who say it is against the Biodiversity Bill and in flagrant opposition to internationally agreed principles for the release of 'exotic organisms' – animals that do not belong in a given eco-system. I felt torn. Li Quan's motto, 'Extinction Is For Ever', was absolutely true. She had invested energy, passion and huge funds in this scheme. I admired her dedication. She had consulted experts. But she seemed to have ignored the world's top scientific advice. She may release a few tigers in a closed reserve but

this will have nothing to do with conservation and will never lead to a viable wild population. It seemed a terrible waste of enormous tiger funds.

The worst danger is that it will divert China from real tiger conservation. International experts have said the urgent priority is a master strategy to conserve *all* China's tigers: north to south, Hunchun to the Indo-China border and Tibet. The wildlife director of China's forestry administration himself suggested an international workshop to discuss an overall Chinese tiger plan. International experts said yes, what a good idea, and wrote offering to help. Chinese authorities did not respond. If you have a superficially glamorous scheme with money in it, why pay to help wild tigers hanging on unseen?

Li Quan also wants to change the name of the South China tiger to Zhongauo Hu. *Zhongauo* means 'Middle Kingdom', the formal name for China: that name would make it simply 'Chinese Tiger ', excluding China's other tigers, the real wild tigers of China today. (I had seen with Wang and Cao how effective that plan would be. The Chinese tiger – of course!) Her English press releases have subtly switched from 'South Chinese Tigers' to 'Chinese Tigers (also named the South China Tiger)'. She hopes to time release of the 'trained' tigers with China's 2008 Olympic Games and make China take the tiger as its mascot. (Shades of Korea, which did that too.) This seemed to me a sick joke when Chinese demand for tiger medicine and skins is decimating tigers worldwide, especially in India, which *has* got viable populations. Save China's tigers? The best way to do *that* would be to use available tiger money to ensure anti-poaching patrols are out all day on every existing Chinese reserve; to whip up political will to pay for removing snares, relocating desperately poor villagers; to help Meihuasan with genetics and relocation, do conservation education everywhere: especially on TV, which is all-powerful in China. And go after everyone involved in the wildlife trade, especially tiger skins, tiger bone. Which would save all other tigers, too.

Still, I now had twenty-four hours on Gulangyu Island, off Amoy. But it was not what I expected. A million Chinese tourists bowled round it in electric chariots tinkling 'Auld Lang Syne'. Restaurants put plastic washing-bowls outside, where turtles waited to be eaten. I watched an agitated one trying, as methodically as a turtle can, to get through the net over the bowl. One shop had a stuffed bear, gibbons and leopard, all illegal, all critically endangered, openly on sale. I looked at the leopard despairingly. Eve said changing attitudes here was going to take time. Did nature have that time?

Back in London, a year since I had broken it off, he suggested lunch in Sicilian Avenue, where we'd once dined under flapping plastic on a rainy summer's night. It had closed. We found another. Across Italian breadsticks, he seized my hand.

'Your hair was darker before.'

His fantasies kept moving the goalposts.

'You overdid it sometimes,' he added with a smirk to an invisible audience. 'I suppose we were very lucky.' He looked earnestly in my eyes. I tried to respond.

'We created something wonderful.'

'Created?'

He looked blank.

I thought of the years of learning, understanding, adapting; forging a joint way of seeing. I thought we'd done that together. But he saw things happening *to* him, like a teenager, not the veteran of a thousand relationships whose end must have been worse for others than for him. I never faced what I thought about all that. Nor what it said about me that I did not.

Looking at his fork he muttered, 'You do something to me. I could be drawn back at any time.'

He had no more way into the person he'd known, the partnership it had been, than into a space invader which might bundle him into its spaceship any minute. My heart had always stumbled after him, excusing. *This isn't really him. He's better than this.* But what he said and did was him. I walked away up Southampton Row.

PART III

SOUTH

South-East Asia, Indonesia

Indo-Chinese, Malayan, Sumatran; and the extinct
tigers – Javan, Balinese and (out of place)
the Caspian

15

VALENTINE NIGHT IN THE GOLDEN TRIANGLE

When buffalo fight, the grass is flattened

ancient Lao proverb

'Come here, Phet,' said Toh. 'I held you in my arms as baby!'

Phet, pronounced 'pet', just went on sunning her white tummy. Rolling on your back shows you are in control. It spreads your scent; it is about owning the ground. Phet did not have much wild tiger grammar left, but she did have that.

She was an Indo-Chinese tiger, whose Latin name *Tigris panthera corbetti* honours Jim Corbett. She started off wild in the Plain of Jars, a grass plateau where Lao kings fought invaders from Siam, Vietnam, China and Cambodia. Then came bigger players, France, Russia, Communist China, America. The Pathet Lao (now Laos's government) hid in its caves. Between 1964 and 1973, American pilots made it a wasteland of craters and unexploded mines. Animals live in it despite the mines, so hunters do too. The big trade is in swallows, for food. Three years ago a hunter shot a tigress. South-East Asian countries cannot protect tigers as well as countries I had seen so far. They have laws, but other things usually outweigh them. Armies log the forests; corruption, poaching and *laissez faire* are everywhere. India, Nepal and Russia have inherited structures of protection from the concept of privileged *precinct*: moneyed hunting. In Indo-China's denser jungles, hunting was for forest tribes, not sport. This hunter got tiger bones, skin, and three tiny cubs whom he sold to a dealer, who sold them to another, whom a Lao official arrested a mile from the Chinese border.

The males were dead. The female survived, scabbed purple skin (I saw the photos) and pods of ginger fluff. An NGO called Care for the Wild gave food and medicine; Louang Prabang, developing its tourism, liked the idea of its own tiger, picked a beauty spot for her by a waterfall sacred to a golden deer, and called her Phet, Diamond.

The grotesque goblin of three years before was gone. In February sunlight, she shone like a jewel. But she was a conservation dead end. Looking after her costs money that could buy jeeps, anti-poaching, compensation, all of which protect *wild* tigers. Yet she was representative of what was happening here. There were supposedly two hundred wild tigers in Laos. I would be lucky to see even tracks.

'Last year part of cliff fell down. People say Deer Spirit unhappy with tiger.'

We walked uphill to the cage into which Phet was locked at night. A woman hit a rod. It rang like a bell: Phet padded in, filling the shed like a bonfire. The woman pushed a bone through bars. Phet pounced and started gnawing like a dog. I crouched eight inches from her tongue, watching it curve along the bone; the most perfectly evolved teeth in the carnivore world tearing, crunching. I stroked her hindquarters. Her skin felt thin like a greyhound's.

'We should bring buffalo. Is expensive to feed. But not pork. Phet not like pork. Not eat.'

Here, too, Buddhism blended with earlier spirits of place. At a shrine to the golden deer, with a plaster hermit in a tiger-skin tunic, bamboo splinters told our fortunes. Toh and I got the same. 'No illness. Very good luck.'

Toh said 'velly'. But that looks comic on the page and I grew very fond of this twenty-five-year-old ex-waiter from south Laos. I was glad we had the same fortune. He was going to take me through a north-western forest on a raft. 'You see more wildlife from the river,' his company emailed. 'No one walks in the forest.' I had books of South-East Asian mammals. I hoped to sit on this raft and glide past trees filled with gibbons and clouded leopards. I did not know of empty-forest syndrome or the scale of the wildlife trade. People trekked in that forest constantly, but this firm specialized in white-water rafting.

*

Louang Prabang's rutted lanes were being resurfaced. Laos was the new Nepal, tourism the fastest-growing sector. In the twelfth century, this town had been the heart of a kingdom full of learning, religion, theatre, sculpture. Laos still admires its culture. Soap operas give intellectuals a Louang Prabang accent. In the 1890s a French explorer, Auguste Pavie, saved the Lao king, a vassal of Siam, from marauding Chinese. 'Louang Prabang is not a conquest of Siam,' the King said, exhausted by fending off China, Siam, Burma, Cambodia, Vietnam. 'We shall give tribute to France!' So the West took final hold of these ancient warring powers. From 1965 to 1974 these people, so in love with ornament, religion, colour, grace, were the most heavily bombed nation on earth. In 1975, the Pathet Lao abolished the monarchy.

I sat beside the wide rubbery Mekong and looked at sunset as gold as Phet. The far bank was a wall of green. Children splashed in the shallows, water-buffaloes held their horns flat along the surface, nostrils at one end, dark lyres at the other. The river curved west, where I was going, into misty beige-blue hills. Along the high street were Buddhist *wats*, temple compounds from the golden age, the fifteenth century, inhabited by novices in orange robes. Laos is as Buddhist as Bhutan, but Theravada not Shambhala; saffron robes, not brown. The *wats* were gold and red with walls of turquoise glass. Down their steps lolled emerald *nagas*, dragons with scarlet eyes and gold flames in their nostrils. In Bhutan, the dragon's medium is air. In Laos, water.

Every *wat* had several buildings, red walls inlaid with cobras, elephants, tigers made of coloured glass. I was overwhelmed by the human urge to decorate what we love, make our source of goodness shine. I remembered how proud he used to be, seeing me wearing jewellery he had given. I had been surprised and touched by his pride. When I wore something he liked that he had *not* given me, he said, 'I should have given you that,' as if everything good in me, should come from him. I thought of the ring he had given, which I took off when I left him and had not looked at since. The ring I gave, which still sat on his left hand. Ornament was a confusing thing.

Twilight. Black-plume silhouetted palms. Sky of bruised oilskin, purple and grey. Wood doors covered with gold: human figures, lollipop trees, gold tigers in gold bushes. There must have been a lot of tigers in the fifteenth century. Two boys with a guitar were practising

Lao rock. Just now my daughter was recording a CD with a producer called Joe Cocaine. How safe was she? What did her father know about where she went? What did I know? In this beautiful place, which she would love, I felt terribly far away. Was it OK, these two-week journeys? She loved being with her dad. She said he worried about her less than I did and cooked different things; we each had good and bad points. But a tigress would never leave *her* daughter.

Novices her age, sixteen, hung over *wat* walls to practise English. They had been in the temple six years and were studying for exams. Laos kept its most explosive sector of society in a temple, heads shaved, hormonal bodies swathed in orange cloth, studying religious texts for seven years. I tried to imagine this happening in Britain. I asked one what he would do when he finished.

'University in Vientiane,' he said longingly, as if talking of his love.

'What will you study?'

'Accounting,' said the novice.

In the palace theatre, women tied white wool round our wrists for luck, to keep for three days. Asia knows too well how we need luck and crave protecting. A tiger spring to drink from; a goddess to save you from tigers; Shan Shin to help you hunt them. But who protected Phet?

The Indian epic *Ramayana* came to South-East Asia with Hindu traders. Java, Bali, Burma, Cambodia, Thailand all evolved their own version. The theft of Rama's wife, Sita, and her recovery was a favourite at the Lao court. The demon king told a servant to disguise himself as a golden deer. Sita's husband went to the forest to catch it; the king approached Sita disguised as a hermit in a tiger skin, like the statue at Phet's shrine.

As I watched, I could suddenly think safely about the way he half invited me to magic him back, and the divided way I felt about him now. The man I had known, tender, warm, vulnerable, funny; and the one I met now who seemed to me to love only his own image. Maybe the split was not in me but in him. His deepest fear (maybe it came from being Greek yet not-Greek) was that he was fake. Could I now forget the outside, the things I shut my eyes to, and just be glad I had known the genuine tenderness within? If *that* was fake, well, it had been true for me, and I had responded truly.

*

'Get in the minibus,' barked Toh's boss in the thunderstorm. 'Nine hours to Louang Namtha.'

'What happens if it rains like this on the river?'

'You get wet!' A hard grin. 'The kayaks are fine.'

'*Kayaks?* You said raft.'

'Really? Toh'd need help. It'd be harder work for you.'

Work? My work would be watching the jungle.

In the minibus Toh slept. His boss had kept him up till three with karaoke. German tourists discussed yesterday's ambush on the Vientiane road: Hmong guerrillas, trained by the CIA for the war, were still fighting the Lao leaders, who called them bandits. At a recent Czech arms fair they had bought military hardware to crush the Hmong. The ambush killed sixteen people, including tourists.

Rain cleared. I saw water-buffalo, palm trees. Never mind bombs and kayaks for the moment: I was off to a *South-East Asian forest.*

In theory, forty per cent of Laos is forest, one of the highest percentage forest covers in the world. Mostly mixed deciduous trees, which deal with rainless heat by shedding leaves to conserve moisture. They are crucial to the Mekong, soaking up monsoon rains, releasing wet into streams and the air. But these hills were secondary scrub. The trees were stacked in piles beneath stilt houses. Or *were* houses, or cooking fires. My bird book was useless. No birds, no raptors over mountains. We drove for hours through hills without a single bird.

At Oudamxai, a crossroads town with shop-signs in Chinese, I ate cabbage soup and sticky pink rice like wet clay.

'Enjoying your soup?' asked a deep American voice.

He had the sapphire eyes and perfect head of Charlton Heston, was lunching off Lao beer and French fries ('Haven't had these in a while') and taught bee-keeping to South-East Asian villagers: who did it badly, apparently. He was Stephen, an apicultural Lone Ranger. Every autumn he let his Alaskan house, left a university where he taught bee-keeping, and walked into Lao villages asking who kept bees.

'I've learned not to ask who *wants* to, just for those who already do.'

Stephen knew many South-East Asian languages but especially loved Laos for its people. He knew a village in south Laos where a tiger had killed a buffalo. They put explosives in the carcass. When the tiger came back to eat he was blown to bits. Laos is familiar with explosives.

'Have a good time in Nam Ha. There's an American in Louang Namtha called Nick, knows the forest like the back of his hand.'

He walked off through banana stalls and glary dust; Gary Cooper in *High Noon*, on pale jean wishbone legs.

In Louang Namtha, where the Nam Ha reserve began, I went to bed scared and angry. I wanted nothing to do with kayaks. I later discovered this Nick ran trekking there; he would have been very knowledgeable. Sweet Toh, with his brown eyes, was not. But four hundred miles the other side of this roadless forest, I had a date with the Mekong.

St Valentine's Day, grey heavy mist. Three black gibbons raged in a cage next door. A baby monkey tied by the leg at a petrol station shrank from cars. In a muddy market we bought water and toilet paper – forest essentials – sticky rice, beans, oil. UNESCO, the New Zealand Government, WCS and the UN Drug Control Programme were helping to develop tourist stays in bio-diversity reserve villages. Guidelines about respecting traditional ways of life were worked out with village elders. No giving to children, it encourages begging. No eating or buying wildlife. And please don't do drugs. This was the Golden Triangle, the name coined in 1971 by Marshall Green, US Secretary of State, for countries growing or refining opium: Thailand, Burma, Laos.

Boys were setting out tables for a Valentine's Day street party. A 'Road Closed' sign showed two pink hearts. An hour later, at the Nam Ha reserve barrier, children played cats' cradle, a soldier listened to the radio and I filled in a form. *Visa Number?* I started searching my passport but everybody had simply put their age. In thirty years of Communism, Laos evolved wonderfully innocent ways of subverting the system.

We stopped at a gravel shoal on the Nam Ha. *Nam* means 'river'. When Americans spoke of going to Nam, they were going to the river. Toh produced two rubber bags; I pressed all my belongings into them. Opera glasses, camera: I would not be able to see golden cats closely or take pictures. No laptop, thank God. For the first time in my life I put on a helmet and life-jacket. I am a wimp about water. Swimming is cold; beaches are stony, full of sea-urchins, jellyfish, things that hurt.

My daughter and friends laugh at me. Even in Greece it has to be really hot before I go in. I walk the dog, and that's it for sport. I had never been on a kayak, or wanted to. It was shorter than a tiger and looked like a turkey-baster. We were going to depend on it for two days, for over a hundred miles, till we reached another boat that would take us three hundred more miles to the Mekong. It all seemed impossible. I picked up a paddle. 'How do you use this thing?'

Toh demonstrated. Up, twist, down. I couldn't get the twist. Could I copy Toh?

'I sit behind. I promise, we not capsize.'

It wobbled. We were going to fall in. Here came a rapid.

'Paddle!' said Toh. 'Right side.' The bottom grated on rock. It was going to puncture us. 'Left side.' The kayak whooshed sideways down a channel between rocks to a whirling wave that washed over us. My sandals floated like otters. I was waist high in the Nam Ha.

'Good OK,' said Toh.

This went on for hours. Sun burned; every rapid was frightening and different. Sometimes we hurried for the bank and caught under branches. Waves curled over the sides. When water came above our waists we stopped on a bank, knee-deep in silky chestnut mud, took out bobbing luggage and emptied the boat. But between rapids we glided alone through forest much junglier than any I had seen, layered with bamboo and vines. If this was anything like what Darwin saw in South America, no wonder he was overwhelmed by the competition for light. There were kingfishers with dark red heads, a small brown heron fishing.

'Hello, Helon!' said Toh. It flew off. 'Lao people eat eggs. Very good.'

Sometimes we passed villages where every house stood on legs, every leg a tree. They had to be renewed each year: a lot of trees each year for just one house. Men and children fishing looked at us like people in *The Snowman* watching the boy fly overhead. Most buffalo were brown. Some were *pink*.

'White,' said Toh. 'White buffalo, black buffalo.'

They looked pink to me. Maybe sunburned. But in the forest there were no animals at all. Darwin had observed animals and plants, imagining how everything fitted together, working out how they came to be, how they interacted. Here was I, 170 years later, learning how they disappeared.

'Who protects this forest, Toh? They say it's protected. Who by?'

'Someone in Vientiane,' Toh said uncertainly.

We stuck on a rock, swirled backwards, Toh got out and spun the kayak, I paddled like mad for ten minutes. Darwin was not constantly watching for the secret water plaiting I had learned to loathe because it meant rocks under the surface; nor pushing a kayak's bottom, *and* his own, off sharp rocks surrounded by raging white.

Laos was my representative South-East Asia. Thailand is more developed, more organized about protection. Vietnam and Cambodia do not quite have the poverty. But Laos had the Mekong, and what was vital for tigers was the relation of forest and river. Tigers need forest. As Ullas's book had told me in Periyar, the key to Asian forest is Asian rivers. Wherever I'd gone for tigers, I'd found rivers: in Kerala, the Periyar, dammed to make that lake, and the Pampa, on whose bank Ayappa was found. In Russia, the Ussuri and Amur; in Bhutan, the Mangde, the only one golden langurs approve of. At Chitwan I learned elephant on the bed of the Rapti, one of those Nepalese rivers created when the rain-god clipped the mountains' wings: in Madhya Pradesh was the Ken with its suttee stone, and the Kanha river I crossed at night, picturing Bagheera drinking. In *The Jungle Book* Kipling calls this river the Waingunga. When the rains fail, Hathi the elephant sees rock in the river: the Peace Rock, which shows in drought. Hathi proclaims the Water Truce, during which no one kills at the river. Ripples like those in the shrinking lakes at Ranthambhore hiss on its sides. Flesh-Eaters and Grass-Eaters drink watchfully from opposite banks.

I had seen for myself that water was crucial to where tigers live. I had come to Laos for the waterways of Asia. Now I was sitting in them. Toh told me to hold a branch while he considered a fierce rapid. Left or right? Sharp rocks and shallows or spiky overhanging trees? But something was moving, a water monitor, head jerking back and forth as it swam.

'Look, Toh,' I whispered.

'Lizard!' shouted Toh, happily. 'We see it because we are quiet!' The monitor vanished. 'We have lunch on bank.'

We pulled towards a space between tangle. A snake shot away, too quick for me to see. 'Lao people eat,' said Toh. 'Make strong.'

He jumped out, sank to his crotch in slippy red mud and pulled the kayak in. We floundered up to where we did not sink. Pale-blue butterflies clustered round the kayak then regrouped on a patch of red earth. It did not seem different from any other bit. To the butterflies it was special. In the shallows were thousands of tadpoles.

'Lao people eat. Boil in water.'

Toh was sad we had seen no monkeys. 'My friends cut monkey's head and drink brains with a straw. They say very good for you. Make you clever.'

I said nothing.

'You believe?'

'No.'

'I also not.' He paused. 'No, I not think so.'

He did not connect us failing to see monkeys with his friends sipping their brains. I was getting more and more worried about what Lao people eat. Thank God for Hinduism. India, with all its problems, does not eat tadpoles.

In late afternoon, unsmiling children watched from a bank as we paddled into a village. Toh had radiated bonhomie all day; to the heron, to villagers. '*Subadi*,' he kept shouting, stressing the *i*. Helloooo! People had smiled and said *subadi* back. Not here. They were Lanten people from South China. Children silent, barefoot, snot-runnels down their fronts. One touched the kayak. Toh tried words; they stared and said nothing.

'Forest people, not river people. Not speak Lao. Not use boats. They think our kayak is *naga*.'

People living on a river without boats seemed all wrong. The tourist board had built guest huts in villages for visitors, but no one knew in advance when visitors might appear.

'We sleep here,' said Toh, in a hut built on earth with a sleeping platform covered with a mosquito net. Outside was a hole in the earth in a cupboard, the village's only toilet. Unused, quite clean. The village was uninterested in toilets. The reserve gave a village a guest hut, school and solar panels. In return, it restricted how they used the forest. Hunt only certain animals; use only dead wood for fires. That was the idea. There was nowhere to wash. Children, girls and women walked into our hut, staring. All women, even baby girls, wore an indigo tunic trimmed with pink piping and tassels. Some had silver bell buttons. Even tiny girls had silver earrings and necklets. They had high bald yellow foreheads and almond eyes. That sounds beautiful, but they were dirty sleepwalkers, mud and snot down their fronts as if each only possessed one garment and never washed. One had a black pipe in her mouth. All faces were utterly blank. Toh shooed them out and then gave up. My wet clothes dried on me.

We walked up a slope through village huts with no fences or benches. No one sat anywhere. The highest hut belonged to the head man. 'We talk,' said Toh, who did know some of the language, though the children had not answered him. We stood in an excruciating group with the head man and his wife, pigs, chickens and blond dogs under our feet, watched by the rest of the village. The wife was a teacher, but they had had no school for two years.

'Someone broke the desks. I haven't been able to teach.'

What about solar panels?

'Not come. Broken. Somebody took.'

My brother's mother-in-law, in Orissa, said everybody in a village near hers turns into tigers at night. Did anyone here do that?

'She say, the Red Hmong believe that. Is it true?' Toh was as frightened by were-tigers as I was by rapids. He tried chatting as we went back. The only man who talked back was taller than most. He was mending his roof: the only person doing anything active except a little boy hitting a puppy.

'Man my tribe,' said Toh, surprised. 'From south. One wife here, one in Louang Namtha. He walk there every week through forest. Six hours.'

This man had stories about tigers. Yes, a tiger round here recently killed a buffalo; had killed his wife's cousin. A bear killed someone too. They had killed it and carried it to the reserve office, which did not give them anything. Not for the bear, or compensation. I did not believe much of this, except for the dead buffalo. Carry a dead bear through forest for six hours, give up skin and body for nothing, just below the Chinese border?

I wanted to try pictures of animals and opened *Mammals of South East Asia*. People pointed to gibbons, tiger, leopard, gaur, sambar, tapir, leopard cat, and nodded. They recognized them all.

Toh had arranged to buy a chicken and pay a girl to cook it. She stood with a silver torque on her neck that would sell for thousands in Bond Street, chickens swirling under her, saying something complicated in depressed singsong.

'She says they cannot catch chicken.'

Even I could have caught one.

'They don't want to lose them.'

Our hut was nearest the river. We had little stools with two-inch legs. The man making a fire inside had dreamed of an otter last night. I asked what it was doing in his dream.

'Catching a fish. Then *he* caught the otter! He likes otter. They found family of otters when he worked on a dam. They had home in the dam. It broke. Everyone ran round catching them.'

Short-clawed otters in South East Asia are on the very-endangered list.

'Ask him, if they didn't eat wild animals, what would they eat?'

'Bamboo. Vegetables. He says, "We need to eat."'

'Chickens?'

'Forest forest,' said Toh. 'They keep chicken long time.' These people were surrounded by chickens, pigs, goats, but those are wealth not food. The girl in Waterstone's who sold me the *Mammals* book would be horrified at what it was here: a menu. The Lanten came from South China, which eats everything that moves, and they were devouring the bio of this diversity reserve. No wonder snake, heron and monitor got away so fast.

'Some animals, office allows to catch. Boar. They eat others too. The office not know. They collect firewood, hunt to eat. That is their life.'

Toh gave up on the cook and slopped sticky rice from our plastic bag into a pan. We husked hairy beans, he stirred them with soy sauce. I brought out a bottle of Gordon's gin. Toh was ecstatic. 'Gin and tonic?'

'Only mineral water to go with it, Toh, I'm sorry. *Half* gin and tonic.'

Gin and water on Valentine's night. I was not sure Toh liked the taste but he was delighted. He learned British culture otherwise from karaoke.

Children watched us cook and eat. We were the show in town. I thought they might sing. Toh sang a Lao pop song, I sang a nursery rhyme. The girls said old people had sung, once, but had forgotten. They had never learned. As Toh sang more, I remembered other Valentine's nights. An Indian restaurant, heart-shaped lanterns and flame; a New York hotel, flowers and champagne. He loved the high life, and I loved him loving it. We had been good at having fun. 'The thing about being fantastically in love,' said a friend, 'is that it's deep and shallow both at once.' Now that I had decided there was a split in him, good and bad, genuine and fake, I could let myself remember the good. More painful – I poured Toh another gin – but better pain. Bereavement, not contempt.

The children knew no stories. I told them 'Little Red Riding Hood', though they might have found it odd that the wolf ate Granny rather than the other way round. We slept in our clothes under mosquito nets. Toh worried about were-tigers, I about rapids. Dirty plates hardened by the dying fire. At least snakes and rats would keep away. Frogs chirruped in the river like sea on shingle; an army crunching through gravel.

Next morning the heavy white mist was bitterly cold. It would not burn off till eleven. I sat by the river watching in vain for gibbons, with a paperback of Emily Dickinson. When I am frightened – dentist, injections, operations – I say poems to myself. It helps to concentrate. Something to hang on to. Because of the rhythm, I think. I did not know Dickinson well. If I learned one it might help with rapids. A little boy stared; I gave him a banana. He took it to his mother; she stared; they went into a hut. Women drifted into ours with unattractive pink-tufted purses to sell. One man tried to sell a crude, barely chipped wood mask, hardly a face at all. They said it was the spirit of the forest. It seemed more like the spirit of the village.

Later, in Louang Prabang, Toh's boss said there were problems with opium addiction in that village. Then it made sense. What the one active man was really doing, going to and fro. In 1900, Arsenev saw tribes who gave opium even to their kids. Why had I not seen?

*

I was glad to get away, but not into that kayak. It bucked sneakily as I climbed in. After five hours we joined a slightly wider river, the Nam Tha, with faster, bigger rapids. Once, when Toh got out to pull us off a rock, the kayak knocked him over and ran away with me through a tumble of rocks. I managed to turn it round in calm water. Was Toh hurt? Would I ever see him again? He worked along the jungly bank, retrieved his paddle, got in. Some people did this for fun! I started saying the nearest thing to a tiger poem I found that morning, hammering it into memory, hour after hour. Dickinson's strange dashes helped through rocks and foam.

Right paddle – *Civilization* – next rock – *spurns the leopard* – left paddle, bump down chute, grab sandal as waves roll in – *was the leopard* – spin, crunch on dry shallow basin, jerk forward, sink sideways down waterfall – *bold?*

Other people would have enjoyed this. I needed something to think of and not be terrified. So what was it about, this leopard?

One, isolation. *Civilization spurns* her. Two, her own nature, *tawny*, wild, spotted. Not like others. When she's alone, that doesn't matter: *deserts* don't *rebuke* her. Should a man – a *Signor, keeper*, some male guardian of convention – complain about her nature? Hell, no – this maculate *dun gown* was what she really was. She would not pretend to be different. Three, loss. The *pard* had *lost her Asia*, some experience she treasured. Four, her *memories* of it will not be *stifled* or *suppressed*, even if they hurt.

So that was it. We emptied the kayak again on a red slime bank. This poem was all about being who she was. Isolated. Never mind what people think. No blocking memories just because they hurt. It was a lesson in bravery.

The river was larger and wider than yesterday, the forest thick and dark on either side but further away. No animals, so Toh and I sang, with sunburning knuckles, pushing on against wind and glare. He sang about a boy who had left a girl behind. 'All best songs are love songs,' he said.

The next village was Khmu people, more in charge of their lives. No toilet, only a track above the village where black pigs ate any deposit;

nowhere to wash, except the river we'd been in all day. But well-carpentered houses on stilts, cheerful faces, vegetables fenced to keep out animals, children who showed us their school, the thatched roof, earth floor, maths on the board, and somewhere to sit: a fallen log. They crowded round *Mammals of South East Asia*; they knew books. Mothers lifted babies to see; men discussed different gibbons, gaur, deer, tiger. I hoped they were not reacting only to food. But a toddler pushing to see was dragging a toy on a string: a small dead bird.

The moon rose over lush blue-green mountains. We ate in the head man's house round a fire. Toh, with his irrepressible sociability, stayed chatting. All I wanted was sleep.

We got up in darkness: we had three hundred miles to go in a long-tail boat. Stilt silhouettes of sleeping houses, over a wall – and there she was. No more kayak! A twenty-foot canoe with an engine, boatman and a bundle of clothes, which turned out to be a baby, sitting in the hull like an egg in a cup. There were no roads: the river was everything. Through long dark hours we gave lifts to people and pigs while Toh explained how the head man, last night, said the tiger was the spirit of the forest. When he died, he would join the tiger.

At a village called Bam Na La we drank black Nescafé beside a pot of bubbling strong-smelling stew.

'Python. Only for man. They think it makes strong.'

It was misty and cold. At a market of rope and rubber flip-flops, with bullets everywhere, Toh bought a woolly hat. We went on. This was much faster than the kayak, the river was broadening, day was coming. There were two boatmen: an old man in the front at the engine, facing us, a young one steering at the back, eyes narrowed against water glare, carving arcs through rocks that lay beneath the river's skin. Toh put his feet on the side and went to sleep. When sun came it was bright but still cold. I had sunglasses; Toh woke and put his on, yellow-glazed black, and inspected himself, Elvis sideburns, brushline moustache, woolly hat, in mine.

'I look like *farang*.' A foreigner.

'You look like a skiing pop star.'

The forest was patchy, gold-flecked green, its reflection lighting coffee-brown water. Ghostly mountains rose before us. Near villages, palm-trees joined the lacy forest, children fished in shallows, women washed clothes, water-buffaloes dozed on banks. A girl in a red sarong stood to her waist with a fishing-line, her reflection a small red blur. We saw other long-tail boats, elegant elongated canoes with one slat on the bottom, a long low brush-glide curved at both ends. Birds too: a buzzard soaring, flame-of-the-forest trees with scarlet flowers had birds in their branches.

Forty years ago, the head man had told Toh, a man in Louang Namtha used to turn into a tiger. One day his wife saw a tiger who told her not to be afraid. She told everyone her husband was a tiger. When he came back from hunting they tied him up. He had the head and tail of a tiger with a man's body. The old boatman nodded; he remembered too.

We shared lunch with two fishermen. One said there were tiger pugmarks an hour's walk away, and four or five tigers in the hills. Sometimes he saw pugmarks on this bank. He traced a perfect pug-mark in the sand. I brought out *Mammals*. Gaur? Yes. He turned pages. Pangolin? Lots. Clouded leopard, yes. Even banteng, the wide-horned chestnut wild ox, biggest of all South-East Asia's wild cattle.

'You know why he know? Was good hunter, catch many. Now catch only fish.'

In late afternoon we puttered into the wide, wind-ruffled brown shine of the world's twelfth-longest river. Tenth-largest in volume. The Mekong, Mother of Waters. The far bank was Thailand. Speedboats slammed past. We had rejoined the world.

The Lao say there were once two dragon kings who lived in an enormous lake. One invited the other to dine on porcupine. (Laos ate wildlife even then.) The other did not believe that anything with such long spines could have so little meat. An elephant, with shorter hairs, had so much. His host must be keeping the best for himself. Their quar-rel threshed the lake: its waters threatened Laos. The king of the gods set them a competition: who could build the bigger river, to restore the land? One made the Nan, one the Mekong. It is a dangerous river with rocks just under the surface, especially in the dry season. Marco Polo crossed it in the thirteenth century. In 1893 it became the Siam-Indo-China border. In 1993 a Thai-Lao Friendship Bridge was built. It was undammed, but impoverished Laos had most to gain by sell-ing the Mekong's hydroelectric potential, for now power-hungry China crouches in the north. And in 2005, against global opposition, the World

Bank will announce it is funding a hydroelectric plant on the Nam Theun, a Mekong tributary east of Vientiane. This will flood a tiger forest the size of Singapore, home also to elephant, gibbons, clouded leopard and many unconsulted tribal people – so Laos can sell electricity.

But what I saw were children splashing on its banks. Women washed, laughing and calling, boys fished from rocks with bell nets like giant courgette flowers. A dead animal floated on its back towards Cambodia and the sea. It looked like a binturong, the largest civet: rare, shy, clumsy-looking, a tree-dweller, and very primitive. The progenitor of all feline predators, millions of years ago, may have looked like that. Was this the tiger's ancestor, floating to sea? Or just a dead dark dog with blown-out eyes?

Houxai was where tourists crossed from wealthy Thailand. Signs were in Chinese, currency was Thai. In a Chinese hotel I kissed the soap, washed *everything*. Restaurants flaunted deer heads on the walls, gaur, muntjac, and – good God – banteng. All illegal; but everywhere. I began to hate Houxai. Later I learned it is a centre of the wildlife trade. It anchors the south-east of the Golden Triangle. In the 1960s it was a major heroin-processing centre run by the Lao army. No one is innocent here. Dragon kings quarrel and lash the waters. The people, forests and animals struggle to survive.

I wanted to phone my daughter, but phones were a problem. Down a dark alley by the river, a Chinese woman had a phone in a cellar under a banteng head. I got through; but it was not a good moment. They were going out, they were late, she was fine but busy with her life.

Next morning Toh and I hugged goodbye on a converted barge taking tourists to Louang Prabang.

'See you've got your priorities clear,' said Stephanie, looking at my feet. In the Houxai bathroom I had painted my toenails blue. We were in wicker armchairs; Stephanie was dark, Charlotte blonde, they lived in California and met their boyfriends on the Internet. Wonderful, to have a laugh with women. We passed deforested red banks, thin teak plantations, and the last working elephant in Laos, Land of a Million Elephants. Charlotte's guidebook said bilharzia was endemic in rivers of north Laos. Stephanie's detailed Laos's unexploded bombs.

American planes dropped two million tons, one B52 load every eight minutes, twenty-four hours a day, for nine years. Over half a ton for every inhabitant, including babies. They did it secretly since Laos was officially neutral. Pilots flew in jeans, free of the rules of engagement observed in Vietnam, like not bombing within five hundred yards of temples or hospitals. When weather was bad over North Vietnam they dumped their bombs on Laos. They left it brimming with mortar shells, munitions, phosphorus canisters, land mines and 'unexploded ordnance', UXO. Today, these cause 130 casualties a year, half of them children under ten. Even in constantly used fields, bombs work their way up and are hit by hoes. Eighty per cent of this five million population live off what they can grow, find or kill on their land. Poverty deepens as the population grows, but fifteen of the eighteen provinces have unmapped minefields. People are scared to open new land. It would take 2600 years to clear the country. The clearance operation is nearly bankrupt. Children learn songs about not touching bombs, about legs being blown off.

A man called Michael Hayes, involved in mine clearance, who had seen tigers on the Ho Chi Minh trail while clearing mines there, had emailed me plans for village-assisted clearance: training and paying villagers to clear mines and UXO. It is happening, but is painfully slow and costs three and a half thousand US dollars a hectare. Eleven thousand in the worst areas. That little boy in the village with a dead bird: how could I tell him it was wrong to tie a bird by the leg and pull it till it died? His culture tied animals with string. Mine, for nine years, had dropped bombs on his home, one ton for every boy like him; left unexploded bombs in his ground, refusing to clear them up. He may die from what they left.

That night in a riverside hotel, a tall Canadian called Peter introduced himself. He was a poet; he and his wife had been teaching at a Thai university. I had a book of his, an epic poem about CIA involvement in Java's 1960s massacres. As a full moon shone on the Mekong we talked poetry. But American foreign policy was his academic subject.

'In those days,' he said, meaning the Vietnam war, 'we liked the

Hmong because they were warlike. We despised the Lao as weak. I see
it differently now I'm a Buddhist. Why shouldn't they be gentle?'

I wished Toh had been there. This was proper gin and tonic. Why,
indeed, shouldn't Lao people be gentle? In my room I tuned to CNN
Asia.

'Wonderful things happen,' said a male American voice in a tourist
ad, 'when you go to Vietnam.'

Next day our boat stopped at caves where ancient statues of
Buddha were stowed. Walking down the rocky path I met Peter walking up.

'Did you see the snake pretending to be a pile of dung?'

It was a twisted olive turd, eyes like orange Smarties. A boatman
came behind me. 'Cobra,' he said, but in my reptiles book the only one
that fitted was reticulated python. This was a young one. It did not
know what risks it was taking with its endangered genes.

'Look,' I said proudly to Charlotte. 'Reticulated python!'

She peered through her long-distance camera lens.

'Well, gross me out,' she said.

16

IF YOU KILL A TIGER, YOU CAN
BUY A MOTORBIKE

'What do you want to do? We have three days and nights.'

'Walk in jungle, as near tigers as possible.'

'Sleep there?'

'Sure.' I knew this north-east was ruggedly mountainous, but *nothing* could be as bad as that kayak. Boatang, a kindly older man who monitored animals for the WCS, went off to organize tents.

Changsavi, a young Lao zoologist with the WCS, first worked here near the Vietnam border in 1995, when conservation took off in Laos. For his Ph.D., he camera-trapped in Phou Loei reserve, got boar and sambar photos, estimated it had up to twenty tigers.

The country's official estimate, two hundred, is guesswork. How can you know, with unexploded ordnance, rebels and poaching everywhere? The forest department supposedly protects, but patrols are rare. The government spends little on conservation; the forest department built an office with the one substantial sum it received. So no funds for jeeps, fuel, weapons or anti-poaching training, as in next-door Thailand. Patrols cause trouble anyway. The government has to be careful: there are rebels already.

Deer hunting is officially banned. This is crucial for preserving tigers, but no one bothers to enforce it. Laos is decentralizing, laws are interpreted differently in different states. In some, the governor is the keenest hunter. Tourists are asked not to eat wildlife but Lao restaurants do not care, and their customers do not realize they are taking food from tigers' mouths. Europeans, having extinguished their own

large predators, have surplus boar and deer; in America, deer-hunting
is an industry.

We drove east for ten hours through birdless mountains while
Changsavi described the wildlife trade, dominated by the Vietnamese,
who buy Lao citizenship cheap. Lao locals catch animals for them.
One stole bear cubs when the mother was taking honey. She caught
him in the act; he spent a year in hospital and emerged without a nose.
But the dangers are nothing compared to the money. Dealers buy king
cobras live, three hundred dollars a kilo, golden turtle for a hundred
dollars; pangolin, tiger bone. Tigers are few and widely dispersed, but
if you kill a tiger you can buy a motorbike.

Houxai's governor levied an illegal tax on pangolins smuggled by
Vietnamese from Laos to Thailand along the road we were on. The
blood is supposed to be medicinal. They put a needle into the pangolin's stomach, draw up blood till it is nearly bled dry, feed it until it
recovers, then do it again.

The driver stopped at a dead jungle fowl, glinting in sun, hanging
from a wicker shack. He was an accredited photographer of wildlife
crime. He photographed it, watched cheerily by the couple in the
shack, and got back in the jeep leaving it hanging. Later, from an international report on the Lao wildlife trade, I saw why he did not fuss. By
1995, Vietnamese dealers had emptied Vietnamese forests and turned
to Laos in enormous numbers, highly organized, with links to drug
and women trafficking. The Lao government refused to criticize
Vietnam. They valued its 'fraternal solidarity' and protected the trade
by ignoring it. High-level officials were also rumoured to be involved.
They did not support people trying to enforce laws; local officials
openly flouted them. It was expected of you, to exploit high position
without punishment. At international cross points Lao officials waved
on Vietnamese jeeps with cardboard over the windows. Occasionally
they peered in and charged something for their own pockets, or
impounded parts to sell. Their salaries were low. For two days in April
1999, undercover investigators watched the Agriculture and Forestry
Office confiscate three thousand dollars' worth of wildlife – to resell.
Over ten thousand dollars' worth of wildlife left Laos at this

checkpoint every day. The trade used every footpath into Vietnam. For tigers, China was the ultimate market. Oudamxai, where I had met the bee-keeper, gave top prices. Louang Prabang was a through-route, though two tigers were killed in its province in 1998–9, one with three cubs.

Many Lao are sickened by the trade. The long-term losers are the very people who poach for the traders: the rural poor, who depend on the forest and receive a tiny proportion of the cash. For porcupine stomachs and macaque bones one dealer shelled out four batteries. They will be left with an empty forest. The trade is out of control nationwide, endangering a very poor country's bio-diversity – which is still, as I write, alive.

Changsavi had worked in south Laos, and used to go to the field with an American scientist. One day the scientist heard a sound, thought Changsavi was creeping up to surprise him and put up his binoculars to see a disconcerted tiger, very close. He shot up a tree with no branches.

'The tiger ran away. He showed me the tree. It was *so high*!'

But most of his work was here in Phou Loei Bio-diversity Reserve, which meets the Nam Et Bio-diversity Reserve to make the second-largest conservation area in Laos. Half of its 4200 square kilometres are over a thousand metres high. Much of Nam Et has been degraded by slash-and-burn agriculture, but the thick secondary forest is cover for bears, leopards, clouded leopards, dhole, silver pheasants, banteng, tigers. Phou Loei has evergreen and deciduous forest, grasslands, bamboo. Short-term foreign help here turned out to be of little use. One international body gave seven hundred thousand dollars for two years of education, but with no follow-up the money was wasted. You have to work long-term. Two years spent educating a few villages is nothing compared to what dealers offer, in this area of no employment. The WCS's small Laos team funded and trained local guards. For ten years, Changsavi had been talking to children, asking men not to hunt, paying hunters to monitor wildlife instead, counting gaur, banteng, goral, tigers, and reporting poachers.

Villagers wanted to move out, closer to a town, but the government will not pay. They release buffalo into the forest, not knowing what happens to them. Buffalo can die from snakebite, for instance. To protect the forest, and tigers from revenge killings, the WCS and the local governor, who was keen on conservation, established a tiger insurance scheme, collecting contributions from all cattle-owners who wanted to join. Each village gave very little, but it mounted and gathered interest in a bank. If someone proved a tiger had killed a properly kept buffalo, the account compensated him. Villagers could also borrow money from the account to send their children to better schools.

The villages we stopped in were delighted to see Changsavi. He checked their poaching, but they trusted him to help them. Conservation depends on people who live far from home and give their lives to science, wildlife, and people who live with it.

We stopped for the night at a checkpoint town on a river; a crossroads near the border just outside the protected zone. Villagers here were allowed to harvest trees, shoot squirrels, rats and wild boar, use arrows but not poison. As we ate in a cellar open to the road, chickens and dogs underfoot, a Customs officer came in: Bita, in an Aertex shirt saying 'Castroville Youth Soccer League'. His job was checking meat for sale, to make sure it was buffalo not venison. He pursued poaching reports, had men jailed for taking sambar. Last week some cat had killed a pig and been shot. The hunter had sold the skin, but he confessed it was a leopard. Here, the laws were making a difference. Changsavi was proud of the local governor. He really had reduced the traders.

'In the mid-nineties, there was open trade in bear gall-bladders, bear cubs, tiger bone, banteng. Last year only python, big-headed turtle.'

'There were many tigers once,' said Bita. 'But how many are left? We don't know.'

At five a.m. the market began and a loudspeaker yelled wildlife laws and prohibitions over and over, in Lao. This was a frontier market, full of forbidden things. If they did not see laws enforced, why should they observe them? In chill mist, Changsavi checked the meat among stalls of camouflage clothes and bullets, and we bought forest provisions.

The WCS station was up the mountain. Boatang was playing

draughts on scribbled cardboard with Lao Beer bottle tops. Black was the tiger-head logo, white was upside-down. Boatang had three queens, the guard none. In an inner room were a banteng's head and a clouded-leopard skin impounded from poachers. When Boatang had won, we drove down a rough track and walked to a village in the reserve, near thick forest, where we would hire men to help carry tents, food and water.

A woman was spinning in the red dust heart of this tiny village. Water buffalo lay under stilt houses; chickens climbed on them, pecking. Women looked at my sun hat, bought in Louang Prabang, and discussed its weave. Laos is famous for textiles. Changsavi said I bought it here, I had come to Laos for tigers. If there was more wildlife, more tourists would come and they, too, could sell things. Boatang wanted a go at spinnning. He sat on the tiny stool and started the thread. It broke. Everyone laughed. He tried again; it broke again. He laughed and stood up; the woman sorted out the mess while we shouldered packs and set off with two men carrying tents.

Rice fields, open scrub, steep open hillside with a few tree stumps, an hour of glary sun: where was the forest? I thought this village was at the jungle edge.

'It was, two years ago. Good-quality secondary forest, last time I was here. Sambar, gaur, tiger tracks. But you can't see this hill from the road. The village has cleared it for rice. I didn't know.'

So much for those internationally funded years of conservation education, supposed to send villages inside the reserve the message Changsavi had just sent out about my hat: *Don't cut trees, don't kill wildlife, and good things will come.* The manager of that project had had an eight-village budget. To reach this village, though, you had to walk. He had picked another instead, outside the reserve, to which one could drive in an air-conditioned car. He also refused to fund a video machine and cassettes for follow-up education. Changsavi had spent ten years so far on these people and forests. He was scathing about short-term projects. As we walked three hours across scorching hillside, which had been prime tiger-forest so recently, I saw why.

The trees began where the hill got steeper and the villagers had stopped felling them. My legs were already water, my pack twice the weight. Changsavi had no hat: his face was streaming, T-shirt streaked

dark with sweat. Bualoy and Vai, the two villagers, stepped lightly in
blue rubber flip-flops as if they had just set off. The forest was a dim,
leathery mix of dry evergreen, deciduous and banana trees; during the
nine years of American bombardment, there were settlements in here.
Banana trees, I found, were treacherous. They toppled when your foot
slipped and you leaned on them; the leaves were slippery. Lianas
twisted everywhere, flowing back on themselves: you had to climb
under or through. The thin ones caught your ankle and held you by
the crotch; you had to fall back and disengage.

In this patchily ancient tropical tangle, the grail above was light.
Steep up, steep down, steeper up. Trail narrower, trees closer. 'Phou
Loei' means 'never-ending mountain': this was a series of ever-higher
folds up raw earth slopes at seventy degrees; then down, then higher,
soaking, panting, scrambling, searching for handholds. We saw
sambar tracks, droppings, and where a stag rubbed itchy antlers on a
branch. Wild boar tracks. Animals that tigers eat were here. How about
gaur on these steep slopes with their bulk and weight? And me? How
would I get back if I twisted an ankle or fell to the side, which I kept
nearly doing, and landed on a Russell's viper? It would be upset to be
rolled on; and I would have six hours to live. Could they get me to
anti-serum? What *was* I doing here? It was four hours to the village;
there were no phones there. Two hours would pass while someone
walked to a driver. Did the WCS have anti-venom? Then ten hours to
Louang Prabang. Still, most vipers had probably been eaten, or smuggled to Vietnam.

The younger villager Vai loved his knife. He would slash at a
banana tree and topple it to check that the blade was OK. He made
Changsavi a hat out of the fronds, slicing shiny veined green, slotting
one leaf inside the other. Once I nearly slipped down the mountain on
leaves he left across the trail. Boatang was a keen botanist, constantly
veering off to look at plants. Once he made a clucking sound and
picked off the ground a ball of ferny wormlike leaves.

'Very rare orchid,' said Changsavi. 'Very expensive. Collectors come
and steal thousands. Everything has a price. Two entomologists from
Czechoslovakia hunting an expensive endangered beetle offered me
money to take one out from the forest. I said no. Why should they take
things from our forest?'

Later I read a report on Lao beetles. In 1997 Japan had a craze for giant stag beetles. Most sold for $500–800 each. One Tokyo pet shop sold one for $50,000. Those, too, had come from Laos. From poaching cascade to trophic cascade . . .

Boatang stuck the orchid on a tree where he hoped no one would see it. He was the caretaker of an enormous garden, pinning back a dangling rose. He had spent ten years in this forest, hiding, during the American war.

We were going downhill, the canopy very high, undergrowth dense: we had to crouch. This forest was tangled all the way down, with an immense variety of textures: flappy, floppy, shiny leaves, spiny ones, tall trees with rough brown bark. It was not entirely pristine, that was higher up, but a mix. We had to bend to our knees through tunnels, lianas dangling at chest height, fallen trees below. At a brown stream with flat rocks we ate lunch. I took off my shoes and paddled. The older villager, Bualoy, was calm; Vai, thin as a willow, intense and restless with hollow eyes and smooth waif face, might have been eighteen or thirty. He wore one of the green army jackets that were everywhere.

'There should be monkeys,' I said, to take my mind off exhaustion, sweat, fear, flies. 'Gibbons. Macaques.'

'Last time I was here, gibbons called two hours in the morning.'

My legs were ribbons. Balance depends on muscle. When muscles are tired you cannot stop the wobble, going downhill. It got steeper. We were on sideways slopes all the time, with a steep drop one side. The air was closer, the ups harsher, the downs more slippy. After a gruelling tunnel of pale beige slippery dead leaves, fallen trees and writhing roots, which you had to pick your feet over while crouching low beneath bushes, then creeping handhold by handhold sideways down a twisty slope, I suddenly felt the exhaustion was dangerous. I was beginning to stumble. My muscles were blancmange.

'Are we nearly at the tiger-track place, the salt lick? I'm not sure I can go much further.'

We were crossing a stream near a river head. The path made a right-angle, looping up, disappearing round a bend. Normally I would have loved to go on. The jungle was feathery rich greens and browns. But it was darkening. The sun would soon set.

'We are only *half-way* to the salt lick they wanted to show you. It is four hours' walk for us, two for them. Sunset will come in two hours. The path gets steeper. This stream,' said Changsavi ruefully, 'is where they take their own first rest from the village.'

He was panting too. I was nearly sobbing with fatigue. Vai was not even sweating. He said something to Changsavi, who laughed. 'He says, "Poor thing, take pity on her." Shall we camp here for the night?'

Never mind tiger tracks. I'd seen lots elsewhere.

'Brilliant idea.'

Vai and Bualoy gathered fallen wood and made a fire. I was too tired and demoralized to say that no animals would come if they smelt smoke. I sat on a stone, fending off flies, imagining a tiger lapping from this stream, padding up towards the salt lick I would never see, where he would leave his footprints and try for a sambar. There was a small waterfall here. The canopy was eighty feet above. The stream's other side had bushes with rosy epaulettes and shiny leaves with holes round the edge, as if a leather punch had made painter's palettes of them all. There were dark shadows behind where brown trunks shot up; light scattered gold dust on leaves of a thousand textures: soft, feathery, shiny, leathery; dark green, light green shot with orange and yellow, emerald fronds layering undergrowth all the way up, packed with pale, licking blades of bamboo. There are more kinds of bamboo in Laos than anywhere in the world, except China and Thailand. I was deep in forest, where I had always wanted to be.

Vai looked up at the trees.

'Civets love this fruit,' said Changsavi. 'We may see civets tonight.'

Hunters find a tree that the animal likes eating and stay till it comes. Civets are great pollinators; South-East Asia has many species. Some live and feed only in trees, some mainly on the ground, eating rodents. The biggest is the binturong, which I thought I saw in the Mekong. But most eat fruit. Ranging more widely than most fruit-eating mammals, monkeys, gibbons, they deposit seeds over a wider area. In the rainy season some move a mile a day, leaving fresh faeces loaded with seeds. They are vital to the forest's diversity. If Vai ate them all, the forest would stop growing.

Bualoy was our chef, Boatang the herb-gatherer, Vai the skivvy. He cut a bamboo, lodged it mid-stream to make a tap, washed pork in the mud pool. Bualoy wrapped rice in bright green leaves.

'Our last expedition,' said Changsavi, 'someone cooked at camp while we checked camera traps. Exhausting! He wrapped our rice in the wrong leaves, so bitter we couldn't eat afterwards! He was *not* popular.'

Vai chopped a bamboo stem into two-foot pieces. Bualoy blocked each at one end and pushed rice parcels into the other, along with wild ginger root Boatang had found. He poured water down the stem and set it in the fire. The bamboo blackened gently, the water inside bubbled, the jungle darkened. Changsavi and Boatang cleared ground for two tents. Bualoy and Vai would sleep in the open, their home. Maybe they were immune to the gathering insects.

My tent had a net window; I crawled in and watched the tree tops grow dark against a fading sky. I was pathetic. I had not reached the salt lick. But this *was* a South East Asian jungle and I was going to sleep in it. Tigers had padded over the stones under my shoulder-blades. Leopard, sambar and gaur drank in this stream when we weren't there.

I looked at the bamboo pipe channelling the water. Brilliant idea. So were rice parcels in bamboo stalk. So was fire. People changed a place. The pipe would rot and fall, the bamboo grow: there was no chemical change. But everything we did would have an incalculable effect on vegetation, and on animals we did not see.

The pork, herbs and ginger-rice were a dream. Boatang brushed his teeth in the waterfall and came back covered in leeches, which he burned off in the fire. But I was glad I was here, not in Nanchang *eating* leeches. The stream was slippery, I could not see where to put my feet. I lay listening to lilting Lao chat and laughter. Boatang and Changsavi crawled to their tent; Bualoy and Vai lay by the dying fire.

'Civets in the trees,' whispered Changsavi, suddenly. 'For the fruit.'

But oh, I could not get up. I was too tired. I could not put shoes on. I had given up. I looked out of the mesh window while Changsavi played a torch in the trees and palm civets disported themselves above. So I missed my chance of seeing the closest thing to a tiger I was likely to see in Lao jungle. But I heard them. They were noisy, chatty feeders. They thought they were OK up there. If we had been hunters . . .

'They are very good to eat,' whispered Boatang.

'There's the small one,' whispered Changsavi. *Eeeeeeeeek!* echoed through the jungle. The baby had overstepped some civet rule and was being chastised.

Bualoy and Vai made a fire at five thirty. Cold wet mist; rice in bamboo pipes; chicken and ginger cooking in the pot. I handed round almonds. Bualoy and Vai were as suspicious as I had been about their pork. They scraped the skin, nibbled politely, looked at each other.

'Maybe we should grow these here,' said Vai.

'I don't think they could take your heat.' I opened a notebook. I failed to climb the mountain but there was something I could do while I waited. I loved the people I had met. But the identification with animals that the West takes for granted was lacking here. It is a luxury: how can you sympathize with animals when you haven't enough to eat? I had been formed by a hundred years of children's literature. Bambi, Bagheera, now translated to film, make children imagine animals' feelings. Vai and Boatang knew wild animals as things to hunt and eat. They never thought how difficult it was to be a tiger. I would write something for Changsavi to use in schools. What could I call a baby tiger?

They decided on Buck Noy. His mother, like Phet's, like Bambi's, was shot. My story was shamelessly message-ridden: a forest full of animals hiding from humans. I threw in a white gibbon, spirit of the forest, who looked after the orphaned tiger till he grew. I read it out over the fire, Changsavi translated. They loved it. I did not have the guts to get out of my tent and watch civets, but I could entertain at breakfast.

We went a different way back. Vai said it was less steep. It did not feel it. Hours went by. The route seemed longer, hotter, tunnels of dense elephant grass, bamboo, banana trees. Watching your ankles at every step, muscle-wrenching plunges through bushes, creeper, mossy tree trunks, stifling bamboo twenty feet above your head where you could not see your own feet and had to watch where to put your hands.

'Thirty years ago there were villages here,' said Changsavi, 'in the American war. This has grown since.'

At the edge of the open we sat and drank water. Vai's faun eyes picked out the Emily Dickinson, small, pale, soft-backed in my pocket. I handed it to him: he held it upside down and looked at Changsavi.

'He did not learn to read. He was in the jungle as a boy, during the war.'

He was much older than I thought. Forty. More.

'His mother was killed by a bomb,' said Changsavi, listening to Vai. 'He lost her when he was very young.'

'Like Buck Noy.' Vai, with his sad eyes, nodded. Yes. Like Buck Noy.

Four hours later we passed a cone-shaped mound built over American mines so children would not step on them. Small boys passed with home-made fishing-guns, bows and arrows. They were allowed to catch fish and shoot birds for the family pot, but not to sell. Then rest! Shade! Village! Vai invited us in but Changsavi led us to the head man's house to wait for the jeep. Up the ladder to the balcony, into a dark room lit through wickerwork slits of light and a small fire on the wood floor. Boatang and Changsavi lay on mats. The head man's wife cooked. On the balcony I watched a sow and piglets flop on to their sides by a woodpile; wiry chickens hopped over them as if they were stepping-stones, pecking parasites. The dogs were biscuit-coloured with tails curled over their backs. They were friendly, mild and rarely barked. No one seemed afraid of them. As we ate lunch I asked Changsavi if people ate dogs. He asked the head man.

'Not their own dogs. They sell a dog to someone else for food. Dog meat is more expensive per kilo than beef.'

In Louang Prabang, I invited Changsavi and the driver to dinner at a French restaurant. The steak was not a patch on pork in the jungle, and there was venison on the menu. Vientiane, reached by plane to avoid Hmong ambushes on the road, was hot, damp, yellow, beautiful. In charge of the Lao WCS programme was Arlyne with her husband Mike, both tall and gentle. Mike looked at me kindly.

'I guess you might like something other than sticky rice,' he said, and took us to an Italian restaurant. They had been here since 1998 and were on their fourth Alsatian. The previous three had been stolen.

'*Eaten?*' In Terney it had been tigers who ate your dog.

'We guess. We're keeping our new dog skinny.'

I phoned my daughter from their office. On the walls were camera-trap photos. Clouded leopard, a rare saola deer.

'Every day, new species are discovered here,' said Arlyne.

'But every day the known ones and their habitat are disappearing. I don't know why you all don't go mad with despair.'

'In graduate school, when we specialized in conservation our professor said, "You're going into the oncology of biology."'

'Ontology?'

'Oncology. Cancer. He said, "*All* your patients are dying. Your job is to judge where your efforts make most difference. Who to help best."'

On the little plane to Bangkok her words ran through my head. I had met bleakness in China but this was the bleakest yet.

London. The birthday of a mutual friend: he was bound to be there. I had to give back an out-of-print paperback from his student days, with his underlinings. He had lent it for a poem I wrote about his mother's childhood.

The party was a long room, full of people. I avoided him, forgot the book, talked to a journalist about tigers.

'Is your book going to be about conservation?' he asked. 'Or will it be more objective?'

By objective, he did not mean describing facts. He meant not minding them. So, did he think conservation was not based on objective views?

'Well . . .'

I moved to a dolls' house in a conservatory. Glass walls bare to a night garden, half-moon bony and bright overhead. Suddenly he was beside me. Alone under the moon. The giving-back-book moment.

'Here.' I pulled out his blue Pelican. 'Put this in your pocket.'

He glanced down nervously. We were completely alien now, apparently, to each other. 'No, no, I've got that.'

'This is your copy. Here's your name in it. You need it back.'

Whatever he had been telling himself about me, I had stepped outside the current script, or had an ulterior motive. I looked at his uncomprehending face. If you live in a world where other people's feelings don't exist, you are knocked sideways when something comes at you out of them. You may even feel aggrieved. 'It's the copy you had at college. You lent it to me.'

He put it into his pocket as if it had fallen from the sky.

A year ago I had warned myself that to stop being sad he'd have to tell himself I was bad. When I saw his blankness now, I understood: he had stopped attributing to me any motive that was not self-interest. Anything else was outside his brief.

A few weeks later a messenger on a motorbike brought books I had lent him over the years. How hard it was, he wrote, to part with them. He gave a sentence to each moment of borrowing, where we had been. Maybe the feeling was not unreal, and this was his version of what I had done on Valentine's night, remember the good things. But the words were advertising copy.

'I'm sorry it had to end. Such a treat, being in love with you and vice versa.'

A *treat*? Let him, in the words of an old film, go bingle his bongle.

17

DEFENDERS OF THE WILD

If we can save the continuity of these forest areas we can bring
back a tiger population to surpass India's
Alan Rabinowitz, Hukaung Valley, Myanmar, 2004

'Thirty years ago people saw leopards here. The military cut all the trees for surveillance. Now they're growing them. You get jail for felling a tree.'

Sunset on Mandalay Hill. May heat: electric velvet on the face. The Chinese had bought up Mandalay, except for two state-owned buildings below. The Lion Palace, restored by citizens' forced labour, and Mandalay jail. A silver tapeworm curled beyond: Kipling's road to Mandalay where flying fishes play. The Irrawaddy, boundary between Bengal and Indo-Chinese tigers.

'I couldn't believe,' said my friend, 'how *small* European rivers are. I'm used to *that*, and what it'll be in two months. Water *everywhere*.'

I can't tell you his name. Most of Asia has dodgy politics. If scientists saved wildlife only in places approved by democracies, the animals would die. Many crucial wildlife areas are governed by corrupt dictatorships: should scientists give up on animals because of that? Scientists *were* protecting animals here, in South-East Asia's largest country, but I was only giving poetry readings and workshops. I hoped to ask about conservation on the side.

In pagodas, bright yellow tigers reflected glaring gold, constantly renewed. Buddhism here stressed different things from Bhutan. Public acts, like paying for gold or pagodas, gained you merit for a better life next time. The generals kept opening new pagodas, while a teacher or doctor's weekly wage (when paid) was one dollar, a thousand *kyats*. (Prostitutes charged fifteen *kyats*, a condom cost fifty.) Outside pagodas, women sold bunches of live sparrows to release: another act of merit. In Thailand, they feed these sparrows opium so they can catch and sell them again. Here, the bunches of brindled feathers were just dazed from heat and trauma.

You are your actions. There was reverence all round me, I felt it, but no religion can prevent its own misuse.

In Yangon, the monsoon broke. We splashed thigh-high through gutters. Aung San Suu Kyi, leader of Myanmar's National League for Democracy, was newly free from house arrest. We had tea. I asked if tourists could come now?

'Not yet. Let them know tourism is waiting to happen if they change policy on human rights. As it is, tourists wouldn't see the truth.'

A year later she was hit on the head and imprisoned. The editor of a sports journal was sentenced to death for helping her League stir unrest – he reported the embezzlement of four million internationally donated dollars intended to promote Myanmar football. Censorship is an industry. There were poem-shaped holes in magazines. A comedian was imprisoned for seven years for a joke about a hat.

Myanmar's tiger experts were away, but a zoology professor met me at the university where Suu Kyi's father had organized student strikes against the British in 1920. In seamless rain I walked with an interpreter through jungly red arches of a campus as empty as the Cold Lairs in *The Jungle Book*. To stop students striking, this regime has put undergraduates in remote campuses out of town whose purpose, so people who taught in them said, is surveillance not education.

Leaking corridors, black umbrellas, an enormous mahogany table, and seven people. I asked about tigers. The professor said Myanmar was Buddhist, ideally placed to preserve bio-diversity. I asked other questions, I got Buddhism and bio-diversity again. My interpreter suddenly said I was related to Darwin. The professor wanted to touch me. We grasped each other's hands. I stopped asking questions. She told me about living alone on this campus with cobra-shadows in twilight. There was a passion for biology here, and communication: but all we could do was touch.

'It was *very* nice of her to see you,' said the poets later, under dry lightning across the Irrawaddy. 'She'll have to write a report on your visit for the military police, to match *exactly* what any staff informing on her said.'

The Padaung, a forest tribe between Yangon and Mandalay, say we have a shadow-soul, a *yaula*, or 'shadow beneath'. It disappears when we are afraid, or in forest where we cannot see shadows. When we die, it comes back as our ghost. How can you look after tigers in a country that treats *people* with such fear?

And yet Myanmar has the world's largest tiger reserve, thanks to officials who genuinely want to preserve, and an American whom the *New York Times* calls zoology's Indiana Jones. Alan Rabinowitz of the WCS studied jaguars in Belize, advised Thailand on conserving big cats; and in 1993 surveyed with George Schaller the Htamanthi sanctuary north of Mandalay. They found few animals, then met the reason why. Hunters, searching for tiger bone and bear gall to sell to Chinese traders. They had already extinguished the rhinos. They had always hunted there: no one had told them not to. Animals were scarce, yes, but they did get a tiger a year. Their technique was metal cable tied to a bent-back tree with a trigger below, which lifted a tiger off the ground. Bamboo spikes pierced him as he swung. Loss of blood killed him. Rabinowitz reported it; Myanmar appointed a new park chief to hire forest guards and involve local people in protection. Rabinowitz began advising Myanmar on conservation. In 1997 he went to the remote north and found pristine forest, tigers, elephants, clouded leopards, hundreds of gaur, golden takin and an unknown leaf deer. It was a transition area, Himalayan habitat overlapping subtropical, tiger and elephant at the north end of their range, red panda and snow leopard at the south end of theirs. It was also precipitous, dense, full of floods, malaria, typhus, venomous snakes. Few people lived there, unsurprisingly, so tigers were fine. But those who did were killing wildlife to sell to the Chinese for badly needed salt.

Rabinowitz advised Myanmar to make some of this valley a

protected area. Why not all? they asked. If he could justify it, they would do it. In 2004 it became the world's largest tiger reserve: 8400 square miles, larger than all India's reserves combined. Eighty to a hundred tigers, which could multiply tenfold if protection and management plans work; continuous forest with cover, prey, water. Tigers can walk long distances to hunt and breed. The buffer zone is used by rattan collectors, gold miners, even some hunters. Rabinowitz wanted to balance things, show you can benefit more from wild animals alive than dead. In the Second World War this was the Valley of Death. Thousands died in it, fleeing the Japanese. Now it had become a valley of life. Because of the tigers, people have salt, medicine, other things they need. It is an answer to Mr Li's key question, how can tigers benefit a local population? But not one he can use in flat, crowded Hunchun.

Myanmar asked the WCS to suggest an overall tiger action plan. With Burmese scientists, the WCS examined seventeen areas of dense jungle, inaccessible except on foot. Each area took two months. Everyone got malaria. They worked with camera traps and 'plot-sampling', monitoring representative sections. They spotlit three key places: Hukaung, Htmanthi and the south-east, Myanmar's scorpion tail between Thailand and the sea. This could support sixty-five tigers. It had moist evergreen forest, water, lots of animals – but also a rampant wildlife trade with Thailand, heavy military security, and officials who cared nothing for wildlife laws.

Tony Lynam, Rabinowitz's successor as WCS director in Thailand, whom I would now meet in Bangkok, helped to direct this survey. 'There *is* political will in Myanmar,' he emailed me, 'to protect habitat and tigers. What we don't have is *time*.' He suggested corridors into Thailand, training rangers in anti-poaching and law-enforcement, monitoring the wildlife trade, especially at border markets, educating local administrators, setting up a compensation scheme, hiring former poachers as protectors. With the Forest Department, the WCS has trained, mapped, developed databases, established a Tiger Team, all modelled on Thailand, where they do similar things.

Rabinowitz felt the Myanmar general he first contacted genuinely wanted to protect. That man disappeared, but Rabinowitz went on working with the Forest Department. Some Myanmar-watchers say this Department is split. Half of its staff are milking the forests, destroying them, sending timber to China. The others are really concerned. Rabinowitz has worked in many countries. Some, like China or Malaysia, 'talk a good game and don't follow up'. But Myanmar has followed up, so far. As a result people in protected areas are better off. One man on his expedition said, 'The animals of our country cannot be saved by putting them in zoos. It is something you have helped teach me.'

Rabinowitz is a hero, to me and many, not just for his books and science but because he has made governments act. His Belize work led to a jaguar sanctuary, his Taiwan work to Taiwan's largest nature reserve, his Thai work to Thailand's first World Heritage conservation site. Because of him there are forests and tigers that would not otherwise be there. 'It breaks my heart,' he says, 'when you go with young people to what you know is denuded forest and hear them say how full of life it is. I want them to know what true wild places are like, and why they are vital to us all.'

In 2001, aged forty-eight with a small son, he was diagnosed with leukaemia. He is determined to do what he can, as long as he can, in the field. 'No more dreams,' he has said, 'of growing old, or thoughts about a house by the lake. I don't know how much longer my working career will be, so I'm pulling out all the stops to make sure things get done and I do what I can do.'

You are your actions. Just because a principle can be debased does not mean it is not good.

After tatty Yangon airport, Bangkok's gloss showed instantly, in airport shops. The marketing of commercial tiger balm. Yes, it is camphor, but it shows what people *want*.

Bangkok is a centre of wildlife trade. There are some good guys in the police, in forestry, but also heartbreaking corruption. Thailand signed CITES in 1973, but did not ratify it. In 1983 it ratified it but did nothing. In 1987 the Eating Out section of *Bangkok and Beyond* gave rave write-ups to restaurants serving tiger penis in whisky. In 1991, threatened by sanctions, Thailand passed laws protecting listed animals, outlawing tiger-hunting and the tiger-parts trade. But it is still a main conduit for that trade. Rabinowitz described the Bangkok wildlife market in the eighties: king cobras hanging up slit open alive, for their blood; a million dying squirrels in the pet section. One Thai child poked a dead flying squirrel, the vendor replaced it with a golden ground squirrel and the parents bought it. Rabinowitz looked at the dead one. How many each day? Things are different now, but Bangkok market still sells endangered species, many from other countries, to Japanese or rich Vietnamese. At least people on the Nam Ha kill to survive. But in the end both mean an empty forest.

Bangkok is also a centre for conservation NGOs. I had no time to go to all countries of South-East Asia but forests in Cambodia and Vietnam are similar to those in Laos. Those of Malaysia are very like those of Sumatra, where I would go next. There are dedicated people working on individual programmes and species everywhere. As my airport cab inched through six lanes of traffic, I thought of their tigers. In Vietnam, the tiger was once respected as royalty: Ong Cop, Lord Tiger. Now prey is scattered and few. In 1995, there were supposedly two hundred tigers; now, there are probably fewer than sixty. The Cambodian government ran poster campaigns to stop trophy-hunting; Khmer pop-stars sang conservation songs on TV; but five tons of wildlife products pass one checkpoint there each day. Illegal logging is even worse: the government catches and tries over and over again the same people operating unlicensed, but barely punishes them. Malaysia has fewer than two hundred wild tigers, Thailand perhaps as many as two hundred and fifty.

In 1986, Rabinowitz studied wild cats in Thailand's Huai Kha Khaeng reserve and saw heavy poaching of animals and timber, ignored by officials and police. He nearly lost a foot in a poisoned trap set for him. Rangers were not paid in summer; the men he trained ate not just his dog but protected species. Returning to camp he found a reticulated python tied between two trees, sobbing as his men ripped the skin from its flinching muscle. They said it was close to camp, they had had to shoot it. Rabinowitz exploded. This was the forest, the python's home! It was endangered, alive, *suffering*! 'Kill it!' he shouted, then did that himself. They were bemused. 'It was easier to skin alive.' 'Buddhists must not take life.'

They knew a report from him could get them fired. *He* knew the park had not paid them for months and snakeskin was valuable. But he could not bear their disregard for animal suffering. The fish they roasted arched away from the flames, eyeballs exploding. Could they not kill them first? They laughed, uncomprehending.

That was the 1980s, in Thailand. Higher up was corruption, illegal timber concessions. A brilliant forest officer took on the reserve directorship, but in the face of corruption killed himself in 1990. Then the sanctuary became a World Heritage Site, forest guards started to report tiger signs, Thai activists founded the Green World Foundation for conservation throughout the country and forced the government to control logging, increase sanctuaries. Border police had been hunting wild animals themselves. Now they collected field data and helped park staff arrest poachers. Rabinowitz showed that change *is* possible.

Tony Lynam was hosting a conference on how to count wild animals. Half Australian, half Burmese, he was tall with a face like those of the Yangon poets. We talked of his hopes for Myanmar, for here. He was camera-trapping in a Thai sanctuary bordering Malaysia, where there were tigers, little poaching, and gaur unfazed by people. Since then, however, that area has become a route into Thailand used by Islamic separatists. The gaur may feel differently now.

Tony led me to the seminar, seven men from all over South East Asia and a familiar face. Ullas! Of course, this was a seminar on counting. He is counting's trailblazer. I would see him next in south India, his home.

'This is *your* home, isn't it?' I asked Tony as I left, looking up at him in sauna-bath night.

'I was brought up in Australia but I love it here.'

Thailand is also a centre of suspiciously many captive tigers. The hundred tigers of Sanya Love World came from one of the many tiger centres in Thailand that look like tiger farms. Their proponents have wriggled on to conservation committees, and argue they do wild tigers good. The owners are so rich that if Thailand closed them they could start again in Malaysia. But China had tiger farms long before. In the early 1990s, China suggested legalizing the international trade in derivatives of farmed tigers. Surprised at the outcry, they withdrew the proposal and researched alternatives to tiger bone. Hence the mole rat. But the farms are still there; now called breeding centres.

In 2001 another NGO operating in Bangkok, EIA,the Environmental Investigation Agency, did a report on Thailand's tigers with photos of battery tiger-farming at the infamous Sriracha Zoo outside Bangkok; of cubs taken away so the tigress comes into season again. Tigresses had twelve cubs a year. The cubs suckled sows.

Superficially, Sriracha was for tourists, who fed cubs and saw tigers do tricks. The professed aim was care and concern for wildlife. Care it is not. Keeping tigers in large groups is against good tiger management, because it is not how wild tigers live. Behind the scenes were hundreds of tigers. Why? They said they had four hundred, but six gave birth every month. Where were they? Were those hundred tigers to Love World the tip of something much larger?

EIA found what was claimed to be bone and tiger products in Bangkok's Chinatown. Tiger-bone pills, whisky, tonic; tiger-penis pills. Some made in China, others in Thailand with factory addresses on the labels: factories which claimed to export all over the world. Norway, the Netherlands. The factories said they imported raw bone from China. But EIA also found their products sold openly at Sriracha. One manufacturer said he bought tiger penis from Sriracha.

Anyone exporting live tigers must have certificates from the Thai Forest Department and CITES. Thailand possessed three hundred captive tigers officially, and unofficially over a thousand. The EIA asked the Forest Department how captive tigers were registered, and got no answer. One breeder said two hundred live cubs were smuggled to China every year, hidden in fruit crates on boats up the Mekong. If an NGO could find this information so easily, what were the enforcement authorities doing? Clearly not fulfilling their obligation to CITES.

In 2001 CITES set up an international Tiger Enforcement Task Force for everyone enforcing bans on tiger products. Countries with wild tigers, *and* countries consuming them. It met in Delhi in 2001. Thailand sent no representative. Next year CITES investigated Thailand. Bangkok's Chinatown was cleaned up beforehand; one tiger-pill manufacturer was busted, others were busted later. The mission confirmed everyone's worries. CITES suggested Thailand create a wildlife crime unit. In 2003, Thailand said it would. The Commander of the Forest Police Division who led enforcement, exposed a thriving illegal trade in tiger meat and live tigers. Tiger breeders complained he was giving Thailand a bad name: it might affect tourism. Thai Royal Police raids found tiger carcasses in freezers, apparently destined for Bangkok restaurants. Not something the conservation community had realized was a significant threat.

Over a Chinese dumpling breakfast I wondered again, *Why not farm tigers?* But I knew why. Everything about the tiger trade comes down to China in the end, and I had met the answer there. It has three prongs. One, if you legalize tiger farms the international community is agreeing that tiger bone works, rather than researching alternatives. Two, the bear-gall parallel: the rich want the wild version anyway, and the product is debased and mass-used in non-essentials like shampoo. Three, it helps dealers launder poached wild animals. How can you know a tiger skin or bone is farmed? Thailand's wild crocodile population became extinct after crocodile farms were introduced. Wild caiman skins, registered as farmed, are laundered here. Farming does not take the heat off wild animals. It just increases demand and validates exploiting them.

Another two-hour cab ride in steamy heat to another NGO. WildAid, like the WCS, worked in Myanmar too, fighting the wildlife trade, protecting, training, educating; helping people and wildlife survive together. And here it was, 'WildAid' on a glass door to a white office high in the sky; twenty people with computers in loose-boxes of grass-green glass.

Tim Redford was a big man with a warm smile, fitter for the jungle than an office. WildAid do protection; they are not science-driven like the WCS. This office was paid for by one immensely generous donor, so all other donations went straight to where money was needed: ranger-training, trucks, jeeps, anti-poaching patrols, monitoring equipment; community work in remote villages – talking to chiefs, teachers, schools; medical care to settlements inaccessible by road; building relationships in places that would otherwise poach and cut forest.

On his laptop, Tim flicked through photos of cable snares, sawmills, his work in every South East Asian country. In each, WildAid pick one park where they protect and run ranger-training courses, teaching patrolling, fieldcraft, tactics when you meet poachers; first aid, forest navigation, photography, camera traps; crime-scene analysis, interviewing, information-gathering; general principles, like law-enforcement, interviewing techniques, crime-scene processing; treating and preventing malaria; UN rules of engagement, self-defence; preparing cases for prosecution.

'God, those courses are tough! Fourteen days of intensive physical and mental activity, starting at five, finishing at eight at night.'

All these Bangkok NGOs are operating in a major wildlife trafficking country that gives little attention to protection. How did *he* cope with despair?

'Switch off on Friday evening. Some people start passionate but burn out in two years. You can't sustain it at that pitch.'

The 'English bar' in the basement was chilly with air-conditioning. Bangkok's image of London: hostesses in red-frogged miniskirts, beefeaterettes. An Australian ex-soldier joined us, WildAid's law-enforcement specialist, who taught arms. South-East Asia is awash with guns. Guards must know how to use them.

'It really is war, isn't it?' I stirred gin with a plastic medieval pike.

'Of course. The men we train are defenders of the wild.'

Back in London, a poet was launching a book in a crowded bar. Soft purple carpet, hard dark wood. He was there by the far wall. The black curls longer now, the glasses tortoiseshell. Parties were where we were in the same room. I was exasperated with myself for even noticing. The person he had been with me was an endangered species. Bit by bit, like species in forests all over Asia, he was leaving the world. But there he was: talking, waving his hands. On his left, the ring I gave him. Soon, he would take it off.

'Writing about tigers?' said an elderly colleague. 'Chap I knew had wonderful tiger stories. Put his wife on an elephant. When she shot the tiger she fell on to it and scrambled up a tree. Tiger came after her! He had to shoot it as it grabbed his wife!'

'Are they stories about tigers, or about shooting them?'

He sniffed what he would call, contemptuously, political correctness. 'Species destroy other species Ruth. It's natural.'

For Darwin, extinction was part of evolution. You cannot understand the origin of species without it. But in his day there was a background level of extinctions. They were part of change. There have been a few mass extinctions in the past, like dinosaurs, but the level of extinction now is a hundred times greater than a 'natural' one. In tropical rainforest, a thousand times. We are the Death Star. And here was a guy with a white wine calling it natural.

I talked to the poet's wife instead.

'I had a drink with – with him the other night,' she said, looking over her shoulder. 'I didn't really know him before. He's very nice. He said how wonderful . . .' She shook her hair in lit wonder. London was full of women charmed by him telling them how much he had loved me. 'I've never *heard* a man talk about a woman like that. Like he talked about you. It's very sad.'

That night I dreamed you could save tigers only by having an operation: gut, bowel or heart cut out and put into tigers. I had the operation: it saved three, a mother with two grown cubs. They recovered quicker than I did and milled round me like horses, eager to go back to the forest. I ran my hands along black spines and red-gold hips. Their passing was a wave of dark flame that did not burn.

18

THE BURNING

I stood on a slope of ash. Black-flecked grey tweed everywhere, up to the wolf-grey horizon. No shadows, nothing tall enough to throw one, just coal-black stumps broken when blazing trunks crashed into flame. Across them a few long white shafts, fallen when fire had passed.

I looked up to the hills, where the psalm says hope comes from. Beyond burnt mountains were tangerine plumes of smoke from still-smouldering forests. At my feet, maimed charcoal scrollwork and one small forked stick whose bark had burned away. A water-diviner or snake-catcher might have found it handy. But here was no water, snake or any animal. Where there had been moisture on every leaf, to a hundred-foot canopy, were broken images where the sun beat.

Before Sumatra, the only volcano I had seen was Vesuvius; and the Phlegraean Fields, named by the Romans from the Greek for 'burning', where extinct craters breathe hot sulphur above Naples. Sumatra's volcanoes are bigger, more numerous and more powerful than Italy's. But this at my feet was man-made.

At Heathrow, on an early August morning, a call from Singapore Airways changed the time of my onward flight to Sumatra. I opened my laptop to find people meeting me, so my daughter could warn them by email. A man beside me hissed in when he saw the tiger desktop. I was so used to it; this tiger face was home. I forgot what a shock it was.

'You have relationship with tiger? Positive or negative?' Italian, Hungarian? 'Your father – you have good relation?'

Really! I looked up. He looked into my eyes. His were gold-flecked hazel.

'When you look in my eyes do you see *tiger*?'

You would have thought I had an erect penis on my laptop.

'Where are you from?'

'Kurdestan. Then Austria.' He said it as if it hurt. Ow-stria. 'Then Has-things, England.' He was visiting family in Turkey, then returning for his English course at Hastings.

'There were tigers in Kurdestan once, weren't there?'

'Many! Is very important symbol in Kurdestan.'

'Of . . . masculinity?'

'*Yes!* You say, my son, he is tiger! You know, our country is wild, very rough, very strong, so we need be wild, strong, rough, to deal with.'

The Caspian tiger, *Panthera tigris virgata*, the westernmost, evolved in west Asia and figured in Ottoman and Persian painting. It lived in forested areas on riverbanks and lakes in Turkey, Iran, Afghanistan, Mongolia, Central Asiatic Russia, the Crimea. The territory was arid as Ussuriland is (for a few months each year) snowy. They were last reliably reported in the 1950s. One was shot in Azerbaijan in 1948, another in 1959 in northern Iran. Fresh skins were seized in east Turkey in 1972. Much hunted for sport in early Russian colonization, and later as a pest, they lost their riverbank forests when water transport increased, and lost their deer to hunters. By the end they were depending on fluctuating numbers of wild boar. In the 1980s the Caspian was declared extinct. Meeting it in the eyes of a displaced Kurd from Hastings seemed apt for Singapore – which is now, like Bangkok, a wildlife trading post. 'Cuddly tiger cub, $20,000, can be delivered to any home in Singapore,' ran a *Singapore News* ad in April 2002, meaning one more cub lost to the wild, and a tigress killed. Beyond Singapore lay extinction. I was flying into battle and loss.

Between Singapore and Sumatra, cloud-wisps trailed over lime-green fried eggs with dark green centres: islands of the Malacca Straits, former peaks of the Sunda Shelf. Here Asia once ran on from Cambodia to Borneo. In the Pleistocene age, seas dropped, rose, dropped. This shelf was often dry land. Vegetation and wildlife changed with fluctuating temperatures. Finally everything warmed, sea levels round the world rose by 120 metres and the high points here became islands.

Islands have been crucial to understanding the evolution of species. Both Darwin on the Galapagos and Alfred Russel Wallace in the Malay archipelago took the island route, mentally, to evolution. Isolation makes species develop separately. Islands are breeding-grounds for the unique and strange, for specialists in closed conditions. They are also crucial to understanding extinction. Biologists use the Sunda islands' wildlife and fossils to show how animals die out when habitat fragments. Smaller islands have fewer species.

But Sumatra, fourth-largest island in the world (after Greenland, New Guinea, Borneo), has soaring mountains, lush lowland, broad rivers, one of the richest wildlife diversities in the world, and *Panthera tigris sondaica*, the Sunda tiger. Sundaland means Borneo, Java, Bali, Sumatra, other islands on the shallow Sunda Shelf, and Malaya, now linked to the mainland by the Isthmus of Krai. It is unlikely that tigers ever existed in Borneo, though a few skeletal parts have been found. The Balinese tiger vanished in the thirties, the Javanese in the seventies. The Malayan tiger, *Panthera tigris jacksoni*, still lives in Malaysia but I had decided to go instead for the two or three hundred tigers (conventionally four hundred, but if counting is hard in India it is even harder here) on Sumatra.

Over Sumatra, the clouds changed to vertical whipped cream penetrated by shockingly tall mountains. Volcanoes! One was my ultimate goal, Kerinci, 3800 metres. Lake Toba, South East Asia's biggest lake, was formed here prehistorically by a volcano in probably the biggest eruption ever. And in 1883 the island of Krakatoa, between Sumatra and Java, blew up. Ash and pumice rose twenty-six kilometres into the air. The sea rushed in, a forty-metre tsunami engulfed Java and Sumatra, and was felt twelve hours later at Aden and in France. For three years Krakatoa's dust circled the globe. America's fire-engines rushed to red glows on horizons. Outside Oslo, Edvard Munch saw a bloody sunset, felt 'a great scream piercing through nature', and remembered it ten years later for *The Scream*. On Java and Sumatra, thirty-six thousand people died. Dead tigers floated in the sea.

Sumatra was my most violent tiger place, earthquakes and land-slides all the time. On Boxing Day 2004, an earthquake off Aceh would send a tsunami over the Indian Ocean, killing a hundred thousand people in Aceh alone. But the violence was not only geological. Aceh's civil war had killed many thousands already, and in Jakarta the Bali bomber was on trial. Here, the breath of dying forests overhung Padang like the pall over Krakatoa. The pilot said it was smoky. 'We'll have trouble getting down. We often do.'

Recently, a tiger had strayed on to Padang university campus so I had arranged to do a poetry reading there. Afterwards I dined with a dean in scarlet trouser suit and matching head-cover, despite fero-cious August heat. Her speciality was sociolinguistics. What was *bahasa Indonesia* (the official Indonesian language, based on Malay) for tiger?

'*Harimau.* But in villages they say *inya* or *nenek.* "Grandmother." Grandmothers are important. This is a matrilinear society. They say, "Sssh, Grandmother's near," so the tiger won't be angry. At least, that's what we're told. Do they really say that now? I don't know.'

My goals were three: a tiger megalith, British tiger research on a plan-tation, and an anti-tiger-poaching operation on Kerinci. Lilik, a wiry guide in his thirties, would escort me to them all. I had a Xeroxed photo of the megalith but he did not know it. Was it in a museum? We would have to go to Mount Dempo volcano, where the photo had been taken in 1932, and see.

The Padang suburbs made Sumatra seem, on the surface, the rich-est tiger country so far; and surface clearly mattered. People on campus had mobile phones flashing purple. Streets had shiny cars. On the edge of town, where houses became shacks, our generator broke. Men gazed at the only tourist in Sumatra, I at mosquitoes in the turquoise sludge of an open drain, till three hours later a man crawled from underneath, beaming, and waved us on our slow way south.

Sumatra measures journeys in hours, not miles. You never know how the road will be. This one, more sieve than road, led over flat cliffs above the sea, through scrubby hills and wooden villages with curtains

of very pink satin, satellite dishes, birdcages. One toddler had a teddy
bear. Compared to children in alpine Bhutan or Laos, they too suggested Sumatra was the wealthiest tiger place. Or was this pink satin
simply a veneer? One village had dainty fencing.

'Javan people,' said Lilik approvingly. 'More civilized.'

Sumatra is ruled from Java, most populated island on earth. It has
sent thousands of settlers here, which caused the Aceh war. Aceh
wants independence from Jakarta. Lilik grew up in a compound. His
father was a Javan policeman here: Javan settlers were unpopular,
police doubly so. Lilik disapproved of Aceh rebels and thought Javan
ways better. My sympathies lay with the unfenced shacks.

Some paddy-fields were under water: coffee-coloured mirrors
sprigged with green rice reflected the mountains. Other fields were
dotted with brown smoke-coils from burning cabbage stalks.

'Not good system. Small fires, but many. Bad for atmosphere.'

This land was fire-obsessed. A nine-foot bank smouldering black
and orange: why burn *that*?

'Just to clean.'

Whole fields were being new-cleared. Trees at the edge, once the
middle of jungle, were now the perimeter to burnt space. Men left a
big tree in the middle, retiring to its shade while others burned;
showing, even as they destroyed trees, how we need them. One
ancient giant was being sawn beside the road, its bole higher than
two men.

'When they fell the big tree, small trees also gone.' Lilik pointed to
other plants. Tapioca. A kapok, the only thing left in a blackened field,
tufts of fluff on its skeleton. 'Once very commercial tree. Now people
use foam mattress instead.'

Sumatra is the beginning of what were once the spice islands.
Kapok and tapioca on the coast, pepper, coffee, cinnamon, cloves
inland. Aceh, an Islamic sultanate, became a major Asian power by
selling pepper to Europe. But the Dutch settled at Padang in 1663, the
British at Bengkulu, where we were heading, in 1685. By the beginning
of the twentieth century, after bloodshed everywhere (especially
Aceh), the Dutch controlled all. They were deeply resented. Lilik preferred the British, especially Thomas Stanford Raffles who invaded
Java for Britain in 1811, governed there till 1816 (discovering

Borobudur, the world's largest Buddhist temple, in the jungle), and governed Bengkulu, then founded Singapore in 1819.

'Dutch only wanted money. Didn't go in interior. Just took. English gave system, education, law. But also took.'

Now the Sumatrans themselves were stripping this botanic wealth. This mountainside was the worst yet. We had seen smoke all day, but here was nothing green at all.

'They clear one hill here, another there. To sell for paddy. For palm oil.'

But who are we to criticize? Malaysia is clearing forest too: its president points out that we have cut *our* forest for millennia. The history of Western civilization is the history of forest destruction. Gilgamesh cut Sumeria's forests to make the city of Uruk. Each civilization, from Knossos to Venice and beyond, was built on timber wealth, and declined as the consequences of deforestation bit. In Britain, forest disappeared as the population rose. The only time it grew back was in the Black Death. 'If woods be suffered to be felled as daily they are,' said James I, in 1610, 'there will be none left.'

Eighteenth-century Britain admired forested landscape and imitated it in landscape gardening. The orientalist William Marsden, who worked in Sumatra, confessed in his 1783 *History of Sumatra* that after wading through miles of jungle he did like a nice formal pepper garden:

In highly cultivated countries like England, we endeavour to
give gardens charm by imitating the wildernesses of nature.
Hanging woods, craggy rocks . . . On Sumatra the irregular
style would attract but little attention. Unimproved scenes on
every side would eclipse such labours.

Back home, trees went on disappearing. In 1879 Gerard Manley Hopkins lamented poplars:

Felled, felled, all felled;
    Of a fresh and following folded rank
        Not spared, not one.

Since 1945, the UK has lost thirty per cent of remaining ancient woodland. In March 2003, at Wigston, south of Leicester, a triangle of
railway track still enclosed woodland full of diversity on the small
UK scale. It was designated for conservation, home to badgers, stoats,
rare marbled white butterflies. In the nesting season, Network Rail
flattened it in a morning. To stop leaves dropping on the line, they
said. They did not tell the local council, made no environmental
survey, and left wood chips on the line, a worse fire hazard than
leaves. They did the same all over England. As I stared at Sumatran
ash, they were probably still going. Ruthless short-termism, contempt
for people who try to protect, evasion and manipulation of laws: all
this happens on my island too. As the biggest investor in Indonesia
after Japan, the UK was now lobbying for British companies to mine in
protected Sumatran forest.

'Long way to Bengkulu,' said Lilik, netting me back to the car. But
within ten minutes the battery failed. We stopped over a jungly ravine.
Something about that new generator? We had a long way to go. The
driver removed the battery. I followed a black butterfly whose open
wings, wide as a tiger's paw, were Guinness-black with orange flashes.
It closed like a book, pretending to be a dead leaf. The grey-brown
underwings were a soft-dragged flame pattern. I stared at tapestried
greens in surrounding trees. We were in mountains now, the slope
above was lathered green, hundreds of near-vertical feet frothing with
the thickest growth I had ever seen.

What was so wonderful was the mix. Colour, texture, shape, the
massy complex jungle vision that had beguiled Darwin, and twenty
years later inspired the concept of bio-diversity. After his first tropical
forest, he wrote in his diary, 'It is not only the gracefulness of their
forms or the novel richness of their colours, it is the numberless and
confusing associations that rush together on the mind, and produce
the effect.' A glorious day, he said, 'like giving to a blind man eyes'.

And I, with a black butterfly for company, was seeing the same
thing. Different continent and plants; same wonder. Wildly various
jewel-slivers of green, wriggling, luxuriant intricacies, any shape and
texture a leaf could be: palm, blade, fluff; tendril, thorn, nodule; floppy,
flat, prickled, freckled, ferny, glossy, furred, runed, spotted, plush. And
within, beneath, who knew what snakes, lizards, insects, voles, frogs,

squirrels and little carnivores? Yet this was not heart-of-the-jungle pristine forest, just run-of-the-mill roadside stuff, intershot with cultivated trees. All, every day, burning.

We were miles from anywhere. You are on your own in Sumatra. We drove on, using the battery as little as possible.

Bengkulu at twilight was larger, more trafficky than I had expected. No graceful colonial port but ring roads, concrete roundabouts, triumphalist statues, shopping centres, coloured lights strung along multi-laned boulevards packed with four-wheel drives and petrol fumes. Indonesia, the world's fourth most populous country, has no coherent environment policy. Thirty million of its children face permanent damage to brain and lungs from lead poisoning.

Next day, inland in south Sumatra, the land rose. Tigers came nearer through hot long hours of green misty gorges and mountains. By afternoon I was looking for Mount Dempo.

There have been tiger-charmers through all the Malay world, but especially Sumatra. In the seventeenth century, when Dutch records began, there were hundreds of real tigers in Malaya, Java and Sumatra but also, supposedly, were-tigers. In human form, Sumatran were-tigers carried spotted knives. Their upper lips had no central groove. (Women unversed in these signs who married one discovered the truth on their wedding night.) Mount Dempo had more than its fair share. Several clans traced their ancestry to tigers. In the 1840s one village was inhabited only by were-tigers.

My megalith was on Dempo, too. A Dutch aviator called Thomassen à Thuessink van der Hoop photographed and described it in 1932, then wrote a Ph.D. on all Sumatran megaliths, which were carved in the first century AD. Most are near Lahat; the tiger one was at Besemah, wherever that was. Two tigers, in fact: mating. The female, under the male, held a human head. Were-tigers and sexy tigers playing with human heads, would be my context for real tigers. But how would we find them?

Outside Pagaralam it began to rain. Fat tropical drops, then glassy sheets. At a guest-house, a boy named Ramla smiled when I said, 'Megalith,' and produced a tatty pamphlet with the same photo. He knew how to get there. From his doorway I saw a lone rainy mountain: Dempo volcano. Did people there turn into tigers?

'Your curiosity is very specific,' said Lilik wearily, before translating. 'Most tourists do not want these things.' But Ramla nodded. He had family on Dempo. He knew.

On the map the other volcano I was bound for, Kerinci, was part of a huge chain. After driving slowly up and down and up next morning, through hairpin bends and ridges, I realized Dempo too was part of a chain: a ring round a great plain. This plain fringed by mountains of tigers and tiger magic must have been settled very early. Our goal was the high slopes: past coffee trees whose white blossom smelt like linden, lime-green secondary forest striped with bare slides where trees had been whooshed down to sawmills; crags, burnt hills, thick bamboo trailing over little streams; and then a bank studded with white pebbles saying BESEMAH. But Besemah was only a subdistrict. On a higher plateau we met Ramla's brother, a twelve-year-old studying in an Islamic boarding-school.

In the aftermath of the Bali bomb, the Western press called Islamic schools in Indonesian hinterlands 'nests of agitation'. These villages looked so poor, education must be the only way out. Ramla's brother guided us to higher villages still: red water-lilies on little ponds, coffee fruit like green sweets spread on the road to dry, domestic cats with strange club tails. (At first I thought they were run over but they could not all have been: it had to be genetic.) Tiny goats, lemon yellow with black stockings, played on woodpiles; stippled chickens, speckly white and apricot, were living pecking sculpture. Of course – Indonesian gamecocks. And outside every shack, birds in wicker cages in hot sun, or empty cages whose occupants had died.

Our village was Rimba Sujud, 'Jungle Reverence' in the Rejang Lebong language. Inland Sumatra has many languages. The names ranged from descriptive ('Big Ditch') to grandiose abstract ('Glory'). This one, considering the burning forests, seemed a bad joke. The jungle was nowhere near. The fields, whose palm-tree edges were etched on morning mist, were paddies of green glass.

Rimba Sujud had sixty-six families. In the head man's house we asked to see the megalith. He said the occupying Japanese had tried to take it but failed: it was too heavy, too magic. He took us over a space where coffee lay drying: gleaming berries, green, yellow, brown. At any other time I would have been fascinated. I had not drunk nearly enough real coffee, looking for tigers. Here it was, the foundation of fortunes and café culture, raw at my feet. But beyond, by a fence of withered palm, was what we were looking for: grey stone mating tigers, last seen to my knowledge by any European who cared, in 1932. Both rearing up; the tigress to get a good hold on her victim, the tiger to get a good hold on her, hugging like a baby chimp clinging to its mother, tail along his back.

With prey they were seven foot, as long as a small real tiger. The stone was ringed with lichen, the faces worn, ears non-existent. They were earless aliens with shadow-pool eyes – but cat bodies, clearly predators. The earth had now been cleared from the base: the human head turned out to be a whole human *baby* in front of an adult human foot. Two, in fact, one each side, under the tigers. The villagers laughed.

'They say tigers are punishing adultery. They have eaten mother, abandoned her foot. The baby is result of adultery. Tiger will eat now.'

'Where's the father? Have they eaten him already?'

Lilik translated. They laughed again.

'One law for woman, one for man. Tigers do not punish man.'

The head man said that when he was a boy a nearby village was attacked by a man-eater that killed only adulterers. There was an outbreak of fidelity. The tiger left.

'He says we must show respect. Tiger is preserver of the law.'

Who knows what the culture that carved this extraordinary statue really believed? All it showed now was that there were tigers here in the first century. But behind these men lay centuries of belief that the fiercest animal of their jungle also patrolled human laws, as the Furies in Greek tragedy pursue the guilty. Those Furies, punishing Orestes for killing his mother, explain their role by saying, 'There is a place where what is terrible is good.' That's the tiger. Terrible, but good. The dread presence that rules your world has to have a purpose. Here, its purpose was enforcing the laws on which human society rested. Maybe the village name was not so ironic. Its people reverenced the jungle's lord as guardian of human law.

Ramla wanted to show me other tiger things on Dempo. We drove to his father's village on a cart track that went higher, wilder. One village was deserted because of tiger attacks. After it, the car stuck in gravel on a steep hill. We got out. They pushed the car back and considered. They would need a long run at that gravel: I said I'd walk on up. I was dying to get out into the air, feel the jungle on my own. 'Jungle Toilet,' I said airily, using Lilik's phrase. Jungle Reverence, Jungle Toilet. It was great walking up, thick undergrowth either side, a drop over cliffs and forest—

'Look behind!' yelled Lilik.

Where I had been a second before, a five-foot piece of green string was crossing the track, so straight I did not think it dangerous to go close. I believed, rightly or wrongly, it would only strike when coiled. It knew I was there but, concerned with getting to the other side, kept yellow eyes with vertical pupils focused on the long grass ahead, black tongue flickering to taste the air. Bright green with a white smile, a line of cream that began on the lips and swept under throat and tummy, tail tipped with pink. In the grass it mostly disappeared, but stopped moving before the tip was covered. This lay motionless, looking exactly like dry grass.

In hot hours of driving I had studied *Snakes of South East Asia*. This was a pit viper. The name comes from a heat-sensitive pit under the skin between the nostril and the eye. I decided it was a female white-lipped pit viper. Other green ones snuggled into branches; this was a ground snake. 'The body of this attractive viper is fairly stout,' said the book. These snakes hunt mice and frogs at night, resting in vegetation by day; they are 'venomous dangerous', widely responsible for snakebites throughout tropical Asia. I went off Jungle Toilet.

The village was on a cliff above a river. We turned into it at a banana tree and parked on open red earth: the village centre, surrounded by stilt houses. Ramla's father, a handsome man with heavy eyelids and a shiny batik shirt, introduced Rahan, clawed by a tiger when they made the village: small, thin in a mustard-yellow T-shirt. Rahan's father too came out, leaning on a stick, his bare left foot twisted inward. He walked on the top knuckles of his toes.

In 1979, Rahan was 'opening jungle' for the village. At ten in the morning, bending to cut bushes where the banana tree was now, he didn't hear the tiger as it leaped from behind, forepaws round him clawing his chest, teeth tearing his scalp. He fought back with his scythe till it ran away, and was ill for two months. He lifted the yellow shirt to show red dots on either side of his chest where the claws had sunk in. I had seen traces of tigers' feet in many places now, but never on a man. Under his hair was a ridged scar.

'The gods do this to us,' Rahan said, through Lilik. 'We have to get over, have to work in forest. I was traumatized but must not let worry me. I have to forget about. Many tigers here before. Very fierce. Afterwards I became more brave not less. Not afraid of criminals. I have survived a tiger, why be afraid anything else?'

Next, a richer village. Stone houses, goats and chickens, a front room of pink carpet, lace curtains, pink plush sofas, empty aquarium topped with a red velvet crocodile, large TV with the sound off. Ramla's older brother, a doctor, was wealthy and had to show it. His wife sat me under a mobile of luminescent fish and summoned people to talk tigers. The TV played; the front door kept opening to let in the inquisitive faces of little goats and a plump young man whose T-shirt said THINK OF SPORT.

The wife's mother, tiny and shrunken with white hair, came in bent double but very alert in striped T-shirt and long orange-and-black skirt. Like an old man with grey stubble, she sat on the floor. Both were barefoot. Their toes spread like wings; they could never have worn shoes. Wealth had come in one generation. Her sister, aged ten, had been killed by a tiger while working in paddy. She remembered flesh scattered around.

Were there tigers now? Yes, in the hills, said the plump man. Many people shot them. He knew a *masu marai*, were-tiger. Lilik translated austerely; this was not his scene. 'The man is sixty, married to a teacher. He turns into tiger when stressed. He eats like an animal. They are afraid of him. His eyes stare like a tiger.' There were many *masu marai*. They had normal children, but food changed them, willy-nilly, into tigers.

I had found my Mount Dempo were-tigers. Now for the only man who had radio-collared a real live Sumatran one: Tom, whom I had first met sitting on the floor of Sarah's London Zoo flat with the research team who worked with him for a month. He collared a tiger immediately afterwards. They had watched his video wistfully, drinking Chardonnay.

*

A few years before, Sean, British manager of a plantation for a palm-oil company called Asiatic Persada, had discovered tigers were living off the wild boar that ate the fallen fruit. What should he do? Similar tigers on Malaysian plantations had been killed.

Malaysia's jungle is very like Sumatra's. Agriculture is eleven per cent of Malaysia's domestic product, palm oil seventy per cent of that. When prices went down in 2001, Malaysia increased production, cut more forest, removing Malayan tigers' homes and bringing them into conflict with workers who, for only a dollar more than they earned in 1965 (well below Malaysia's poverty wage), had to gather two tons of fruit each day. Tiger meat is forty dollars a plate in tourist areas. (The director of WWF Malaysia has said people are more likely to eat tigers there than the other way round.) Poaching, of course, is a temptation. A tiger killed someone on a plantation near Kuala Lumpur and was shot. After maulings in the state of Kelantan, workers stayed at home, terrified; the governor said the army would kill tigers. 'Tigers must not be here. This is well populated, no longer virgin jungle.'

But Malaysian plantations work differently. They are let seasonally to smallholders, who keep livestock to supplement their living, attracting tigers. On Asiatic Persada, the tigers had lots of prey and did not bother humans. British companies are keen on conservation. No one wants to be the one with a bad name. The pressure to be ecologically sound makes a difference. The British owned fifty-one per cent of Asiatic Persada, Indonesians forty-nine per cent. *They* did not want land set aside for conservation; it lowered profits. But Sean contacted Sarah at the Zoological Society of London, who set up a study project there under Tom, who had just done his Ph.D. in Africa.

Tom found ten to fifteen tigers living in dense scrubland full of bamboo. They did not go right into the plantation, just along the edge. This is marginal habitat for tigers. But marginal habitat may be the answer in the future. If all original forest vanishes from Malaysia and Indonesia, tigers can survive if there are trees that give cover and food for animals they eat. Scientists can help them by studying them now in those conditions. The more you know, the better you can protect.

The video showed Tom finding the tiger. To tranquillize in this terrain you have to use snares, but if an animal stays in one long, even caught lightly by the foot with no skin-wound, it may die afterwards

from the hours of pressure. These were humane cables with transmitters. Tom checked the signals every hour at night, when tigers move
most, and deactivated them in daytime. After two months of sleeping
in the jeep, waiting, a signal came at four one morning. This video
began at night, jeep-bonnet nosing over a jungle track of runny red.
The rains had just stopped. We saw Tom walk forward with a torch,
not knowing what lay ahead. A male tiger, larger and yellower than
Sumatran tigers are said to be, caught by a paw in bushes lit to jade by
the torch, watched him come in the archetypal warning mask: ears-
back fury, intended to terrify. If I had been Tom, it would have worked.
To tranquillize, they had to arc round, guessing the cable's stretch,
upsetting the tiger as little as possible. The more stressed he is, the
more tranquillizer you need, and the more harm it might do. So much
can go wrong. Wildlife films show things going right.

Suddenly the tiger was asleep.

'How much did you give him?' asked John Lewis, the brilliant
wildlife vet I had talked to. He had been on the team and, as it happened, saved Sean's dog.

Sean, the manager, lived on the plantation with his family in a compound guarded by the family Doberman. One night they heard the
dog gasping. He had amazingly wide fangmarks on his throat, from an
enormous cobra, or krait. Incredibly, John saved him. Now he and
Tom discussed dosage as we saw Tom on video bend to the great head,
move the snare to another paw, gently rope the terrifying front ones.

They recognized the tiger from camera-trap photos. The advantage
of tigers is stripes. They are all different so you can identify both sides
of every animal. This was the male-with-a-wound-on-his-neck. He
must have been trapped before, and got free. He was six or seven.
They called him Slamet, 'Lucky'.

'Should be Plonker,' said Tom now. 'He keeps walking into snares.'

They checked that the neck wound was healing, checked teeth,
weighed, measured, checked for parasites, poured antibiotics into
scratches. The girl on the team kissed Slamet's head. You could feel
awe and excitement as well as professionalism in every movement.
They took a blood sample. Then . . .

'Take your finger out of his arse, Tom,' someone said.

The real Tom took another swig of Chardonnay. He was six foot and blond. His hands were speckless. In the film he wore surgical gloves for the tiger's anus.

'Internal parasites. Sample.'

They knew that, really; they just wished they had been there. The video broke off and was replaced by the map of *EastEnders*.

'That's where we released him,' said the joker from the floor.

Sarah put on lights, Tom showed camera-trap shots of tigers they had *expected* to find in that snare. A tigress with two grown-up cubs. Flash, the male whose territory they thought this was. Tom was surprised that Slamet had been on Flash's patch. He bore no marks of a fight. How differently do tigers behave in marginal habitat? Tom was there to find out.

They were all scientists, except me and the man beside me on the floor: Jeremy, a wildlife photographer based in Sumatra. He had accompanied the team, worked in South-East Asia, and had taken unique photos of rare creatures: the only one of the Sumatran striped rabbit, and many in my *Mammals* book. He adored his work.

'I could spend five years just photographing frogs. People have no idea how long it takes. Tomorrow I'm off to Malaysia: FFI want photos of one particular small bird. If I don't get it in five days they'll be annoyed but I can't order it up like pizza. If I see one it may not show itself clearly. It takes days. *Weeks.*'

A poet in disguise. That '*I could spend five years just photographing frogs*' went to my heart.

'I'm going to Sumatra. When's the best time?'

'July's good. After Tom, stay in my house in Kerinci. There's a spare bed. Tell Debbie, whom I share it with.'

That was why I was here now. This barmy highway, this unsafe car. Sarah, Tom, Jeremy, John. Conservationist, scientist, photographer, vet. Working together. The cutting edge of conservation.

We drove for eight hours without turning off the engine, even when filling up. The Trans-Sumatran Highway had wonderful views. Green velvet stairways fading to spangled mist. Trailing tendrils in a thousand shades of green. It was also hundreds of miles of stony lace. Once, as we bumped at two miles an hour into a particularly deep crater, a crocodile barged down at us from a high grass bank: no, a giant monitor lizard, six foot long with a barrel chest, arms like those of a Sumo wrestler, a beaky smile. Monitor lizards are carnivores, very intelligent by lizard standards. This was a clouded monitor; they live from Pakistan to Java. It stopped, looked at us outraged, whipped away at a waddly canter. Thank heaven for holes. This disgrace of a road was excellent for wild animals. Lilik had seen a truck here going equally slowly – axles break in the pits – meeting a vast python head on. It overturned. The python departed, unhurt.

We stopped for food in a cement shopping complex. Sumatra was a jarring mix of beautiful jungle and ugly towns, where other engines ran in parked cars to keep the air-conditioning going. Ours ran because it might never start again. Waiting for Lilik and the driver, I watched a gibbon chained to an iron bar. 'Siamang,' said a man. I was not sure. Siamang, the largest gibbon, has under its chin a leathery pouch that inflates when it calls. This was small: black fur, tiny sad face, furry throat, palms and inside wrists shammy smooth for swinging. It picked up its chain and grabbed a branch, leaving one toe on the bar below, slim hairy leg making a long black line with its right arm. A black hairy star against clouds of exhaust. A pipe-cleaner acrobat, arms as long as body and legs combined.

In Pleistocene times, gibbons diversified through South East Asia in places isolated by rising sea. They are smaller than the great apes, but still our close relatives. Unlike them (and us) they are monogamous. As in other monogamous animals, male and female are the same size. Their pure, elaborate songs echo, or used to, through eastern jungles. Males sing to defend their mate from other males. The energy of their song shows potential rivals how tough they are. Females sing even while launching themselves through air, to defend territory (and fruit trees) against other females. Couples also sing duets. Maybe the male is helping her defend her territory, but as in any musical partnership the duet's complexity also shows how long they have been together. Like tigers, gibbons depend on the forest for food. Since different trees fruit at different times they eat fruit all year, playing a vital role in seed dispersal and regeneration. Trees depend on them; they, on the trees.

There were so many gibbons in my book. Javan, Bornean, pileated, Hoolock, agile, white-handed, white-cheeked, buff-cheeked. This one was all black. Black gibbons lived only in China and Vietnam and had crests. Maybe it was Kloss's gibbon, from the Mentawai Islands off

West Sumatra; very endangered because those forests, too, are going. Its solo songs have the most complex structure of all gibbon calls. A male can sing for forty minutes non-stop. But this one had no mate to defend. It was not badly cared for. Not in a cage, like those in Laos. But it should have been with a mate in the forest. A single animal on a chain is a genetic full stop. How species become rare, then extinct.

When darkness fell, we drove without lights. I mistrusted our electrics and did not fancy getting trapped in a burning car so I kept my door-lock up. Lilik kept pressing it down. Apart from Aceh, this was the worst stretch in Sumatra for *bajing lompak*, 'flying squirrel' brigands. They used to jump from overhanging trees but now just held you up, with weapons. Luckily we met only the police, paid for an escort and limped into Jambi with policemen fore and aft.

Tom in a dusty jeep looked even larger among the slight Sumatrans. On the two-hour drive to the plantation I met his training assistant Elva, the Indonesian girl who had kissed Slamet, and Tom's official counterpart Satrio. The Indonesian government oversaw ZSL's research. The Department for Conservation of Natural Resources (BKSDA), under the Ministry of Forestry, was responsible for forest outside protected areas, and Tom operated within their rules: genetic samples stayed here, photos were developed here, Indonesian personnel were involved at every level.

Elva spoke good English, Satrio a little. Tom's *bahasa* was, he said, coming on. Another thing defenders of the wild must do: learn languages. In remote places and physical emergencies, you need words.

Squat chunky palm-trees, every one the same; a dirt road running through and a mustardy cobra on it, split by a wheel. Satrio carried it to the roadside. I touched the dry black head. The pupils were round, not vertical like the viper's. Satrio spread the skin to show ochre scales black-edged like crystals outlined in kohl. A yellow snake in a black net tube. Equatorial spitting cobra, said my book. Tom, the professional, smiled. Snakes are hard to tell apart; there is enormous variation in one species. But two of Sumatra's three cobras do spit. They aim at the eyes. It is agonizingly painful, but does not blind. The bite kills, though, within a few hours. They eat lizards and rodents, which here would eat fallen fruit. It is accident that the poison with which they paralyse tiny prey kills big animals too, like us. I looked at the ground between the all-surrounding palms with more respect, but Tom had not worried about snakes here so far.

'In Africa, working on meerkats, I saw puff adders everywhere. The meerkats alerted me. Also scorpions. Some were enormous, but the venom is supposed to be in inverse ratio to claw size. The smaller the claw, the more venom. A friend visiting, who used to work out a lot, sat with us round the fire one night and got stung. We found a big-clawed scorpion. Shouldn't have been a problem, he was tough, said he'd be OK. But someone heard him making amazing noises in the night. His lungs were so paralysed he couldn't shout. We got him into a car. He said afterwards that was excruciating – we didn't know, he couldn't talk. We phoned the hospital, miles away, to meet us with adrenaline. They gave it to him on the road. Otherwise he wouldn't have made it. In three days he was OK. Then the anti-venom arrived. When they gave it he nearly died again.'

After Mount Dempo, staying in Tom's small bungalow surrounded by plantation workers' homes felt like an English country weekend, despite the muggy heat, capture equipment, geckos, cockroaches, data sheets, papers on tiger biology and a conservationist's manual mostly on what goes wrong with jeeps. Currently Tom was trying to do something just as important as tagging tigers: radio-collar wild pig. Prey animals are not glamorous but you cannot understand tigers without them. Boar on camera all look the same. They are intelligent and wary; Tom had not got one yet. When he interviewed candidates for Satrio's job, people said no one would want to work with pigs. One candidate said he would if he did not have to see their faces.

'He's not going to go far in tiger conservation,' said Tom.

Someone knocked at the wire-mesh door: Volta, tall, dark, with beautiful winged eyebrows, the plantation's Environment and Conservation officer. He ensured its work was environmentally sound, did conservation education, monitored poaching and illegal logging, liaised with all kinds of people, including those opposing conservation, to explore ways of working so that people could make money without harming the environment. To encourage Jambi's youth to feel proud of their environmental heritage (rather than dad's new car), he set up a Conservation Club and

Café. They were making a difference, he said, to background awareness. There were wildlife TV programmes now. But his deep concern was marginalized native people, facing similar problems to tribal people in India.

Who do forests belong to? When Indonesia became a sovereign state, 'the land belongs to us' was *the* big anti-colonial slogan. But the government gave rights to loggers, not to the native tribes. Deforestation increased. Today, there was a push towards regional power, but local politicians did not stop entrepreneurs claiming forest land in the tribe's name and clearing it.

The tribes round Jambi, the original inhabitants (once called Kubu, Malay for 'Sumatran tribes', but this was now a non-PC word), were Orang Dalam (*orang* is 'man', as in *orang utan*, 'person of the forest'): nomadic hunter-gatherers traditionally living off forest produce. They had never killed tigers. The tiger was a god.

'Their young men know it is valuable, but still avoid it. Seeing a tiger is a curse, for them and the tiger.'

They are surrounded now by sawmills, logging, plantations. Jambi was booming from timber, rubber, palm oil, coffee. Plants the Orang Dalam depended on were disappearing. The Trans-Sumatra Highway brought thousands of Javan migrants. They have adapted to agriculture, a little; crops attract boar and deer so hunting is easier; they work on farms, trade rattan, honey and baskets for medicine, guns, torches, radios, tobacco. Instead of biodegradable litter round their homes there are now batteries, plastics, bottles, tins. Farmers who employ them, sedentary Muslims who feel part of developing Indonesia, cannot sympathize with half-naked non-Muslim nomads. Missionary organizations build houses; the Orang Dalam abandon them to camp on village edges, alarmed by mandatory schooling, political activity, community duties.

Asiatic Persada was enlightened. Another palm-oil company, PT Agricinal based in Bengkulu, also had tigers on a plantation; others too had conservation programmes. With Agus Priambudi, formerly head of BKSDA in Jambi but now transferred to Bengkulu, Volta began to link NGOs with industrial companies. There was deep resistance to conservation: they worked tactfully to get the rich and powerful on board. Most thought tigers should not be conserved. Using land fully helped local taxes, increasing the local government's budget. The

Department of Agro-business had stated that Asiatic Persada should *not* use for tigers land earmarked for commercial purposes.

Volta was descended from a tiger. His family said there was a sign in the toenail. He wiggled his toes at a reflective cockroach. I told him about *masu marai* on Mount Dempo. Here, were-tigers were *harimau jadi-jadian*, 'made-up tiger', but these too had no gully in their top lip. Could he change into a tiger? Volta's top lip was sharply indented.

'We aren't *harimau jadi-jadian*, just descended from the tiger god so tigers protect us. If pugmarks are seen by the house, a tiger has come to stop something bad happening to the family.'

A European in his early forties came in: Ian, the company's environmental manager. I was lucky to catch him: Asiatic Persada's parent company, Pacific Rim Palm Oil Ltd, had plantations all over Indonesia. Ian went from one to another, checking human rights, workers' living conditions, conservation. By getting a large company to move in environmentally good directions, he could make things happen in other companies too. Large players like Unilever were pressured by environmental and human-rights groups. At conferences, Ian now had a new important thing to bring to the table: tigers and their science on plantations. Other companies had different aspects of conservation to share.

'To make things happen *well*, we've got to get maybe seven hundred different people to see things in a positive conservation light.'

'Do you ever despair?' I refilled his vodka. I had brought it for Tom. Not much was left.

'Sometimes. Then I see they really did listen, *did* bind pipes to stop spills into rivers. Yes, there's still degradation going on. But we *can* push things in a positive way.'

And poverty here? The villages looked poor, but I had seen a teddy bear . . .

'Poverty's difficult to interpret. Even teddy bears are confusing. People go without more important things to buy one. Most are *very* poor. Logging started seriously in the late sixties. By the late nineties *more* people were below the poverty line, so the forests went with no benefit to the people.'

He loved this country, had married into it; loved the people. There were businessmen here as well as scientists, helping tigers and the wilderness to survive.

That night among camera traps I dreamed I had a pet cobra. Its temperament was so sweet it was hard to remember it could kill. Then it disappeared. Suddenly – help, loose cobra, and a little girl down the road! If I found it would I dare pick it up? Would it recognize me? Had I been wrong to trust it? Something you are fond of, think you know; when it's out of sight you realize its true nature. I woke sweating, looking out at oil palms and dark mist. First I dreamed him a skunk. Now I was dreaming of cobras. But did this have to be about him? He was so unimportant now, compared to what I was learning. God's sake, wasn't this just a dream about a snake?

Elva brought coffee in the dark. We were going to check transects, a basic tool of wildlife research. Transects are lines through habitat on which you regularly record animal traces. Like plot samples, they reveal the *density* of different animals: animals that tigers depend on, like prey, but also others whose lives tigers indirectly affect and which indirectly affect them by pollinating, fertilizing. Transect-checking is a vital, exhausting, sometimes dangerous activity. Scouts, originally appointed by Asiastic Persada to check on snares, now helped Tom's research by walking these every two weeks, checking camera traps marking tracks and faeces, recording their position then kicking them away so they did not record them again. This built up the long-term data. Tom walked them himself as often as possible.

We drove through the dark plantation, past security men at crossroads, past Tom's boar trap disguised as brushwood.

'They're much too clever,' said Tom, gloomily. 'Jeremy said use truffles! We'd be looking at a slightly larger budget next year then.'

Claustrophobic palms marched in all directions, with no horizon or variation. The only animals that liked them were civets, snakes and Western tarsiers, primates thirty-five centimetres long with big night eyes and gecko-ish feet, which inhabit only south Sumatra. The current Miss Indonesia, keen on their bush-baby appeal, was sponsoring a protection programme for them.

Now one side opened on to scrub. Satrio had seen a tiger there.

'We cut a transect here in very dense cover,' said Tom. 'Afterwards we found tigers using it too. "Thanks, folks," they must have said.'

Tigers are large and have soft feet. They like comfort, like conserving energy, like a decent path. A frozen stream. A transect, cut to study them. Land they used regularly here was undulating iron-orange heath: Cézanne colours, violet flowers, pink curlicues, leaves like scaly claws, and no deep shadow. This was low opportunist scrub, grown when a logging company felled big trees in the 1970s.

'Last time I was here I tried to get Slamet's signal. We knew afterwards, from camera traps, he was down there in the riverbed, but I couldn't pick him up.' The undergrowth was much denser than Russian *taiga*, the land low-lying: signals were difficult. There had been none recently. Slamet was, said Tom, locationally challenged. Tom climbed the jeep-roof with the aerial, a thin wire H against blue sky. Nothing. Elva got out the Global Positioning System, like a TV remote control. It speaks to satellites, knows their patterns through the sky, gets accurate readings for transmitting tiger collars. This was what Sasha had used with Lidya.

'There were problems with GPS at first. The US military scrambled everything, worried about terrorists. Then they found anti-coding devices cost six thousand pounds and stopped scrambling. Ours went haywire during the Gulf War. It's OK now. We take GPS readings for faeces and pugmarks.'

The first transect began as a stony track in burning sun. The territory belonged to a tigress called Wendy. Next door was Tiga Jari, with three toes. Hard ginger sand, three weeks since rain, so no tracks, only a speckled nightjar pretending to be stone. Tom's team had found no sprays, scrapes or boundary marks: tigers must make them in denser cover. Suddenly we saw tracks fifteen centimetres across, but not petalled and round like a tiger's. Four stubby toes – tapir, a few hours ago.

Tapir, tiger and bear were the big mammals. Sumatra is the only place apart from the Sundarbans (soon, alas, maybe Russia) where tigers live without leopards. No one knows why leopards skipped Sumatra and populated Java. The one I was scared of was bear, although if Slamet had put his huge head round the next bend I would have been petrified. Delighted afterwards, of course. If there was an afterwards.

The first camera, on a tree above a river he bathed in, had taken him most often. The cameras were made for the US and hated Sumatra's strong sun. They were supposedly heat- and movement-sensitive but they misbehaved here, bleaching out in daylight, omitting date and time, sometimes not flashing at all. People stole them, slicing them off with machetes. The Indonesian plantation manager said this was Orang Dalam; Tom pointed out they were only stolen outside their area; he didn't listen. A ripped notice said, 'Property of ZSL and Asiatic Persada. Surveying wild animals. Please do not disturb.'

The track got smaller, with boar tracks; then bushes and grass closed in, over our heads, and our feet. That cobra . . . Elva was behind, Tom ahead out of sight. Did Elva mind if I sang, to warn snakes? She laughed.

'This bit's pretty hairy,' came Tom's voice. A rotten log across a gully. Bushes either side, thick scrub beyond. I remembered the pit vipers, photographed snuggling in branches. I tested the slippery log. This gully was deep and tangly. It was not the drop – if this had been Britain I would have skipped across in a moment – but it might be stiff with cobras. I grasped a thin stem. It could not have held me. But you need something to hang on to, even if you know it is not enough. Ants cantered indignantly towards me from a nest.

A couple of hours later we met a violent smell. A kill? No, a boar, spread-eagled, no trotters left, front legs under its bronze chin. The inside was black with heaving saffron maggots. Human work.

'Satrio said two men were camping here. I'll tell the conservation office.' Tom picked up a porcupine quill. 'Something else they killed.'

We joined Satrio at a transect starting from a mound where Tom had slept in the jeep, listening to snare transmitters, waiting for a signal.

'One boar on camera here was nearly as big as Flash, our biggest male. We got them both at the same angle. Wouldn't fancy a tiger's chances with him. Lots of *very* well-fed pigs; which means well-fed tigers.'

Pigshit heaven. Tom, Elva and Satrio bent over blobs of dark green, chocolate, daffodil, mauve. Smelly, backbreaking work. They put samples into envelopes, marked positions by GPS, recorded in notebooks. I felt they needed more interesting names for these colours.

'Misted Pearl. Amber Oval. Knobbled Rust. This slippery one,' it was gliding into an envelope, 'is Midnight Algae. Don't need laxatives, do they?'

'Piggy piggy,' said Elva, who knew all grades of pigshit.

'Tubular Straight, Tubular Spiral, Conch, Labyrinth. Oh – how do you like this? Off Opal.'

'Off Putrid, rather,' said Tom, trying to concentrate on his work. 'If it's white, it may be carnivore. I want to know what small carnivores use this path.'

Faeces for zoologists are like potsherds for archaeologists: basic currency. They tell you DNA and what animals eat what, who uses a trail, how often. There were dozens of small tracks. Elva had a diagram of comparative tracks: brush-tailed porcupine, long-tailed porcupine, short-clawed mongoose, badger, leopard cat. Little curls of faeces lay beside runways in long grass. I wandered ahead, unscientific and useless, guiltily aware that I was more interested in impressions than in accuracy.

'Silver Jade,' I said, triumphant because it was white and might be carnivore. 'A little bit of fur in it! Tubular with a twist. Fresh.'

'Maybe tiger?' said Satrio.

'Very small tooth in it,' said Tom. 'Prey only just bigger than a rodent. Could be a cub's shit. We'll analyse it.'

Elva produced an envelope. I started up a slope.

'Odd,' I said to Tom, behind me. 'After all those tracks, absolutely nothing here.'

'Except,' said Tom, looking at me and the slope, 'a row of tiger tracks.'

I was standing on them! Once he spoke, I could see ahead of me large hollyhock-flower prints, lightly indenting orange sand. Horrified, I hopped on to the grass. The tiger had walked where I walked and on up, laying huge feet over tyre tracks. You could see the prints from below where Tom was, but the sun was so high they disappeared when you were on them. Tom went ahead to see where they led; Elva and I tried measuring. I stood below where I could see them, pointing to the edge with a reed; Elva squatted close and put bark where I said. But the reed wobbled. It did not work.

Now we knew that a tiger was near, everything felt different. Those run-holes of mongoose or leopard cat could be replicated in large: what was cover for porcupines might be cover for tigers. On one side were thick trees with bushes under them. Tom went in. Tigers rested in there sometimes, he said. I was terrified. However calm, they might not take kindly to being walked in on while lying up. I came to a place where three tracks met. Hollyhock Paws could be anywhere. Long grass rustled. A breeze, or something else? Tom joined me.

'Wendy had two cubs in April last year. This is her area. That shit could be a dispersing cub. Maybe the male. Males usually go first. That would fit the small tooth. Could have been his first kill alone.'

'Maybe those prints were his dispersing walk.'

There were two cameras here, one on the track's continuation, angled to cover the crossroads. If he had kept on, he'd have walked past it.

'Sometimes they turn themselves off,' said Tom, unfastening the camera. So many things to let you down. He was very calm about it.

'We'll reset them. I'm sure he's around somewhere.'

One tree was too fat; the chain would not go round it. Another was perfect for the tiger's track. Tom and Satrio hammered in nails to hold the camera. Elva looked at a mud bulb on a high branch. 'Tom, I think you must try another tree.'

Suddenly Tom was dancing up and down, brushing long limbs. Satrio slapped his shirt and carried on hammering, which enraged the ants even more.

'These ones are red-hot needles on me,' said Tom. 'For some reason their bites don't bother Indonesians.'

Elva found a safer tree, but we had to pull out undergrowth so the camera could see the path: it must be shaded from direct sun, but have no leaves in front. Tugging bushes, we disturbed red-winged beetles who flew round our hands, distracted or angry.

'Are these things OK or toxic like everything else?'

'Since I read about one that shoots out of its abdomen liquid boiling at a hundred degrees, I've had a lot of respect for beetles.'

At last the camera was stable, shaded, clear.

'But if that was his dispersing walk, he may never come this way again.'

Tom brushed ants and glared politely. 'Thanks.'

It turned out there was a tiger in that camera already. Just before we got there, Wendy had walked down our track and posed for a second. Then her son walked up it, out of her life.

19

NEVER SAY YOU ARE NOT AFRAID

*I once saw a tigress stalking a month-old kid. The kid saw her
and started bleating. The tigress gave up her stalk and walked
straight up to it. The kid went forward to meet her and stretched
out its neck to smell her. For a few heartbeats the month-old kid
and Queen of the Forest stood nose to nose. Then the queen
walked off in the direction she had come.*

Jim Corbett, *My India*

'We get cobras in the kitchen in our other centre. Only civets here.
Sorry, *clean* out of olive oil. Got some *gorgeous* oil last time in England.
Jeremy used the lot! He thinks I'm an uncivilized cow, said it was his.
So, *much* as I disapprove, it's gotta be palm oil.'

Tall, dark and in her forties, with the cheekbones of a *Vogue* model,
Debbie dispensed amazing stories in dry, gruff telegraphese. The main
room in her house in Sungai Penuh on Mount Kerinci had a bare bulb,
peeling ceiling, an orphaned leopard cat kitten rescued from poachers,
and impounded tiger bones.

Kerinci and Gunung Leuser are two of the world's most important
tiger areas. One, in north Sumatra, was in the middle of civil war. This
one is horribly steep. At a recent research conference someone who did
a pilot study said research would be impractical here: it was too vertical. Kerinci reserve and surrounding forest, an area bigger than Wales,
have about ninety tigers, and the poaching is unremitting. It is illegal
to kill tigers or buy their parts, but the park loses thirty a year. The
bones go to China, the local market is for skins. That yen for display:
politicians, army chiefs, businessmen, civil servants want stuffed ones

for their vestibules. Stuffed tigers say you are Mr Big, above the law. An aggrieved politician recently arrested for tiger-skin trading actually said so. Taxidermists are protected by senior policemen, some of whom are their biggest clients. Jambi is a major trafficking centre, with big tiger-dealers. A conservation officer from Gunung Leuser said there was no poaching there while his driver was whispering to Debbie that he had just been offered two pelts.

I held up a tiger skull; teeth showered out. Another pelt: an eight-month male. Most tigers poached were dispersing males killed within six hours of the forest edge. A dead tiger is hard to lug.

When Debbie started here she had no idea things were so bad. With Indonesian colleagues, she had set up a unique espionage-cum-protection system. They researched other species protection systems (orang utan, rhino, elephant), run by foreign NGOs working with forest rangers. Then they created their own: a tiger unit that uniquely belonged to this national park. Debbie is its adviser, Fauna and Flora International fund it, but it is the park's own Tiger Team. Each unit is led by a ranger with power to make an arrest. They began in 2000 with two units, now had three; there would soon be five. There were community members, training members, cooks, base-camp cleaners, a network of informers and agents, one of whom had once watched a tigress giving birth.

'He fled to his village gibbering! Someone asked why he didn't take a cub. He punched him. *Such* a stupid question!'

They *had* made a difference. The first year they destroyed twenty-eight tiger snares; this year they found three. They worked closely with police, who were mostly *not* law-breakers, and made arrests outside the park. Debbie even helped police cash-flow problems. Last week she paid their phone bill; the week before, the Xerox paper. During an operation she paid police petrol and food; after arrests she helped prosecutor and judge with administration costs and any suspect's subsistence in jail.

Police now realized tiger-poaching was linked to the traffic in drugs and arms. But since the Indonesian government had given each province more autonomy, there had been more corruption. Convicted bigwigs bribed their way out. A major trafficker caught with skin and skull got one year's jail instead of the statutory five. In any tiger country, relations between the Forest Department, police and judiciary are crucial, and often problematic.

You cannot protect tigers without protecting deer. The peak deer-poaching season here was before Ramadan. Free meat for feasts. To convict, they have to get hard evidence. Poachers caught with snare-wire in the forest say they were mending bridges. And operations can go wrong. The worst poachers, in Tapan, just over the mountain, were single-handedly responsible, Debbie felt, for driving the Sumatran rhino to extinction. On one operation there, the team had used Kerinci police because the more local people know of it beforehand, the greater the risk of leaks. Especially in Tapan. But a hundred people came to back up the poachers. The Kerinci police fled, not having had permission to be there from the locals. One team member was beaten up.

How had Debbie got into this? From Gloucestershire, apparently. Having grown up with ponies, wellies, pheasants in the scullery, she had become a journalist, came here for a story in 1989, loved it, hated the devastation, and came back for tigers: camera-trapping, monitoring, learning Kerinci dialect.

Everyone in conservation deals with heartbreak their own way. Giving her life to save tigers in a whirl of corruption and violence, Debbie clearly kept sane through black humour and a taste for lunacy. Beneath was passionate loyalty to people she trusted, in the park, police, forest office and villages.

'There's *real* poverty here but one mustn't show it. A farmer buys vegetables at market because otherwise people'd say he's too poor to buy 'em.'

Of all places I had seen, tigers lived closest here to people. Last week Debbie was rung by a man who used his van as an ambulance for mountain villages. He said, 'Come quick, there is a tiger on my ambulance!' When the team got there, the tiger, sleeping on the bonnet like any cat, had woken, realized it had overslept, and left. There were muddy pugmarks on the bonnet. Another tiger stopped worship by sitting beside a mosque, new-built on his trail. People asked Debbie, their tiger guru, what he wanted. She suggested he wanted to turn Muslim. 'Then someone said something *very* indelicate about circumcision.'

There are human deaths, of course, and tigers are most at risk when this happens. It must be proved to have been tiger. Recently a

murderer faked his crime to look like a tiger, tracing pugmarks, clawing the face with a rake. 'But *downwards* not up, the clot! So when a call
came saying a tiger'd killed a woman now, we *had* to take photos.'
Debbie drove at night to a high village in the rains and found the dead
woman with bitten-through eye and throat, and a crushed cheek.

'First dead body I'd seen. Very nasty. Jeremy complained I hadn't
done a good composition! Photographers are *not* as other people. Then
he had to photograph roadkill and shut up about composition.'

It had been an accident, witnessed by the woman's fourteen-year-
old son. She had been planting chillies and was walking downhill as
the tiger was stalking a pig. The boy saw the tiger, but his voice dried,
he could not shout. She simply got in the tiger's way. Knowing police
would turn up, Debbie drove down to meet them. It was slippery,
their tyres were bald; they accepted her lift.

'But was the chief pissed off to see us! He'd already said he wanted
the skin!'

All night it was stand-off: Debbie, team, corpse; police, crying
family, drumming rain. The law is clear. No tiger-killing, not even in
self-defence. The death had obviously been an accident. Eventually the
chief left the report to Debbie's team. The family got no compensation,
but the team did what it could. Its job is to mediate between people
and tigers. For injuries, they pay medical bills. Here they resolved
other problems – they even stopped fish-poachers poisoning the river.
Some villagers afterwards wanted to burn the national park offices
(punish the tiger by punishing its protectors), but the people they had
helped said no. They also told Debbie about illegal chainsaws. The
tiger team were known. They were people-who-help.

'That's the important thing, being there when they need you. If
you help, you make a friend for tigers. Can't protect tigers without
protecting people. Dear me, this is very nice!' I had brought vodka.
'Arak's filthy, but helps after a hard day. Oh, the privations of the
field.'

If the team heard about problems early, they tried to stop them esc-
alating, explained how to behave with a tiger around and why it was
there, so people would be less likely to kill it. Often tigers enter farm-
land because of pigs, or because chainsaws have disturbed other prey.
But some tigers did kill deliberately. In Tapan, a tiger killed a couple

while the team was in the forest reporting on illegal logging. They came out to shouts of 'Harimau nggamuk!' Tiger amok!

Villagers live in villages, but also own farmland, a *ladang*, nearer the forest. One Friday this couple went to their *ladang* for vegetables to sell. On Sunday, their son found his mother by a river, mostly eaten; his father part-eaten. She had been attacked while getting water; he had triggered the tiger's chase mechanism by running away. The village was screaming as if Dracula had struck.

'The tiger's such an archetype here. But if we find a *reason*, people start being sensible again. It can be plain bad luck, like that other woman. But when a tiger goes amok, *harimau nggamuk*, it's seriously terrifying. It'll break doors, anything. Tigers are normally nice animals. But when they lose it, boy, do they!'

As on Dempo, tigers were terrible but good, linked to a long list of social and moral prohibitions. Living so closely with tigers, people here had always needed specialist mediation, and tiger magic was everywhere, related also to healing. A *dukun*, tiger-caller, used incense, *kemanyan*, to open the door to the spirit world. He could summon a *harimau roh*, soul-tiger, spirit-tiger. The cheapest *dukun* was a witch-doctor, a roadside herbalist, but one of Debbie's friends was a high-grade *dukun*, Pak Yerti, who taught men how to protect their skin against knives. Debbie watched a lesson. The men had sharp machetes, they sliced banana leaves with them; then he made them attack their own arms and the skin didn't break.

'They were *milking* those *parangs*. I saw milk dripping out of them! Some of the tiger team have done self-protection with that *dukun*. The more educated ones can't get it as well as the village-based people.'

Another evening she watched men going into a trance, growling, roaring, entered by tiger spirits, then heard growls in an empty corner.

'*Very* freaky. Logically, you could say the sound was bouncing off the wall. Men were growling elsewhere. But it didn't *feel* like that.'

Apart from *dukuns*, villages had a *pawang*, a shaman linked to a particular species. The *pawang harimau*, tiger shaman, was a tiger specialist. A *dukun* could be a *pawang*, a *pawang* could be a *dukun*. Both were in touch with tigers you could not see (though some people did see soul tigers), but when they 'called', what came might be a soul tiger or a real one. You never knew.

Because real tigers are territorial, most old villages had a village tiger, *harimau kampung*, which they recognized. Our tiger, they called it. Or *harimau nungu*, the waiting tiger. It was probably an ancestor spirit, and would give a sign, or advise, when the village had a problem. It was part of the community. The tiger they were generally afraid of was *harimau luar*, the tiger from outside; the *other* tiger.

But they were petrified if the community tiger killed someone: its role was to protect the village. So now Debbie asked the *pawang* what had happened. He said the couple had cut timber in tiger nests, *sarang harimau*. 'Tiger nests' belonging to the village tiger were sacrosanct. The whole village instantly relaxed. Rules had been broken. Everyone understood. There are reprisals for breaking tiger rules.

Everyone felt it was not natural for tigers to kill people. Tigers made magic to catch their normal prey. *But* if you accidentally acquired tainted blood, or a bad aura, you might get caught in the tiger's magic so it saw you as a deer or a pig. If that happened, you had (assuming you survived) to ask the *dukun* to repair your aura. Then it would see you as human again. Debbie had to know both zoology and magic, and pay for tiger exorcisms. The system worked because people trusted the team to listen and help at every level.

Debbie's *dukun pawang* friend Pak Yerti referred to his three tiger familiars as *sahabat'*, 'friend'. He also had a big black leading tiger, a *harimau kumbang*. Last year, he came to get an offering from Debbie before an important Islamic feast (the Tiger Team contributes to his annual ritual feast for these tigers) but later came back in tears. Only the *harimau kumbang* had attended. The other three complained the black tiger wouldn't share the feast. If he went on like this they would not help lost people out of the forest or drive transient tigers away from farmland. Pak Yerti was horrified. The village's whole well-being was at stake! These tigers were crucial to the village. If they went on strike, wild pig would cavort unchecked in the rice fields, TVs would break down, final-demand income tax letters would arrive . . . The ancestors suggested he hold two tiger-feeding feasts a year, one for the black tiger, one for the others. He consulted the Tiger Team. Debbie diagnosed sibling rivalry. The black tiger was always being called up to sort out land disputes, government failures to repair the village bridge, suspected poisoning. The 'friend tigers' only showed people lost in the forest the way home. If Pak Yerti were the black tiger, *he* would be pissed off at sharing his feast with a bunch of lazy poseurs while he did all the work. Next day Pak Yerti turned up beaming. He had talked to all four tigers. They shared the yellow rice and betel nut. (Supernatural tigers are not obligate carnivores.) Black tiger said he was sorry he was hasty, the errant three agreed to a heavier workload: annoying poachers by breaking snares and terrifying them. They also agreed (Debbie's input had gone further than patching up sibling rivalry) *not* to help people out of the forest if they had been 'breaking' the forest, or poaching. The Tiger Team encouraged even magic tigers to declare war on poaching.

Tigers ate domestic animals, of course; most often dogs. One tiger took two off a solitary old woman. Like the wolf in the Little Pigs fairy-tale, he beat her door down and grabbed the third, the old woman's favourite. She hung on to its head till the tiger retreated. The dog survived. Crippled and retarded, but alive. Tigers were in most danger when they took the smallest things, chickens and ducks. The park heard of attacks on people or cows, the team rushed to resolve things, protect the community *and* the tiger. But fowls were not reported.

'I'd be scared too if I had a family and found a tiger close to my house. When people react, we don't know till too late.'

Reacting meant poisoning meat with organophosphates, which used to be illegal and now were not. You could buy poisons banned elsewhere twenty years ago. Debbie wanted to organize a poisons register.

'People say tigers don't eat carrion: *bullshit*! That's how they get poisoned. They put it in pigs mostly. One tigress I followed left faeces, blood and vomit all over the place. She didn't eat enough to die *fast*.'

A golden cat, smaller than a leopard, had died recently because it ate a goat killed by a tiger; villagers had poisoned it.

'Another was snared. We kept it in a holding-cage till it healed. Wanna see the video of the release?'

The team carried a large box past a green pit viper curled smugly among leaves at eye level, staring at Debbie's camera like a baby. Then: put the box on the ground, stand back, lift the lid and whoosh, a peach-coloured head, a gold flash into the grass. The one that got away.

'Worst was a month ago. *Perfectly* hideous day. Urgent phone call: *melanistic* golden cat, only the second known on Sumatra, only the third in all South East Asia. It died two hours before we got there. Snare wasn't even illegal, just a farmer trying to stop boar eating his crops. Guy who rang couldn't get through at first. We probably couldn't have done anything. Haven't got veterinary supplies yet: whatta y'*do* with a large hostile mammal in a snare when the nearest anaesthetic is in, say, Jambi? John Lewis gave a *graphic* demonstration, had to translate his slide-show with my eyes shut, about what snares do! But – we could have *tried*.'

'Trauma every day. *Waste* every day. Debbie, how do you stand it?'

'Better than the check-out at Safeway's? Cor, I don't know. At least I'm trying to *do* something? But that day was pretty bloody. Then there's the forests. Bus ride I did in 1989, eighteen hours through burnt nothingness – *that* made me a conservationist.'

Two men came in. Amadeus, a soft-faced boy in denim: an intelligence agent or *hantu*, ghost. He sat on the floor, settling the kitten in his lap. A lawyer in his village, already suspected of poisoning one tiger, had bought poison and said he was going to his *ladang* to poison another. The team would protect that tiger if possible; otherwise get evidence to prosecute him, without compromising Amadeus. No one knew he worked for the team except his brother, who was the lawyer's brother's best friend. A tiger skin is heavy, especially fresh. They would watch for him returning with a suitcase, phoning the 'boss'. Poachers sell to a broker, who is integral to the wildlife trade.

'I *loathe* brokers! Loathe educated men doing this stuff, too. Can't prosecute unless you catch 'em in possession, and in the sting you've gotta have the poacher plus the broker. Which the broker tries to avoid, in case poachers learn how much *he*'s selling skins – or bones or tusks – for.'

Twenty-four-hour surveillance in villages is hard: Amadeus had to be careful. He could ask for tiger meat or hair, for magic. If the lawyer said he'd have some soon, he must have active snares, or had killed the tiger already. On one operation, Amadeus gave sweets to the dealer's children. The arrested dealer complained that Amadeus had seemed such a *nice* boy.

'Dealers say it's not fair, our men should be in uniform. But all's fair

in love and extinction, as far as I'm concerned. I got an MI6 guy to give
us lessons but he said we're doing all the classic things already.'

Syamsul, a founder member of the team, was older with sharp black
eyes and a small round head. He had helped Debbie before 2000, with
camera traps, monitoring and transects. He had taken part in the
Tapan operation that went wrong. They had entered the suspects'
house and there was a fight, the poachers' hundred-strong reinforcements arrived, police fled, the seven-man team escaped on motorbikes,
poachers chased them ten kilometres. Then they realized they were
only six. Andy was missing. He had been beaten up. He was off work
for three months, unable to play his guitar for six.

Syamsul most loved being in the forest, but that had its moments
too. One evening in rain at dusk, having finished a transect, he
returned to camp past a fallen log. A tiger was sheltering under it.
They startled each other, the tiger spun round to run away and its tail
hit his face.

'Like me and Suderman, another team member,' said Debbie. 'I saw
a yellow-black pheasant – God, no – a tiger *right* beside us! It was
spooked and came at us. Suderman was brilliant: jumped on a log,
screamed. It somersaulted mid-run and galloped away.'

Syamsul was so small and quiet, the dangers he faced so large. In
his village most people felt killing tigers was wrong, but they wanted
to use their own forest. Why not make money from it? There were so
many trees! People poached less, because of the penalties. 'But,' he said,
'if we say, don't use more forest because of tigers, they would resent
them. We must be careful not to foster resentment of tigers.'

The food market rippled with vegetables, tubular, shiny, yellow, red,
black. Debbie joked with the women; they roared with laughter, joking
back.

'It's my ambition to get 'em all saying, "*'Allo, darlin'*."" Everyone
needs a minor ambition in life. That's mine. An anthropologist complained I'd ruined the purity. All over Kerinci, people were saying,
"*'Allo, darlin'*"!'

In the chilli aisle was a handsome young man with a chicken under
his arm. It raised a fierce, wattled head and glared. Whoops, no

chicken: this was M, one of Debbie's most brilliant men. He was from Tapan, the most dangerous poachers and the best men in the forest. He was carrying his prize-winning fighting-cock. Last year his wife, now ex-wife, cooked a prize-winner. M was taking no chances with this one.

In the jeep, cock on knee, he reported on another operation, involving two tiger skins and ivory. M had found the man who bought them from the poacher and got an ounce of tiger flesh as proof. The aim now was to use another agent, with no Tapan connection, who could lure this man with promise of a sale, to drive somewhere else so they could arrest him without anyone getting hurt.

'M knows a lot of were-tigers,' said Debbie, casually.

I said I heard they were called *masu marai* on Dempo. And in Jambi, *harimau jadi-jadian*. They looked at each other.

'Dempo's *impossible*,' said Debbie. 'Mad language.'

'Best word,' said M, 'is *cindaku*. Their homeland is Kerinci. That's the truth of the matter, though people in Kerinci don't agree.'

A *cindaku* walked head down. M's friend Ilias was a *cindaku*, who also mended broken bones. He told M if they met when he was a tiger he must call '*Ilias!*' and he would change back. His wife once forgot to do this when they had a quarrel. He turned into a tiger and mauled her; she called '*Ilias!*', he became a man and let her go. As a boy, M was fascinated by *cindakus* and wanted to learn how to do it. Did he truly want to? Ilias asked.

'He said he would give me the wisdom of tigers. But then everyone started shooting tigers. I decided I didn't want this thing. A tiger was killed in my village. I thought this gift would be danger to me.'

I had thought Dempo special, but were-tigers were everywhere. When the Tapan couple were eaten, Debbie's team returned to the forest to finish their logging report. An official asked if she was afraid of the man-eater.

'I didn't say no. How could I? I said we had to be careful. He asked me to teach him my mantra! Even a civil servant thought I had a charm against tigers!'

People in Tapan believed she had released thirteen tigers into the forest and went back because she had lost one. They asked if she had found her tiger. The district director himself asked her to teach him to

talk to tigers. Having finished the report, she waited for the bus to
Sungai Penuh. Someone told M, 'She shouldn't wait there, I saw a
tiger on that road.' M said, joking, 'Oh, that was Debbie, waiting for
the bus!' But no one in Tapan thought it was a joke.

Debbie's new jeep was filthy, battered, but working. Her old one
had been borrowed for a film on illegal logging in Tapan. The owner of
an illegal sawmill bussed in a gang – mob rental is an Indonesian tradition – who burned the jeep and held the film crew hostage. The
soldiers protecting them ran away; a ranger was badly hurt. Debbie
asked a garage to repair the burnt jeep and paint it tiger-colours, for
show occasions. The garage-owner was sitting on a sofa surrounded
by welders. A toddler played with a hula-hoop beside the welding
sparks. They were all watching TV with a plain-clothes policeman and
a fat young man comfortably cupping his genitals.

'Ask the policeman about wildlife crime,' said Debbie, and
explained that I was interested in tigers. I smiled encouragingly. The
policeman looked at my notebook. He was dizzy. He had a headache.
Malaria coming on.

'He's scared to talk.'

'Er – yes.'

Behind them was a Hallowe'en jeep, black stripes rampaging over
orange bonnet down to white mudguards. The painters of Sungai
Penuh knew all too well how gold shades to white on a tiger's skin.

A sparkling white building, marble staircase: the Forest Office for
Kerinci-Seblat National Park, one of Indonesia's largest, shaped like a
long, thin Belgium, embracing four provinces and many subdistricts.

'Lystia the director's got very good rangers,' said Debbie, joking
with some guards, skirting others, 'but also *very* dodgy ones! They
don't know she's investigating them.'

In principle, the Indonesian protection system was the best, she
said, in Asia. *Much* better than India. A park director is responsible to
the Secretary-General of protected areas and the Minister of Forestry;
the Central Forest Office removes inadequate heads of park. But just
now there were few suitable heads of park. There were lots of very
bright young trained guys with Masters degrees, but they were not yet

senior enough to direct a park. Also, in the face of all the pressures, laws tend to stay in law books.

This was a critical moment for Kerinci's park. Three provinces had proposed new roads, which would carve the forest into bite-sized morsels for loggers, plantations, poachers. Forest reduction was constant everywhere. The Western plywood, pulp and paper industries had expanded so much that demand for wood fibre here exceeded legal supplies by forty million cubic metres a year. Holland had just exposed sawmill companies exporting Lystia's trees to the UK and Europe by laundering them in Malaysia and Singapore. Mining companies and palm-oil conglomerates were eyeing the park; central government issued licences to log protected areas; district heads owing money to businessmen and contractors for election help repaid it by granting logging concessions. Or wrote logging licences for new bribes.

The Forest Department can license a company to take timber from an area, but if that place is already cleared the company trots off and chops the park instead. Rangers can *ask* where the wood comes from – obviously not where the licence said – but what can they do? Under the ex-dictator Soeharto, forestry companies paid huge bribes just to do business, but they at least followed laws. Since government had decentralized, corruption had too. All forests, protected or not, became fair game.

The largest company cutting here was Tegal-Kerinci owned by Prabowo, Soeharto's son-in-law. In his thirty-two-year rule, Soeharto amassed fifteen billion US dollars himself. For his family he got forty-six billion: three billion more than the IMF's rescue package to Indonesia when Asian markets fell in 1997. Prabowo married a daughter who owned banks, financial services, shopping centres, cement businesses and a Jakarta Fashion Café. He was head of Indonesian Special Forces. Implicated in engineering the 1998 Jakarta riots, he was removed from ministerial office and became the second Indonesian general to face a court hearing. But he was not jailed: he went overseas. Now he was said to be back. His palm-oil company (selling to an international company) cut five thousand acres from the park. (They claim that on their map it was outside the park.) Critical tiger habitat. But she had only three hundred dollars to fight each case. And no lawyer would take on Prabowo.

Debbie said Lystia was brilliant, a fighter of complete integrity. They had had other good directors, but she was the first who wanted to be *here*, not advancing her career in a Jakarta office. Lystia was in a meeting.

'She *hates* smoking – this'll fetch her.' Debbie lit up. A door opened: a tiny woman, sizzling with command, said, 'Debbie, come in but no smoke!' Debbie grinned and stubbed it out.

Lystia's office looked out over the mountains she was trying to protect. She fought illegal licences and illegal logging. There were hundreds of sawmills everywhere. Even when they were legal, who knew what wood went into them? Chainsaws could only be operated by someone with a licence to saw a particular area; nobody checked. No one recorded who owned them. Middlemen were sometimes arrested. Big men never were.

'It will become war. Nobody cares. Conflict increases. It is so frustrating for me and my rangers. We must tell the truth. I *love* Indonesia, it is my country. I am sad because people are apathetic. Everyone knows heads of district are involved in illegal activity: why do they do nothing? We *must* investigate! One day people *will* mind, will turn round and say, "Why didn't you protect the forest?" I have to show I did, that I *said* they were breaking laws.'

She had set up an information centre, education programmes, a conservation puppet theatre. She was grateful for international assistance but passionate about local responsibility. In the drought, people shouted for the World Bank but she, like Mr Li in Hunchun, felt they must solve their own problems in *their* place.

'I am proud of my staff. We get appreciation all over the world, and international money. We get that trust, because we are *working*.'

Three months later, she was transferred to Jakarta. She was not compliant. She stood up to corruption. Moving her stopped fights with powerful men for whom protection got in the way. Her last official task was introducing Kerinci as a candidate park for World Heritage status, something she worked furiously to achieve. We did not know this then. Nor that her successor would average five days in his park every three months, or try to release illegal loggers the team caught, when they threatened to burn the park building. 'Finished, this park and our team,' Debbie would email, 'if people capitulate.'

In Sumatra's parting shot to someone who had done so much for its wildlife, Lystia would be forced to leave behind her pet tortoise with Debbie. Jambi airport said he had to be X-rayed.

'Must get my *parang*. Never go into the field without a machete.'

At last we were going into the forest: Mount Keronsong, in the Kerinci range. Her neighbour handed over a squat, curved scythe. Debbie looked. 'The team's got mine: this is my second-best. Bit blunt. Oh, well.'

What was it for? If a tiger charged, it would be hopeless against that reach. I was more scared of this forest than I had been of any other. Sumatra felt, all round, the most violent place I had been. Defenders of the wild were charming, knowledgeable, brave. Great company, doing great work. I had never met people I admired so much. But they were much, much tougher than me, and I suspected Debbie of being the toughest of the lot.

We drove up a hairpin mud track where a young man climbed in, smiling. Iwan, one of Debbie's radio operators. Radio was essential; most mobile phones worked only in towns. Last month the team had found illegal chainsaws in the forest. The loggers had run for reinforcements, the team circled the chainsaws through the jungle, radioing Debbie to get them out. Since radio can be listened to, they used code words. Snares were 'washing-lines', elephant, 'bulldozer', chainsaws 'crickets'. A jeep, as in 'I need a jeep fast', was 'wheelbarrow'. Debbie once heard someone demanding a wheelbarrow for a broken bulldozer.

'Haven't been to the forest with Iwan before. Don't know how he'll do. He lives by mending radios but he's passionate for wildlife.'

I was their cover. An agent had reported people coming down this ridge at night: what for? It might just be ganja, but tiger-poaching often goes with ganja. (They once found tiger snares round marijuana grown in forest.) I was a tourist, Debbie was showing me round.

The highest village was where the dog-fancying tiger had worked. The old lady's hut, the last, had a new wicker door. Then the track turned to grass and we came to a dead-end, a small house. An old man came out, with two women and children. Debbie waved, parked by the stream, talked to them, checked what we were taking: *parang*, leaf-packed lunch, water. Watched by the family, she turned an imaginary key in the jeep door and slipped it into her pocket.

'Lock doesn't work. How are your shoes?'

We took a steep path beside poplar-like trees topped with red leaves: a cinnamon plantation. A nineties cinnamon boom had led to over-production. In 1997, before Asia's financial crisis, cinnamon was three dollars a kilo. Now it was forty cents; another reason for illegal logging in former cinnamon areas.

'In older plantations, boar ruffled the ground and stopped lower vegetation growing. But they don't like wild pig round their houses. It attracts tigers.'

Kerinci had two species of wild pig. The bearded kind migrated; tigers came closest to villages when they arrived.

'People call it *musim harimau turun*, time-when-tigers-come-from-mountain. I don't think tigers follow them *hundreds* of miles, but they do follow large movements of prey.'

When people poach sambar there is less prey in deep forest, which sambar prefer. Pigs hang round the forest edge and come into farm-land, so hungry tigers go after them instead. This is the edge effect: when most prey collects at the forest edge, the most dangerous place for people and tigers, where there is most interaction.

We were in forest edge ourselves now, crossing a stream. Debbie had no socks. I supposed they were no use against cobras but what about thorns? In the next stream Debbie and Iwan stopped to argue. Iwan seemed to win.

'Tigers use the ridge routes. Iwan says left is the quickest way up. But his way means *this*!' *This* was a gigantic tree slide: bare earth down which thousands of trees had crashed. It stretched above, a near-vertical fifteen-foot-wide ribbon of loose earth.

'If this were a ski-run, it would be a black slope.'

I did not know what a black slope was and did not care. I am feeble about snow sports as well as water. I followed, sticking to the edge where you could hold live branches as well as the odd tree root; where wild pigs, who did not like slipping either, had runkled the earth. It was slow work, squirming vertically on your stomach, thanking God for roots, hanging from hands, letting torso, legs, knees and toes worm up behind, finding what hold they could. When dead branches broke, you lost painfully gained height. Sometimes all that held you was a dip in the soil where a knee could lodge. Two-thirds up, I stuck. I could not reach the next handhold. Every time I tried, I slipped further down. I was a gecko on a glass mountain, stranded, cheek against bare earth like a lover. I would hang there for ever.

'You all right?' Debbie shouted. They were nearly at the top. 'Want Iwan to come and give you a hand?'

'*Absolutely not!*' Whenever they moved, stones and earth bounced down on my hair. At last a branch held: I inched up beside them and sat panting on a stone. We must have squirmed five hundred feet.

'Iwan asked why you didn't want help. I said, "Because she doesn't want to be a mattress." All those stones!'

'Glad metaphors are such fun,' I said, 'in Kerinci dialect.'

We pushed through scrub and found a knife-edge trail. The other side, light-green bushes overgrowing another slide, was as steep as ours. We met an old man with a dog and sat with him on grassy lumps. He was cutting grass for his buffalo: drought had withered all the grass lower down.

'He says there are five tigers up here, maybe three. I don't believe it. Andy saw a large adult tigress up here recently, that's all.'

'Could be a mother and two grown cubs.'

She listened to the old man.

'He says they're large *and* small. A tiger sleeps on a rock overhang here, and looks for food by the stream where we parked.'

The black-and-white dog sat with his head against the old man's knee. Dogs here were loved companions. I had seen a man bathing a pony's broken knee. Relation to animals was different from in Laos.

'What's your dog's name?'

'Blang,' said the old man through Debbie, stroking Blang's head.

'Is Blang afraid of tigers?'

The old man thought. 'You must never be arrogant when you go in forest. You must be humble. Blang will be careful so he will not meet a tiger. But you must never say, "I am not afraid." Last week I saw a tiger very close. I saw he wanted to eat my dog. I said, "Please, sir, do not interfere with my dog." After I said that, the tiger went away.'

There was a swish of bushes where the trail led higher. Something parting grass, coming towards us . . . tawny . . . The man's other dog, with the old man's wife, binding long grass. She put down a bundle and turned back for more. The old man said if you were lost in the forest and a *dukun* was with you, you could call up a tiger to find your way out. Otherwise, search for scrapes and pugmarks. A tiger's trail helps you to get out.

'Yup,' said Debbie. 'Tigers like a wide trail. They hate really dense undergrowth except as a place to lie up, stow cubs, or wait for dinner. They don't like it steep any more than we do.'

The old man said you could call a tiger to help you, but you must keep on being afraid.

'They say here their tigers are *sopan*, polite,' said Debbie. 'My question going into new forest is always, are your tigers *sopan*? A polite tiger is one you don't see. The other scares the shit out of you, or worse.'

The old man said tigers were not supposed to meet people. If they did, they had to travel seven hills for forty days.

'Very unfair on the tiger, in my opinion,' said Debbie.

Tigers as well as people should obey forest rules, but traditional laws round Kerinci were all designed not to annoy them. That was why the old man had said, 'Please sir,' to the tiger. As on Dempo, the tiger was preserver of the law. Different areas had different rules but all ended 'otherwise *harimau marah*. Tiger will be angry.'

Jungle reverence, Kerinci style.

'These laws maintain *adat*: forest safety,' said Debbie. 'We always stress *adat* when we try to resolve conflicts with problem tigers.'

The old man snapped a bamboo stalk, showing me how spear-sharp the spike was. Alan Rabinowitz had nearly lost his leg in a trap set with a bamboo spike like this, but poisoned.

'Everything is dangerous here,' the old man said. 'You must never be arrogant. Always afraid.'

That was no problem. Every time I went into tropical hill forest my legs wobbled, muscles ached, feet slipped, and I was – is scared the word? Thrilled, nervous, privileged. Like entering a beautiful cathedral wired for bombs.

Iwan and Debbie plunged into a tiger-shaped tunnel of bushes, the ridge trail. Bamboo, high grass, and then tall trees, a mix of secondary and, at last, primary forest. Olive-dark air breathed bark and leaf.

Brown earth, dark roots, silver moss, ochre boulders; splashes of light on leaf-surfaces. This, said Debbie, was where the dog-eating tiger was snared. Awful to know where and how the animals you protected died.

A red bird, with white cheek flashes like a Nike logo, fussed round a branch in fluttery darts like embarrassed hands.

'Silver-cheeked mesia.'

Up, up, a faint path through bamboo covered in long thorns.

'No touch,' said Iwan sternly.

'Hairy bamboo,' said Debbie. '*Seriously* ghastly if it gets in your clothes. Stings like fire.'

Thorns: I had never seen such variety. Even lianas had them. In Laos, lianas were friends to hang on to. Not here. A thin type was studded with little prickles all the way up; a silver-white kind had thorns with pink points, like my pit viper's tail.

'No touch,' said Iwan, more firmly.

Even plants were poisonous. I shut my mind to snakes.

'Another forest rule,' said Debbie, laughing. 'If you fall, you land in these. If you grab a handhold in a hurry, it's these.'

I had never seen vegetation so out to get you. Iwan plunged inside a hollow tree with the *parang*, and came out with shit on a leaf.

'*Very* fresh. Cat, definitely,' said Debbie. 'I've seen tigers produce something like this when there's not much in their intestines. But could be anything. Marble cat, jungle cat, golden cat, fishing cat, flat-headed. Or leopard cat. They climb in for bats.'

Monkeys peered down, each with a dark cap of Venetian velvet. Pig-tailed macaques, which travel through the forest in groups. Debbie put her hands to her mouth and called: one snapped back a fierce chirrup. We climbed higher, leaving secondary forest behind. There were fewer mosses than there were lower down where it was wetter. This was the real thing: high, pristine, tropical evergreen forest; equatorial forest about as thick, though not as wet, as it gets.

'Terribly dry. We're *really* short of water.'

The light was lavender and silver-green, the air grainy. The canopy closed in: protecting or menacing, you could feel it as either. A canopy gets lower as the altitude goes up, but these trees were many times higher than any I was used to. Sometimes a light-ray slanted in, an eerie firework strand from a stained-glass window. The leaves they lit were furry, ochre-green, smoke-coloured, shaggy. The atmosphere and light were almost underwater hazy. Tall slender trees, with a white flesh bloom like moonrise on oddly smooth trunks, had epiphytes half-way up like a muezzin platform on a minaret. There were delicate changes in undergrowth between them; a thousand different greens, blackberry shadows, cocoa spandrels, tasselled seedpods, ovals, trefoils, a wild inner movement of bark and leaf untouched for millennia. Cutting this would be like blowing up Notre Dame.

But to look and wonder you had to stand still. Every step was dodgy; it was so steep and so tricksy you needed handholds all the time. Those had to be checked too, for pit vipers or thorns. Hours later, we came to a place where, behind undergrowth, we could see out over the valley.

'I just wonder,' said Debbie. 'My God, I've got a signal! Look, Iwan!'

Iwan got out his mobile. They started laughing, texting people. Here I was, pristine tropical forest, and they were dancing about texting like teenagers.

Debbie laughed at my expression. 'Signals are rare anywhere – it's just *amazing* there's one up here. I'm texting Lystia. She gets so depressed at what's happening to her park and it'll cheer her up to know there's lovely forest so close – *and* a signal!'

A trail came in from the right, Debbie brushed aside dead leaves.

'Yes!' she said. 'There, Ruth!'

A tiger footprint. Very light: the soil was so dry. About a month old, but pointing our way. It had walked up to join our trail. Ten minutes later there was another, much fresher. Toes rounded or pointed? They were too blurred in fine soil to see. But there was the width, the pressed weight.

'You should never not respect a tiger,' whispered Debbie. 'As the old guy said, you should never *not* be afraid. But they are OK animals normally. It's the other things to be afraid of, at least in daylight. The landslide, the inadvertent pit viper.'

'And if we hear a growl?'

'If it's loud, the tiger's probably far away. The softer the growl the nearer, the more dangerous. First time Jeremy and I heard that – we were very green – we went straight up into trees. Later I asked Jeremy what he'd done on *his* tree. He said he'd recited Blake.'

'"The Tyger"?'

'No, the words wouldn't come. Some other Blake. Dunno. Jeremy's a poet, really. Always quoting the stuff. The joke here is, if you hear clucking like hens in the bushes, don't go looking for eggs: you'll find a tiger! They make a chuffly noise, like chickens.'

Sumatran tigers really must be pretty different. *Nobody* else, Russia, India, Nepal, anywhere, had said tigers sounded like hens.

'Worst I ever heard, I was going up a *hideously* muddy track ahead of the jeep, see if it was OK to drive up. A stream crossed the track, I sloshed through and heard the jeep driver revving like crazy behind me. I was going to yell down he mustn't do that or he'd blow a gasket. Then I saw *very* small tiger pawmarks filling with water at the edge of the stream I'd just walked through. That noise was no jeep! It was on *my* side of the stream.'

'You were between the mother and—'

'Er, yes. The cub had followed the stream across the path just after I followed the path across the stream. I walked quickly back across, down to the jeep, kept going past the noise, not looking back. Told the driver we couldn't go up there. That was *really* loud growling. And *near.'*

Our whispers were soft as breath. A giant ancient tree had fallen, tearing up a crater of earth as it uprooted. A landslide had eaten part of the ridge, but trees had grown back: the old tree lay like the lintel of a fallen temple across a basin looped with creepers. New trees bent over and under, crafting a way to the light, making architraves above.

'When you hear a tree start to go and you're camping, it's really scary,' breathed Debbie. 'You don't know where it is, what it'll bring down. We nearly lost two members when a tree fell on their camp. Arifin, leader of one unit, and Edy Johann, a trainee. Arifin fractured an ankle, Edy cracked ribs and a shoulder.'

'Do you camp often?'

'When I can. Tied a bit, at the moment. Used to go a lot: four- or ten-day treks. Found a ridge trail last year where I saw two clouded leopards, and the bathing-pool of a male tiger I was keeping an eye on. *Longing* to go there again. But I have to sit and man the radio, be the central reliable person. Can't get to the field.'

Debbie motioned us off the trail. We sat down screened from it in bushes, silent. Debbie went further into undergrowth. We listened.

Iwan lit a cigarette. Debbie, unusually, did not. The forest was still with a full, live stillness: a packed concert hall before the conductor comes. A hushed sea of branches where gods lived, tigers walked. Heart of the world. If there was meaning to the universe, a non-man-made meaning, this was it.

A little brown tree-shrew jumped to a branch, ran down like coffee pouring, leaped away. The macaques had been rustling overhead, calling and grumbling. Now they moved away and fell silent. Debbie motioned Iwan to stub out his fag. From behind the trees where Debbie sat came a light cough. A twig snapped. On the trail we could not see there was a presence. The jungle was differently still, as if holding its own breath. Something was listening to us breathe, watching us listen.

It lasted about ten minutes. Then we felt it fade. Debbie, nearer to it, looked at me and smiled slowly as if waking from a dream.

'What was it?' I breathed.

'Some large mammal,' she said quietly, getting up. 'You feel the forest go still. When there's a large mammal around, usually a predator, there's a *feeling*. Even when you can't see it, and you usually can't, you find later it was *there*. Could have been a golden cat. Or a sun bear: they like dense forest. But the pig-tails were *definitely* not happy bunnies; and they wouldn't have worried about a bear. People here say when a tiger wants to tell you it's there, it snaps a twig.'

She picked one up and snapped. The sound that came in the stillness.

'Could well have been a tiger going along our path, stopping to check us out. Probably was. If I'm worried a tiger's near I have a cigarette. It indicates human presence.'

'It smelt Iwan's?'

'Oh, yes.'

We left our hiding-place and came out on the trail.

'Can't go further up. Be dark before we got back. Er – *not* a good idea, coming down in the dark. We'll turn back.'

I started down; Debbie pointed. In soft earth, over the imprint of my Tunisian trainer, was laid, like a love-token, a *very* large, deep, fresh pugmark. We had been at a tiger's mercy. A polite tiger, maybe the tigress that Andy, whoever he was, had seen here. Observing *adat*, forest safety, her own and ours, she had seen us, heard us, smelt us, *known* us, and gone her way, leaving us to go ours. I thought of my first tiger, and Hoon saying, 'We've been blessed.' This was a blessing from the tiger itself. A gift. My cup was full.

You never know when arrogance may strike. We felt so happy walking down, Iwan cutting lianas for a nephew's hula hoop, Debbie and I chatting as if we owned the world.

Coming up, we turned left from the old man's ridge, meeting the tiger's trail from the right. Now, without noticing, we took the other fork. After half an hour Debbie realized. They conferred. I just thought, Great, no tree slide. I had no idea what missing a trail means. Especially near sunset.

'We know where we *are*,' said Debbie. She said that a lot, the next few hours. 'We're not *lost*. But this'll take us down *miles* away. We'll strike across to meet the other trail.'

Iwan hefted the *parang* into a wall of thorns which all had a single aim: stopping us. Undergrowth two metres above our heads; places human bodies could never get through. Tertiary forest, growing after total clearance. Usually, when villagers clear forest for farming, they leave some original trees. After thirty years there grows up a mix of original and pioneer vegetation. But if all is felled, two-metre scrub grows back with dense ground cover. Eventually things die beneath it, making fertile loam. Over fifteen years, if original forest is still near, seeds dropped by birds or civets fall in, bigger trees grow, scrub dies back in the shade. (Pioneer scrub hates shade.) This slope had not nearly reached that point. The bushes were high and close, above, between, behind, below. We were ants in a stifling green haystack, walking on springy bushes four feet above any ground.

'The trail's up there!' Debbie pointed to a dense wall of twisted thorns spaghetti-ing round huge boulders. We had to detour down; a cathedral of impenetrable roots and rocks forced us even lower. All treacherous. Every handhold, every step.

'Debbie,' I shouted an hour later, not knowing which way they had hacked. 'Right or left round this lot?'

'Just follow the trail of broken skin!' I knew now that you really,

really, have to like as well as trust the people you go into the field with. You have to forgive them when you are furious and afraid. 'Trail's near now, twenty metres above!' she yelled. An hour later, I caught up. 'Fuck it, we'll *have* to go down to the river. We know where the trail *is*, just can't get through to it.'

'That way's easier.' I could even see earth there.

'Leads to a waterfall! Can't get over the river that way.'

They plunged ahead. For hundreds of metres I slid on my bottom over bushes, looking for handholds to stop sliding too fast on a poisonous liana. Even handholds you knew to be rotten could steady you, for the second it took to find a foothold. Momentum was all. If you stopped and breathed, despair hit. Nothing to do but go on. The others were out of sight. I was alone with vegetation; and God knew what else.

Lower was hotter, undergrowth thicker. Then came slippy, mossy, loose boulders, the river's old bed. I caught up at the water's edge.

'The climate's changed so much! Iwan remembers when this was a *real* river. These boulders were in it.'

Now the only problem was loose stones and aching muscles. I fell back again, and found them sitting on the mud track, bushes either side. Six o'clock, a peach and lemon sky. The sun, setting.

'Funny place to sit.' But even they must be tired.

'You don't leave your friend alone this time of day.'

Of course. That tigress might not be so *sopan* now.

'You've met the best and worst of tropical evergreen forest. Primary, and perfectly *bloody* tertiary. We didn't do *rintiss*: mark trees on our trail. The *parang* was too blunt.'

'We were arrogant.'

'That's just what we were saying.'

The leopard cat kitten, alone in the dark with the flashing red eye of the answerphone, spat desperately when we came in, her face a tiny mask of ferocity, doing her best to be a fierce leopard cat: how she, or a small tiger cub, would defend herself alone in the wild against predators. Then she recognized us. She was moving on from milk to solids; Debbie chopped chicken and she fell on it messily, purring.

I got out the snake book. What had I missed on Mount Keronsong at 1100 metres? A paradise tree snake, one of the so-called flying snakes that flatten their bodies and glide. Debbie saw my book.

'Ah. We *were* keeping an eye out. The *scorpions* up there! When I first saw them, thought they were lobsters! But *anything* can do you. Rescued one trainee with a *huge* allergic reaction to a furry caterpillar! Told the team I'd dock their wages if they don't take anti-histamine to the forest.'

'But – snakes? You can tell me, now we're back.'

'We see four kinds of pit viper there. Hand height. People grabbing branches get bitten on face, neck and hands – I've got pictures, you *don't* want to see! Poison's necrotic. Kills and blackens flesh. *Quite* disgusting! But you don't usually *die*.'

I knew about green pit vipers now, but the brown-blotched mountain pit viper, apparently, liked highland up to 1740 metres and was happiest under the forest litter and stones I'd been cheek-to-cheek with all day. Pit vipers, though, were only *venomous dangerous*. Over the page was *venomous fatal*. My friend the equatorial spitting cobra loved thick forest to 1500 metres. King cobras, largest poisonous snake in the world, liked streams. 'Very potent neurotoxin,' said the book. 'Fatal if not treated. Forests and mountains to 2135 metres.'

'Yes, we were watching for cobras. And kraits. Seen three species there.'

I'd forgotten the purest poison in the world.

20

THE TIGER SHAMAN

'Debbie, how much do you believe the tiger magic?'

'Well, now . . .'

A few years ago she had surveyed an isolated valley with a student and a local guide, Pak Yus. They were directed up a vertical slope, to wriggle on their bellies under overhanging rock on cliff over a river. One mistake and you'd be dead. Debbie decided against it and led them down. An old man told them a different way up, across a fresh landslide. Afterwards they camped for the night.

'It's usually me and three or four blokes. I like to sleep on the outside. People who know me know this. Others say take the middle, it's safer.'

'What, from tigers?'

'Er – yes. But it isn't. When people *are* taken, it's from the middle.'

Next morning they found pugmarks, and a scratch. A tiger had walked round the camp. They went up, down another valley, up and up. Next night they camped in a horribly damp place; again there were fresh tiger pugmarks round the camp. When they finally got down, the old man asked, 'Why did you make her camp *there*? You should have camped on the ridge. That place is *so boggy*! And why did you let her sleep on the outside? You should put her in the middle!'

Pak Yus looked at him blankly. Debbie asked how he knew.

'I came to see. I thought you heard me,' the old man said.

I looked at Debbie hard.

'He was simply saying what he knew,' she said.

A small man came in with dark eye pouches and shiny darty eyes.

Zul, an informer. I dabbed TCP on scratches and pulled out thorns while they talked through an operation. I happened to mention *dukuns*. Zul pricked up his ears. He said the *dukun* in his village called his tiger behind an abandoned bus station. Debbie's *dukun* friend Pak Yerti was out of town. Could Zul's friend call a tiger for me?

This required money. There were two types of tiger-calling, said Zul. If the *dukun* called his tiger from the wild, he must go up the hill. His tiger might be too far away. He fed it once a month, and had fed it last week. Well – could he call a soul-tiger for me? Maybe.

'I don't know this *dukun*,' said Debbie.' Anything might happen.'

Zul's village, on the outskirts of Sungai Penuh, was richer than I expected, more suburban. People worked in Malaysia and were sending money back. Zul led us up a cul-de-sac in warm, drizzly dark where the *dukun*'s neighbour Pak Rusti had a large house suitable for foreign visitors, a tiger séance.

Pak Rusti, a smooth gentleman in a white and blue anorak with COMMUNICATION down one sleeve, checked wraparound skirt, Indonesian glitter hat and big white smile, sold and mended TVs. His living room had eight TVs banked up the walls. His stout wife, in her early thirties, wore a grubby, straining white dress dotted with pink peonies. They ushered us past a sofa area to a floor mat overlooked by four more TVs. One, whose electronic entrails dangled below like a catheter, was showing *Police Academy* in Indonesian. A white cat with orange hindquarters strolled in and started washing. Little fluent Zul sat down beside us and introduced the *dukun*, a small man of about forty, cross-legged in front of a glass ashtray, two unused cigarettes, dry leaves and a pot of charcoally embers. He had glossy black hair, huge eyes, a waif-like face, and did not look as if tiger wisdom earned him a lot. This was traditional village Kerinci, on which Debbie's operations depended, meeting *nouveau* Kerinci rich.

'There's a language problem,' said Debbie. 'This village has its own language. I don't get much the *dukun* says, so Zul will translate between the Kerinci dialect of Indonesian, which I speak, and this language. I'll translate the upshot into English. OK?'

'Brilliant.'

'Pak Hamzin was my *dukun*,' began the *dukun*. 'He bestowed this blessing on me. He got the gift from his father, who still calls the tiger.'

The *dukun* closed his eyes. The TV switched to football with Indonesian commentary. The *dukun* chanted; Zul and Debbie whispered their chain of translation. 'I apologize for any sins.'

He sang a long soft note, like an oboe giving the A for an orchestra. 'Ohhhh . . . I am your grandchild, I have given you these gifts, I am your grandchild, I have given you these gifts.'

He was calling his ancestors, said Zul, Simpación and Patipadang, who controlled his tiger. 'Your grandchild asks your help.' He smacked the mat with his palm. Zul said that was correct: you make a request, then hit the ground to show it is also a command. The *dukun* looked at me.

'If we know where the tiger has come from it is easy to summon. All tigers come originally from Beginda Ali, who married Sitibitimá, a child of the prophet. They had three children, a tiger, a snake, a crocodile. These were the offspring of Sitibitimá: Hai Ali Linta, ancestor of all snakes; Hai Ali Sintis, ancestor of all crocodiles; Hai Ali Lias Ana Enkau Verperang, the First Tiger. We must show respect if he comes.'

The wife leaned back against the cupboard under the TVs.

'Once, this tiger fought in the mountains with another of the prophet's children. The prophet threw a spear to stop them fighting. It hit the tiger on the spine. Now, when he walks, his spine goes from side to side with a click, like this.'

He touched his own spine, clicked his tongue and smiled affectionately. Vividly, I saw a tiger walking through forest. The long back moved, the fur swayed. The *dukun* closed his eyes, praying to First Tiger.

'Please guard these children of yours that they may not die.'

He opened his eyes, lifted the leaves, piled them up, stretched his hands to me. I stretched out mine: he pressed the leaves between my palms.

'What do I do with them?' I whispered to Debbie.

'Haven't a clue. Hang on and see.'

'Now give them back,' said the *dukun*. He put them into the ashtray and took my hand in a long handshake, closing his eyes, his palm warm and small against mine. Everything was silent. He muttered. Something was passing between us. The wisdom of tigers.

'Now he will guard you. If you are in the forest and have a problem, you must put *kemanyang* on your cigarette end.'

'Better learn to smoke,' muttered Debbie.

'If you have a problem, he will come to help. If you have no *kemanyang*, put earth on the end of the cigarette, or a slice of wood, and the tiger will come. Do you have a question?'

Stumblingly I explained I was writing a book about tigers. Writing a book was like . . . going into the forest. You don't know what you will find, you may miss your path, meet dangerous things. You come out changed.

I saw Zul's face, then the *dukun*'s, light in understanding. For me the forest was often metaphor. For them it was real. I said I wanted to help tigers, not only in Sumatra, show people how tigers lived, what happened to them. Could my spirit-tiger help me do it well?

The TV switched to a programme compèred by a hostess in gold lamé and gold-metal bunny ears.

'Extraordinary,' murmured Debbie. 'She's giving out *polygamy awards*!'

'You must write your question,' said the *dukun*, 'on a bit of paper.'

He put what I had written under the leaves.

'You're right,' he said. 'We must not be arrogant in the forest, we must be patient. If you are lost, ask your guardian. The path will open for you. When we go into the forest we must ask permission. If we do, he will look after us.'

'Does the tiger come to you when you do not call?'

'If we forget tigers, yes, they will come. If we are frightened, he can make other tigers run away. But, very important: if you ask the tiger to help, you must thank him after.'

'How?'

'Side of raw beef I should think,' whispered Debbie. She listened. 'Put crudely, you say, "Thank you, you helped me, now please go away."'

'It doesn't matter if you bathe without clothes on, this tiger doesn't mind,' said the *dukun*. 'If you want the tiger to come quickly, eat out of a saucepan because that is against the rules.' Everyone smiled. The atmosphere was lightening. 'But then it is hard to get him to go.'

'There are lots of saucepan rules,' said Debbie. 'Old rules. You mustn't wash them directly in the stream.'

The tiger was *the* magic in everyday life. The dangerous helper, guardian of taboos enforced by ancestors, governing even kitchen rules. But you do sometimes want to relax. A guardian ancestor spirit-tiger is not a thing you want round all the time.

'Your spirit-tiger will help you now,' said the *dukun*. 'Even in Malaysia and South Sumatra.'

'What about India? England?'

He closed his eyes as if hearing a crackly phone line.

'*Wherever* you go, he will always try to follow you. If you don't call, he will move round for himself. But you are one of his children now. He will recognize you, if you call. Call his name, Hai Ali Lias. The name is not secret, but he will not hear others call. Only you.'

'Please tell him he has given me a great gift. I will try to use it well.'

The polygamy contest continued. The *dukun* and I were absorbing what had passed between us. Zul and Pak Rusti took over, talking fast to Debbie. I had to pay a hundred thousand *rupiah*, ten US dollars. Zul and Pak Rusti were muscling in; but the *dukun* was genuine. Ten dollars for a spirit-tiger guardian? I only had a hundred-thousand-*rupiah* note; I hoped the *dukun* would get some of it. I put it in the glass ashtray. The note, with a translucent pink rose in the middle, lay between us like a Valentine heart.

'Well,' said Debbie, 'as far as they're concerned, you've been given something immensely valuable.'

I thought of all the luck and protection I'd been offered on my journey. Prophecies, wool bracelets. A guardian spirit-tiger upped the stakes.

'Sumatran tigers are nice, polite, loyal creatures. People who have a *harimau roh* like you are jolly lucky.'

'Even if I can't see it,' I said sadly.

'Maybe you will one day. *I* haven't got one. Well, I haven't asked.'

'You *are* a tiger, anyway,' I said.

21

WALLACE'S LINE

Baggy silver clouds, Mount Kerinci's soaring outline, lesser peaks draped in misty blue-green forest, and a bright new orange gash on Mount Keronsong. A landslide in the night, exactly where we had been! Sumatra does not let you forget its violence.

'Bus I was on had to drive over a *really* fresh landslide. Driver got out and said prayers before driving on.'

The edge of this mountain road to Tapan was unsupported earth, dry as biscuit over a three-thousand-metre drop. A bus fell over it last year. Debbie kept to the centre. Round a hairpin bend was a lorry with a broken gearbox and a load of rotting fruit. The driver, waiting glumly for help, had made a little fire. The road was notorious for tigers. Not polite Kerinci tigers but Tapan tigers, who are into meals on wheels. One jumped a motorcycle and carved up the saddle although the rider escaped. A Sungai Penuh student, riding home from Tapan at night for an exam, was snatched from his bike. They found a leg and a shoe.

'You hear *siamang* calling here. People say they call up the rain.'

Fat drops of rain began, but no gibbon songs. Instead, a small man with a bamboo birdcage on his pedal-bike. Debbie interrogated him. He gripped my rolled-down window with short black nails.

'He *says* he's not after anything rare, just birds beside the road. Maybe green magpies for the pet trade. Or bulbuls. They're easy to call up.'

Bird-catching is one of the biggest direct threats to bio-diversity in Indonesia. People take hundreds of thousands of songbirds each year from Kerinci. In 1989 Debbie saw white-rumped shama at the forest edge. Now you walk two days in deep forest to see them. I saw figures of folk myth in a new light now. Papageno in *The Magic Flute*, wood-cutters, charcoal-burners. They were OK when the world was young, and forest was for ever.

'In Jakarta you *must* go to the wildlife market, the Pramuka.' Debbie parked in dust-clouded Tapan. 'I was offered a tiger cub there. Guy said he'd have it next week. He had a leopard coming too. Someone had ordered it; I could have it if I paid more. People I've got to see. *Ciao.*'

Her black-jeaned figure disappeared among the pony-carts and chilli-powder stalls of Tapan market.

The Sunda Strait. Broken cones of Krakatoa through scattered pewter cloud. Coming down South East Asia, I followed the tiger's ancient route south. It had come through Java, where I was heading now, and ended at Bali. Fifteen miles beyond Bali was the island of Lombok, but there the tiger never came. Lombok is a different continent.

The man who discovered that was Alfred Russel Wallace, in the 1850s. He intuited a deep-sea rift between Bali and Lombok from their birds and animals. Bali had monkeys, and birds like the rosy barbets of the Malay archipelago. Lombok had Australian birds like white cocka-toos. A line had been crossed. In 1868, T. H. Huxley called this 'Wallace's Line'. Modern geophysics (of which Wallace is the father) has shown this is where two ancient super-continents bumped into each other. Lombok lies just off the Sunda Shelf, Bali just on it. East are marsupi-als, kangaroos; west are monkeys, bears, leopards, tigers. The tiger's long quest for territory ended on Bali, this tiny island at the end of Asia. But that was also where its light started to go out.

Tigers disappeared from Bali just after my grandmother went there in 1936, with Margaret Mead and her husband, the anthropologist Gregory Bateson. They stayed there to work; my granny came back in December 1936, bringing with her a box carved into a crouching animal. I have known it all my life. She kept rubber bands in it on her desk at Boswells and filled the chipped tail with red wax. She liked mending broken things. It now stands on my desk, and at last I see what it is. A Bali tiger: round ears, staring eyes, wavy brows. A private morsel of family history, made when there were still tigers on Bali. Nine months after my granny returned, on 27 September 1937, someone photographed Bali's last recorded tiger. A young tigress, paws crossed, hanging upside-down from a pole. European hunters from Java had found her last retreat.

Before the mid-nineteenth century, Java had thousands of tigers. The tiger magic I met in Sumatra was also deep in Java's blend of cultures, Hindu, Buddhist, Muslim. A 'white tiger' was associated with the vanished Hindu kingdoms, with ghosts and spirits. It was also the icon guardian of the seventeenth-century court. Javanese kings did not hunt tigers, but enjoyed tiger-stickings, *rampogs*, which sometimes killed two hundred tigers a day.

The Dutch began tiger-hunting there as a sport. By 1900, animal collecting for zoos and circuses all over the world was already depleting Javan tigers. But a blurry photo of a *rampog* survives from 1900, when tigers were already scarce, showing a palm-fringed gymkhana field, parasol-sheltered crowds. The tigers are in the field in hen-coop-like cages. If a tiger did not come out, men set fire to it. Three coops are still intact, five destroyed. So, four tigers have been killed. One is in the open, where tigers hate to be, dazed, with drooping hindquarters. Everyone round the edge holds a spear. They will pierce it till it dies.

The other traditional Javan entertainment was a fight between a water-buffalo and a tiger. This symbolized the conflict of good and evil, but in colonial times locals cheered the buffalo. It stood for the colonial power, the Dutch.

Java is half the size of England and has twice its numbers, four times its population density. It is the most thickly populated island in the world. Even so, it was forty years after Bali's tigers disappeared that Java lost its tigers, too. The last documented sighting was 1972.

Jakarta was jumpy. A bomb outside the Marriott Hotel yesterday had killed twenty cab drivers queuing for work. People linked this to the Bali bomber's trial, currently taking place here too. Seventy neolithic cities with altars and temples lay under Jakarta. Today it was a temple to pollution and fear. An anxious man called Rachman drove me for two hours, at five miles an hour, through a million four-wheel drives

on six-lane highways to the Old Harbour, port for the last Hindu kingdom on west Java, where hundreds of cargo boats unloaded on to old
Dutch wharves, in muggy dazzling haze, hundreds of thousands of
enormous ancient logs.

'Where does that wood come from?'

'Many places,' said a guide proudly, keen to show me round.
'Borneo! Myanmar! Sumatra!' Six months later an EIA report would
expose a billion-dollar trade in smuggling illegal timber from
Indonesia to China. China – always China.

'Can we go?' I asked Rachman.

I woke in the night, about the time that a bank manager exposed in
a corruption scandal jumped from a nearby fifty-first-floor window
and broke every bone in his body. I looked out of my own window, at
roof-tiles in dim lamplight. Jakarta swirled secrets and shadows behind.

Before my plane left for Singapore, I wanted to see the wildlife market
and Wayang museum. Rachman said I had to see Monas first. This
obelisk symbolized Indonesia's 1949 independence. A hundred and
thirty-two metres high, topped by a gold flame, it was one of the archi-
tectural extravaganzas on which Sukarno, Indonesia's first president,
spent the new republic's exchequer as the price of a kilo of rice rose to
a worker's daily wage. It was begun by Sukarno in 1961, but com-
pleted in 1975 by Soeharto, whose 1965 coup crushed Indonesia's first
frail guided democracy. The help given *him* by Western arms, CIA,
foreign banks and oil companies was the subject of the poem I owned
by the poet I met on the Mekong. Soeharto himself fell in 1998, when
hundreds died rioting against army snipers' shootings of students
demonstrating against his regime.

'Bigger than Houses of Parliament? London Eye?' said Rachman.

'Much. Can we go to the Wayang now?'

I wanted to see this museum because tigers sometimes figured in it
and it is the core Javanese art. *Wayang kulit*, leather shadow-puppet
shows, traditionally play at night, till dawn. On a journey begun under
the auspices of St Lucy, I had to see an art whose medium was *wayang*,
shadow.

As in the Lao court, the stories came from Hindu epic, but Indonesian characters, clowns, contemporary jokes and references piled in too. *Wayang* encapsulates Java's Hindu-Buddhist-Muslim heritage. Stone reliefs from the fourteenth century show the traditional characters realistically. During the fifteenth-century rise of Islam, with its resistance to the human image, they were stylized into insect-like grotesques.

This cobbled square was the colonial heart of old Jakarta. A Dutch painting in tropical haze, with auto-rickshaws. Here Michiel, the Dutch conservationist running the Tigris Foundation in Vladivostock, had picked up a bullet as a child when his father had brought him to visit the island he himself had grown up on. Of course a bullet. What else would it be, given the history here?

The museum was in an old Dutch church on a side of the square. An elderly man with inflamed eyes struck a gong in the dark hall to bring luck and showed me antique buffalo-hide puppets in glass cases. One, a red stripy giant called Kalasinga, had tiger claws, a tiger head. What about actual tiger puppets? I had seen photos . . .

The old man had firm views on this. 'We believe the spirit is in the puppet. Tiger too dangerous. No one wants.'

Every set of figures included a leaf-shaped fan, which the puppeteer waved to signal the end of a scene, or passage of time. The back showed hell, a demon head with lolling tongue. The front was the gate of heaven, a temple façade with tiger fighting buffalo. Good and evil? Not according to my guide.

'Tiger is powerful like king. Buffalo is man who works, is responsible.'

Above was a gold tree with birds in its branches.

'Bird is for singing. A bird takes away stress, makes joyful the universe to humans.'

Hence birdcages. Papageno. Forests emptied of their pollinators.

'Fan shows tree of life. We believe you cannot live without a tree.'

And the burnt forests, the logs in the harbour?

People were making puppets, cutting buffalo hide, painting figures, stuccoing them with coloured glass. It takes three weeks to make a puppet.

'But you won't *see* this in front of the screen! If you only see shadows, why the paint and jewels, this glitter-gold brightness?'

'Is spiritual. Is down-to-earth, like life. We only see the shadow, the outline. But the real thing must be as beautiful as we can make it.'

There was a theatre with a musician mending a drum, and *wayang*'s two basic ingredients, the screen and the lamp. A white cotton sheet hung from a carved frame, a bare bulb beside it. The old man said he would do a performance for me. No wonder he thought so brilliantly with symbols: he was the *dalang*, the puppeteer.

'Traditional is coconut oil, cotton wick. We use electricity. But the lamp is like thought. It illuminates.'

He turned out the overhead lights and sat behind a banana-wood bole, in which the puppets' pointed horn handles stuck like toffee apples at a fair. I went round the other side. I had never had theatre done just for me. I heard him mutter the *dalang*'s opening prayer, 'May silence prevail; may the strength of wind and storm be mine.'

This single lamp was St Lucy. Light in the dark, when other lights go out. I saw his trousers beneath the screen; then Rama's lacy shadow appeared. Rama and Sita again. This Rama was in the forest already, and far more talkative than in Laos.

'I am very lonely in the middle of this forest,' said Rama, in English. 'I hope nothing happens to me or my family. I will meditate.'

His wife, here called Sinta, was kidnapped. Hanuman the monkey-god saved her. When a puppet came on, its filigreed silhouette had shadows on two sides for a second, like wings fading in and out of focus. Scenes switched between forest and palace. When Hanuman returned Sinta to Rama he said, very excited, 'I must go now! Not to my family in forest! No no *no*, much more important: to Afghanistan, Iraq! Find Bin Laden, Saddam Hussein, weapons of mass destruction!'

Wayang specializes in contemporary references. And jokes.

In Bangkok and China I had ducked the wildlife markets. Pet trade or cuisine, it comes to the same thing: doomed animals in cages, not reproducing in the wild. Now I had to see one.

Rachman drew up by a black canal, one of many the Dutch had built through this estuary's swamp. Young men in bright shirts. Birdcages; an unwise male pigeon showing off swelling neck-feathers to females in cages on the ground.

I told Rachman I'd be an hour, got out into the heat, watched by hundreds of eyes, and walked along the canal behind the edge of slums. Here were the smells masked by spray in airports and hotels. Sludge, foetid sewage, rotting vegetables.

But the bird market smelt of birdseed and straw: a vast, covered market with cages stacked far higher than I stood. Some ornate, beautifully painted – a lot of craft and love had gone into their making, as into the puppeteer's explanation: birdsong makes the universe joyful for man. But the cages held hundreds of thousands of wild dead-end captives. Songbirds.

I walked through endless bird sections, followed by increasing numbers of boys trying to sell. Out of the corner of my eye, I realized this was not the callousness of Laos. They enjoyed handling birds. They stroked feathery breasts. Loving animals takes many forms, but can be lethal to the animal and its species.

I wanted to see mammals. The only *bahasa* I knew apart from *harimau* was, God knows why, the word for slow loris. I thought if I asked for that I would see other mammals.

'*Coucang*?' The word was repeated like rifle shot through the bird alleys. A man brushed the boys aside and led me further. The place was enormous. Here was a baby palm civet, frantic in its little black mask. Rows of small squirrels. A red tree squirrel; baby squirrels clunched like shivering black pasta on the floor of a cage. A pacing beige cat, an adult. Fishing cat, jungle cat, flat-headed cat? Leopard cat kittens everywhere. Debbie's was lucky, most would die before they were sold. *All* on the endangered list. Illegal to catch or trade in them *all*. I felt like Jesus in the temple with the moneylenders. But what would freeing them do here?

The *coucang* broke my heart. In the loris section, in each cage, the inmate would turn round very slowly – they are *slow* loris, after all – to fix saucer eyes upon me. *Why are you troubling me in my misery?* A particularly small one half sat up like someone exhausted by shopping, a bend in its despairing little back. The slow loris is a primate, like us.

'Baby baby baby,' men kept saying. 'You want to buy *coucang*?'

How did Debbie stand it? I heard Lystia saying, 'I love Indonesia because it is my country. But I think people do not care.'

I walked rapidly back through the maze of stalls, ignoring shouts. The man followed me right to the car calling, 'Baby! *Baby*!'

'You want to buy *coucang*?' asked Rachman, when we got the door shut. 'I get you good price.'

'No, thank you. Not any price.'

'I had a perfectly dreadful time, thanks, in the Pramuka,' I emailed Debbie from London. 'Didn't dare ask about tiger cubs. Just fled.'

'I know,' she emailed back. 'Sorry to do it to you but it's another face of Indonesia. The worst are hidden *behind* Pramuka, where the seriously protected species are stashed. And if you think that's bad, you should see warehouses where they stack snakes and tortoises in filthy boxes and leave them, and primates wait to be killed for rich bastards who think it's cool to eat the brains when they're still alive.'

'Did you see a tiger this time?' asked my daughter.

'No. But a tiger in the forest saw me, and let me pass. I've got a guardian spirit-tiger now too.'

'Yeah, right,' she said. But kindly.

Then a last lunch with the man I had left. Why? Was this a good idea?

'I'll take you to a fab place where you can eat zebra. Or tiger if you like.' He did not know that this was no joke in other places.

'Against the law,' I said. 'Endangered species.'

But in this Turkish restaurant there was nothing more endangered than an aubergine. Over Ottoman lamb he grabbed my hands, checking rings.

'That one I know. This?'

'A family ring. My mother's.'

He still wore the ring I had given him, but others also, two on each hand.

'You will tell me,' he said, 'if . . .?'

He once said other people, by which he meant women, were salvation. I knew there was a girl around, thirty years younger than him. I made an opening for him to talk about it, if he wanted.

He considered yellow-taggled fibres in his cooling garlic bread.

'My left foot keeps on tapping.' He looked at me critically. 'Nothing you're wearing matches. Nice jacket, but doesn't go with the blouse. And the earrings don't go with any of it.'

He convinced himself of things by saying them to other people.

Now he was telling himself, by telling me, that he too had crossed a line; had finally fallen out of love.

Back home my daughter looked at my face and said I needed a pedicure. She had an after-school job as a salon receptionist.

'First time?' said Yasmin next day, plonking my feet in a vibrating footbath of bubbles, then taking one on her knee. 'Do you look after your feet yourself?'

Tigers licking pads, healing cracks, cleaning mud, pulling thorns. Dealing with impacted snow in China, love-mud in the Sundarbans, boiling rock in Rajasthan.

Sun-patched from Sumatra, my right foot dripped on Yasmin's towel. These feet had carried me up krait-laced mountains, soaked in the Nam Ha, frozen in rhododendron forest, escaped pit vipers in *taiga*. They had looked after me, not the other way round.

'Yes,' I said. 'Entirely by myself.'

PART IV

RETURN TO SOUTH INDIA

Tigers Today and Tomorrow

22

THE NO AND THE YES

In wilderness is the preservation of the world.
Thoreau

Cows nose the gutter. Beggars shove pink stump arms through the taxi window. Sari shops, pavement cafés. 'Meet India's Most Intelligent Washing Machines.' I am going to the Bombay Natural History Society's centenary conference in a campus just outside Bombay, near a reserve that is suffering from man-eating leopards. They killed fifteen people last year, one on this campus. There is carnivore–human conflict right in front of me, and yet I have come back to India for hope. With all its suffering and secrets, this city makes sense to me where Seoul, Bangkok, Jakarta did not. India feels like home – which is silly: I know nothing of its depths. But I have depended, all through, on two people here who know tigers intimately, and India is the tiger's likeliest long-term home. No accident that here I saw tigers themselves, not just their signs.

Russia is maybe their next best bet, and the only country with a nationwide tiger crime unit. If only all tiger states had one; all as incorruptible, knowledgeable, culturally sensitive and espionage-driven as Debbie's in Kerinci. But maybe only small operations *can* be incorruptible, and who knows what will happen in Russia politically? Everywhere tigers depend on political will. They occupy a country's greatest natural wealth, its forest. Here, they live on squeezed islands surrounded by unimaginably large human seas. The population of Uttar Pradesh is bigger than Russia's whole electorate.

Good things have happened – to me. My daughter is making her life in a way I admire, takes her boyfriend to Trafalgar Square to climb the lions, show him they can have fun on no money; has refused universities her father and I know, and found one of her own that really wants her. She is kind, intuitive, generous. I am proud and in awe of all this. My personal quest for disenchantment is done, though I'd like some final goodbye. Not to the real person now, but to the one in my head.

But tigers? Why did I not see from the beginning I had blundered, for personal reasons, into a worldwide war for the wild? And since I have been questing, it has got much, much worse.

Tigers have all been poached from Sariska. Panna is back below the numbers it had before Raghu began his research. The skin trade has grown tenfold. Skins as well as bones go to China now, mainly through Lhasa, capital of Tibet, and on to other Chinese provinces where the Environment Investigation Agency found skins openly on sale, expertly tanned to fold, light as lingerie, into suitcases. Not only Chinese but Westerners are buying them. Diplomats, expats, businessmen, tourists; £5500 a skin. Sungai Penuh is the crude new blueprint for everyone. It is cool to have a tiger on your sofa. Or your bed, as in a photo featured in a recent e-Bay tiger-skin ad. Andy Fisher, head of wildlife crime at New Scotland Yard, showed me a stuffed ten-week-old cub mounted on olive wood, impounded from a British film director. The Western market is out of control and its hub is China, to whose tune Asian wildlife crime dances. Thirty-one tiger skins, 581 leopard skins, 778 otter skins seized in Tibet in one Nepalese truck, going to China but killed in Indian forests.

Tibet, roof of the world, water source, spiritual and cultural source for so much of Asia: you cast a new shadow now. In your own tragedy, you are a route of death to tigers, too. And since 2003, all has got even worse. Fresh skins were found drying on a deputy head man's house near the edge of Madhya Pradesh, the tiger state. Two tigers were electrocuted in Bandhavgarh: the poachers quarrelled and betrayed each other. Such seizures are accidents: they come from gang warfare, tip-offs from rival poachers. In only three weeks of June 2004, ten tiger skins, twenty-five leopard skins, four sacks of tiger bones, and claws from thirty-one tigers and leopards were found in eleven seizures in India and Nepal.

The people I have seen are a fraction of those working to save tigers and yet in most of South-East Asia, except possibly north Myanmar, this could be the last moment before wild tiger extinction. To change policies on logging, mining and roads in countries where corruption, violence and poverty are the norm would need fourteen separate political miracles. Someone going where I have been ten years hence may find no tiger traces. Have I been writing about tigers? Or about people and what they do to the world with their symbols, fear and greed? 'Enjoy the wilderness of the world while it's around,' Valmik emailed. 'It won't be for long.'

Ullas and Valmik: I learn from both. Emotionally, I swing between. Will wild tigers survive? Valmik and Ullas, my no and my yes.

Pessimism does not blunt Valmik's furious energy. He now sits on a new Central Empowered Committee, set up by India's Supreme Court in 2002. Its four other members are a lawyer, an ex-bureaucrat, two serving forest officers. They investigate forest misuse. Valmik is a passionate advocate for tigers but looks at their future with very dark eyes. His hope now lies in India's legal system.

Ullas believes with equal passion in science, rationality, education. That the middle classes will see that people as well as animals need forests and will act to save them, like Green World in Thailand. He believes that in India at least, tigers *can* be saved. As long as prey and trees are there, tigers survive some poaching: it is habitat that counts. He believes Asia must and will save its remaining forests. 'The tiny amount that's left from what *was* there won't help developing countries. The only thing that can is to conserve. Nature can still surprise.' As in Darwin's favourite line from Wordsworth, 'Nature never did betray the heart that loved her.' As Ted Hughes said about his poem 'River', 'Nature keeps all options open.' But if we have closed them all?

I have come back for hope, but even India offers little now. The forest service is anxious mainly to cover up. 'The reserve does not sufffer from poaching, I am sure there are tigers,' a Sariska officer will tell the *Indian Express* when all tigers vanish from Sariska: a level of denial worthy of China. 'While tigers cannot be individually identified thirty-four were counted in a census,' another will announce from Panna, where the once-rising numbers have plummeted. In Delhi I met P. K. Sen, ex-Director of Project Tiger, round-faced with glasses; an angry man. Project Tiger's steering committee is supposed to meet every six months. Two and a half years after he left it still has not met. The new director has been planning to spend $150,000 on celebrating thirty years of Project Tiger. No one else thinks there is anything to celebrate; that money would be better spent on anti-poaching patrols everywhere. 'The tragedy is,' said P.K., 'we are still patting ourselves on the back for Project Tiger. But today forty per cent of tiger reserves are out of management control! No one enters them: there are militants, Naxalites, criminals, land mines. What can guards do against poachers there? And everyone is trying to dilute wildlife and forest laws. Politicians, bureaucrats, industrialists, ordinary people: they're all against the forest! They want the land. Do tigers have a future in this country? *No!* No future!' And now in this lecture hall the chairman is saying, 'We are at war. The government owns the land and the animals. *Nothing* the forest service has done gives me hope for the future. India's wildlife laws *are not enforced*. If a forest officer is competent and honest and takes on local politicians, he is moved to make way for someone more compliant. There are no forest officials here . . .'

Someone puts up a hand. 'One man. That's the trouble. No one from the Environment Ministry and,' he bows courteously, 'the forest service not adequately represented. When a good man directs a reserve, good things happen. He does poaching patrols. The next destroys all he's done. We have no support from the people in charge of wildlife.'

Valmik's colleagues on the CEC explain how that committee began, what it does. There was no political will to enforce wildlife laws. Railways, state governments and police were all involved in illegal logging. Forests were vanishing – which threatened ecological security, human food, human water. In 1995, the judiciary set up an investigation team and closed thousands of sawmills, over half unlicensed. In 2002 they created the CEC to investigate abuse of forest land and refer prosecution to the Supreme Court. It is greed versus conservation everywhere. There is so much money to be made. ('Wish *we* had something like this,' mutters a British ornithologist beside me.) A state's chief minister pressurizes its chief wildlife warden to say there is no significant wildlife so the trees can go. Honest people in state environment ministries are traumatized. The CEC checks law enforcement on all forest land, twenty-one per cent of India. Mining can be allowed on such land, but only with the consent of central government. Everywhere they went, they found abuse. In one tiger reserve, forest staff had not been paid for fourteen months. In others, forests were being harmed by vested-interest mafias exploiting tribal people's rights, making money in the tribals' name by building roads that assisted logging and poaching. In the Sundarbans, people profiting from mass trawling pretended to help poor fishermen. The CEC went to see, allowed small fishermen to work but not big trawlers.

The CEC also scrutinizes bureaucrats in federal and state governments. You can do far more harm with pen and ink than axe or snare. In 1995 in a small sanctuary called Jamua Ramgarh beside Sariska tiger reserve, a company asked permission to open a marble mine, backed by Rajasthan's chief of forests, who is responsible for this state's wildlife. He said in his opinion the area did not 'fall in the route of migrating fauna'. (This was a red herring. The migration-routes argument applies only outside designated wildlife areas.) In September 1996 the Ministry rejected the request, which clearly violated the law. Then the federal minister changed. In October the new one asked to see the file urgently. In March 1997 he gave the mine permission. For three years the two bureaucracies played ping-pong as people in power changed. Good ones voiced doubts; the mine continued under 'Temporary Working Permits' supposed to cover clearing debris. (Many mines simply carry on working under a series of TWPs.) Its supporters said the mine was a 'legacy of the past'. In October 2000, those in power clearly did think the law was violated, mining supporters started back-tracking, and the case went to the Supreme Court, today's ultimate protector of India's forests (and therefore the tiger). The worst breakers of India's wildlife laws are the permission-givers, the lawmakers themselves.

I lunch with the CEC members. The younger one looks like the young Gandhi. Why, when this country has so many brilliant, highly knowledgeable and qualified concerned people, is all this such a mess?

'People in charge of forests treat wildlife as a penance, a chore,' says the older judge with heavy jowls, grizzled hair. 'They prefer to do anything but. Anything that makes money.' He says there are moves afoot to review and change this. As we stack our trays he says, eyes shining behind his glasses, 'Know what? On this campus last night I saw *two leopards*!'

Hot conference days go by. Detailed problems faced by defenders of the wild in the world's largest democracy are all different. So many remote places with different languages, conservation worries, histories of forest protection, resistance to it, corruption, armed insurgents. So many species to protect, so many vested interests to fight.

The last evening I am in blue silk with pink beading. This is speeches and dinner night. The audience is shepherded by young men and women in green: naturalists, scientists, activists from all over India. Valmik talks ferociously, brilliantly, on how conservation began here, how the society was founded, what is happening now. He shows film: a Ranthambhore tigress attacking a crocodile who tried to steal her kill. She leaps on its back, jaws on its neck, gold toes spread like someone playing octaves on a harp in boxing gloves. Then an image of tenderness: that tigress at Panna, suckling tiny cubs, film taken by Raghu long distance in early morning. Such things are *still here* – just. We have to fight that they will stay.

The society is giving George Schaller a lifetime award.

'Conservation must be integrated,' says Schaller, 'with the needs of people and cultures.' He talks of Vishnu the Preserver, Shiva the Destroyer: of that dangerous word 'sustainable', which often means what the market not the earth will bear. 'Development often means destruction. Shiva and Vishnu must go hand in hand.' Society must respect humanity's need for wild places, for the pristine; for places where pillaging is forbidden. 'Gandhi said there is enough in the world for everyone's need but not everyone's greed. Understanding is not enough, even science is not enough. Reaching a new insight is wonderful but scientists today must defend: must act, as well as gain knowledge.'

He focuses, as anti-poaching reports do too now, on Tibet. There are maybe a dozen tigers in its south-east. But in mountains prey is less, so the tigers take more livestock, especially in winter. 'What do you do when wild animals harm crops and livestock?' People find solutions: compensation and insurance schemes, as in Bhutan, Laos, Vladivostock. Giving people clinics and schools in return for not killing tigers, as in Ranthambhore, the Sundarbans. 'But how many of these are long-term solutions? Problems of implementing protection laws are always *local*.'

He talks of the Tibetan antelope, the chiru, whose throat-hair is made into shatoosh shawls in Kashmir. It is illegal to make, sell, buy or own shatoosh. Yet shawls are bought by rich Westerners in Rome, New York, Paris. Shatoosh is linked with the tiger trade: dead chiru are exchanged for tiger skins at the Tibetan border. Poachers with automatic rifles shoot females giving birth at the calving grounds and sell skins to middlemen, who take them to Kashmir, sell them to weavers and get rich.

'You'd think one solution would be captive breeding. But you can't shear them, the throat hairs are too short. To get that fur, the animal must die. OK, protect wild ones and cull them legally, once there are enough. The state, and the weavers, will make money. But no. Instead there is constant illegal slaughter and a beautiful animal is endangered. One day no one will make money from them. They won't *be* there.'

His voice is American, with occasional German vowels.

'There are no victories in conservation. We must simply fight on and on. Express our loyalty to the earth by helping other species endure.'

Society is Canute. Scientists and conservationists risk their lives all over Asia. I have seen them. They are not sitting watching the waves, but stepping in. Yet the waves roll higher all the time. I remember the wildlife vet John Lewis, talking me through tiger diseases beside a young tigress in Chessington Zoo, saying, 'You have a choice: do nothing or do something. I know what I decided.'

Like Valmik, Schaller ends with a tiger: a moment when he was working at Kanha and a tigress stepped out of dawn mist.

'She was *so beautiful*. That is what we are fighting to preserve.'

Tears in my eyes, I head for the dinner queue, a buffet for a thousand in a garden. Dusk has come, high-rise buildings around are lit. I queue beside a white-haired woman in immaculate green and gold, a donor from Bombay's élite. I feel hot, obvious, Western in my blue dress. 'Those are the most expensive flats in Bombay,' her husband says.

What did they make of the talks? She says she likes animals.

'I used to breed dogs. I made a white Alsatian.'

That is conservation to her. She heard Valmik and George, but thinks tigers should go, they destroy other animals. The tiger and its forests are in India's hands, but every country has people who will not care; like one sarcastic leader-writer who said in the *Calcutta Telegraph*: 'Most Indians believe there are more important things than being considerate to flora and fauna.' He was talking about polluted water endangering human lives. Yet uranium waste from a proposed mine in an Andhra Pradesh tiger reserve is less than one kilometre from the Narjuna Sagar dam, source of drinking water for Hyderabad. The same things that threaten tigers threaten people. Protect fauna and forest in the tiger's name and you protect people, too.

None of this interests the white-Alsatian lady. But I see hundreds of young naturalists coming to Schaller for autographs, stars in their eyes. Forget her. *They* are India's, and the tiger's, hope.

23

THE BATTLE OF FLOWERING BAMBOO

'What will you do when you get your research permit back?'

I am with Ullas in Bangalore. His study, full of books, is open to a roof-garden. Trees round a little lawn rustle with Bonet macaques. They are terrible bullies. When Ullas's white cat appears, they chase her in. Fire-crackers go off below and they whoop away. Diwali is coming, the Festival of Lights, the victory of good over evil; the clearing of backlogs, the new account book. Like St Lucy, this is light from the dark, a new beginning. People light lamps, give presents.

Ullas is one of the minds that lit my journey. I love his fierce passion for science in whatever circumstance. I felt the same with Dale in Russia. In Sumatra I watched Tom, earlier in his career, taking that burden on. They all think about what science is, and can do. Making it work in the field means languages, political sharpness, diplomacy, action, partnerships, bodily endurance. Here in Karnataka, Ullas's home state whose stamps commemorate his poet father, I will see in the field, for the last time, this vision of science in action, before answering my own question: tiger no, or tiger yes.

Biology, says Ullas, begins with natural history, that love of nature I grew up with, but must prove and disprove, find new ways of collecting and interpreting evidence, be ready to say it does *not* know. A pilgrim towards God, a Buddhist on the mountain path. 'Good science goes forward to truth but never gets there.' He looks for tools developed in other sciences that might help biology: the more you know about tigers and their prey, the better you can protect them. He writes research papers with statisticians, mathematicians, sociologists, seeking new ways not only to monitor tigers and prey but to study humans, who have taken the earth away from them. He gets science to partner law, too, and local communities. For years he has trained volunteers all over Karnataka: architects, businessmen, lawyers and doctors who realize their countryside is in danger. They do transects in dangerous terrain (there are elephants here, as well as bear, cobras, kraits), and monitor what is happening in each national park.

Karnataka has many parks and maybe four hundred tigers. The tiger places are Nagarahole, Bandipur, Kudremukh, Bhadra. I will see the last two, where villagers have newly left the forest. How are they recovering, now humans have left? Kudremukh Park has an iron ore mine in it. The Supreme Court found it violated the law and has ordered it to close in 2005.

To protect tigers you protect forests. To make sure forest laws are enforced you must keep a hard edge even – especially – against its official protectors: the state and some foresters. Foresters make no extra money from essential protection, only by doing something intrusive. As with a clinic paid to keep patients healthy, basic protection makes nothing, surgery does. If you take things out or put things in, to a body or forest, you profit from each stage of operation. Sell contracts for extracting cane, which is some animals' main diet. Make a road with a commission, tweak the work register to say you paid twice as many workmen as you did. Some forest officers are wonderful. They care about preserving wildlife. Like Valmik, Ullas supports such people fervently.

'The honest forester's job is very difficult. He's everyone's enemy. He's isolated, a target. NGOs must help him, with law-enforcement skills, for instance.'

Saving wildlife is now a last-ditch battle: police the wild or it will fray away. Ullas is the inspiration behind an NGO called Wildlife First whose members all over Karnataka monitor the forests and challenge destructive work like mining, logging, roads. They stand for protection. They cross political borders, arguing simply that in designated reserves the interests of wildlife, especially large extinction-prone animals, tiger, elephant, must override human interests. The burning *human* issues of the world's largest democracy must be resolved on the other ninety-six per cent of India's land, where wild animals have no rights.

Wildlife First makes powerful enemies. The worst threat to forests is from development operations which enrich local politicians and foresters working with them, who get away with bogus arguments to defend their work: sell acres of a tiger reserve and say this manages tiger habitat better, build dams and say they are good for marsh crocodiles or birds. Wildlife First constantly questions what happens in Karnataka's forests. *Why are you clearing this? Why cut such large view-lines? Thirty feet each side is OK, sixty feet not.* They did the science to prove that sixty feet upsets the balance of grass species and endangers deer. Believing that activists must understand the issues properly, Ullas taught them good science. In Kudremukh, they collected proof that the iron ore was polluting the forest and fields; evidence on which the Supreme Court ordered it to close. Today there is another issue, flowering bamboo.

Bamboos vary. Many species flower once every forty-five years, then die and fall. Wildlife First did a study that proves the fallen stalks form a cage protecting new growth from grazing animals. This is how the forest was made. The regenerating clumps give food, shelter and homes to birds, rodents, reptiles and insects, who sustain the forest and larger animals. The canes dry in March; in April, May and June, new shoots appear. Each clump is a continuous micro-habitat. But foresters can make money by removing and replanting flowering bamboo. You write a proposal to extract bamboo, cost each element of the operation, take a percentage on each stalk cropped, on transport, stacking, cane storage, cane sales, buying seedlings, plastic bags, mud, digging, planting, fertilizing. All this is ten times more expensive than letting it flower and regenerate, but you make money. You say dead canes are a fire hazard. So why not extra fire protection? No, instead you pay for propaganda. North India had flowering bamboo this year. On street stands today a magazine called *Outlook* carries a piece headlined 'BUDS OF POISON!!!' Flowering bamboo is 'ravaging our forests'. The 'race is on' to cut it before it flowers. We must reclassify it, urgently, as agricultural, because it is illegal to cut forest plants.

Bamboo flowered this year at Bhadra, too. Wildlife First is blocking its removal. In the war between science (and true protection) and management which exploits rather than cherishes the forest, regeneration itself is now the battleground.

You can imagine how popular Ullas is. His car and office have been burnt before now. For twenty years he has argued, and then proved, that pugmark-counting tigers is unreliable compared to estimating their density. For ten years, he has camera-trapped and radio-collared tigers in a long-term study. Raghu and Ullas are the only people in India researching tigers long-term. An Indian scientist with a British passport was refused permission by the MOEF because 'tiger conservation is a sensitive issue'; how could he ensure tiger information was not 'disseminated'?

Ullas's work in Nagarahole monitoring the tiger population was unique research that should never have been broken. His methods have been copied by scientists all over the world. But here he is resented, ignored, envied, maligned. Like Raghu, he criticized forest works: illegal logging licences, the removal (for sale) of dead wood providing food and shelter to thousands of species. After a terrible fire at Nagarahole he used a satellite survey to prove exactly how much forest was burnt (far more than the forest authorities claimed) and how fire-fighting was mismanaged. Authorities do not forgive being shown up. They cancelled Ullas's research permit, saying he had interfered in departmental management matters, raised issues like fire and destruction or illegal grazing and complained to outsiders, 'which was not appreciated by the Department'. I have seen their deposition. Stories are planted in local tabloids saying his research is a cover for smuggling tiger bones. He is killing tigers not protecting them. His radio collars give tigers cancer.

And people like my brother's friends believe them. Many human-rights activists demonize wildlife laws. The tiger is the enemy because land was taken from people in its name. Again an Indian issue is played out in my family; but in my absence, at my mother's table. A visiting friend of my brother says Ullas killed sixty tigers. ('Wildlifers' and 'people people' have a common enemy: mining and timber lobbies, politicians exploiting forests. But these lobbies divide and rule.) I expect my mother snorted. *Fairly* politely; I cannot vouch for it. She is outspoken, and she studied biology. Scientists have radio-collared animals everywhere for decades. It does not cause cancer. And *sixty* tigers? It is expensive enough radio-collaring one. But there is not enough background scientific education here yet for people to disbelieve such accusations, so libel suits, bail bonds, legal warrants and court hearings take up the time of scientists desperate to study, monitor, protect. Ullas is not teaching arms in South East Asia, but he is fighting the same war.

Soon he will get back his research permit. The CEC said Karnataka's grounds for refusing it were frivolous, arbitrary, without basis. Then Ullas will restart work in Nagarahole. He suspects up to a quarter of tigers older than a year die naturally each year, wounded in fights, hunts, dispersal accidents, and through starvation. 'We need to understand basic data about their natural life cycle. That's what should drive our understanding. We'll monitor their population across the whole state. And at Bhadra, monitor recovery.'

I ask the most naïve question. How many tigers does he think India still has?

'Maybe three and a half thousand. Unlikely to be less than two and a half. The tiger's resilient. We could have fifty thousand if the land was managed competently. That's not a dream. I'd be happy with half that. You can say, let the tiger go. OK, I'd respect that position. That would be a decision. But to try to save it and do it badly! I can't respect that.'

More fire-crackers. A macaque on the lawn flashes off to a tree.

'Bhadra could have thirty to forty breeding tigresses. It's ideal habitat. We don't know yet. Can't work there till the permit comes through.'

Downstairs, his wife brings Diwali sweets and sits me at her computer in their daughter's bedroom. I email my own daughter, studying for A levels in dark November London.

Next day, high up again in Mangalore, on Karnataka's west coast, I hear a rushing of wings. A Brahminy kite lands on the hotel windowsill. They circle this city as they circled the boat in the Bangladesh Sundarbans. So close: hooked yellow beak, fierce lemon eyes, a lord of creation, resting. For minutes we stand unmoving. Fire-crackers snap below, and the bird floats off into a white Diwali sky.

Behind Mangalore are the Western Ghats, one of the globe's eighteen bio-diversity hotspots designated for conservation. In 1987 the

Karnataka government declared a national park here. It is unique tiger habitat, high, rolling hills and folds of pristine tropical evergreen forest called *sholas*, with leopard, wild dogs, king cobras, gaur, sambar, and highly endangered lion-tailed macaques.

'Ghats' means 'steps', as in stairs. The Western ones are an enormous mountain range. They run down south-west India through Kerala and Tamil Nadu. Periyar is at their southern end. Ullas's man here in Mangalore, Niren Jain, is a tall architect. His gentle face belies his embattled position as leader of the Kudremukh Wildlife Foundation – passionate amateur naturalists, hand-trained by Ullas, who challenge anything that might harm their unique wilderness.

I dine with them: a fortyish surgeon with wide girth and smile, a businessman (in electrics), a bookseller. Would their equivalents in a provincial British town think getting eaten by ticks and leeches in dangerous jungle the ideal way of spending two weeks away from their families? Ullas wanted people who could operate delicate instruments and behave responsibly around dangerous animals. These men responded.

The bookseller has a book by Ullas translated into the state language Kannada, saying why tigers matter, how people can help. He loves rock-climbing, knows the Western Ghats intimately and writes about them in the papers, most recently against a scheme for diverting rivers. Wilderness gives its defenders a rough time: he was once attacked on a cliff by the largest sort of wild bees. Four hours he and his friends were stuck there, stung hundreds of times, unable to move for bee-clouds. When the bees got tired, the men climbed down and were rushed to hospital, swollen and vomiting.

And the transects? I had been nervous of snakes on Sumatran transects and that was only scrub. These men had learned in thick jungle. The businessman was once finishing a transect with Ullas when they saw their jeep waiting, lights flashing. Ullas was furious. Then, suddenly, a tiger was in front of them, coming down the trail, not realizing they were there. Ullas hissed, 'Don't move!' Movement gives you away. They froze. The tiger walked.

'Ullas was gripping my arm, I didn't know which I was more afraid of, the tiger or Ullas! Then it turned its head at the jeep noise, flashed off the trail and was gone.'

Tigers, bees – and something more dangerous still. Niren, finishing a transect with a friend, was charged by an elephant. It galloped five feet behind him. You cannot outrun them; Niren swerved into thorn bushes.

'I didn't care *what* was in them! Then it veered off, I didn't know it was going after my friend, I thought he'd got away.'

When all was quiet, he crept out. There was his friend, dishevelled, dazed. He had tripped and lain still. It hit him, he never knew how – tusk, trunk, foot – went away, came back, hit his back and head again. He just lay. Their pick-up colleagues thought both of them were dead.

The surgeon once brought fifteen ten-year-old children in forest to train them with a colleague. They communicated by whistles. Human voices alarm wildlife, whistles do not. He heard a whistle across a stream, thought his friend had something special to show the kids, took them carefully across, heard him whistle deeper, then deeper. A hill mynah, brilliant at imitating calls, had lured them into the middle of a herd of elephants. The elephants had not noticed or smelt them but one, browsing, had closed the gap in the herd. He backed the children out slowly between the widest-apart elephants. Later, hoping to see tiger at night from a *machan* (a viewing platform) on a lake, he climbed up at twilight with a guard.

'The *machan* was swaying and frail. I'm pretty much an elephant myself. I like my food.'

When they got up there, the guard fell asleep. A young tusker turned up. Even young males are at risk for ivory now: Saudis like the small tusks for dagger-hilts.

'He didn't know he was at risk but like all young males he was confused. Even more so when I stupidly switched on my torch. He trumpeted and charged. I threw the torch away; he swerved and went after it!'

The torch lay beaming to itself in the bushes, the tusker tried to trample it, bellowing, slashing bushes, unable to put it out.

'I could see everything in the light! The guard slept. Luckily the elephant made too much noise to hear his snores.'

After an hour the tusker went away. By daylight they saw he had torn bushes apart and uprooted trees. A miracle he had missed them.

*

Green mountains, caressing drizzle: Niren and I are two thousand metres up at the Ghats' most northerly point. Nobly, he lends me his leech socks. 'They're only important for transects and *long* hikes.'

We walk up through forest over gaur tracks in mud, and out to mountain grass like no landscape I've ever seen. Something like the Lake District, but greener, larger: light huge restless geological shoulders of grass and bracken studded with dark-green pockets, the fragile, crucial evergreen jungle, *sholas*.

We walk up through mist-shreds to a ridge where three sambar are silhouetted against white muslin; outposts maybe of a herd. Niren once saw a tiger there against the mist, sitting on a rock slowly lashing its hanging tail. Maybe it, too, was watching sambar.

In *sholas* it is dark, leechy, mossy; the green-brown writhing stillness of Kerinci forest, but damper. Hanging swags, ferny fronds, a bright tree palm, mixed, close, overgrowing each other. Leeches wriggle up my legs. Something shakes a branch: langurs, not the endangered lion-tailed macaques that Ullas nominated to have this reserve created. He walked it, found their densest populations, and recommended the reserve.

'One troop,' whispers Niren, 'hangs about here. I hoped it might be them. Other troops are deeper in, further from the road. Wildlife is coming back slowly, now it's protected.'

A millipede curls before my feet into a ball like a striped wooden toy, yellow, black and shiny, trying not to be eaten. When we reach the ridge the sambar are gone. We sit on the tiger's rock, flip off leeches, look down on green, swooping mountainside. Sudden lightning comes, and thunder; the mist is darker, lower, we cannot see the peak. Half-way down a massive gaur bull, tall, humped, glistening and maroon, walks out of a *shola* below us and glares at a clump of bracken. It is November, fighting time for gaurs. He lowers his horns, tosses a bush, lifts his head, ears out like radar, creamy nose in cottonwool mist, and bellows.

He does not know we are there. We are voyeurs. There is something magical but unfair in watching a wild animal who does not see you. Alone, restless in his huge green luminous canvas, he attacks the bracken; we creep closer. Walking, freezing. Grandmother's Footsteps with a gaur. He swings his head up. We freeze. So does he, trying to make us out. He badly needs something to challenge. We are four legs on a slope. His eyes see movement, not shape. Like sambar, he is ideal tiger prey, any tiger that dared. He is what Sarah rudely calls cat food; but a miracle.

'*Huge* horns,' I breathe. 'Do gaurs charge people, much?'

'One gored a tourist to death: someone taking close-ups,' whispers Niren. 'A flash startled him. Usually they just move away.' We are close enough to see purple silky shadows ripple his skin. You tell their age by horn rings. I wouldn't like to try. Suppose he thinks we're another bull? Niren smiles, coughs politely, and the gaur trots off. He turns to stare, humphs to himself, trots further. Is gone, is mist.

'You only have to show you're human. I did that with a tiger once.'

Back at the car we flip off more leeches. My feet are fine. Niren's are threaded with blood. It drips on blue-grey stones.

'Niren, *thank* you! I'm sorry – I'm such a wimp.'

'Doesn't matter, a few leeches. Not like ticks. You have to be careful when you take *them* out. The heads break and stay embedded eight months. Very embarrassing, scratching all the time.'

Ticks usually go for the groin. As we drive off a leech waggles from my bare arm. You have to admire their cheek, waving with one end while sucking your blood with the other. I flick it out of the window. The mark stays for a week, a tiny badge of tropical zoology.

The evil road is steel-smooth through copper-green mountains, opening the forest to anyone who wants to damage it. God knows how much money was made in its construction.

'The forest officer used such *stupid* arguments to make it! His last was, "I've had twenty years' experience managing forests!"' When that man first came he was good. Now he's done more long-term damage to this unique terrain than anyone. Now he and his deputy are both against us.'

He stops to photograph a dead krait. Roadkill. Evidence. Thank God the Sumatran highway is full of holes. My first krait up close: three feet long, charcoal grey with ivory bands. You can see the lower flange frilled with the muscles that propel a snake forward. Snakes are all length. The car mashed it in two places; the lower belly is broken, neck severed, exposed windpipe white in red. The neat black head has flipped, black shiny eyes look back the way it came, the dangerous mouth, pearly cappuccino, a little open.

'This road was originally built for the mine. Now they want to upgrade it to a national highway! That would more than double the traffic. The highway department is so used to priority they don't bother about other departments. Would be the end of the king cobras. I saw a juvenile here trying to cross. It thought better and drew back.'

Some bends have lurid painted signs. A gaur. 'Save Bison!' A snake. 'Save King Cobra!' Then 'Save Blackbuck!' There are no blackbuck here, but the forester wrote a budget to get these signs, and also for unnecessary water gullies. This park has streams everywhere. But in India water projects always attract money. Gullies are a prime head of expenditure. They have them in Ranthambhore, so build them here, too.

At the Bhadra's source, the shallow riverbed is burnt brown sugar on a toffee-apple, letting green skin glow through. Niren scoops his hands and drinks from the river whose purity he has fought to save. I am trying to feel this strange double landscape, steep open hills and secret *sholas*, from a tiger's point of view. Light, then dark. In Nagarahole, Ullas found three tigers per square kilometre. Here, the density must be lower. All this open grass for prey, no cover for stalking (no wonder the tiger Niren saw was lashing its tail), but super-dense inside. The territory-battle here must play differently from the Sundarbans, or Kanha.

Round a bend is a fence, a monument. Pillars, graffiti, a dustbin! Years ago, there was a tiny wooden shrine here. Then a notice appeared on it: 'This should be restored.' The deputy warden, the DFO, said she'd look into it. Niren called a second time; again she stalled him. Three months later a stone plinth appeared. 'I thought I told you,' she said. 'I gave them permission.'

Shrines mean people, disturbance, traffic, commerce. Two and a half thousand people a day visit the temple in Sariska. Millions visit the one in Periyar; a million, the one in Ranthambhore. Shrines start small. Someone sees an odd-shaped stone, people feel spiritual in the wild. Then they destroy what they feel spiritual about by building a shrine. It goes commercial: you get litter, cars, a fair. Human excreta becomes a major problem.

Afraid they would lose the ridge above, source of the three main rivers, Niren asked the DFO asked to put up a fence, show that the foresters had *some* authority. He got calls from religious organizations saying not to interfere. But one dead krait today is king cobras gone tomorrow, and dead tigers the day after, like those at Terney.

Going down, the Bhadra keeps us company, sparkling through dense, steep, whiskery greens, jungle beside and below us: thousand-foot drops of mountainside. The loneliest, wildest place. A waterfall bursts out snow-white, flirting through sixty-foot tree-tops.

'He wanted to cement underneath that, so people could bathe! He built a pit; we stopped the rest. He's forgotten what the forest's *for*.'

We stay in bungalows by silky, rustling jungle. In the morning I am speckled with bites up to my waist. I fling back the sheet; dark ginger scatter silts away under the folds. I had lit a mosquito coil, sprayed repellent, never thought about *inside* the bed. I dress in the bathroom where a last leech from my clothes stands up on the tiles, a miniature elastic periscope. People in London say, *'Tigers?'* never thinking of sloth bears, kraits, elephants. But it's the invertebrates that get you.

Kudremukh mine is a dark red gash across two mountains where there should be grass, gaur, sambar. These huge green mountains and tropical *sholas* with their dark intricacies are so fragile. Wildlife First has a hydrologist sampling the water to show how iron ore sediments in the Bhadra river. In hard rain, he tests every hour. He sends everything off to be tested, posting the report to the Karnataka minister. The mine will appeal, and, one hopes, be rejected. A mining website is already indignant about the closure of this 'prestigious industry' which transports slurry concentrate by pipeline down the Ghats to Mangalore. The Supreme Court acted 'most casually'. This was 'the only mine of its kind in Asia'. Well, those slurry pipes leaked in the middle of fragile jungle, causing terrible damage, as Michiel in Vladivostock warned an oil-line might in the Amur leopard's last habitat.

Recently the company cut a new road into a *shola* without telling anyone. When Niren queried it, the new forester said, 'Well, we should listen to them, they've had a lot of experience.' Niren took photos, went to the media. 'The road was stopped – but the damage was done.'

The ministry supposed to protect this environment was granting constant extension permits to the mine. With the Forest Department's consent, Wildlife First took video evidence of the damage it does, showing villagers dipping hands into their fields and bringing them out black. This place has India's highest rainfall. In monsoons, the Bhadra sweeps iron sludge everywhere, saturating the soil's substructure. This builds up each year, solidifying in summer. Nothing grows. Local media showed it polluting the fields.

Before the court case, the company planned to cut into new hills. The mine had already caused massive erosion. Niren looks at it now with an architect's eye. 'To continue mining is madness.'

I am seeing Ullas's point in action. You need hard science. Qualified professionals who know technology can fight with genuine knowledge the vested interests defending damage they do by fake argument.

Now we stand above an enormous dam of silt, red unproductive schlock. A dam should make a resource for what is precious. This is its negative: a sump of barren waste, left when iron is extracted. They have cut down one mountain, wrecking the valley below, and dumped this in another valley, wrecking two. They raised the dam illegally, extending this stuff into a *shola*. I step to the edge with my camera. A guard runs out of a sentry box. 'No photo!'

'Because you're with me! I took photos and had them published before anyone knew it mattered. They're on our website now. *And* you're a foreigner.'

I stand and look. The top is a sheet of cracked silt. If the dam broke, this barren pinkness would bury the valley deeper than Pompeii. They wanted to build another silt dam, in a valley like the one where we saw the gaur. 'Excellent idea,' said their environmental consultant. His one small paragraph on wildlife said there was nothing significant there, just crows and rabbits. Rabbits? India has no rabbits. Wildlife First said an *independent* consultant should be appointed. Their own study of that valley showed thirty-four sambar, many gaur and tiger tracks.

'One ranger, when he began, thought animals were brought from Africa and put here! That's how dissociated city people are from the country. People don't know their own wilderness.'

We get in the car. The guard watches to make sure I take no photos. I see now. There are no victories. People are always trying to harm; you are always trying to stop them. They are always trying to stop you stopping them.

Another mountain, a different warden. Niren strides to the chief ranger's bungalow. I sit in the car. Two young heifers, chestnut and grey, eat grass; a cattle egret darts in and out of their feet as they crop. We are refused permission to enter. Niren has stopped them doing so much: he had to argue for permission to take me up the first mountain – that guard, too, had been afraid of what his boss would say. This one is a nice person but worried. He told Niren to ask the deputy conservator.

'It's ridiculous! The public has a right to enter the forest if they ask. He said, "You take photos of roads, print them in papers, make trouble for us in media. We can't let you in."'

In 1987, people were going in with guns, hunting. Niren nagged them to put up fences, gates. Now they close these against him.

'As soon as Ullas gets permission, all this will change.'

Indeed it will. The proof that conservation *can* stop damage will become unbearable. Next April, forest officers will raid Niren's office. From eleven in the morning till late at night, they will take documents, files, discs, a computer with private emails. Pointless time-wasting cases will follow, accusing Niren, Ullas, Wildlife First, people who have worked in Karnataka with approval (and thanks from the foresters) for years, of alleged trespass, photography, and monitoring without obtaining approval. Many charges will reflect what happens on the other side of the fence. Wildlife First are 'habitual liars'. They malign foresters' images 'through false news in newspapers', 'carry out systematic false information, show upright officers in bad light'. That hydrologist who sent water-sample reports to the state minister was 'trespassing'. So was the reputable cameraman (often used by the forest service itself) who made the film which established the pollution. All these were 'heinous criminal crimes'. Eighteen criminal cases will be put in the Karnataka courts. Litigation will be part of Ullas's and his team's lives for years, draining energy and manpower from protection and research. WWF India will warn Karnataka's chief minister the state is telling the international conservation community that India intimidates, harasses and defames great conservationists while the lobbies that harm wildlife flourish. Tigers *and* their defenders, in red weather.

Hearing all this from London, I will stupidly feel *I* am more upset than anyone. *They* knew it was war. So shocked – Niren and Ullas are the epitome of integrity – I email Debbie in Sumatra. She has just rescued a baby tapir from a poacher and lodged it in her bath, to the leopard cat's fury.

'Eeeeee,' Debbie emails, when she untangles them. For everyone in the international community, Ullas's work is a beacon. 'You certainly know how to depress a girl. Of course you're right about what's behind. It's not just interfering that gets up people's noses, it's *showing what should be done and isn't!* Everyone you've seen spends too much time dealing with local jealousy! Government, bureacracies . . . You identify and support good people, avoid useless ones. But, believe me, Ullas and his people will fight on. You lose a skirmish here, get a black eye there, but have to keep pushing. *Don't be dispirited!'*

She is right. The CEC will exonerate them. But poachers have it easier, meanwhile. The forest, elephants and tigers pay.

The last thing Niren shows me is a place from which villagers have recently moved. We drive through a gate, guarded by a boy on a water tank, to Bhadra's bank. Everything, grass and drizzle, is soft. Collapsed mud houses are returning to red mud. Grassy hillocks and hollows were once rubbish heaps. It said in the contract they wouldn't get a penny for their new houses till they demolished the old ones. The shallow river crossing, lushly overgrown, was where munching cows once stood. Now there is a heron, but Niren has seen gaur here, elephant, tiger.

We walk along the bank to a small hut. A young guard comes out, one of the anti-poaching team, thin with red-veined eyes. He speaks to Niren urgently. The state language is Kannada; many speak only Tulu. Niren speaks both; and Hindi, and English. We smile and shake hands; the guard gives Niren a sleeping-bag. Niren goes round the park constantly, watching, camping, while somehow keeping his architecture practice going.

'It's a big park. It takes a long time to go round. Soon as I've finished, it's time to start again. Last time I slept here I left this.'

The guards have not been paid for five months. They want Niren to help them get their salary. Relations with the lower field staff are fine.

Wildlife First encourages guards, runs anti-poaching camps, gives cash rewards for outstanding work, gives uniforms: caps, belt, shoes, socks.

'We got these men insurance policies too. They were on day contract, no insurance if injured by poachers! Why should they risk themselves protecting, if they're not helped when hurt?'

The boy at the gate says a tiger was right here yesterday morning. It jumped on that tank, saw him, jumped down and went away. Throughout my journey, if I'd been a day, an hour earlier, I might have seen dozens of tigers. Too bad. What matters is that they are there.

Chikmagalur is a country town surrounded by coffee plantations, India's biggest coffee-growing area. Except in Sumatra, my journey has run on instant coffee. Over real coffee I meet Praveen, who runs Wildlife First's website. Tall, luxuriantly black-bearded, with formidably tailored pale slacks, a thirtyish cosmopolitan with a Bangalore advertising business, he has survived Ullas's transect tuition, knows the zoology, and will introduce me to Bhadra, the regenerating forest. Niren hands me on like a baton. Tomorrow I go to Girish, the Bhadra man. Not my London friend; Girish is a Karnataka name.

Like Kanha, Bhadra is moist deciduous forest. It also has king cobras, a hundred and fifty elephants. Several hundred families left it last year. Praveen and I stop to get permission at the forest guardhouse. Relations are easier here. Wildlife First suggested building a free hostel for the guards' families. Otherwise, guards rent. They do not often see their families, but at least they are nearer now.

This air is soft, dark green, wet. No more open mountain. We drive up a lane that was formerly full of people and grazing cows. The meadow behind once held crops; Praveen has already seen chital there. The plaster in roofless mud walls flakes like cracking ice as roots take hold. Bushes wave from walls, others claw up to meet them. The forest is taking back its own. In *The Jungle Book*, elephants destroy the village that stoned Mowgli's human mother. A month later it is a dimpled green mound. After the monsoon, it is roaring jungle in full blast.

We drive into the jungle. Dozens of chital, grazing the view-lines, raise their heads. Some dart off, turn, look, vanish. Others stay. They are calming down, less afraid now that the villagers are gone and poaching has stopped. Spotted doves squat on the ground, Malabar parakeets flash blue underwings in tall trees, grey Malabar hornbills clatter in to roost. It is Malabar everything here, the world that Go A Way gave me two years ago. Malabar squirrels pour up and down trees. A thrush zooms past, sits on a high branch whistling like a kettle. The Malabar whistling thrush.

'We call it the Idle Schoolboy.'

The round brown drums in the branches are bee-hives. When honey buzzards and bee-eaters pierce them they fall and burst with furious bees. Now a rustle: a monitor lizard, the size and colour of a mongoose, flashes into a bush. Muntjac, red in the shadows. At a bend in the slippery mud track a langur hops over elephant dung, a serpent eagle is chased by a racket-tailed drongo and two sambar look up. One puts up her tail in alarm, then puts it down. The other does a soft stamp with her foot, another alarm sign. But they do not leave. Sambar are calming too, their numbers growing. The main tiger prey here is gaur and chital. Gaur were nearly wiped out by rinderpest, but are recovering.

Huge stands of bamboo, sixty feet above us, are brown and brittle after flowering, falling pale sprays rattling in wind, with jungle babblers flicking in and out. I touch a dead flower, tiny empty cases left by fallen seeds. Beneath is dark fresh tiger scat, but too much vegetation for pugmarks. Regenerating bamboo, regenerating tiger.

We bump along the track beside the Soma Wahini, one of the Bhadra river's main tributaries. This village was a kilometre long, a hundred metres wide, with paddy-fields beyond the river. Wild animals could not drink here: the village fenced off the river so that elephants would not enter the paddy. Now there is grass, and a thousand different plants roil over the track. More the grass, more the tiger. Praveen sighs.

'Grass! Ten years Girish has come here, talked to them about moving, checked poaching. This was bare earth, grazed by cows, three kilometres into the forest.'

Ullas's daughter did a scientific study on how this village fragmented the habitat of tigers and prey. Now behind green bamboo is a vast dark gaur bull. He looks at us, steps forward, eats more. There are others behind: a whole herd. Two calves skip. They lower white muzzles and graze.

'I've *never* seen gaur here! It's a critical tiger-conservation need, this voluntary resettlement. Everything's healing and regenerating here while the people are much better there. With Girish, you'll see.'

The gaur slip soft into shadows. Our wheels spin in sloshy red ruts; we get out and look at the flood of wrinkled amber, hidden rocks breaking its surface to spidery whorls. The other bank is a solid wall of bushes, trees, bamboo. Living here, villagers worried about snakes, sloth bear, leopards, tigers. One man carried his sick brother across here in the rains when the flood was twice as high, three times as fast; then ten miles to hospital. And carried the corpse back.

In the next abandoned village something moves in the gloaming.

'Elephant,' breathes Praveen, 'in what was a paddy-field. See his trunk swing? The villagers *wanted* to move. Said, "We can't live here. Elephants ruin our crops." They were consulted about the design for their houses. Different packages were worked out: everyone wanted different things. They're happy now. They were agriculturalists: when they were given land they knew what to do with it. You can't disrupt people everywhere. But protecting wildlife seriously means putting space between it and people.'

I hear Ullas saying, 'Human-rights groups say they live in harmony with nature. Rubbish! Crops where elephants take three-quarters and you spray them with shot so they die is not harmony! Outsiders see an illusion: idyllic peace. Not the conflict and damage.'

People, often tribal, live in most protected wildlife areas. It would be impossible and unjust to evict them all. Many have a long history of conservation. But traditional forest living evolved in pristine forest, not today's pressurized forest. No one I met in Bombay wanted to force them out, but felt that if they chose to stay they should not have roads. If you bring them roads, communication, power, schools and hospitals, the forests will go. And if the bamboo forest goes, the sound of the bamboo flute goes with it.

But people wanting to make money from road contracts ask for roads on forest-dwellers' behalf. Many NGOs are wonderful, but some have got rich by seeming to help tribal people. With a road, poachers take animals and exploit the people in whose name the road was made.

At Nagarahole, the villagers were tribal, not Hindu. They wanted to leave, but an NGO got hold of disaffected boys and persuaded them to say they would stay, promising self-rule, which they would only have got if they were over fifty per cent of the population. *Their* lives didn't change, but those of the NGO employees did. First they came on push-bikes, then in air-conditioned four-wheel drives. One got money for a tribal people's ambulance, refitted it as a van and sold it.

Most people in forests are agricultural communities with the same aspirations as people outside. India is developing fast. If you cannot put in roads, because the forests will die, you must take the people out. In the past, resettlement had a bad name; it was often more like eviction. Here it has been done well. Three hundred tribal families left Nagarahole. Rajendra Singh, well known as a people's leader, went down and talked to the resettled families. He said it was excellent. 'This is what *we* should be doing.' One of his party asked, how could he betray their cause? He said, 'Have you *been* to Nagarahole? I have. I trust what I've seen. I've betrayed nothing.'

Twilight. Shadow chital, gaur, a great horned owl. A teak plantation, near where a village had been. On the ground, in our lights, is a dappled yellow-brown snake, nine feet long. A python. As it slides away, cloud-rings on its skin elongate then shorten, glimmering in our lights' penumbra. It rests when it reaches shadow. The village used to burn along here; the pythons' eggs burned. Now they are safe. More regeneration.

I get back in. Can I stand on the back seat? I am a child with wind in my hair. Pristine forest now: the red track winds between pale, flanged, flying-buttressed trees, the dominant tree of this part of the forest, crocodile bark tree; then the Naked Maid of the Forest, a shining, ginger-pink ghost. The canopy is black-green tracery on primrose silk sky.

'Gaur,' Praveen whispers. 'No, *elephant.*'

Ahead is a long glade. At the end, crossing it, is a large grey shape, a young male with small tusks. Then comes a baby. Then a female who stops, turns, looks long at us. Her ears flap. A danger sign. She has a very young calf. She stands still, looking at us, takes a step forward – then turns, walks after the others. We drive to where they were. Three huge animals, vanished. Valmik calls the tiger the soul of Asia, but the elephant is too. I saw my first tiger from the back of an elephant. Except in China, Russia and the Himalayas, the two belong together.

The Forest Rest House on a red hill, surrounded by crimson blossom in the dusk. The caretaker leads me to a first-floor room with a paraffin lamp. From the terrace, Bhadra forest is deep indigo under dark sky. No lights.

'Five years ago, here at night you heard gunshots.'

After supper we drive to a neighbour: Roy, a retired coffee-planter. Jungle presses on his veranda. Tendrils throw cerise shadows on distempered walls.

'I found twenty wire traps yesterday on my perimeter,' he says. 'And tracks of a tiger and cub behind the house.'

Dressing for the forest in pre-dawn dark, I rummage for a torch. My canvas handbag is on the floor. It has bobbed in a kayak, sat on my back up that tree-slide in Kerinci; it never lets me down. I put my hand in and *zam*! The base of one finger is on fire. I pull it out in disbelief. Can't see anything in the dark. A pin? Thorn from the forest? I tip it out on the bed, find the torch, turn it on. Nothing. The usual junk, passport, mosquito spray, notebook, dead leaves. All through the jungle – mist, hush, wet trees, waking birds, pouring rain – my finger throbs. No tigers, but two hundred chital, enough for three or four tigers for a year. Sambar, muntjac, gaur. Tigers are sensibly sheltering from rain. Back in daylight, I see a scorpion on my bed. No African monster, just three inches, tail curled smugly to the side like a crochet hook. Never leave your handbag open on a tropical floor.

'We're having lunch with the Wildcats,' says Praveen, smiling. 'The next generation. The ones we'll hand on to.'

For ten years around Chikmagalur and Bhadra, Girish has organized younger volunteers, planters, lawyers and businessmen: the Wildcats. Trained by Ullas, these men now work in the community, explaining tiger conservation, watching what happens to the forest.

We drive up a crescented ridge above the reserve. This outspur of the Western Ghats, studded with coffee plantations, is the Bababudan Hills, which cut the reserve nearly in two. The sanctuary's centre is a narrow corridor, bounded on the west by Bhadra reservoir.

These hills are called after a fifteenth-century Sufi saint. He went to Mecca, pocketed five coffee beans from Arabia's closely guarded stores, and planted them here, where coffee has grown ever since. The British grabbed the best places, leaving a legacy of plantations that exists today. Karnataka has up to sixty thousand.

My eyes have changed since Kerala's tea plantations. Then I just reacted to landscape. Now I wonder how wild animals use it. With low tea plants it is civets, jackals, muntjac, leopard. With coffee it can be tigers. Coffee grows best under bigger trees, so the big animals come. Three wild tuskers went walkabout here recently.

We drive up the greenest hill, on a road of shiny dark coffee leaves fronted by blazing poinsettias thirty feet high, and reach a large, low brick house. Sloping tiled roof, white walls, pierced brick, a rose-garden. Below is the blue-mist undulating canopy of Bhadra forest. Tall trees dance in the foreground, shadow-puppets against a screen. A smiling young man of twenty-five comes out, wearing a loose turquoise shirt. Shreedev, one of the Wildcats: this is his plantation. Inside is cool, low-ceilinged, shadowy. 'This is our old house,' he says. 'I was brought up here. We've built another where my parents live but this is our centre of operations.'

My first coffee plantation. I love it. I am staying here tonight, for the forest ranger has booked his yoga class into the Rest House. We walk down the road to where a tiger killed a cow. The smell hits us at the bend. We crouch through bushes into a grassy dell where villagers cremate their dead. The smell is *much* stronger. 'Under here.' We peer in. Just a few flies and that smell. The tiger dragged it here, ate crouching like us, and returned to finish its meal.

This is outside the reserve. Shreedev often gets transient tigers. A young one died recently of starvation, as Ullas says many tigers do. But one has a territory here. Shreedev has seen it far off, too distant to tell the sex. All plantations have wild animals; low densities, but there. The neighbouring plantation has a tigress with a cub. People accept that tigers kill cows; the Wildcats help them get compensation fast. But it is so easy to take revenge. Pesticide or fertilizer in the carcass and that's that. Poaching here depends on the social level. A villager gets two dollars for a chital; people want meat at festivals. For tigers, here, poaching is not organized. Five tigers are known to have died in the last few years; all were accidents. One in a deer snare, one at night when someone fired at eyes.

'At higher levels, it's changing,' says Shreedev, as we walk back. 'My friends, plantation-owners' sons, thought it macho to take lanterns, jeeps and guns into the forest at night. But that's declining. The shame of court is a big deterrent. You're finished in the community. A father's shamed if the son is seen arrested.'

Shreedev can eel up to a cousin, whisky in hand at a party, saying '*What?* Do *you* do it too?' and shame him from within. Ullas's point again: eyes on the forest, *informed* conservation at every social level.

24

TO A GOOD PATH THROUGH
THE FOREST

'That's the school closed because of man-eating leopards.'

There is a mystique about Girish. People speak of him with a smile but a touch of awe. He is kindly, but I suspect pure steel beneath. He has a neat, close beard, hair like a black velvet cap, hunched shoulders, deep laugh-lines around his eyes, and is driving us in his Gypsy jeep to the northern part of Bhadra sanctuary. We gaze at a beige building in Kardu, a railhead town en route. In 1994–5 leopards killed old people and children in villages around here. First a six-year-old girl, then an old lady. Her son was a forester; Girish begged him to keep the part-eaten body so that the leopard – they thought just one, then – would return and they could shoot it. He refused. Eight more died, one only six kilometres from the town centre. No one left home after dusk. Anyone falling off a bike claimed insurance from leopard injury. Professional hunters shot two leopards, but then a boy was taken from behind his mother as she washed clothes at a well. Villagers gave chase, the leopard dropped him; he survived. Then a leopard took a boy watching his parents winnowing. Hunters shot two more leopards. One had a human organ in its stomach. Then a toddler, crossing the road with his brother and sister, was taken before his sister, walking behind him, reached the kerb. Then they shot twenty-two leopards. Two more contained human organs.

'We had no idea there were so many in twenty built-up kilometres!'

No one knows why that man-eating started. But leopards in such areas have no forest for normal prey like boar and hares. So it is dogs, sheep . . . There had also been illegal quarrying and railway-gauge widening. Both used migrant workers who did not cremate. They were working illegally, so left their dead in scrub. Leopards must have found them, as in India's flu epidemic of 1918 which killed a million people. Villagers in western Uttar Pradesh, where two rivers meet to form the Ganga, normally cremated their dead, but unable to cope with the numbers they started to put live coals in corpses' mouths and tip them off cliffs. After the flu died out a male leopard, used to this easy diet, began to kill people. In eight years, he killed 125. He clearly liked the taste: he killed goats Jim Corbett put out but left them uneaten and went on to human prey.

He was outrageously stealthy, this leopard. To get one woman victim he walked over fifty sleeping people, then carried her back over them, just scratching someone's foot as he passed. He took one of two men smoking on a balcony. The other only noticed when the hookah fell. He was unusually large, very strong, and killed instantly, four teeth in the throat. Or so Corbett found, tracking him. In 1926 he shot it, and gazed at it dead. It had been the most feared animal in India, and scared him more than any other. But,

> Here was no fiend, who while watching me through the long night hours had rocked and rolled with silent laughter at my vain attempts to outwit him . . . Here was only an old leopard . . . whose crime, not against the laws of nature but the laws of man, was that he had shed human blood that he might live.

'We get power here,' says Mallaiah, grinning, a small old man with springy grey hair and a baggy, very clean white shirt over khaki shorts. These men have been resettled from Bhadra forest. Girish worked with an excellent forest officer, Yatish, who arranged the resettlement. They solved the complex problems together: nothing could have happened without the forest service. One man in check shirt-sleeves and knitted waistcoat sweater now talks anxiously to Girish: his brother has taken money for land due to him. All watch Girish as if he delivers miracles. Girish listens, head forward, with a smile. We walk past maize belonging to Raju Shato, a middle-aged man in slacks and flip-flops. Smiling, he spreads a silky stalk on my hand like gold coin. In the forest he got ten bags a field; here he gets ninety-five. I know Mallaiah means electricity, cooking and light, but 'power' means more than that. This young man on a shiny motorbike is Najendra, once one of the worst poachers in the forest. But he had no motorbike there. Anyone with money lived outside. There have been twenty weddings since they moved. No one wanted their daughters to go into remote forest.

'They hated me before: I stopped them poaching. Now they love me because I've brought them this.'

There are 373 families, a bus station, shopping complex, school. The white houses around a hill in rows, off a tree-lined main road, have tiled roofs and little gardens. Some one window, some two. Green paddy-fields behind, a belt of trees. Extraordinary, to have moved from forest where they never saw open sky, except in the fields raided by wild animals, to this openness and safety. Three thousand years of civilization in one bound. How do the children like it? They are at school so I get the parents' perspective: the hospital is nearby. 'In the forest, it was forty kilometres to walk.'

Everyone clings to Girish. To save wildlife, he has become a rehabilitation agent. These people have joined the world for the first time. He spent months winning their trust, getting their input into house design. They have never been part of a wider community and want all problems to disappear at once. He listens, encouraging them to do things themselves. Encroachers have already built thatched shacks nearby, taking advantage of the settlement. They break a law when they put up a roof, but once it is on, it is against the law to remove it. The villagers resent them.

'They want me or the government to solve all problems, don't understand when officials change and the new one's less friendly. Before, I was the problem. I kept turning up to see they weren't poaching. Now I'm the solution. All for wildlife.'

Two old men stand under a tree, waiting for granddaughters to come home from school. Off a bus now, not walking through jungle with elephants and bears. In the forest, these men lived in different villages. If they wanted to chat, they walked for three hours. Now they have a social life.

'The forest was a cocoon. It was specially hard on women. Here if a man beats his wife he gets booked in the courts. We've had some cases already, they are seeing the law at work. In the forest nothing was done. Socially, they are getting more aware.'

Girish has known them for twenty years. Their life before was hunting and illegal liquor-making. Now they sell sugar cane, eight hundred rupees a ton, money they have never seen. The Kudremukh forest-dwellers asked to move when Niren showed them this and they saw how pleased the Bhadra settlers were.

'How did you start all this?' I ask Girish, as we leave.

'I heard about Ullas's work. He and his friend Chinappa did transects at Nagarahole between 1986 and 1989. People like me, worried about what was happening to our wildlife, turned up. They trained us. It was *very* tough. Both were exacting masters. They saw who couldn't cope, who kept coming back despite ticks, leeches, elephants. Then we helped train others.'

A pink-striped caterpillar inches over a puddled yard to the unsafe shelter of Girish's Gypsy, standing by the Forest House at Bhadra reservoir. The caretaker says three poachers have been caught in Bandipur with a dead elephant, bear, otters, langur: they are confessing, naming five more.

Wildlife First educate villagers, show them why poaching is against their own long-term interests, support forest officers enforcing the laws. There are 162 villages around Bhadra sanctuary. Up here they steal mainly timber. Until 1987 there were no gates or protection. Men went in openly with guns to shoot and get drunk. When the dam was built around 1960, some villages were submerged and the people relocated.

'Only time a dam did any good. They were *very* hardcore poachers. Timber smugglers. But they're at the forest edge now, and still come in.'

They used to come seventy at a time, and hitch logs to bullocks who pulled them home. Girish stopped a bullock cart once; they ran away and left him with it. But the area now has an excellent forest ranger.

'He's tough. In this year's drought, people wanted to graze cows in the forest. He said no! You can graze *there* but not *here*. He kept them out. It's difficult for him. The Forest Department is the only one that says no.'

Light fades on blue hills across the reservoir's lapping grey smiles.

'People in cities don't think where water comes from. They turn taps. Water is priceless but we make it freely available. Only when you put a cost on a thing do you think where it's from. Rivers come from forest.'

We set off for the forest in the Gypsy. I hope the caterpillar is gone. At the sanctuary gate a semi-tame crippled chital hangs round the guardpost. Then we are on a red cart-track full of puddles. Some warden kept part of the budget for repairing the road and did a bad job, but that bit of percentage-taking is good for wild animals. Better a bumpy road than the new ones being built through Chinese reserves.

'But if he cuts down on anti-poaching patrols, we're after him.'

Tiger pugmarks flower in red mud. Was it after that lame chital? No, here's scat; it dined extremely well on something else. I didn't know when I began how piles of shit lift the heart. We stop at a bridge on a creek.

'I saw a tiger here with Ullas. Early morning. We were standing on the bridge and it came out from under, just here. We woke it up. It was sleeping beneath. It walked off up the stream.'

Forest closes in. We are very close to a bull gaur standing in mud. Much bigger than the Gypsy. Mud-splashed ivory stockings, ivory muzzle. The foresters put a salt lick here two days ago. We have stopped him enjoying it. His massive beautiful cow-face, framed in wide ears and heavy horns, turns towards us, tense. A langur calls an alarm; he flicks to listen. Tigers, Ullas has found, eat bulls when they can. Now poachers are gone, tigers are what this one-ton animal really fears. He needs to read the forest all the time: smells, movement, calls. He snorts softly. His nostrils bubble mud. He looks completely menacing, but humps round, unsticks himself from the mud, walks away.

Through the open window, wet bushes lash in. So does a wood spider with lemon-flecked knees, bigger than my hand. Girish scoops it gently out, but it likes the interior, or its filaments do, and it swings back in at my window. I gather it up in Girish's cap and float it into wet leaves. It sits there deciding where to try next.

A remote guardpost, two brick huts where guards sleep and cook.

Three slight men in flip-flops run up: their kitchen has been assaulted by an elephant, who smelt something he liked, probably vegetables, knocked in the wall, got hurt, was furious, charged, pinned them in the other hut all day. The kitchen looks as if a bus ran into it. He tore off half the roof, trampling pans and dish-racks into the rubble. Of all things in the jungle, says Kipling, an enraged elephant is the most wantonly destructive:

> They heard a crash of falling beams and thatch behind the
> walls. They saw a shiny, snaky black trunk lifted for an instant,
> scattering sodden thatch. There was another crash, followed by
> a squeal. Hathi had been plucking off the roofs of the huts as
> you pluck water-lilies, and a rebounding beam had pricked
> him. He needed only this to unchain his full strength.

But that was at Mowgli's suggestion, letting in jungle on the village that stoned his mother. This real elephant, like the bees in Kudremukh, attacked his own protectors. Don't expect thanks from the wilderness. Your thanks is that it is still here.

It is darker now. A great horned owl is a grey-fawn bug-eyed Buddha on a branch. Two gaur bulls click each other's horns in a slow-motion fight more ritual than lethal. Lightning runs vibrato overhead. The canopy is black wriggle-silhouettes against pink sky. Little frogs leap over the path.

'Can we stand a moment in the forest, Girish?'

We get out. Around us are red trunks and stillness. A mongoose hustles across the trail. Between trees, three chital tilt their heads, ears moving like loose leaves. They float away. Far off a gunshot, then silence. 'Maybe a fire-cracker,' Girish breathes, 'or poachers. I'll tell the guards.'

We get back into the Gypsy. Two sambar leap over the track. What are they running from? I have only seen tourist tigers, this is my last forest, oh, I would love to see . . .

Childish, I tell myself fiercely. You cannot *plan* to see a tiger: it is like planning to fall in love. It is a privilege to be in this darkening forest where tigers whose footprints I have seen are on the move. Somewhere. They are what matters. 'We've seen so much, maybe it's better if there are some things we *don't* see,' Schaller said to Peter Matthiesson in *The Snow Leopard*. Still—

'A tiger,' I say, as we bump between pink-ginger trunks, Naked Maids of the Forest blushing in the headlights like tinted sepia, 'would look wonderful coming along that path, between red trees.'

Girish's voice is that of my own better self: 'How can you ask for a tiger? We've seen wonderful things.'

'I just thought,' I say lamely, 'those colours . . .'

Girish stops. Switches off the engine. Walking down the trail towards us is a leopard. By the time I see, it is aware of us. In that first split second only Girish sees that wonderful thing, a wild animal thinking itself alone. I see it leap and crouch behind grass five feet away, close as the stove is to my kitchen table at home. It stays there motionless, ears down, unblinking: even a blink can betray. Leopards do not have white eye-patches above the eyes, do not growl or make themselves look big and frightening, as tigers do. The tactic they evolved is to flatten themselves and hide. That is why they are killed in villages; villagers surround and clobber them.

'A female,' breathes Girish. 'They're that size.'

Emily Dickinson's pard. But this one has kept her Asia. Spotted dun gown, clear mustard eyes whose *tapetum lucidum* condenses us, for her, in this dim light. And she, for us, is gold jigsaw in grass, and also an emblem of hope. We are utterly still, all three of us, watching.

Look for a tiger and you find a leopard. If you do not go into the forest you find nothing. I am a world away from those wine-bar leopards where my journey began. You have to go into the dark and trust that loss will turn into vision, light will come.

'You can understand the true conditions of life,' says Darwin, 'only if you use your imagination to hold on to a sense of the ruthlessness of the natural forces that could waste the bright surface.' He spent a lifetime pondering the structures beneath, but he loved that surface passionately. In June 1832, it delighted him outside Rio de Janeiro. 'No art could depict so stupendous a scene,' he wrote in his diary. Climbing Corcovado mountain he could not walk a hundred yards without 'being fairly tied to the spot by some new & wondrous creature'. It was there that he began formulating in diaries the insight into what was later, in 1873, named ecology: 'how exactly the animals and plants in each region are adapted to each other . . . Nature, when she formed these animals and these plants, knew they must reside together.'

A hundred and seventy years later, we walked there too. Corcovado now had a mountain car and a giant Christ statue, cocooned in mist. But afterwards, in drizzly twilight, we went up a forested mountain, secondary jungle grown back over a Portuguese plantation. This really was rainforest. Fritz our guide plunged off the main path through trees, demonstrating relentlessly in a downpour the hollowness of the Telephone Tree, which Indians tap to send messages. Umbrella wheels above our heads, green against black. I had open sandals, he wore trainers, but Fritz had stout boots and, suddenly, two sticks. He led us up mossy boulders by a stream.

In Rio Zoo, a notice in the reptile house had said Brazil had seven kinds of *cascavel*. 'Let's sing,' I said suddenly. Hand in wet hand, single file, stopping each other slipping, we sang every song we both knew. Rain drummed, the stream splashed, Fritz led us up slippery jungle in the dark. Then a clearing, a hut, a fireplace of blue tiles, a surprised guard making *caipirinhas* of sugar liquor. Round the walls were posters of far more than seven kinds of *cascavel*. Now I knew what that word meant. Did they come in here? Fritz and the guard laughed. One got in here two days ago. It had coiled under the chair I sat in.

'Fritz, *were there rattlesnakes on that path?*'

'I've often seen them there. They lie in wait for frogs by the stream. You're all right if you don't get between them and their frog.'

One best description of how it feels to be with the person you love is by Louis MacNeice.

> Time was away and she was here
> And life no longer what it was,
> The bell was silent in the air
> And all the room one glow because
> Time was away and she was here.

All the room aglow; even soaking wet with seven kinds of rattlesnake beating at the door.

Now, gazing at the leopard as she looks at us – *will they hurt me, will I hurt them?* – I suddenly think: I can leave him there now, in that forest, along with the person I was with him. Let them drink *caipirinhas* on that mountain unaware of snakes in their Eden: unaware that we will leave them behind, our shadow-souls, and waste the bright surface of what we made.

And to the real person living his separate life I can say what I am saying fervently in silence to this leopard: go in peace. Like a medieval saint, holding one hand open, to show there is no weapon. It's all right. I wish you a good path through the forest.

But where do I stand now on the big question: tiger no, or tiger yes? This leopard is not a tiger, I was not given that to see. But she is a miracle herself. I can never see the forest as she does, know her consciousness, but I need her to be here. She is real, not a Borges fiction. Wonderful to know, as Auden said, even when we can't see or hear you, that you are around. And she *could* have been a tiger. Thirty to forty breeding tigresses, said Ullas. A population of over a hundred, if Bhadra is well managed.

No hope in hell of that, Valmik would say. And oh, maybe pessimism is right: in six months' time, spring 2004, as the series of cases begins against Niren, Ullas and Wildlife First, the worst fire Bhadra has ever seen will rage, destroying the dark peaceful secret mass I looked down on under the moon with Praveen. For *twenty-four hours* it will be left to burn. People will suspect, Valmik will say, it was begun deliberately. Those who wanted to remove bamboo were making their point. (Dead bamboo? Fire hazard. Must be removed.) Big animals will run. Little ones, hiding fawns, reptiles, small animals, baby birds, maybe this leopard's future cubs, will burn.

So what do I think now? Tigers *yes if*? That word, title of the poem in Mr Reddy's study, is vital. *If* the CEC monitors and enforces India's laws, the best wildlife laws in the world? But it sees only one in a hundred violations, it needs more staff; by 2005 it will be spending much of its time on central government files, which demonstrate tragically how makers of the law become breakers of the law. More harmful than any poacher are people putting their initials to proposals releasing forest land to mines, roads, irrigation projects.

By March 2005 even Ullas's optimism will be dimmed. There will be rumours that the Director of Wildlife Preservation (and Project Tiger's Director's boss) wants to ban radio telemetry and bird banding, the kind of scientific monitoring which is vital to keep track of what is happening to the wildlife, on the grounds that such studies are invasive and 'bad'. That is how far apart the bureacracy is from proper science-driven conservation. Our tiger population is like someone wasting away gradually from leprosy, Ullas will tell the *Indian Express*. Failures are covered up by official 'reviews' of tiger reserves and tiger projects, generated by lucrative consultancies given to people of dubious ability and integrity.

If bureaucrats managing India's forests start respecting real science, stop seeing forest management as making money? But can they, ever? In 1992 the poaching crisis was revealed. Thirteen years later it is worse, and there is no national wildlife crime cell to enforce the law. Meanwhile livestock increases constantly. Villagers have to graze cows in forest land because powerful local interests illegally grab common village land; so tigers eat cows and are poisoned. We cannot save India's forests with today's system, says Valmik. Good NGOs and scientists have no say in running forest land. There are some fantastic forest officers, maybe eighty out of eight thousand. But many are dropouts from other services, third-rate graduates of engineering colleges. Good ones are harassed, get shifted to where they cause state politicians less trouble; greedy corrupt ones are encouraged. There is no central control to whom they are responsible.

If India can change its system? Russia banned tiger shooting first, but in 1973 India saved its tigers from the brink. If only, with all the brilliance and knowledge there is here, India could make another such leap now. Get itself, like Russia and Kerinci, a Tiger Team which acts immediately on tiger–human conflict and masterminds the never-ending war on wildlife crime. Unless a strong *political* commitment to reversing the decline is demonstrated now, says Ullas, by political leaders cutting across party lines, tiger decline will continue to its logical conclusion in the next few decades. There are many senior forest officials who get extra money by dismantling nature piece by piece, promoting commercial penetration of protected areas on superficial 'pro-people' grounds. But protection at the grass roots, guards, equipment, vehicles, patrolling systems, wages paid to lower staff, is less than half what it was in the mid-1980s. Tigers are dying because of tiger poaching, deer poaching, the fragmenting and disturbance of forests. Ullas wants a professionally trained wildlife service. The current anti-science culture in the forest bureaucracy means MOEF officials can inject their personal whims into wildlife policies. Overseeing science in reserves should be given to the Ministry of Science and Technology. At higher levels, forest officers should have five years' training in biology, management and law enforcement. Lower positions should be manned by genuine forest-dwelling people with traditional skills suited for nature protection. This should make my brother and his friends happy: turn the original forest inhabitants into the forest's government-backed guardians.

Is the *if* a dream? This is not my country. Mine is not innocent here, either in the past or now. The problems are so large.

My journey was about stopping being wilfully blind but also about survival and hope. Eyes wide open, you have to go on hoping. All over Asia I have seen people making a dangerous stand to protect wilderness in the tiger's name. Against greedy men who think they are above the law, against ignorant people who want to feather their nest and do things the way they always have without interference, and also desperately poor people who eat only rice, need food for their cows and children, and are hammered by the corruption of the greedy and the ignorant. Sumatra's rural poor are worse off since the forests were felled. What will Lao villagers do when they have emptied the forest and sold all the wildlife to Vietnamese or Chinese dealers for batteries that will also die?

This war will go on as long as human civilization stays the way it is. There are no victories. But in wilderness is the preservation of the world. I believe in India, with all its brilliance, science, justice, passion. It saved tigers once. Can't it do it again? Maybe it's bashing my head against a few hundred facts but I also, still, believe in the good.

Here, so close to this wild leopard, I'll go for hope.

The red trail shines with puddles, trunks are roan pillars against black velvet, rain is soft Morse on the canopy. I am hardly breathing, nor is Girish; we are watching, she is watching, everything is still except shushing rain. It is possible to fall out of love and find riches along the way. Nature, outside and in, can still surprise.

An ancient Tamil poem I saw translated in London's Underground, but composed very near here two thousand years ago, runs through my head, linking itself more to this leopard than past love:

> What could my mother be to yours? What kin is my father
> to yours? How did you and I ever meet? But in love
> our hearts have mingled like red earth and pouring rain.

The leopard makes a decision. She springs up and away into the shadows. Her coat is smoke-rings closing and opening on gold, a festival of lights.

POSTSCRIPT, FEBRUARY 2006

Since I finished my journey, the tigers' weather has become redder.

In India, in March 2005, Sariska tiger reserve in Rajasthan said it had no more tigers, that they had all been poached during the monsoon. India's prime minister said that their country was facing its "biggest crisis in the management of wildlife". I saw two tigers in November 2005, one in Nagarahole in South India, right beside me and one in Corbett National Park, Uttar Pradesh: a young tiger, climbing out of a pool, shaking itself like a dog.

In any case, India's tiger numbers fell drastically in 2005. A new market has arisen for tiger skins and the poaching mafia is happy to oblige. Today, the people buying fresh tiger skins in large quantities are Tibetan entrepreneurs, newly enriched by selling caterpillar fungus to China and Japan for Asian medicine. They wear the hides at festivals where fresh leopard and tiger skins are on open sale in their markets. As I watched tigers in Karnataka and Kumaon, poachers in Rajasthan admitted shooting twenty-two others (out of a likely thirty) in India's star reserve, Ranthambhore. "The tiger cries until it dies", the ringleader explained when caught. He shot them at night with home-made bullets, twenty yards from forest guards.

Panna has lost half its tigers. Raghu Chundawat, one of India's two internationally acclaimed tiger biologists, who pointed out the high levels of poaching to the forest service, is still refused permission to research there.

In November 2005, Namdapha reserve in Arunachal Pradesh said it had only one tiger left, and that had not been seen for some time. Namdapha, a unique biosphere, once had all four of the subcontinent's big cats; snow leopard, clouded leopard, tiger, leopard. Back in 2002, it claimed to have 61 tigers – this was probably a lie. The figures were massaged to cover up poaching by the Lisu tribe (originally from Myanmar) who have settled inside the reserve and killed its tigers. When evicted they burn forest posts and camps. When caught they wriggle free and attack patrols in revenge. Even the staff are said to poach deer and feast on them. Both infrastructure and morale are in tatters.

Twelve, in fact, out of India's twenty-seven tiger reserves are in ruins. To cover up how much poaching there is, forest officers say tigers have "migrated". (Something tigers do not do. They stay in the territories they fight for.) In despair, Valmik Thapar brought out a book documenting India's tiger conservation until October 2005, showing that the bloodiest battles for the tiger are against its legal protectors, the forest service, and that the reason India is losing its national animal is the service's mismanagement of wildlife. He documents forest officers persecuting anyone who exposes poaching, accusing conservationists of smuggling tigers, prosecuting them for trespass, trying to open false files on them – anything, to smear people exposing how at risk India's tigers truly are.

Thapar now believes armed guards must police the forests, and human

beings be entirely separated from tigers for the safety of both. But India is currently debating a "tribal bill" to give land to all human forest dwellers, which
would wreck forests from within and destroy the tribal societies which could,
under a different system, provide forests with expert protection. Today, says
Thapar, India's tiger protection is "a shambles". Project Tiger has not yet
released funds to pay for a new relocation of villages (who are keen to leave)
out of the forest at Nagarahole. But it *has* paid for a costly update to its pugmark count: a count of tigers who are vanishing daily and can only be protected properly by frequent patrols. Project Tiger's Steering Committee, supposed
to meet regularly, did not meet for over two years until the prime minister con-
vened it in April 2005. Every institution connected with protecting tigers, says
Thapar, "requires reform."

In Russia, poachers have killed Dale's longest-running radio-collared tiger,
Olga. And in July 2005 China was reportedly considering revoking its ban on
selling bones of captive tigers from tiger farms, arguing that this could "fund
conservation". The WWF has reminded the world of what this threat means for
wild tigers and hopes the Chinese government will, said a spokesman, "come
out and say they are not going to do it".

Sumatra has the most dramatic after-story. Kerinci Seblat National Park,
where I saw tiger footprints, is one of the largest and last unfragmented blocks
of forest in Asia: 10,000 square miles of tropical hill, montane and lowland hill
forest. It is recognized as one of the most important tiger reserves in the world,
and the last best chance of Sumatran tigers surviving into the twenty-second
century. There are known to be more than eighty: the largest single tiger population in Sumatra. In 2005, Unesco gave this park World Heritage status. Jambi
province has twice pledged its commitment to conserving it, and in return
received World Bank support for sustaining the forest edge communities.

But in mid-2005, one village asked permission to make a footpath to the
coast through what researchers always urged should be part the secure core
zone. The park director, unfortunately, said yes. This started an orgy of road-
planning. Agricultural interests had wanted roads for years: this was their
chance. One road would bisect the park in the north; another would go through
Sipurak, the park's most important biodiversity hotspot, with many species
that depend on intact original habitat, and one of the most important areas in
the world for tigers, where in 2004 Sumatran tigers were filmed in the wild for
the first time. But Jambi's deputy governor announced as confirmed a major
road building plan, not discussed with the park, less than a year after the park
got World Heritage status. "If roadbuilding goes ahead," Debbie emailed,
"tigers will be extinct here in twenty years. It will open up their last safe havens
to poachers, loggers and farmers. Jambi province has taken the tiger for its mascot – but it will be responsible for the extinction of Indonesia's last surviving
tiger species."

The ecological damage would also mean social disaster. The only people to
benefit would be illegal loggers (whose syndicates are already logging the
park), plantation owners (they began staking land along the expected routes),

and hunters, who would now be able to get at tiger, elephant, clouded leopards and bird species that have been almost wiped out in more accessible areas.

And, as in the Amazon, traditional local communities, already marginalized and intimidated by migrant farmers and illegal loggers, would suffer. Crime has rocketed, and in some villages local people are outnumbered by newcomers taking political control; local people have lost their land rights; Jambi Province does not protect them. Hundreds of thousands of farmers depend on the watershed forests; people in riverside communities are already being drowned and killed by flash floods and landslides caused by illegal land clearance and logging, which always go with new roads; fish have been killed off by floods and sedimentation. The people orchestrating land clearance pay no taxes or reafforestation duties on illegally logged timber, so local communities get nothing back from the loss of their own forest.

In February 2006, bulldozers began clearing a five metre wide road (with massive damage and disturbance), moving three kilometres a day into pristine forest of the kind I walked in. Twenty men working by day, ten at night. All, allegedly, funded by the (very poor) forest edge communities. All started by that fatal original permission for a small gravel path.

But a miracle happened. The road *is* being stopped. Conservation, of community and forest, pride in forest heritage, has taken real hold in Sumatra. Some people in local and central government do support their unique park. The meeting at which they acted was a wonderful demonstration, said Debbie, of how local governments, forestry officers and local NGOs *are* achieving things. The Bupati, head of district government in Sungai Penuh (where I stayed), was the only local government leader who stood up on World Tiger Day in October 2005 and demanded action to stop tiger trafficking. Now he was incandescent with rage. He said Kerinci would be "shamed in the eyes of the world" if they let this happen!

"I feel more optimistic today for the future of Sumatra rainforest and conservation in general than for years," Debbie emailed. "I have seen local government leaders shrugging off the demands of their monied constituents and business lobby, bravely and actively supporting conservation of their national park."

The eyes of the world. By a biological geographic accident, the eyes of the world *are* on the tiger range states, above all on the one that has most tigers. Each state has bitter vicious local problems which all come down to greed versus integrity in the end. It is still not too late. The tigers are there and they are resilient animals. If India can act to protect them as decisively as Kerinci has - if reforms can happen - India could still, even now, have twenty thousand tigers.

The tiger cries until it dies. I began my journey five years ago. Today, Februray 2006, does seem to be a turning point.

"You have a choice, do something or do nothing," said the wildlife vet John Lewis.

You are your actions.

POEMS

John Donne 'A Nocturnal upon St Lucy's Day, Being the Shortest Day'

'Tis the year's midnight, and it is the day's,
Lucy's, who scarce seven hours herself unmasks;
   The sun is spent, and now his flasks
   Send forth light squibs, no constant rays;
     The world's whole sap is sunk;
The general balm th'hydroptic earth hath drunk,
Whither, as to the bed's-feet, life is shrunk,
Dead and interr'd; yet all these seem to laugh,
Compar'd with me, who am their epitaph.

Study me then, you who shall lovers be
At the next world, that is, at the next spring;
   For I am every dead thing,
   In whom Love wrought new alchemy.
     For his art did express
A quintessence even from nothingness,
From dull privations, and lean emptiness:
He ruin'd me, and I am re-begot
Of absence, darkness, death: things which are not.

All others, from all things, draw all that's good,
Life, soul, form, spirit, whence they being have;
   I, by Love's limbec, am the grave

Of all that's nothing. Oft a flood
   Have we two wept, and so
Drown'd the whole world, us two; oft did we grow
To be two Chaoses, when we did show
Care to aught else; and often absences
Withdrew our souls, and made us carcasses.

But I am by her death (which word wrongs her)
Of the first nothing, the elixir grown;
   Were I a man, that I were one
   I needs must know; I should prefer,
     If I were any beast,
Some ends, some means; yea plants, yea stones detest,
And love; all, all some properties invest;
If I an ordinary nothing were,
As shadow, a light and body must be here.

But I am none; nor will my sun renew.
You lovers, for whose sake the lesser sun
   At this time to the Goat is run
   To fetch new lust, and give it you,
     Enjoy your summer all;
Since she enjoys her long night's festival,
Let me prepare towards her, and let me call
This hour her vigil, and her eve, since this
Both the year's, and the day's deep midnight is.

Emily Dickinson 'Water Is Taught by Thirst'

Water – is taught by Thirst –
Land – by the Oceans passed –
Transport – by Throe –
Peace – by its Battles told –
Love – by Memorial Mold –
Birds – by the Snow.

John Donne 'Song'

Sweetest love, I do not go
   For weariness of thee,
Nor in hope the world can show
   A fitter love for me;
     But since that I
Must die at last, 'tis best
To use myself in jest
   Thus by feigned deaths to die.

Yesternight the sun went hence,
   And yet is here today;
He hath no desire nor sense,
   Nor half so short a way:
     Then fear not me,
But believe that I shall make
Speedier journeys, since I take
   More wings and spurs than he.

O how feeble is man's power,
   That if good fortune fall,
Cannot add another hour,
   Nor a lost hour recall!
     But come bad chance,
And we join to it our strength,
And we teach it art and length,
   Itself o'er us to advance.

When thou sigh'st, thou sigh'st not wind,
   But sigh'st my soul away;
When thou weep'st, unkindly kind,
   My life's blood doth decay.
     It cannot be
That thou lov'st me, as thou say'st,
If in thine my life thou waste,
   Thou art the best of me.

Let not thy divining heart
   Forethink me any ill;
Destiny may take thy part,
   And may thy fears fulfil;
     But think that we
Are but turned aside to sleep;
They who one another keep
   Alive, ne'er parted be.

Jorge Luis Borges 'The Other Tiger'

(translated by Cheli Durán)

'And the craft that createth a semblance'
   William Morris, *Sigurd the Volsung* (1876)

I imagine a tiger. The semidarkness heightens
the vast working library
and seems to make the stacks recede.
Strong, innocent, blood-stained, new,
he'll move through his forest and his days
leaving his traces on the mud banks
of a river whose name he doesn't know
(in his world there are no names or past
or future, only the certainty of now).
And he'll cover immense distances,
and nose in the braided labyrinth
of scents for the scent of daybreak
and mouth-watering scent of deer.
Between the stripes of bamboo stems I decipher,
his stripes and intuit the skeleton
under his splendid, pulsing skin.
In vain do the curving seas and deserts
of our planet come between us:
from this building in a distant port
of South America, I follow you and dream,
O Tiger of the Ganges riverbanks.

Afternoon deepens in me, and I reflect
how the tiger I summon in my poem
is a tiger of symbols and shadows,
a series of literary metaphors,
and memories of encyclopedias;
not the deadly tiger, star-crossed jewel,
which, under the sun or changing moon
in Bengal or Sumatra, follows a course
of love and languor and death.
Against this tiger of symbols, I've set
the real-life, red-blooded tiger,
the one that culls a buffalo herd
and casts today, the 3rd of August '59 –
a lengthening shadow on the plains;
though the very act of naming him
and guessing at his habits turns him
into a work of fiction, not a living creature
among the many wandering the earth.

We will look for a third tiger.
He too will be a figment of my dream,
an arrangement of human words
and not the tiger with a real backbone
which far beyond the old mythologies
paces the earth. I know that for sure,
and yet something forces on me
this shadowy, absurd, remote adventure,
and all afternoon I keep hunting
the other tiger, the one not in my poem.

William Blake 'The Tyger'

Tyger! Tyger! burning bright,
In the forests of the night,
What immortal hand or eye
Could frame thy fearful symmetry?

In what distant deeps or skies,
Burnt the fire of thine eyes?
On what wings dare he aspire?
What the hand dare seize the fire?

And what shoulder, & what art,
Could twist the sinews of thy heart?
And when thy heart began to beat,
What dread hand? & what dread feet?

What the hammer? what the chain,
In what furnace was thy brain?
What the anvil? what dread grasp,
Dare its deadly terrors clasp?

When the stars threw down their spears
And water'd heaven with their tears,
Did he smile his work to see?
Did he who made the Lamb make thee?

Tyger! Tyger! burning bright,
In the forests of the night,
What immortal hand or eye
Dare frame thy fearful symmetry?

Wallace Stevens 'Disillusionment of Ten o'Clock'

The houses are haunted
By white night-gowns.
None are green,
Or purple with green rings,
Or green with yellow rings,
Or yellow with blue rings.
None of them are strange,
With socks of lace
And beaded ceintures.
People are not going

To dream of baboons and periwinkles.
Only, here and there, an old sailor,
Drunk and asleep in his boots,
Catches tigers
In red weather.

Ezra Pound 'Erat Hora'

'Thank you, whatever comes.' And then she turned
And, as the ray of sun on hanging flowers
Fades when the wind hath lifted them aside,
Went swiftly from me. Nay, whatever comes
One hour was sunlit and the most high gods
May not make boast of any better thing
Than to have watched that hour as it passed.

John Keats 'La Belle Dame Sans Merci'

'O what can ail thee, knight-at-arms,
  Alone and palely loitering?
The sedge is wither'd from the lake,
  And no birds sing.

'O what can ail thee, knight-at-arms,
  So haggard and so woe-begone?
The squirrel's granary is full,
  And the harvest's done.

'I see a lily on thy brow
  With anguish moist and fever dew,
And on thy cheeks a fading rose
  Fast withereth too.'

'I met a lady in the meads,
  Full beautiful – a faery's child;
Her hair was long, her foot was light,
  And her eyes were wild.

'I made a garland for her head,
And bracelets too, and fragrant zone;
She looked at me as she did love,
And made sweet moan.

'I set her on my pacing steed,
And nothing else saw all day long,
For sidelong would she bend, and sing
A faery's song.

'She found me roots of relish sweet,
And honey wild and manna-dew,
And sure in language strange she said –
"I love thee true!"

'She took me to her elfin grot,
And there she wept and sighed full sore,
And there I shut her wild, wild eyes
With kisses four.

'And there she lullèd me asleep,
And there I dream'd – Ah! woe betide! –
The latest dream I ever dream'd
On the cold hill side.

'I saw pale kings, and princes too,
Pale warriors, death-pale were they all;
They cried – "La Belle Dame sans Merci
Thee hath in thrall!"

'I saw their starv'd lips in the gloam,
With horrid warning gapèd wide,
And I awoke, and found me here,
On the cold hill's side.

'And this is why I sojourn here,
Alone and palely loitering,

Though the sedge is wither'd from the lake,
    And no birds sing.'

Ilya Sielvinsky 'Tiger Hunt'

(*translated by Myles Burnyeat and Ruth Padel*)

A roar in the redbrown forest: a stag, calling hinds.
Another crowned head answers roar for roar.
Through bracken, over streams, they gallop
to a duel. He stands, the doe behind him,
insulting his rival, plastered mud staining
his roan coat, shoulders and breast.

He snorts through webbed nostrils, rolls his eyes.
The other walks out in the open: three-tined antlers,
tall as a moose: a wapiti throwing his head back
twice in the roar. His eyeballs are red
with a dream of his only beloved.

On such days, up to your thighs in undergrowth,
you take the birch-bark deer trumpet and practise
blowing through a reed martial harmonies
of the red deer's love. And we, putting out the camp
fire, sit in the hide all night. A Gol'd,
myself, and Igor Ivanitch, the Natchdir hunter.

All of us listen to the dark. Blue dawn comes
but no deer. The hunter blows his birch-bark horn.
Artificial love blares through the *taiga*
up and down. But silence. Blows again. No answer.
Is the forest deaf? We'll try somewhere else –

but suddenly in the distance comes an answer roar.
Blood pounds in my ears. Blow again – he's nearer –
here – just *by* us! We are sure a magnificent stag
is coming to our call. It's daylight. Sky already blue.

He's treading the skeletal deer trail over the moss
and stones, bellowing as he moves. We sit, don't breathe:

three rifles ready. Suddenly, between tree roots and grey
underbrush, a red-gold whirlwind, whiskered like sun.
Hot glare of a tiger – full epiphany,
Blessed Assumption. No time to shoot. The deer
we waited for all night is nothing now.

We rush down the tiger track. Wait. Wait an hour.
From a ditch we hear a deer roar, see the tiger's face.
Burning orange, scrawled over with black,
grey over gold, his shadow-and-mountain-ridge spine.
He goes down the hill: a dragon, leaving the temple.
Sometimes he stops, glances round, and switches his tail.

Weightless, enormous, a lazy banner under sky
and ruffling wind, he comes slowly to meet us.
For him red rags of the villagers fly from the branches.
They glorify Amba like God. *Shen. Ten. Met. Bay.*
Here he comes, a General of all Chinese dynasties,

breathing his fire. Seagulls fly over him, black notes
on a new-gold keyboard. He is elderly, not old.
Does he have to eat carrion? His tigery smell
scatters other living things in all directions. He walks on
down the slope, bold warrior, pressing enormous
shoulders forward, searching the ravine for deer.

From between his blue-string whiskers comes the call
of a stag. O beloved, O clever one! He is a hunter like us.
He uses the deer-trumpet too! Antlered princes
canter up to the challenge. With a whistle, a low growl,
he rears up with his claws, open-mouthed, desperate,

but misses. Only the deer's love call can feed his tongue.
just as a Chinese monk might stroke his own hair,

plaits glossy as those of a girl. But now the Gol'd
takes up his trumpet, blows the deer call.
The tiger looks, looks up. For a second, two gold fires
bore into me. But there's no mercy. Comrade Igor

throws up his rifle. One blast and the tiger falls
in mud. But he's up again, in front of us like myth.
His own roar is thunder, an organ in church.
He spits at us and vanishes, gold legend with new red
ribbons on his shoulders, into the mist.

Emily Dickinson 'Civilization – spurns – the Leopard!'

Civilization – spurns – the Leopard!
Was the Leopard – bold?
Deserts – never rebuked her Satin –
Ethiop – her Gold –
Tawny – her Customs –
She was Conscious –
Spotted – her Dun Gown –
This was the Leopard's Nature – Signor –
Need – a keeper – frown?
Pity – the Pard – that left her Asia –
Memories – of Palm –
Cannot be stifled – with Narcotic –
Nor suppressed – with Balm.

Gerard Manley Hopkins 'Binsey Poplars (felled 1879)'

My aspens dear, whose airy cages quelled,
Quelled or quenched in leaves the leaping sun,
All felled, felled, are all felled;
   Of a fresh and following folded rank
      Not spared, not one
      That dandled a sandalled
   Shadow that swam or sank
On meadow and river and wind-wandering weed-winding bank.

O if we but knew what we do
  When we delve or hew –
Hack and rack the growing green!
  Since country is so tender
To touch, her being só slender,
That, like this sleek and seeing ball
But a prick will make no eye at all,

Where we, even where we mean
    To mend her we end her,
  When we hew or delve:
After-comers cannot guess the beauty been.
Ten or twelve, only ten or twelve
    Strokes of havoc únselve
    The sweet especial scene,
Rural scene, a rural scene,
Sweet especial rural scene.

Louis MacNeice 'Meeting Point'

Time was away and somewhere else,
There were two glasses and two chairs
And two people with the one pulse
(Somebody stopped the moving stairs):
Time was away and somewhere else.

And they were neither up nor down;
The stream's music did not stop
Flowing through heather, limpid brown,
Although they sat in a coffee shop
And they were neither up nor down.

The bell was silent in the air
Holding its inverted poise –
Between the clang and clang a flower,
A brazen calyx of no noise;
The bell was silent in the air.

The camels crossed the miles of sand
That stretched around the cups and plates;
The desert was their own, they planned
To portion out the stars and dates:
The camels crossed the miles of sand.

Time was away and somewhere else.
The waiter did not come, the clock
Forgot them and the radio waltz
Came out like water from a rock;
Time was away and somewhere else.

Her fingers flicked away the ash
That bloomed again in the tropic trees:
Not caring if the markets crash
When they had forests such as these,
Her fingers flicked away the ash.

God or whatever means the Good
Be praised that time can stop like this,
That what the heart has understood
Can verify in the body's peace
God or whatever means the Good.

Time was away and she was here
And life no longer what it was,
The bell was silent in the air
And all the room one glow because
Time was away and she was here.

Gerard Manley Hopkins 'Inversnaid'

This darksome burn, horseback brown,
His rollrock highroad roaring down,
In coop and in comb the fleece of his foam
Flutes and low to the lake falls home.

A windpuff-bonnet of fáwn-fróth
Turns and twindles over the broth
Of a pool so pitchblack, féll-frówning,
It rounds and rounds Despair to drowning.

Degged with dew, dappled with dew
Are the groins of the braes that the brook treads through,
Wiry heathpacks, flitches of fern,
And the beadbonny ash that sits over the burn.

What would the world be, once bereft
Of wet and of wildness? Let them be left,
O let them be left, wildness and wet;
Long live the weeds and the wilderness yet.

PEOPLE

Bangladesh

Mowgli, aka Rubaiyat Mansur, guide, the Guide Tours, Dhaka

Bhutan

Karma Tshering, Head of International Conservation and Development
    Program Management Planning, Nature Conservation Division,
    Department of Forestry, Thimphu, Kingdom of Bhutan
Hishey Tshering, his brother, eco-tour operator, ornithologist
Sharap Wangchuk, Tiger Programme, Nature Conservation Division
Sangay, forest warden in Thrumshingla National Park
Tsaung, forest warden in Tintibi National Park
Dr Sangay Wangchuck, Nature Conservation Division
Chadho Tensin, Director, WWF, Bhutan
Parents of Karma Phuntso (a theology student at Oxford, UK), Ura
Princess Kunzang Choden, author, Bumthang

China

Endi Zhang, Country Director, WCS China Program until 2004
Eve Li, Ph.D. student of Dr Endi Zhang, working for WCS in Shanghai
Wang and Cao, tourism students, Nanchang
Mrs Zhang Xiaoying, officer at Yihuang Reserve, Jiangxi province
Mr Li Zhi Xing, Director of Education for Hunchun Reserve, Jilin
    province

Liu Yu (Leo), MA student of Dr Endi Zhang, doing tiger research in
Jilin province, working with WCS

India

Kerala

Rama Iyer, director of Margi theatre company, Trivandrum
Ayappa Paniker, poet, Trivandrum

Panna

Dr Raghu Chundawat, zoologist
Joanna, his wife
Dr Malik, wildlife vet
Vinny, runs the Ken River Lodge, a visitors' camp on the Ken River
Anil, his assistant

Kanha

Anil, naturalist; manager of a Kanha hotel
Hoon, his Singapore girlfriend

Ranthambhore

Fateh Singh Rathore, ex-director of Ranthambhore National Park
Dr Goverdhan Singh, doctor, his son
Terry, manager of Sher Bhag, a visitors' camp at Ranthambhore
Stephen and Lee, visitors to camp at Ranthambhore
Vipul Jain, government-approved guide to Ranthambhore National
    Park

Delhi

Valmik Thapar, author, conservationist, has spent thirty years working
    with issues concerning the natural world of India, currently serves
    on the Central Empowered Committee constituted by the Supreme
    Court of India
P. K. Sen, ex-Director of Project Tiger, head of WWF's Tiger Programme,
    India

Karnataka

Dr Ullas Karanth, zoologist, Country Director, India Program, WCS

Niren Jain, architect, Co-ordinator of Kudremukh Wildlife Foundation and member of Wildlife First, Mangalore

Praveen Bhargav, Trustee of Wildlife First, Bangalore

Shreedev Hulikere, Trustee of WildCat-C and plantation owner, Chikmagalur

D. V. Girish, Trustee of Wildlife First, Chikmagalur

Sundarbans

Mrinal Chatterjee, Project Director, Project Lifeline Sundarbans, Institute of Climbers and Nature Lovers, Kolkata

Indonesia

Sumatra

Lilik, guide and interpreter

Ramla, of J. L. Sumur, Aceh Village no. 34, Lahat, working in Losmen Mirasa Guest House, Pagaralam, with family on Mount Dempo

Rahan, villager in Talang Datar on Mount Dempo, survivor of tiger attack

Dr Tom Maddox, directing zoologist, ZSL Tiger Project on Asiatic Persada plantation, Jambi

Jeremy Holden, wildlife photographer, specializing in South-East Asia and Indonesia

Sean Marron, President Director, PT Asiatic Persada, Jambi

Ian Rowland, Environment Manager, PT Asiatic Persada and Pacific Rim Palm Oil Ltd

Volta Bone, Environmental and Conservation Officer with Asiatic Persada

Elva Gemita, assistant to Tom Maddox

Debbie Martyr, working for Flora & Fauna International, advisor to Kerinci-Seblat National Park's Tiger Protection Team

Amadeus, intelligence agent for Kerinci-Seblat Tiger Protection Team

Syamsul, founding member of Kerinci-Seblat Tiger Protection Team

Ibu Lystia Kusumardhani, forestry officer, Director of Kerinci-Seblat National Park until 2004

M, member of Kerinci-Seblat Tiger Protection Team

Iwan, radio mechanic (radio name Timbul): radio operator for Kerinci-Seblat Tiger Protection Team

Zul, informer for Kerinci-Seblat Tiger Protection Team

Java

Rachman, guide in Jakarta

Laos

Arlyne Johnson, Country Director, Laos Program, WCS

Changsavi Vongkhambeng, biologist working for WCS

Toh, guide

Vai and Bualoy, villagers in north-east Bio-diversity Reserve

Boatang, working for WCS as monitor in Phou Loei Bio-diversity Reserve

Nepal

Dr Charles ('Chuck') McDougal, Director of Wildlife and Conservation, Tiger Tops, Chitwan

John Roberts, his assistant

Ramdin, naturalist at Tiger Tops

Sukrun, tracker at Tiger Tops

Tenzing, antique dealer in Kathmandu

Russia

Dale Miquelle, Country Director, WCS Russian Far East Program

John Goodrich, Director, WCS Siberian Tiger Project

Irena and Boris, guides in Khabarovsky Kraij

Nikolai Evdokimovich Spizhrvoi, Director of the Museum for Indigenous Cultures of the Amur

Sergei Zubtsov, head of Inspection Tiger, Vladivostock

Michiel Hötte, Director and Founder of Tigris Foundation

Sergei Bereznuk, Director of Phoenix Fund, Vladivostock

Olga Bekhtereva, physicist, tour guide to Primorye with Dalintourist Travel Agency

Leonid, her driver

Yevgeny, bee-keeper in Terney

Tamara, his wife

Sasha, working for WCS in Terney

Katya, working for WCS in Vladivostock

Yevgeny Smirnov, tiger biologist, Terney *zapovednik*

Dimitri Pikunov, tiger biologist

Olga, his wife

Thailand

Bangkok

Tony Lynam, Country Director, Thailand Program, WCS, until 2004

Tim Redford, Director, Surviving Together Program, Wildaid, Bangkok

United Kingdom

Amanda Bright, Chair of Trustees, Global Tiger Patrol

Carole Elliott, Trustee of Global Tiger Patrol

Sarah Christie, Programme Manager, 'Carnivores and People' Conservation Programme, Zoological Society of London

Andy Fisher, Wildlife Liaison Officer, New Scotland Yard, London

Girish Karnad, playwright, Director of the Nehru Centre, London, 2000–2003

John Lewis, wildlife vet with International Zoo Veterinary Group

United States

Dr George Schaller, Vice President for Science, WCS

Dr Alan Rabinowitz, Director of Science and Exploration, WCS

CHARITIES

Giving money to help protect wild tigers is a complex business. Large organizations have enormous overheads and many different conservation programmes that do not involve tigers; some turn down projects which will not deliver the X per cent overhead required for cars, secretaries, offices; some borrow from one project to pay another; some also pay for advertisements, T-shirts, posters, which is what your money may end up doing. Below are organizations guaranteed to help tigers in the field. Either I have direct knowledge of them and have seen them in action, or someone I trust knows their work. I have put them in three categories.

1. Agencies that give only to tigers, and guarantee to send 100% of donations to field projects

CANADA

The Tiger Foundation (Canada), www.tigerfdn.com
    Suite 1780–999 West Hastings Street, Vancouver, British Columbia V6C 2W2, Tel. (604) 893-8718. Email: info@tigers.ca
    Directed by Ron Tilson, this fund helps to fund the Sumatran Tiger Conservation Programme.

HOLLAND

The Tigris Foundation, www.tigrisfoundation.nl
    Laagtekadijk 135, 1018 ZD Amsterdam, The Netherlands
    Tel. 31-20-6206274. E-mail: mhotte@inter.nl.net
    Directed by Michiel Hötte, it funds protection of Amur tigers and leopards. You can send a cheque or make a credit card donation using the account 'Wild About Cats' (donations are tax-deductible

for US citizens). For donation forms, see www.wildaboutcats. org/form.htm. Put 'Tigris Foundation' in the 'Comments' space; Wild About Cats will forward your donation to the Tigris Foundation.

INDIA
Wildlife Protection Society of India, www.wpsi-india.org
  M-52 Greater Kailash Part 1, New Delhi 110048,
  Tel. (91-11) 2621 3864 & 2629 2492. Email: wpsi@vsnl.com
  Directed by Belinda Wright, this organization focuses on anti-poaching, capture and prosecution of poachers. Mark donations 'for tiger conservation'.

JAPAN
Japanese Wildlife Conservation Society, Tiger Trust Fund, www.jwcs.org/ English-page/index-e.html
  This organization funds tiger protection in Russia, investigates Japanese trade in tiger parts and monitors the enforcement of CITES in Japan. Reliable contacts say they are small but effective. For email, see the website. Ms Kumi Togawa is in charge of the Tiger Trust Fund.

UNITED KINGDOM
21st-Century Tiger, www.21stcenturytiger.org
  Zoological Society of London, Regent's Park, London NW1 4RY
  Tel. 44 20 7449 6444. Email: 21stCenturyTiger@zsl.org
  For credit card donations see website.
  They focus on scientifically driven field projects to conserve tigers in Sumatra and Russia.

Global Tiger Patrol, www.globaltigerpatrol.co.uk
  87 Newland Street, Witham, Essex, CM8 1AD
  Tel. 44(0)1376 520320. Email: globaltiger@compuserve.com
  They fund field projects in India.

USA
Save the Tiger Fund, www.SaveThe Tiger Fund.org. National Fish and Wildlife Foundation

1120 Connecticut Avenue, NW Suite 900
Washington DC20035

Environmental Investigation Agency, www.eia-international.org (click on Tiger Campaigns)

The Tiger Information Centre, www.5tigers.org, sponsored by Save the Tiger Fund, hosted by Minnesota Zoo and maintained by Dr Ron Tilson, Director of Conservation at Minnesota Zoo.

2. Organizations that channel funds to tiger projects on request. A percentage of smaller donations may go to administrative costs

USA
Wildlife Conservation Society, www.wcs.org
Normally, donations to WCS/Tiger Conservation Program go to tiger field programmes at WCS direct. But if you give over $1000, you can direct your donation to a country programme (any of those run by the officers mentioned in this book, for example), as long as your instructions are clearly written on the cheque or in a covering note.
Send to Asia Program, 2399 Southern Boulevard, Bronx, New York 10450. For credit card donations, see website or call 1 (718) 220-689.

UK/ USA/THAILAND
Wildaid, www.wildaid.org
They fund many projects but can accept dedicated donations.
450 Pacific Avenue, Suite 201 (headquarters)
San Francisco, CA 941 33
Tel. (415) 834-3174. Email: info@wildaid.org
or Environmental Justice Foundation
5 St Peter's Street, London N1 8JD, UK
Tel. 44-207-359-3543. Email: askacapuk@wildaid.org
or UBC II Building, 10th Floor, 591
Sukhumvit 33, Wattana, Bangkok 10110, Thailand
Tel. 66-2-204-2720. Email: info@wildaidasia.org

3. Organization with a more general brief; donations mainly benefit tigers indirectly

Flora and Fauna International, www.fauna-flora.org
Email: ffi-usa@fauna-flora.org

All donations generated by this book are guaranteed to be spent on tiger team activities in Kerinci, Sumatra, if made by cheque or bank transfer, specifying 'Kerinci Tiger conservation Project in Sumatra'.

Great Eastern House, Tenison Road
Cambridge CB1 2TT, UK
Tel. 44 (0) 1223 571000. Email: info@fauna-flora.org
or PO Box 42575, Washington, DC
20015–0575, USA.
Tel. 1 202 329 1672

BIBLIOGRAPHY

PART I   OUT OF THE WEST

Anton, M. and A. Turner, *The Big Cats and Their Fossil Relatives: An Illustrated Guide to Their Evolution and Natural History*, Columbia University Press, 1997

Borges, J. G. 'The Writing of the God' (*The Aleph*, 1949), 'Dreamtigers' (*The Maker*, 1960), 'Blue Tigers' (*Shakepeare's Memory*, 1983) in *Selected Fictions*, trans. A. Hurley, Penguin, 1999, pp. 250–4, 294–5, 494–593

Carter, Angela, 'The Tiger's Bride' (*The Bloody Chamber and Other Stories*, 1979) in *Burning Your Boats: Collected Short Stories*, Chatto & Windus, 1995, pp. 154–69

Champion, F. W., *With a Camera in Tiger-Land*, Chatto & Windus, 1928

Chaudhuri, A. B. and A. Choudhury, *Mangroves of the Sundarbans*, Volume One: *India*, IUCN–The World Conservation Union, 1994

Choden, Kunzang, *Folktales of Bhutan*, White Lotus Press, 1994

Christie, S., P. Jackson and J. Seidensticker, eds, *Riding the Tiger: Tiger Conservation in Human-Dominated Landscapes*, Cambridge University Press, 1999

Corbett, Jim, *Man-Eaters of Kumaon*, 1944

—— *My India*, Oxford University Press (Delhi), 1952

—— *The Temple Tiger*, Oxford University Press (Delhi), 1954

—— *Jungle Lore*, Oxford University Press (Delhi), 1990

De, Rathindranath, *The Sundarbans*, Oxford University Press (Calcutta), 1990

Dinerstein, E., E. Wikramanayake, J. Robinson, U. Karanth, A. Rabinowitz, D. Olson, T. Mathew, P. Heddao, M. Connor, G. Hemley and D. Bolze, 'A Framework for Identifying High-Priority Areas and Actions for the Conservation of Tigers in the Wild', WWF–US, 1997

Dorji, Sithel, *The Origin and Description of Bhutanese Masked Dances*, KMT Press, 2001

Gittleman, J. L., S. M. Funk, D. W. Macdonald and R. K.Wayne, eds, *Carnivore Conservation*, Cambridge University Press, 2001

Gurung, K., *Heart of the Jungle: The Wildlife of Chitwan, Nepal*, André Deutsch, 1953

Hahn, D., *The Tower Menagerie: Being the Amazing True Story of the Royal Collection of Wild Beasts*, Simon & Schuster, 2003

Hussain, Z. and G. Acharya, *Mangroves of the Sundarbans*, Volume Two: *Bangladesh*, IUCN–The World Conservation Union, 1994

Ives, R., *Of Tigers and Men: Entering the Age of Extinction*, Mainstream Publishing, 1996

Karanth, U., *The Way of the Tiger: Natural History and Conservation of the Endangered Big Cat*, Voyager Press, 2001

Khan, M. and H. Monirul, 'The Sundarbans' in P. R. Gil, ed., *Wilderness – Earth's Last Wild Places*, CEMEX, Mexico City/Conservation International and Sierra Madre, 2002, pp. 280–9

Lipton, M., *The Tiger Rugs of Tibet*, Thames & Hudson, 1988

Matthiesson, P., *The Snow Leopard*, Chatto & Windus, 1979

McDougal, C., *The Face of the Tiger*, Rivington Books and André Deutsch, 1977

McDougal, C. and K. Tshering, *Tiger Conservation Strategy for the Kingdom of Bhutan*, WWF, 1998

McDougal, C., *et al.*, 'Tiger and Human Conflict Increase in Chitwan Reserve Buffer Zone', *Cat News*, 40, 2004, IUCN, Berne, Switzerland

Mills, S., 'A Family Affair', *BBC Wildlife Magazine*, October 2002, pp. 28–33

—— *Tiger*, BBC Books, 2004

O'Brien, S. J. *et al.*, 'Phylogeography and Genetic Ancestry of Tigers', *Public Library of Science: Biology*, 2 (12), December 2004, pp. 442–60

Quammen, D., *Monster of God: The Man-Eating Predator in the Jungles of History and the Mind*, Norton, 2003

Schaller, G., *The Deer and the Tiger*, University of Chicago Press, 1965

—— 'A Face Like a Bee-Stung Moose', *International Wildlife*, 16 (6), 1986, pp. 36–9

Sen, Mala, *Death by Fire: Sati, Dowry, Death and Female Infanticide in Modern India*, Weidenfeld & Nicolson, 2001

Study Report on Human–Wildlife Interactions in Relation to the Sundarban Reserved Forest of Bangladesh, 'Internal Notes No. 78', submitted to Sundarban Biodiversity Conservation Project (Forest Department, Ministry of Forest and Environment, Bangladesh) by Jagrata Juba Shanga, Khulna, 2003

Sunquist, F. and M. Sunquist, *Tiger Moon: Tracking the Great Cats in Nepal*, University of Chicago Press, 1988

Thapar, V., *The Secret Life of Tigers*, Oxford University Press, 1989

—— *The Cult of the Tiger*

Thapar, V. and Fateh Singh Rathore, *Wild Tigers of Ranthambhore*, Oxford University Press (Delhi), 2000

Ura, K., *The Hero with a Thousand Eyes*, Centre for Bhutan Studies, Thimphu, 1995

PART II   EAST

Arsenev, V., *Dersu the Trapper*, trans. M. Burr, Recovered Classics, McPherson & Co., 1996

Cao, Dan, 'Reducing Demand for Tiger Medicinal Products', www.tcmwildlife.org

—— 'Ancient Traditions, New Alternatives: Endangered Species Do Not Belong in Traditional Chinese Medicine', WWF 2001

Cat Specialist Group, 'Saving the South China Tiger', *Cat News*, 38, IUCN, Berne, Switzerland

Chekhov, A., *The Island of Sakhalin*, trans. L. Terpak and M. Terpak, Folio Society, 1989

Chungliang Al Huang, *Embrace Tiger Return to Mountain: The Essence of Tai Ji* [1973], Celestial Arts, 1997

Covell, A. C., *Folk Art and Magic: Shamanism in Korea*, Hollym Corporation, 1985

Goodrich, J. with L. Kerley, D. Miquelle, E. Smirnov, H. Quigley and M. Hornocker, 'Effects of roads and human disturbance on Amur tigers', *Conservation Biology*, 16 (1), February 2002, pp. 97–108

—— 'Reproductive parameters of wild female Amur tigers', *Journal of Mammalogy*, 84 (1), 2003

Harrington, A., ed., *The Placebo Effect*, Harvard University Press, 1997

Insob, Z., ed., *Folk Tales from Korea* [1952], Hollym Corporation, 1982

Kandell, J., 'Korea: a house divided', *Smithsonian*, July 2003, pp. 38–48

Kim, H. and Y. Yun, *The Korean Tiger* [1986], 4th edn, Yŏrhwadang Press, 1995 [in Korean]

Lever, C., 'The impact of traditional Chinese medicine on threatened species', *Oryx*, 38, January 2004, pp. 13–14

Li, Eve and E. Zhang, *Bringing up Public Conservation Awareness in China 1996–2003*, WCS, Shanghai, 2003

Lynas, M., *High Tide: News from a Warming World*, Flamingo, 2004

Mason, D. A., *Spirit of the Mountains: Korea's San-Shin and Traditions of Mountain Worship*, 1999

Matyushkin, E. N., ed., *The Amur Tiger in Russia: An Annotated Bibliography 1925–97*, WWF Publications (Moscow), 1998

Miquelle, D., 'Vladimir', *Wildlife Conservation*, August 2001, pp. 44–7

Miquelle, D. and E. Zhang, *A Proposed International System of Protected Areas for Amur Tigers*, WCS, Shanghai [in preparation]

Schaller, G., *The Last Panda*, University of Chicago Press, 1994

Schrire, C., *Tigers in Africa: Stalking the Past at the Cape of Good Hope*, University of Cape Town Press, 1999

Sullivan, M., *Symbols of Eternity: The Art of Landscape Painting in China*, Oxford University Press, 1979

Tilson, R., with Hu Defu, Jeff Muntifering and P. J. Nyhus, 'Dramatic decline of wild South China tigers: field survey of priority tiger reserves', *Oryx*, 38 (1), January 2004, pp. 40–7

Whitfield, R., ed., with Y. Yoon and W. Nam, *Handbook of Korean Art: Folk Painting*, Yekyong Publishing, 2002

Xuanbing, Zhou, L. Chunmei and P. Feng, *The National Forest Protection Project, Forest Management, and Its Relation to Tiger Protection*, Heilonggyang Forest Industry Bureau

PART III   SOUTH

Banks, D., *Thailand's Tiger Economy*, Environmental Investigation Agency 2001, www.eia-international.org

—— *The Tiger Skin Trail*, Environmental Intelligence Agency, 2004, www.eia-international.org

Berry, A., ed., *Infinite Tropics: An Alfred Russel Wallace Anthology*, Verso, 2002

Boomgaard, P., *Frontiers of Fear: Tigers and People in the Malay World, 1600–1950*, Yale University Press, 2001

Dale Scott, P., *Coming to Jakarta: A Poem about Terror*, New Directions, New York, 1989

Darwin, C., *On the Origin of Species*, John Murray, London, 1859

Fink, C., *Living Silence: Burma under Military Rule*, Zed Books, London and New York, 2001

Gargan, E., *The River's Tale: A Year on the Mekong*, Vintage Departures/Random House, 2003

Grabsky, P., *The Lost Temple of Java*, Orion, 1999

Hoagland, E., 'Wild things', *Granta 57: India, the Golden Jubilee*, Spring 1997, pp. 39–58

Hough, Robert, *The Final Confession of Mabel Stark* [Random House, 2001], Atlantic Books, 2003

Khoo Thwe, P., *From the Land of Green Ghosts: A Burmese Odyssey*, HarperCollins, 2002

Kingsolver, B., *Small Wonder*, Faber & Faber, 2002

Koch, C., *The Year of Living Dangerously* [1978], Vintage, 1998

Marsden, William, *The History of Sumatra*, London, 1783

Marshall, A., *The Trouser People*, Viking, 2002

Meacham, C., *How the Tiger Lost Its Stripes: An Exploration into the Endangerment of a Species*, Harcourt Brace, 1997

Nooren, H. and G. Claridge, *Wildlife Trade in Laos*, Netherlands Committee for IUCN, 2001

Orwell, G., *Burmese Days* [1934], Penguin, 1989

Perlin, J., *A Forest Journey: The Role of Wood in the Development of Civilization*, Norton, 1989

Quamman, D., *The Song of the Dodo: Island Biogeography in an Age of Extinctions*, Touchstone Books/Simon & Schuster, 1996

Rabinowitz, A., *Chasing the Dragon's Tail: The Struggle to Save Thailand's Wild Cats* [1991], Shearwater Books/Island Press, 2003

—— *Beyond the Last Village: A Journey of Discovery in Asia's Forbidden Wilderness* [2001], Aurum Press (UK), 2002

PART IV   RETURN TO SOUTH INDIA

Corbett, J., *The Man-Eating Leopard of Rudraprayag* [1947], Oxford University Press (Delhi), 1988

Karanth, U., 'Ecological Status of the Lion-Tailed Macaque and Its

Rainforest Habitat in Karnataka, India', *Primate Conservation: Journal of the IUCN/ SSC Primate Specialist Group*, 6, July 1985, pp. 73–84

—— 'Analysis of Predator–Prey Balance in Bandipur Tiger Reserve with Reference to Census Reports', *Journal of Bombay Natural History Society*, 81 (1), April 1988, pp. 1–8

—— 'Conservation Prospects for Lion-Tailed Macaques in Karnataka, India', *Zoo Biology*, 11, 1992, pp. 33–41

—— 'Behavioural Correlates of Predation by Tiger, Leopard and Dhole in Nagarahole, India,' *Journal of the Zoological Society of London*, 250, 2000, pp. 225–65

Karanth, U., with W. A. Link, 'Correction for Overdispersion in Tests of Prey Selectivity', *Ecology*, 75 (8), 1994, pp. 2456–9

—— 'Estimating Tiger Populations from Camera-Trap Data Using Capture and Recapture Models', *Biological Conservation*, 71, 1995, pp. 333–8

Karanth, U., with B. M. Stith, 'Prey Depletion as a Critical Determinant of Tiger Population Viability' in Christie *et al.*, 1999, pp. 100–13

—— 'Debating Conservation As If Reality Matters', *Conservation and Society*, 1, 2003

—— 'Science Deficiency in Conservation Practice: The Monitoring of Tiger Populations in India', *Animal Conservation*, 6, 2003, pp. 141–46

Karanth, U., with Mel Sunquist and Fiona Sunquist, 'Population Structure, Density and Biomass of Large Herbivores in the Tropical Forests of Nagarahole, India', *Journal of Tropical Ecology*, 8, 1992, pp. 21–35

Sahgal, Bittu, ed., 'Saving India's wildlife – the pioneering role of the Supreme Court of India: extracts from the Supreme Court of India's orders', *Sanctuary Magazine*, Mumbai, 2003

Smith, J., S. Obidzinski and I. Suramenggala, 'Illegal logging, collusive corruption, and fragmented governments in Kalimantan, Indonesia', *International Forestry Review*, 5 (3), 2003, pp. 293–302

Thomas, Keith, *Man and the Natural World: Changing Attitudes in England 1500–1800*, Allen Lane, 1983

www.wildlifefirst.com

INDEX